—出口成章，脱口而出！

英文诵典

Selected English
Articles For Recitation

主编 / 北京大学 李震

审订 / [美]Stephanie Diamond

世界知识出版社

中国图书（CIP）数据

英文诵典/李震主编. —北京：世界知识出版社，2005.4

ISBN 7 – 5012 – 2537 – 0

Ⅰ. 英… Ⅱ. 李… Ⅲ. 英语 – 语言读物　Ⅳ. H319. 1

中国版本图书馆 CIP 数据核字（2005）第 030090 号

英文诵典

责任编辑	吴健生　依　露
责任校对	程宏齐
责任出版	赵　玥
封面设计	大象工作室
出版发行	世界知识出版社
地址电话	北京市东城区干面胡同 51 号　　（010）65265928
邮政编码	100010
经　　销	新华书店
排　　版	北京笃志科技发展有限公司录排部
印　　刷	世界知识印刷厂
开本印张	787×960 毫米　1/32　15 印张　400 千字
版　　次	2005 年 5 月第 1 版　2006 年 9 月第 5 次印刷
定　　价	18. 00 元

In Reciting We Learn.

FOREWORD

❖ 序 ❖

In classes, in bookstores, on trains, anywhere that I meet Chinese people studying English, I am asked the same questions — "How can I improve my spoken English?" My answer is always the same, "Open your mouth and speak." Your mouth is a muscle and needs to be exercised just as you need to exercise the rest of your body to make it strong. The exercise best suited to helping your mouth feel more relaxed speaking English is to speak it.

There are many ways you can open your mouth and speak, English Corners, foreign friends, conversation classes and recitation are just a few ways. *Selected English Articles for Recitation* encourages you to use recitation as a way to improve your spoken English. This book provides interesting and useful articles that you can use to practice your spoken English anywhere you are. But there is an additional advantage to this book, the contents of the articles themselves. These articles are thought provoking and challenging. They can encourage you on your life's journey and also cause to stop and think.

I hope that you will find *Selected English Articles for Recitation* not only a useful way to improve your English but also a way to improve your character.

Stephanie Diamond *

---

* Stephanie Diamond is from northern New York in the United States. She has her B. S. in Chemistry from Rochester Institute of Technology and her Master of Education from Boston University. Ms Diamond is currently living in Beijing, China and has been teaching English to Chinese college/university students since 1989. She has and continues to encourage her students and other students in China to not only grow in their knowledge of English but also their knowledge of life.

PREFACE

前言

The limits of my language mean the limits of my world.（我的语言的局限意味着我的世界的局限。）

— Ludwig Wittgenstein（路德维格·维特根斯坦）

　　勿庸置疑，任何一门语言的学习，都有一个从模仿到逐渐学会运用的过程，是一个在头脑中大量储存语言信息，并在实践中练习和提高的过程。根据克拉申的"输入假说"理论，模仿就必须先有大量的信息输入、积累和储存，只有在输入、积累和储存到一定程度时才会有信息的输出。语言不是无本之木，必须依赖"源头活水"，循序渐进，方可"水到渠成"。

　　众所周知，朗读和背诵是我国源远流长而又行之有效的学习语言的方法之一。而英语作为一种世界通用语言，要想对其熟练地掌握和运用，同样离不开朗读和背诵。它有助于我们对英语单词、词组、句型及习惯用法的积累，有助于我们对语法的精熟掌握和运用，有助于我们提高英语口语的流利程度，有助于我们英语语感的养成和加强，有助于我们写作水平的迅速提升，真可谓"一箭数雕"。而且，许多英语成功者的实例已经充分证明了这一点。毫不夸张地说——

　　朗读和背诵是英语学习的彻底革命！

　　朗读和背诵是最终征服英语的强力武器！

　　朗读和背诵是到达英语学习彼岸的必经之路！

　　朗读和背诵是素质教育理念对于我们最终攻克英语的根本要求！

　　《英文诵典》正是为了满足广大读者这方面的需要，是编译者历时三年、精心策划编写而成，其间曾听取十多位来自北京大学外国语学院、教育学院、社会学系、心理学系、欧美文学研究中心和跨文化研究中心资深教授的意见而进行选材。

PREFACE

　　本书编选文章的主要原则是"经世致用"，亦即"理在书中，题目在书外"。本书选材范围甚广，内容丰富多彩，包括隽永婉约的散文，音韵优美的诗歌（对其朗读和背诵尤其可以锤炼自身英语口语的节奏），撼人心魄的演说，感人肺腑的书信，发人深省的时文，经典名著的名篇，圣人智者的名言和千年传诵的谚语等等，或者展现世态万象，或者阐释生活哲理，或者抒发缱绻情怀，或者演绎精彩人生，是"原装正版"英语的大观园，是纯正地道英语篇章的大本营，是西方国家灿烂思想的万花筒。本书可以完全突破一些英语老教材的"思想禁锢"，既可以锻造各位读者"出口成章"的真功夫，又可以开阔眼界，拓宽思路，还可以帮助大家洞察自己的内心世界，从而从精神层面上更加深入地认识自己和改善自己。可以说，本书是一座无穷无尽的宝藏，它正等待着各位读者去发掘和开采。

　　本书特别适用于各类大专院校公外英语一至六级水平的学生、英语专业一至三年级的本科生、非英语专业的研究生、学有余力的高中生以及那些对英语抱有热望的自学者等等。

　　本书的编排方式决定了其既可以作为朗读和背诵的最佳范本，又可以作为练习笔译的绝好素材，也可以作为提升自己文学修养的经典读本；并且，既可以用作各类相关培训课程的培训教材，又可以用作各位读者业余或课下的自学资料。

　　美国英语学会课程部主任 Stephanie Diamond 女士担纲了本书的审订工作，对于本书的篇章安排和体例设计等方面提供了诸多宝贵的建设性意见。承蒙协助，谨致谢忱！

编译者

2005 年 3 月于北京大学

CONTENTS

⊙　向左走？　向右走？——〈英文诵典〉背诵方略指津……………… 1

001. **Life Is to Be Whole**
人生在于完整 …………………………………………… 9

002. **Home**
家 ………………………………………………………… 14

003. **Too Dear for the Whistle**
得不偿失的哨子 ………………………………………… 17

004. **Youth**
青春 ……………………………………………………… 22

005. **On Punctuality**
论守时 …………………………………………………… 25

006. **Work and Pleasure**
工作和娱乐 ……………………………………………… 28

007. **April Days**
四月的日子 ……………………………………………… 32

008. **Man and Nature**
人与自然 ………………………………………………… 35

009. **Who Moved My Cheese?**
谁动了我的奶酪？ ……………………………………… 39

010. **The Smile**
微笑 ……………………………………………………… 44

011. **Love**
爱情 ……………………………………………………… 48

CONTENTS

012. **Hope Is the Thing with Feathers**

希望是长着羽翼的东西 ·········· **52**

013. **The Story of Life**

生活的故事 ·········· **55**

014. **Night**

夜 ·········· **59**

015. **Lady First**

女士优先 ·········· **63**

016. **A Better Tomorrow**

一个更好的明天 ·········· **67**

017. **The Watch**

手表 ·········· **70**

018. **True Nobility**

真正的高贵 ·········· **75**

019. **A Mother's Letter to the World**

一位母亲写给世界的信 ·········· **78**

020. **A to Z**

从 A 到 Z ·········· **81**

021. **Successful English Learning**

英语学习成功之道 ·········· **84**

022. **Science and Art**

科学和艺术 ·········· **90**

023. **Tactics for Job-hunt Success**

求职胜略 ·········· **95**

024. **Ambition**

抱负 ·········· **99**

025. **To —**

给—— ·········· **104**

026. **Learn to Live in the Present Moment**

CONTENTS

学会生活在此时此刻 ······ 107

027. The Telephone
电话 ······ 111

028. Courage
勇气 ······ 115

029. The Gift of Love
爱的颂歌 ······ 118

030. Be an Optimist
做一个乐观者 ······ 122

031. On Lying
论说谎 ······ 126

032. My Heart's in the Highlands
我的心呀在高原 ······ 130

033. The Road to Success
成功之路 ······ 133

034. Eyes Can Speak
眼睛会说话 ······ 138

035. Relish the Moment
品味现在 ······ 142

036. On Motes and Beams
微尘与栋梁 ······ 146

037. A Leap in Thought
思维的飞跃 ······ 150

038. Our Family Creed
家族的信条 ······ 154

039. Mother's Day and Father's Day
母亲节与父亲节 ······ 159

040. Expressing One's Individuality
个性的表达 ······ 163

CONTENTS

041. **If**

如果 ………………………………………………………… **168**

042. **True and False Simplicity**

真正的纯朴与虚假的纯朴 ……………………………… **172**

043. **Last Letters Home from an American Soldier Who Died in Iraq**

一名在伊拉克阵亡美军士兵的最后家书 ………… **176**

044. **Jimmy Carter's Nobel Lecture（Ⅰ）**

吉米·卡特的诺贝尔和平奖受奖演说（一） ………… **180**

045. **Jimmy Carter's Nobel Lecture（Ⅱ）**

吉米·卡特的诺贝尔和平奖受奖演说（二） ………… **186**

046. **A Visit to an American Court**

到美国法庭看一看 ……………………………………… **191**

047. **The Man and the Opportunity**

人与机会 ………………………………………………… **195**

048. **The Daffodils**

水仙 ……………………………………………………… **198**

049. **Man Will Prevail**

人类必胜 ………………………………………………… **202**

050. **An October Sunrise**

十月的日出 ……………………………………………… **207**

051. **The Art of Living**

生活的艺术 ……………………………………………… **211**

052. **The American Character**

美国人的性格 …………………………………………… **216**

053. **The Pleasure of Reading**

读书之乐 ………………………………………………… **221**

054. **A Knack of Wal-Mart's Success**

沃尔玛发迹妙诀 ………………………………………… **225**

CONTENTS

055. Gettysburg Address
葛底斯堡演说 …………………………………………… 229

056. The Love of Beauty
爱美 …………………………………………… 232

057. The Road Not Taken
未选择之路 …………………………………………… 235

058. On Leadership
论领导 …………………………………………… 238

059. Address to the Millennium Summit
在千年首脑峰会上的演讲 …………………………… 242

060. Napoleon to Josephine
拿破仑致约瑟芬 …………………………………… 248

061. Questions Asked in an Interview
求职面试题 …………………………………………… 251

062. What I Have Lived for
我为何而生 …………………………………………… 257

063. Cars
汽车 …………………………………………… 261

064. The Lover and the Beloved
施爱者和被爱者 …………………………………… 265

065. Human Life Like a Poem
人生如诗 …………………………………………… 269

066. Benjamin Franklin
本杰明·富兰克林 …………………………………… 273

067. Perseverance
坚持不懈 …………………………………………… 277

068. Paris: a Romantic Capital
巴黎:浪漫之都 …………………………………… 280

069. Eulogy for a Dog

CONTENTS

狗的颂歌 286

070. **The Reward of Solitary Life**
独身生活的回报 290

071. **Life Is a Game**
生活是一场游戏 293

072. **Globalization**
全球化 298

073. **Self-control**
自制 303

074. **The Four Freedoms**
论四大自由 306

075. **A Psalm of Life**
人生礼赞 310

076. **Conservatism of the English People**
英国人的保守 315

077. **You Are What You Do**
你是你的所为 319

078. **April Fool's Day**
愚人节 322

079. **Bill Gates' Speech to Qinghua University（Ⅰ）**
比尔·盖茨在清华大学的演讲（一） 326

080. **Bill Gates' Speech to Qinghua University（Ⅱ）**
比尔·盖茨在清华大学的演讲（二） 332

081. **Love Your Life**
热爱生活 336

082. **Privacy as Border**
隐私如国境 339

083. **Of Studies**
谈读书 344

CONTENTS

084. The Urgency
紧迫性 ……………………………………………… 348

085. The Happy Door
快乐之门 …………………………………………… 352

086. Success Is a Choice
成功是一种选择 …………………………………… 355

087. Living in Big Cities
住在大都市 ………………………………………… 359

088. Speech Given by Colin Lucas at Bejing University
牛津大学副校长科林·卢卡斯在北京大学的演说 ……… 363

089. O Captain! My Captain!
哦，船长！我的船长！ …………………………… 367

090. The Strenuous Life
艰辛的人生 ………………………………………… 371

091. On the Fear of Death
谈怕死 ……………………………………………… 375

092. On the Instability of Human Glory
论人类荣誉之虚渺 ………………………………… 378

093. A Message to Garcia
致加西亚的信 ……………………………………… 381

094. Autumn
秋 …………………………………………………… 385

095. Tribute to Diana, Princess of Wales
致威尔士王妃戴安娜的献词 ……………………… 388

096. Tips for Getting Promoted
晋升的诀窍 ………………………………………… 391

097. The Other Side of the Olympics
奥运会的另一面 …………………………………… 394

098. Liberty Is Order

CONTENTS

自由就是秩序 ···································· 398

099. We Were Dear to Each Other

我们相亲相爱 ···································· 401

100. Born to Win

天生赢家 ···································· 404

101. Leaning into the Afternoons

倚身于暮色中 ···································· 408

102. On the Future of Africa

非洲的未来 ···································· 411

103. Man Is Here for the Sake of Other Men

人为了别人而活着 ···································· 415

104. Game Playing

玩游戏 ···································· 418

105. Paradox of Our Times

我们这个时代的尴尬 ···································· 422

106. Fleeting Time（Ⅰ）

似水流年（一）···································· 427

107. Fleeting Time（Ⅱ）

似水流年（二）···································· 432

108. I Have a Dream（Ⅰ）

我有一个梦想（一）···································· 436

109. I Have a Dream（Ⅱ）

我有一个梦想（二）···································· 444

110. I Remember, I Remember

我记得，我记得 ···································· 451

向左走？向右走？
——《英文诵典》背诵方略指津

现今，无数国人已经踏上英语学习之路，会说几句英语的人也比比皆是；可是，会说几句英语就算是掌握英语了吗？事实上，绝非如此。

我们认为，英语的"学有所成"绝不意味着仅仅会用其进行日常的寒暄问候，这是远远不够的。能够进行一些基本话题的交流固然可喜，可是相信各位读者还是不时会感觉"话到用时方恨少"。其实，我们更需要的是能够大段大段地讲英语，是能够"如滔滔江水，连绵不绝"，是能够练就英语"出口成章"的硬功夫！我们坚信——

出口成章才到家！

出口成章才是硬道理！

出口成章才是真正的竞争力！

那么，怎样才能练就英语"出口成章"的"绝技"呢？

他们如是说

学习英语（或任何一门外语）没有任何捷径可图，老想找捷径的人是永远学不好的，要想学好必须定下心来打一场持久战。……要从阅读中学到好的，地道的英语，我们不妨读细一点，甚至对好的句子、段落加以背诵。但阅读不应该只限于写一些漂亮句子，更重要的是得到知识，不仅是专业知识，而且是广泛的人文知识，这是学好英语的关键所在。

——熊德輗，曾任教于北京外国语学校（今北京外国语大学），现已退休

学语言光听不说，光读不写，是学不好的。现在，有不少学生只知戴着耳机听英语，埋头读英语书，却不开口朗读、背诵名

篇、名段,不开口练着说英语,也不动手做笔头练习,写英语文章。只有语言的"输入"(通过听、读吸收语言),却无语言的"输出"(通过口头和笔头表达思想,应用学到的语言),是学不好语言的。

——张中载,北京外国语大学英语系教授、博士生导师

背诵是惟一真理!背诵是真正的英语速成捷径!背诵让你的英语突飞猛进!背诵让外语真正成为母语!背诵让你拥有最好的语言环境——不用出国胜似出国!背诵让你大大缩短征服英语的时间!背诵让你成为口语大师!背诵让你成为绝对的考试高手!全国的高考状元、四六级高手都是背出来的!著名英语教授和学者都是背出来的!赶紧来背诵吧!……在中国学英语,背诵是惟一的真理!背诵才是硬道理!背诵是钢、是铁、是生产力!其他都是"假"的!其他都是辅助的!其他都是虚幻的!背诵让你每天都是最快乐的人!背诵让你每天都是最有成就感的人!背诵让你的记忆力和智商每天都在增长!

——李阳,"疯狂英语"创始人

同样,在我看来,多背诵好的文学作品,无论是中国的,外国的,都大有益于自己的写作。就是在阅读一些小说时,有些好的句子、段落,也可以背下来。……处处留心皆学问。只要肯读书,多背诵,自己的感受能力、表达能力必会长进。……想想看,一旦你把课文都背下来,学习时会多么轻松啊!考试时,很多语法即使记不清,也可以从背诵的文章中找出一些相似的例句,举一反三,就明白了。我从此找到了英语学习的信心。

——秦朔,《南风窗》总编辑

要学好英语,就要对语言本身及语言所传达的各种文化信息感兴趣。当你读到或听到别人用简洁的英语表达深奥的思想时,兴奋不已,立即记住,这就表明你已对语言产生了兴趣。没有这种兴趣,难以在语言学习中登堂入室。……

学习英语跟做任何学问一样,没有捷径可走,不下苦工夫是不行的。……学习语言有一个累积过程,在听、说、写、读四项技

能中,阅读是关键。应该大量阅读简写本文学名著和其他简易读物,培养对英语的感性认识,了解英语社会的文化背景知识。如果把自己感兴趣的文章或诗歌或名篇背下来,那对以后写地道的英语会有很大的好处。

学习英语是为了使用。在大量阅读的基础上,要想方设法使用自己学到的东西。最简便的办法是用英语复述自己感兴趣的阅读材料和用英语写日记。这两种办法可以促使我们在阅读时有意识地寻找我们想用的语言素材和表达方式,而长期坚持的结果会提高我们理解原文的能力和用英语正确表达思想的能力。

——何其莘,北京外国语大学副校长、教授、博士生导师

在基础阶段后期,或高年级,要努力背诵名篇,譬如说,背50—100 篇。无论从语言还是内容来说,这都是精华。背熟了,对了解西方文化,对研究文字的运用都有好处。

——梅仁毅,北京外国语大学教授、博士生导师、美国研究中心主任

……我将把好的课文念得正确、流利、烂熟,睡梦中会说出来,作文中会用出来。我还要读课外读物,并用简单的英语向我的同学复述故事的内容。我将学一点基本语法知识,以加强学习的自觉性,但绝不去钻牛角尖。

——薄冰,北京外国语大学英语系教授,英语语法教学与研究专家

在没有语言环境的情况下,外语是不可能"习得"的(但作为一种教学手段,必须尽量创造习得环境),只能"学得"。必须下艰苦的功夫。我一向主张要"背"。不仅儿童,成人更加要背。且看郑板桥在《自叙》中所说:"人咸谓板桥读书善记,不知非善记,乃善诵耳。板桥每读一书,必千万遍。舟中、马上、被底,或当食忘匕著,或对客不听其语,并自忘其所语,皆记书默诵也。书有弗记者乎?"(人们都认为我郑板桥特别擅长记忆,他们不知道,我不是擅长记忆,而是擅长背诵。我每读一本书,都

要重复很多遍。无论是在船上、马上、被窝里，还是在吃饭的时候，还是在招待客人的时候，我常常走神，忘记了自己在干什么，这都是因为我在默默地背书的缘故。读书哪有不背的道理?)一代大师尚且如此，何况我辈凡人，更何况他背的大概不是外语。

——陈琳，中国老教授协会外国语文专业委员会理事长

在没有语言环境的情况下背熟几十篇文章。让这几十篇文章形成一个有效的、生动的语言小环境。单词和词组只有在句子中才有生命力，才能显示其内涵、色彩、格调。而句子结构只有在上下连贯的意义中才能显示出内在的理由、作用和功能。背熟了几十篇课文，学过的单词和句型才能活起来。我们在阅读的时候才能读了上半句就能在大脑中预感到下半句，读了前一句就能够预感到下一句，根本无须暗暗译成中文之后再思量意思，这样就提高了阅读速度。背熟了几十篇文章，我们要动口的时候，各种各样的表达就能更快地来到我们的嘴边而无须去搜肠刮肚。

——俞敏洪，新东方学校创始人，现任北京新东方教育科技集团董事长

Move your mouth! Understanding something doesn't mean the muscles of your mouth can produce the sounds. Practice speaking what you are learning aloud. It may seem strange, but it is very effective. (让你的嘴动起来吧! 理解了某些东西并不意味着你的口腔肌肉能够发出相应的声音。练习将你所学到的大声说出来。或许那看上去有点怪异，但是却很有效。)

Be patient with yourself. Remember learning is a process — speaking a language well takes time. It is not a computer that is either on or off! (对自己耐心一点。记住，学习是一个过程——说一种语言确实要花费一些时间。那可不像打开或关掉电脑一样轻易!)

——from *11 Ways to Improve Your English*(选自《改善你英语的十一种方式》)

　　几年的学习中，令我印象最深的是我在朗读上下的功夫，朗读从一开始就成了我的习惯。只有在高三最后阶段才暂停，到了大学里又保持了下来。它的效果令我至今受益匪浅。我认为朗读的关键有三点：一要音准，二要理解，三要流利。……在一遍一遍的朗读过程中，句意渐渐清晰起来。对于已经弄懂的句子，我反复朗读到成诵，使之成为自己的东西；对于难懂的句子，我从不轻易放过。这仿佛是在有路障的道路上开车，碰到一处路障，就倒车再试，不行转向，直到顺利通过。一旦意思清楚了，以后的每一遍诵读就成了巩固，印象深了，以后再碰到相似的问题就不会被难倒。久而久之，理解与思考能力就加强了。……我不是为了背书而背书，我是多读而自然成诵。这就要花大量的时间，直到每句话都朗朗上口，一滚而出方满意。这样做的目的不是要记课文内容，而对语音、语调、语速、听力、理解以及舌头的灵活性的综合训练。现在常常有人说我的语音语调好，听上去像美国人说话。原因就在于长期的训练口形与舌头，初步掌握了它们的运动方法，从而做到说者轻松，听者舒畅。

——刘欣，中央电视台四频道英语新闻节目主持人

　　多背优美的英文篇章。我们学习汉语写作是从背诵开始的，这一点不言而喻。对于学习英语写作来说，背诵就更加重要了。不下苦功夫在……阅读的基础上背诵数百篇的优秀篇章，英文思维能力就不可能培养起来；而不能用英语进行思维就无法超越翻译式的写作阶段，也就永远不可能真正用英语进行创造性的写作，即创作。

——孙远，留美学者、教授

　　背诵对于语感的培养具有重要的作用。从初中一年级到高中的英语部编教材的课文，我都做到了逐课背诵，现在看来，这对于英语学习帮助非浅。通俗地说，背诵的过程，也就是将别人的东西化为自己的东西。背诵一些英语国家作者的作品，有助于培养标准英语的思维，只要有坚持不懈的精神，必然会实现从"量变到质变"。

——俞弘，毕业于南京大学外国语学院英语系，后赴美留学

背诵要领"五步曲"(建议)

【第一步:扫清拦路虎】弄清楚每篇文章之后所列单词和词组的发音、拼写和意思。

【第二步:奠基工程】理解文章中的每一句话以至整篇文章。

【第三步:热身运动】一板一眼、大大方方地轻声慢读全文二到三遍,注意体会句与句之间、段与段之间的脉络关系,通过慢读尽量达到琅琅上口。

【第四步:核心环节】放开声音、心无旁骛、清清楚楚地朗读,不要过多考虑文章的内容,朗读速度越快越好,快到一口气能读完四五个句子,直到不假思索就能倾泻出全文的内容,亦即出口成章。这样可以使自己的口腔肌肉充分活动起来,改变多年来形成的汉语发音的习惯性口腔运动模式,使嘴与大脑逐渐协调起来,从而逐渐建立并巩固全新的英语发音的口腔运动模式;同时,这样做还可以磨练自己的自信心,增进自己学英语的动力。否则扭扭捏捏地嘟囔英语就是"小和尚念经,有口无心",自己的口形自然不会到位,长此以往,就会形成恶性循环。

【第五步:坚实保障】如果时间充裕,我们建议您默写全文,将文章内容落实到笔头,然后对照原文,一丝不苟地进行订正,进一步深化对文章内容的理解,锤炼自己掌握语言的精确程度,全面提升自己用词造句、布局谋篇的书面表达能力。

　　值得注意的是,方法就是方法,它始终无法替代勤奋刻苦的练习与实践。Practice makes perfect,而不是 Methods make perfect. 对于这些精彩的篇章,我们建议您逐句识记,逐篇背诵,直到完全可以出口成章,达到"流利、清晰、完整、准确和恰当"的英语口语新境界。这样做表面上看起来有些慢,实际上对自己英语综合能力的培养有百利而无一害。当然,如果觉得时间不够用,那么您完全可以从这些篇章中挑选出一些您最感兴趣的实用句子,反复记诵,举一反三,这同样可以给您带来意想不到的收获。

我们知道，朗读和背诵具有很强的记忆性质，而人脑又不是电脑——人是会遗忘的，所以在我们朗读和背诵的过程中，一个无法回避的问题就是记忆问题。

德国著名心理学家艾宾浩斯（Hermann Ebbinghaus，1850—1909）对人类的遗忘现象做了系统的研究和测试，得出了一些统计数据。（见下表）

时间间隔	记忆保持量
刚刚记忆完毕	100%
20 分钟之后	58.2%
1 小时之后	44.2%
8—9 个小时之后	35.8%
1 天之后	33.7%
2 天之后	27.8%
6 天之后	25.4%
一个月之后	21.1%

后来，艾宾浩斯将实验数据绘制成一条曲线，即著名的"艾宾浩斯遗忘曲线"，其横坐标代表记忆天数，纵坐标代表记忆保持量（百分数）。（见下图）

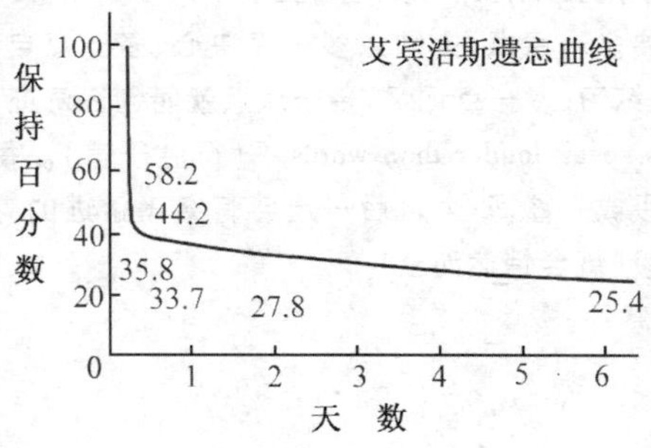

这条曲线表明了人类遗忘发展的一条规律:遗忘进程是不均衡的,先快后慢——在1天时间里遗忘得很快,以后逐渐变缓。这是一个具有共性的群体规律,但是记忆规律可以具体到我们每一个人,因为我们的生理特点、生活经历不同,可能导致我们有不同的记忆习惯、记忆方式、记忆特点。

那么,怎样才能有效战胜遗忘这个敌人呢?

根据中国人学习英语的特征以及朗读和背诵的学习规律,我们可以从这条遗忘曲线中得到如下启示:当天朗读和背诵的内容最好能够在当天复习一次,并且建议各位读者能够在之后的第2、5、15、30、60天各复习一次,这样对于记忆量的保持极有帮助,甚至于达到终生不忘的程度。

这样,我们记忆的"雪球"会越滚越大。久而久之,反复消化,积少成多,集腋成裘。你会发现自己的记忆速度越来越快,同样长度的篇章所需要的背诵时间越来越短。而对于英语的领悟力和感受力,就在这一天天的朗读和背诵中大大加强。你会产生一种"立体学习"的感觉,不知不觉中已经跳出了枯燥记单词和背语法的束缚,身临其境,高屋建瓴,站在一个全新的层面上学习英语,学习英语俨然已经成为一种享受!

说做就做(**Just Do It!**)

一本书读三遍要比三本书读一遍好得多!

学英语就是要用,要在用中学,在学中用!

每天只要多一点点,比别人多一点决心、多一点自律、多一点行动、多一点练习、多一点记忆,多一点点就能创造奇迹!

"Actions speak louder than words."(行胜于言)。每天坚持朗读或背诵一段或一篇,四个月后一定会有突飞猛进的感觉,"用英语思维的阶段"就会悄然而至!

Life Is to Be Whole[*]

Once a circle missed a wedge. The circle wanted to be whole, so it went around looking for its missing piece. But because it was incomplete and therefore could roll only very slowly, it admired the flowers along the way. It chatted with worms. It enjoyed the sunshine. It found lots of different pieces, but none of them fit. So it left them all by the side of the road and kept on searching. Then one day the circle

---

* 作者佚名。每个人都渴望自己的人生完美无瑕，可是真实的情况却往往是"人生因不完美而完美"。一位先哲这样说过："我的人生不完整，因为我的人生太平静，没有大的波澜。"也许更多的时候，丰富我们的经历才是人生中最重要的东西。如果我们将生活中不同的特定境遇连续起来，便构成了一个完整的人生线段。这个处境线段既不可能是圆的，也不可能是直的，你会遇到逆境、顺境和无奈的俗境，你也会因此而产生种种不同的心态。因而，我们不妨"不求'完美'，也不求'永不犯错'，而是求得人生的'完整'。"

found a piece that fit perfectly. It was so happy. Now it could be whole, with nothing missing. It incorporated the missing piece into itself and began to roll. Now that it was a perfect circle, it could roll very fast, too fast to notice the flowers or to talk to the worms. When it realized how different the world seemed when it rolled so quickly, it stopped, left its found piece by the side of the road and rolled slowly away.

The lesson of the story, I suggested, was that in some strange sense we are more whole when we are missing something. The man who has everything is in some ways a poor man. He will never know what it feels like to yearn, to hope, to nourish his soul with the dream of something better. He will never know the experience of having someone who loves him give him something he has always wanted or never had.

There is a wholeness about the person who has come to terms with his limitations, who has been brave enough to let go of his unrealistic dreams and not feel like a failure for doing so. There is a wholeness about the man or woman who has learned that he or she is strong enough to go through a tragedy and survive, who can lose someone and still feel like a complete person.

Life is not a trap set for us by God so that he can condemn us for failing. Life is not a spelling bee, where no matter how many words you've gotten right, you're disqualified if you make one mistake. Life is more like a baseball season, where even the best team loses one-third of its games and even the worst team has its days of brilliance. Our goal is to win more games than we lose.

When we accept that imperfection is part of being human, and when we can continue rolling through life and appreciate it, we will have achieved a wholeness that others can only aspire to. That, I believe, is what God asks of us — not "Be perfect", not "Don't even make a mistake", but "Be whole".

If we are brave enough to love, strong enough to forgive, generous enough to rejoice in another's happiness, and wise enough to know there is enough love to go around for us all, then we can achieve a fulfillment that no other living creature will ever know. ✻

 ## Vocabulary List【词汇清单】

wedge /wedʒ/ *n.* 楔子(一块如金属或木头的材料,一端粗至另一端逐渐变细以便插入狭小的缝隙内,用于劈开、绷紧、固定或用杠杆撬动某种东西)

admire /ədˈmaiə/ *v.* 钦佩,羡慕,赞美

perfectly /ˈpəːfiktli/ *adv.* 完美地,完整地,完善地

incorporate /inˈkɔːpəreit/ *v.* (使)结合,(使)并入

in some sense：在某种程度上,在某种意义上

yearn /jəːn/ *v.* 渴望,向往,想念

nourish /ˈnʌriʃ/ *v.* 怀有,孕育

unrealistic /ˈʌnriəˈlistik/ *adj.* 不现实的,不切实际的,幻想的

go through：忍受,经受,经历

tragedy /ˈtrædʒidi/ *n.* 悲剧,不幸,灾难

trap set：(捕捉野兽的)陷阱,圈套

condemn /kənˈdem/ *v.* 谴责,责难,怪罪

spelling bee：<美>拼字比赛(一种将拼错了指定字词的比赛者淘汰出局的比赛,亦作 spelldown)

disqualify /disˈkwɔlifai/ *v.* 使无资格,使不合格,取消比赛资格

brilliance /ˈbriljəns/ *n.* 辉煌,显赫,杰出

aspire /əsˈpaiə/ *v.* 渴求,渴望,追求(知识、名誉等)(to,at,after)

rejoice /riˈdʒɔis/ *v.* 欣喜,高兴(at,in,over)

fulfillment /fulˈfilmənt/ *n.* (事业的)成就,(希望的)实现,(义务、诺言的)完成、履行

 参考译文【Suggested Translation】

人生在于完整

从前，有一只圆圈缺少了一块楔子。圆圈想要保持完整，于是四处寻找失去的那块楔子。可是，由于它不完整，所以只能很慢地滚动。一路上，它对花儿露出羡慕之色。它与蠕虫谈天说地。它还享受到了阳光之美。圆圈找到了很多不同的配件，可是没有一件能够完美地与其相配。所以，它将它们全部弃置路边，继续寻找。终于有一天，它找到了一个完美的配件。圆圈是那样喜出望外。既然它已经成为了一个完整的圆圈，所以滚动得非常快，快得以至于无暇观赏花儿，也无暇与蠕虫倾诉心声。圆圈飞奔急骋，发觉眼中的世界变得如此不同，于是，它禁不住停了下来，将找到的那个配件留在路旁，又开始了慢慢地滚动。

我认为这个故事告诉我们，从某种奇妙的意义上说，当我们失去一些东西的时候反而感到更加完整。一个拥有一切的人其实在某些方面是一个贫穷的人。他永远也体会不到什么是渴望、期待以及对美好梦想的感悟。他也永远不会有这样一种体验：一个爱他的人送给他某种他梦寐以求的或者从未拥有过的东西意味什么。

人生的完整性在于一个人知道如何去面对他的缺陷，如何勇敢地放弃那些不现实的幻想而且又不以此为缺憾。人生的完整性还在于一个男人或者女人懂得这样一个道理：他（她）发现自己能够勇敢面对人生悲剧而继续生存，能够在失去亲人之后依然表现出一个完整的人的风范。

人生不是上帝为谴责我们的缺陷而给我们设下的陷阱。人生也不是一场拼字游戏淘汰赛。无论你拼出多少单词，一旦出现了一个错误，你便前功尽弃。人生更像是一个棒球赛季。即使最好的球队比赛也会输掉 1/3，而最差的球队也有春风得意的日子。我们的目标就是多赢球，少输球。

我们接受了不完整性是人类本性的一部分，我们不断地进行人生滚动并能够意识到其价值，我们便会完成完整人生的过程。而对于别人来说，这只能是一个梦想。我相信这就是上帝对于我们的要求：不求"完美"，也不求"永不犯错"，而是求得人生的"完整"。

假如我们勇敢得能够去爱，坚强得能够去宽恕，大度得能够去分享他人的幸福，明智得能够理解身边充满着爱，那么我们就能取得其他生物所不能取得的成就。◆

（《英语沙龙》许歆 译）

● You never know what you can do till you try.（在尝试之前你不会知道自己能做什么。）

● So said, so done.（言必信，行必果。）

● Better be envied than pitied.（宁为人妒，不受人怜。）

● Deliberate in counsel, prompt in action.（考虑要仔细，行动要迅速。）

Home[*]

What makes a home? Love and sympathy and confidence. It is a place where kindly affections exist among all the members of the family. The parents take good care of their children, and the children are interested in the activities of their parents. Thus all of them are bound together by affection, and they find their home to be the cheeriest place in the world.

A home without love is no more a home than a body with-

---

* 作者佚名。有一首歌这样唱道："我想要有个家,一个不需要华丽的地方,在我疲倦的时候我会想到它;我想要有个家,一个不需要多大的地方,在我受惊吓的时候我才不会害怕。"另外一首歌也唱道:"给我一个小小的家,蜗牛的家,能挡风遮雨的地方,不必太大。给我一个小小的家,蜗牛的家,一个属于自己温暖的蜗牛的家。"家——多么亲切而温馨的字眼!有家,又何尝不是一种幸福呢? 作为其中的一员,我们每个人都有责任让自己的家更温暖,更舒适,更惬意。

out a soul is a man. Every civilized person is a social being. No one should live alone. A man may lead a successful and prosperous life, but prosperity alone can by no means insure happiness. Many great personages in the world history had deep affections for their homes.

Your home may be poor and humble, but your duty lies there. You should try to make it cheerful and comfortable. The greater the difficulties, the richer will be your reward.

A home is more than a family dwelling. It is a school in which people are trained for citizenship. A man will not render good services to his country if he can do nothing good for his home; for in proportion as he loves his home, will he love his country. The home is the birthplace of true patriotism. It is the secret of social welfare and national greatness. It is the basis and origin of civilization. ✳

Vocabulary List 【词汇清单】

sympathy /ˈsimpəθi/ *n.* 同感,认同,和谐

confidence /ˈkɔnfidəns/ *n.* 信任,信赖

affection /əˈfekʃən/ *n.* 感情;(对人对物的)爱,喜爱

bound /baund/ *adj.* 受约束的;被联结在一起的

cheery /ˈtʃiəri/ *adj.* 快乐的,喜气洋洋的

prosperous /ˈprɔspərəs/ *adj.* 繁荣的,富裕的,兴旺的

prosperity /prɔsˈperiti/ *n.* 繁荣,富裕,兴旺

by no means：决不,毫不,一点也不

personage /ˈpəːsnidʒ/ *n.* 要人,名流

humble /ˈhʌmbl/ *adj.* 简陋的,寒伧的

dwelling /ˈdweliŋ/ *n.* 住所,寓所

citizenship /ˈsitiznʃip/ *n.* 公民权,公民身份

render /ˈrendə/ *v.* 给予,提供

✓**proportion** /prə'pɔ:ʃən/ *n.* 比例；(in) 相称
✓**patriotism** /'pætriətizəm/ *n.* 爱国主义，爱国精神
welfare /'welfɛə/ *n.* 幸福，福利，救济
civillization /ˌsivilai'zeiʃən/ *n.* 开化（的过程），文明

 参考译文【Suggested Translation】

家

组成家庭的因素是什么？答案即爱、认同和信赖。家是一个所有家庭成员凝结情感的地方。父母亲悉心照料孩子，而孩子们也对他们双亲的活动感兴趣。他们为爱所联结，因而发现家是世界上最令人感到欢乐的地方。

一个没有爱的家便不再称其为家，如同没有灵魂的躯体不再是人一样。每一个有修养的人都是社会性的人。没有人能够脱离社会独自生存。一个人也许过着成功而宽裕的生活，但是荣华富贵决不能保证幸福快乐。在世界历史上，许多名人都对其家庭怀有深情厚意。

你的家也许贫穷而简陋，但那正是你的职责所在。你应该努力使其愉快和舒适。你遭遇的困难越大，所得到的报偿也就越多。

家不仅仅是一个供家人居住的地方。它还是一个培养人们成为公民的场所。一个人假如无法对家庭做出有意义的事情，也就无法为国家提供优良的服务，因为爱家和爱国是成正比的。家庭是爱国主义精神的真正发源地，是社会福利和国家昌盛的秘诀，是文明的基础和起源。◆

Too Dear for the Whistle[*]

When I was a child of seven years old, my friends, on a holiday, filled my pocket with coppers. I went at once to a shop where they sold toys for children. Being charmed with the sound of a whistle that I had seen by the way, in the hands of another boy, I handed over all my money for one. I then came home, and went whistling all over the house, much pleased with my whistle, but disturbing all the family.

---

　　* 作者本杰明·富兰克林（Benjamin Franklin，1706—1790），18 世纪美国最伟大的科学家、著名的政治家和文学家，美国独立宣言的起草人之一，资本主义精神最完美的代表，其代表作有《富兰克林自传》、《穷理查年鉴》等。他一生最真实的写照是他自己所说过的一句话："诚实和勤勉，应该成为你永久的伴侣。"在《得不偿失的哨子》一文中，作者由孩提时代发生的一件天真而愚蠢的小事谈起，然后过渡到后来汲取的教训，进而感叹世界上各种各样的人在做着得不偿失的事情，耽搁了生活，甚至贻误了一生。

My brothers and sisters and cousins, when I told of the bargain I had made, said I had given four times as much as the whistle was worth. They put me in mind of what good things I might have bought with the rest of the money, and laughed at me so much for my folly that I cried with vexation. Thinking about the matter gave me more chagrin than the whistle gave me pleasure.

This, however, was afterwards of use to me, for the impression continued on my mind, so that often, when I was tempted to buy something I did not need, I said to myself, "Don't give too much for the whistle," and I saved my money. As I grew up, came into the world, and observed the actions of men, I thought I met with many, very many, who "gave too much for the whistle." When I saw some men too eager for court favour, wasting his time at court gatherings, giving up his rest, his liberty, his virtue, and perhaps his friends, for royal favour, I said to myself — "This man gives too much for the whistle." When I saw another fond of popularity, constantly taking part in political affairs, neglecting his own business, and ruining it by neglect, "He pays, indeed," said I, "too dear for his whistle."

If I knew a miser who gave up every kind of comfortable living, all the pleasure of doing good to others, all the esteem of his fellow citizens and the joys of friendship, for the sake of gathering and keeping wealth — "Poor man," said I, "you pay too dear for your whistle." When I met a man of pleasure, who did not try to improve his mind or his fortune but merely devoted himself to having a good time, perhaps neglecting his health, "Mistaken man," said I, "you are providing pain for yourself, instead of pleasure; you are paying too dear for your whistle." If I saw someone fond of appearance who had fine clothes, fine houses, fine furniture, fine earrings, all above his fortune, and for which he had run into debt, and ends his career in a prison. "Alas," said I, "he has paid dear, very dear, for his whistle." In short the miseries of mankind are largely due to their putting a false value on things — to giving "too much for their whistles". ✱

 ## Vocabulary List【词汇清单】

whistle /ˈwisl/ *n.* 口哨,哨子

copper /ˈkɔpə/ *n.* 铜币(英国口语,相当于 penny, halfpenny)

be charmed with：为…着迷的,被…吸引的

disturb /disˈtəːb/ *v.* 打扰,扰乱

bargain /ˈbaːgin/ *n.* 成交商品(的行为),交易

folly /ˈfɔli/ *n.* 愚蠢,蠢笨

vexation /vekˈseiʃən/ *n.* 烦恼,忧虑,苦恼

chagrin /ˈʃægrin/ *n.* 懊恼,悔恨

be tempted to：想要去做…,一心要去…

court favour：朝廷的恩宠(下文的 royal favour 与之同义)

virtue /ˈvəːtjuː/ *n.* 德行,美德

popularity /ˌpɔpjuˈlæriti/ *n.* 名望,声望

constantly /ˈkɔnstəntli/ *adv.* 经常地,不断地

neglect /niˈglekt/ *n.* 忽视,疏忽

ruin /ˈruːin/ *v.* (使)荒废,毁灭

miser /ˈmaizə/ *n.* 守财奴,吝啬鬼

esteem /isˈtiːm/ *n.* 尊敬,尊重

for the sake of：为…起见,为了…

merely /ˈmiəli/ *adv.* 仅仅,不过

devote oneself to：专心于…,致力于…

mistaken /misˈteikən/ *adj.* 犯错的,误入歧途的

furniture /ˈfəːnitʃə/ *n.* 家具,设备

earring /ˈiəriŋ/ *n.* 耳环,耳饰

✓ **fortune** /ˈfɔːtʃən/ *n.* 财富,财产
run into debt:负债,欠债
alas /əˈlæs/ *int.* 唉,哎呀(表示悲哀、惋惜等)
✓ **misery** /ˈmizəri/ *n.* 痛苦,苦恼,不幸
largely /ˈlɑːdʒli/ *adv.* 主要地,在很大程度上
due to:由于…,由…引起(造成)的

参考译文【Suggested Translation】

得不偿失的哨子

当我还是一个七岁孩子的时候,有一次过节,朋友们往我的衣袋里塞满了铜币。我立刻向一家卖儿童玩具的店铺跑去。半路上,我却被另一个男孩手中的哨子声吸引住了,于是就主动要求用我所有的铜币换了他的哨子。然后我回到家里,吹着哨子满屋子转,非常得意,却打扰了全家人。我的哥哥、姐姐和表姐们知道了我所做的这笔交易,便告诉我,为了这个哨子我付出了比它原价高四倍的钱。他们还使我懂得,用那些多付的钱可以买到多少好东西啊。大伙儿都笑话我傻,竟使我懊恼地哭了。回想这件事给我带来的悔恨远远超过了那只哨子所给我的快乐。

不过,这件事情后来却对我很有用处,它一直保留在我的记忆中。因此当我常常打算买一些不必要的东西时,我便对自己说,"不要为哨子花费太多",于是便节省了钱。当我长大走进社会,观察了人们的所作所为,我感到,我遇到许许多多的人,他们都"为一只哨子付出了过高的代价"。当我看见一个人过分热衷于恩宠荣禄,把自己的光阴牺牲在侍候权贵、谋求接见之中。为了得到这种机会,他不惜牺牲自己的休息、自由、品德,甚至自己的朋友。我便对自己说,"这个人为他的哨子付出了太高的代价"。当我看见另一些人醉心于名望,无休止地投身于政界的纷扰之中,而他自己的事情却被忽视、被耽误了,我说,"他的确也为了他的哨子付出了过高的代价"。

　　如果我听说有个守财奴，他为了积累财产而宁愿放弃各种舒适的生活，一切为别人做好事的乐趣，所有的同乡们对他的尊重，以及慷慨无私的友谊的欢乐。"可怜的人啊"，我说，"为了你的哨子，你付出了过高的代价。"当我遇到一个寻欢作乐的人，他不愿使自己精神上或命运方面得到一切可赞美的改善，而仅仅为了达到肉体上的享受，为了这种追求损害了自己的身体。"误入歧途的人啊"，我就说，"你真是有福不享自找苦吃；为了你的哨子，你付出了太高的代价啊"。如果我看到一个人沉迷于外表，或者是漂亮的装束，讲究的住宅，上等的家具，精致的耳环，这一切都远远超出了他收入的水平。为了得到这一切，他举借外债，最后以被投进监狱而告终。"天哪！"我说，"为了他的哨子，他付出了太高太高的代价。"总之，我认为，他们所遭受的人类很大一部分的悲苦都是由于他们对事物的价值所做出错误估价而造成的，都是"为他们的哨子付出了太高的代价"。◆

● He laughs best who laughs last.（谁笑到最后谁笑得最美。）

● Deal with a man as he deals with you.（以其人之道还治其人之身。）

● It's never too late to mend.（亡羊补牢，犹未为晚。）

● Pride goes before a fall.（骄兵必败。）

Youth[*]

Youth is not a time of life; it is a state of mind; it is not a matter of rosy cheeks, red lips and supple knees; it is a matter of the will, a quality of the imagination, and a vigor of the emotions; it is the freshness of the deep springs of life.

Youth means a temperamental predominance of courage over timidity, of the appetite for adventure over the love of ease. This often exists in a man of 60 more than a boy of 20. Nobody grows old merely by a number of years. We grow old by deserting our ideals.

Years may wrinkle the skin, but to give up enthusiasm wrinkles the soul. Worry, fear, self-distrust bows the heart

---

　＊　作者塞缪尔·厄尔曼（Samuel Ullman，1840—1920），生于德国，童年移居美国，参加过"南北战争"，曾经是五金制造商，并热衷于公益事业，是著名的教育家和社会活动家。他的名篇《青春》美妙绝伦，曾被美军名将道格拉斯·麦克阿瑟以及日本实业家松下幸之助等要人视为座右铭。

and turns the spirit back to dust.

Whether 60 or 16, there is in every human being's heart the lure of wonder, the unfailing childlike appetite of what's next and the joy of the game of living. In the center of your heart and my heart there is a wireless station: so long as it receives messages of beauty, hope, cheer, courage and power from men and from the Infinite, so long are you young.

When the aerials are down, and your spirit is covered with snows of cynicism and the ice of pessimism, then you are grown old, even at 20, but as long as your aerials are up, to catch waves of optimism, there is hope you may die young at 80. ✱

Vocabulary List 【词汇清单】

rosy cheeks：玫瑰色的双颊, 粉红色的面颊

lip /lip/ *n.* 嘴唇, 唇缘

supple /'sʌpl/ *adj.* （身体）柔软的, 柔韧的, 伸曲自如的

vigor /'vigə/ *n.* 精力, 活力

emotion /i'məuʃən/ *n.* 情绪, 情感

freshness /'freʃnis/ *n.* 清新, 新鲜, 生机勃勃

spring /spriŋ/ *n.* 源泉, 起源, 渊源

temperamental /ˌtemprə'mentl/ *adj.* 由人的气质引起的, 性情的

predominance /ˌpri'dɔminəns/ *n.* 主导, 支配

timidity /ti'miditi/ *n.* 胆怯, 羞怯

appetite /'æpitait/ *n.* 欲求, 渴望（for）

desert /di'zə:t/ *v.* 放弃, 抛弃

wrinkle /'riŋkl/ *v.* （使）起皱纹, 起皱褶

enthusiasm /in'θju:ziæzəm/ *n.* 热心, 热情, 热忱

self-distrust /ˌselfdis'trʌst/ *n.* 缺乏自信, 自卑

bow /bau/ *v.* 压弯,(使)扭曲、屈服

lure /ljuə/ *v.* 吸引,引诱

unfailing /ʌnˈfeiliŋ/ *adj.* 经久不衰的,无穷尽的

the Infinite /ˈinfinit/ *n.* <修辞>上帝

aerial /ˈɛəriəl/ *n.* (用于接收电磁波的)天线

cynicism /ˈsinisizəm/ *n.* 玩世不恭、愤世嫉俗的态度,爱讥讽
　　人的习癖

pessimism /ˈpesimizəm/ *n.* 悲观(论),厌世主义

optimism /ˈɔptimizəm/ *n.* 乐观主义,乐观情绪

 **参考译文【Suggested Translation】**

青　春

青春,并非人生的一段时光,而是一种精神状态;亦非粉颊红唇和冰肌柔骨,而是刚强的意志、灵秀的想像和充满活力的情感;它是使生命之泉永不枯竭的常青树。

青春,意味着一种非凡气质:敢做敢为而不怯懦退缩、甘冒风险而不贪恋安逸。在一位 60 岁老者的身上,这种气质的存在可能甚于 20 岁的小伙子。没有人会单单由于岁月的流逝而衰老,有的人却因为放弃理想而老态龙钟。

流年时光可以在皮肤上留下皱纹,而熄灭热情则会使心灵起皱。忧虑、恐惧和缺乏自信只会使人心胸狭隘,心灰意冷。

不管是 60 岁还是 16 岁,每个人的心里都会被新奇事物所吸引,都会像孩子一样对未来洋溢着无穷无尽的憧憬,都会在生活的游戏(境遇)之中获取欢乐。在你我心灵的深处,都有一座无线电台:只要它从人群中间和造物主那里接收到美、希望、鼓励、勇气和力量的电波,你我就会青春常在。

一旦这座电台的天线收拢,一旦玩世不恭的冷雪和悲观绝望的寒冰覆盖了你的心灵,即使你只有 20 岁,也未老先衰了;但是只要它的天线始终竖立在你的心中,捕捉着每一个乐观向上的电波,纵使你 80 而逝之时也会青春永驻。◆

On Punctuality*

A punctual person is in the habit of doing everything at the proper time and is never late in keeping an appointment.

The unpunctual man, on the other hand, never does what he has to do at the proper time. He is always in a hurry and in the end loses both time and his good name. There is a proverb that says, "Time flies never to be recalled". This is very true. A lost thing may be found again, but lost time can

---

　　＊ 作者佚名。时光如流水,岁月不待人。时间本身就是生命! 守时就是遵守承诺,按时办妥要做的事情,没有例外,没有借口,任何时候都做到。守时既是对自己生命的一种责任,又是对他人生命的一种尊重。守时表明诚信,这样才能严于律己,有所建树。如果你不守时,你就没有影响力或没有道德的力量。"如果你想结交朋友和有影响力的人就要准时。"(戴尔·卡耐基) 面对"逝者如斯"的时光,你又该如何去做呢?

never be regained. Time is more valuable than material things. In fact time is life itself, and the unpunctual man is forever wasting and mismanaging his own valuable asset as well as others'. The unpunctual man is always complaining that he finds no time to answer letters, or to return calls, or to keep appointments promptly. But the man who really has a great deal to do is very careful of his time and seldom complains of want of it. He knows that he can not get through his immense amount of work unless he faithfully keeps every appointment promptly and deal with every piece of work when it has to be attended to...

Failure to be punctual is a sign of disrespect towards others. If a person is invited to a dinner and arrives later than expected, he keeps all the other guests and the host waiting for him alone. This is great impoliteness.

Unpunctuality is very harmful when it comes to doing one's duty, whether private or public. Imagine how it would be if those who are entrusted with important tasks failed to be at their proper place at the appointed time. A man who is known to be habitually unpunctual is never trusted by his friends or fellow men. And the unpunctual man is a source of annoyance both to others and to himself. ✳

Vocabulary List 【词汇清单】

punctuality /ˌpʌnktʃuˈæləti/ n.　严守时刻, 准时

proverb /ˈprɔvəːb/ n.　谚语, 格言

regain /riˈgein/ v.　收回, 复得, 重新获得

mismanage /misˈmænidʒ/ v.　处置不当, 管理不善

promptly /ˈprɔmptli/ adv.　立即地, 果断地, 迅速地

immense /iˈmens/ adj.　极大的, 巨大的

disrespect /'disris'pekt/ *n.* 无礼，不尊重

impoliteness /ˌimpə'laitnis/ *n.* 不礼貌，失礼

entrust /in'trʌst/ *v.* 委托，托付

habitually /hə'bitjuəli/ *adv.* 习惯性地，惯常地，通常地

annoyance /ə'nɔiəns/ *n.* 烦恼，恼怒

参考译文【Suggested Translation】

论　守　时

一个守时的人养成了按时做事的习惯，这样的人言必信，行必果。

另一方面，不守时的人却从不按时完成他应该做的事情。他总是匆匆忙忙的，到头来却既浪费了时间、又败坏了自己的名誉。有句谚语说道："光阴一去不复返。"此话千真万确。一件东西丢了可能找回来，而弄丢了时间可就永远找不回来了。时间较之财富更加珍贵，实际上，时间本身就是生命！因此，那些不守时的人既在浪费自己的宝贵财富，同时也是在浪费他人的珍贵财产！那些不守时的人总是在抱怨，说自己没有时间去写回信、没有时间回电话、或者没有时间按时赴约。然而那些真正有大量事情要处理的人则会小心翼翼地利用时间，很少抱怨说时间不够用。他们知道，除非自己按时赴约和按时处理好应处理的每一件事情，否则他们是不可能做完这一大堆事情的……

不守时是对他人极大的不尊重。如果一个人应邀去参加晚宴，却没有按时出席，结果让所有的客人和主人等他一个人——这就是非常的无礼。

履行义务的时候——无论是公事还是私事——不守时是非常有害的。设想一下，如果把一件重大使命委托给一个不守时的人，结果他没有在恰当的时间和地点完成这项任务，那么结果会怎么样呢？如果一个人以不守时而"闻名"，他怎么可能得到朋友和同事的信任！不守时的人既惹别人生气，又弄得自己不快活。◆

Work and Pleasure *

To be really happy and really safe, one ought to have at least two or three hobbies, and they must all be real. It

---

* 作者温斯顿·L·S·邱吉尔(Winston L. S. Churchill,1874—1965），英国著名政治家,而且还是一位著名的演说家和作家 ,其著作有《第二次世界大战回忆录》、《英语民族史》、《世界危机》等。由于《第二次世界大战回忆录》等历史著作和演说,他以政治家身份获得 1953 年度的诺贝尔文学奖。邱吉尔曾经这样说道:"男孩子必须能够选择自己的道路。我从父母那里得到的只是我的名字而不是财产,我必须寻找机会。我的特殊不是继承来的而是我通过拼搏争取来的。"作为世界历史上的一位伟大人物,他的伟大之处就在于:当国家需要他献身的时候,他会站出来担当神圣的使命;当国家不再需要他的时候,他也会站出来牺牲自己,并且回归平常。在退休之后,邱吉尔多次强调"永远不要放弃",其实他所坚持不放弃的是对生命的追求,而不是对权力的无限追求。2002 年 10 月,温斯顿·邱吉尔被英国人民选为"最伟大的英国人",排在他身后的英国伟人依次为莎士比亚、牛顿、达尔文等。

is no use starting late in life to say: "I will take an interest in this or that." Such an attempt only aggravates the strain of mental effort. A man may acquire great knowledge of topics unconnected with his daily work, and yet hardly get any benefit or relief. It is no use doing what you like; you have got to like what you do. Broadly speaking, human beings may be divided into three classes: those who are toiled to death, those who are worried to death, and those who are bored to death. It is no use offering the manual labourer, tired out with a hard week's sweat and effort, the chance of playing a game of football or baseball on Saturday afternoon. It is no use inviting the politician or the professional or business man, who has been working or worrying about serious things for six days, to work or worry about trifling things at the weekend.

It may also be said that rational, industrious, useful human beings are divided into two classes: first, those whose work is work and whose pleasure is pleasure; and secondly, those whose work and pleasure are one. Of these the former are the majority. They have their compensations. The long hours in the office or the factory bring with them as their reward, not only the means of sustenance, but a keen appetite for pleasure even in its simplest and most modest forms. But Fortune's favoured children belong to the second class. Their life is a natural harmony. For them the working hours are never long enough. Each day is a holiday, and ordinary holidays when they come are grudged as enforced interruptions in an absorbing vacation. Yet to both classes the need of an alternative outlook, of a change of atmosphere, of a diversion of effort, is essential. Indeed, it may well be that those whose work is their pleasure are those who most need the means of banishing it at intervals from their minds. ✸

# Vocabulary List【词汇清单】

aggravate /ˈæɡrəveit/ *v.* 使（病情）恶化，加剧，加重

relief /riˈliːf/ *n.* 减轻（痛苦，焦虑等），慰藉，宽慰

toil /tɔil/ *v.* 苦干，辛劳

manual /ˈmænjuəl/ *adj.* 手的，手工的

rational /ˈræʃənl/ *adj.* 理智的，有理性的

industrious /inˈdʌstriəs/ *adj.* 勤劳的，勤奋的

compensation /ˌkɔmpenˈseiʃən/ *n.* 补偿，报酬

sustenance /ˈsʌstinəns/ *n.* 推持（生计），支撑（生活）

harmony /ˈhaːməni/ *n.* 协调，和谐，融洽

grudge /ˈɡrʌdʒ/ *v.* 勉强给，不愿给

vacation /vəˈkeiʃən/ *n.* 假期，度假

interval /ˈintəvəl/ *n.* （时间）间隔，间隙

# 参考译文【Suggested Translation】

工 作 和 娱 乐

要想真正得到幸福与平安，一个人至少应该有两三种业余爱好，而且必须是真正的爱好。到了晚年才开始说"我对这个或那个感兴趣"是毫无用处的，这种尝试只会增加精神上的负担。在与自己日常工作无关的某种领域中，一个人可以获得渊博的知识，但是他几乎得不到实在的益处或者放松。喜欢干什么就干什么是无益的，你得干一行爱一行。广义而言，人类可以分成三个阶层：劳累而死的人、忧虑而死的人和烦恼而死的人。对于那些体力劳动者来说，在经过一周精疲力竭的工作之后，周六下午给他们提供踢足球或者打棒球的机会是没有意义的。对于政界人士、专业人士或者商人来说，他们已经为棘手的事务操劳或者烦恼了 6 天，在周末再请他们为琐事劳神，同样是毫无意义的。

　　或者可以这么说，理智的、勤奋的、有用的人可以分为两类：第一类，他们的工作就是工作，娱乐就是娱乐；第二类，他们的工作和娱乐是合二为一的。当然，很大一部分人都属于第一类人。他们可以得到相应的补偿。在办公室或工厂里长时间的工作，带给他们的不仅是维持生计的金钱，还带给他们一种渴求娱乐的强烈欲望，哪怕这种娱乐消遣是以最简单、最朴实的方式进行。命运的宠儿则属于第二类人。他们的生活自然而和谐。在他们看来，工作时间永远不够多，每一天在他们看来都是假期；而当正常的假日到来时，他们总会抱怨他们正在全神贯注地休假被强行中断。然而，有一些东西对于这两类人来说是十分必要的，那就是变换一下视角，改变一下氛围，努力做一件别的事情。事实上，每隔一段时间，那些把工作看做娱乐的人们很可能最需要以某种方式把工作驱赶出他们的大脑。◆

●Wise men are silent; fools talk. （智者沉默寡言，愚者滔滔不绝。）

●A bird in the hand is worth than two in the bush. （一鸟在手胜过双鸟在林。）

●Business is the salt of life. （事业如同人生之盐；事业是人生的第一需要。）

●Care and diligence bring luck. （谨慎和勤奋才能抓住机遇。）

April Days *

Days of witchery, subtly sweet,
　　When every hill and tree finds heart,
When winter and spring like lovers meet
In the mist of noon and part —
　　In the April days.

Nights when the wood frogs faintly peep
Once — twice — and then are still,
And the woodpeckers' martial voices sweep
Like bugle notes from hill to hill —

＊ 作者哈姆林·加兰(Hamlin Garland, 1860—1940)，美国著名小说家和诗人，其主要作品有《破碎的偶像》(Crumbling Idols)、《中部边疆的儿子》(A Son of the Middle Border)、《中部边疆的女儿》(A Daughter of the Middle Border)等，1921 年荣获普利策奖(Pulitzer)。从加兰的作品来看，他从未全心全意皈依现实主义，故渐而抛弃了它，其晚期作品转向唯灵论。本诗清新灵巧，饶有趣味，是其诗作中的精品。

Through the pulseless haze.

Days when the soil is warm with rain,
And through the wood the shy wind steals,
Rich with the pine and the poplar smell,
And the joyous earth like a dancer reels —
Through the April days! ✳

 ## Vocabulary List 【词汇清单】

witchery /ˈwitʃəri/ *n.* 魅力,魔力

subtly /ˈsʌtli/ *adv.* 微妙地,轻微地

mist /mist/ *n.* 雾气,雾霭

peep /piːp/ *v.* （小鸟、小鸡等）唧唧叫,啾啾叫

woodpecker /ˈwudˌpekə/ *n.* 啄木鸟

martial /ˈmaːʃəl/ *adj.* 英勇的,威武的

bugle /ˈbjuːgl/ *n.* 军号,喇叭,号角

pulseless /ˈpʌlslis/ *adj.* 不跳动的,无声无息的

haze /heiz/ *n.* 薄雾,烟雾

reel /riːl/ *v.* 翩翩起舞（reel 原指一种轻快的苏格兰双人舞,在此作动词）

 ## 参考译文【Suggested Translation】

四 月 的 日 子

迷 人的日子,发出飘逸的幽香。
每座山和每株树都焕发出生机,
冬天和春天像情人一样
在正午的雾霭中相聚又分离——
　在这四月的日子里。

夜晚，树蛙在轻轻地叫，
一下——两下——接着一片寂静，
啄木鸟威武的嗓音
像军号声越过重重山峦——
　　穿过无声无息的雾气。

在那些日子里，雨水浸润的土地发出暖气，
羞怯的风悄悄地穿过树林，
满载着松树和白杨的清香，
还有欢乐的大地，像舞蹈家一样翩翩起舞——
　　在这整个四月的日子里！◆

（徐栋良 译）

⊙A straight foot is not afraid of a crooked shoe.（身正不怕影子斜。）

⊙Complacency is the enemy of study.（满足是求知的大敌。）

⊙Every man is the architect of his own fortune.（每个人是其自身命运的建筑师。）

⊙If you want knowledge, you must toil for it.（要想求知，就得吃苦。）

Man and Nature *

The intimacy between man and Nature began with the birth of man on the earth, and becomes each century more intelligent and far-reaching. To Nature, therefore, we turn as to the oldest and most influential teacher of our race; from one point of view once our task-master, now our servant; from another point of view, our constant friend, instructor and inspirer. The very intimacy of this relation robs it of a certain mystery and richness which it would have for all minds if it

---

* 作者汉密尔顿·怀特·马堡(Hamilton Wright Mabie, 1846—1916)，美国著名的散文家和社会批评家。人与自然的关系是人类存在和发展所必须面对的最基本的关系，也是人类永恒的主题之一。实现天人合一、人与自然和谐共处，是人类社会的理想境界。本文文笔瑰丽，逻辑缜密，将人与自然的关系演绎成一段韵律十足的交响曲。

were the reward of the few instead of being the privilege of the many. To the few it is, in every age, full of wonder and beauty; to the many it is a matter of course. The heavens shine for all, but they have a changing splendor to those only who see in every midnight sky a majesty of creative energy and resource which no repetition of the spectacle can dim. If the stars shone but once in a thousand years, men would gaze, awe-struck and worshipful, on a vision which is not less but more wonderful because it shines nightly above the whole earth. In like manner, and for the same reason, we become indifferent to that delicately beautiful or sublimely impressive sky scenery which the clouds form and reform, compose and dissipate, a thousand times on a summer day. The mystery, the terror, and the music of the sea; the secret and subduing charm of the woods, so full of healing for the spent mind or the restless spirit; the majesty of the hills, holding in their recesses the secrets of light and atmosphere; the infinite variety of landscape, never imitative or repetitious, but always appealing to the imagination with some fresh and unsuspected loveliness; — who feels the full power of these marvelous resources for the enrichment of life, or takes from them all the health, delight, and enrichment they have to bestow? ✳

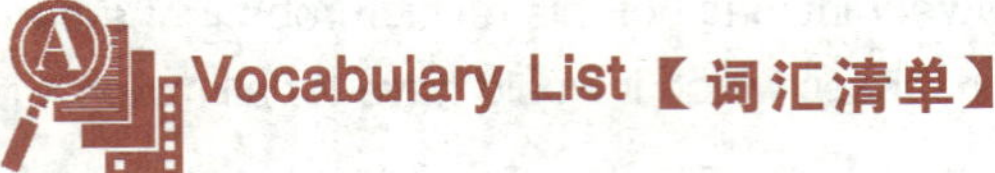

Vocabulary List 【词汇清单】

intimacy /ˈintiməsi/ *n.* 亲密,亲近,友好
far-reaching /ˈfaːˈriːtʃiŋ/ *adj.* 远大的,影响深远的
influential /ˌinfluˈenʃəl/ *adj.* 有(巨大)影响力的,产生影响的
instructor /inˈstrʌktə/ *n.* 教员,指导者
privilege /ˈprivilidʒ/ *n.* (某些个人、阶层享有的)特权,优惠

splendor /ˈsplendə/ *n.* 光辉,壮丽

repetition /ˌrepiˈtiʃən/ *n.* 重复,反复

spectacle /ˈspektəkl/ *n.* 景象,奇观

dim /dim/ *v.* (使)变暗淡的,(使)变朦胧

awe-struck /ˈɔːˌstrʌk/ *adj.* 敬畏的,畏惧的

worshipful /ˈwəːʃipful/ *adj.* 尊敬的,崇拜的,虔诚的

sublimely /səˈblaimli/ *adv.* 卓越地,超凡地,无比地

scenery /ˈsiːnəri/ *n.* 风光,景色

dissipate /ˈdisipeit/ *v.* 使分散,消散,消释

subdue /səbˈdjuː/ *v.* (使)屈服、驯服,(使)折服

recess /riˈses/ *n.* (常用复数)隐秘处,幽深处

imitative /ˈimitətiv/ *adj.* 伪造的,模仿的

repetitious /ˌrepiˈtiʃəs/ *adj.* 反复的,重复的

appeal /əˈpiːl/ *v.* 引起兴趣,吸引(to)

marvelous /ˈmaːviləs/ *adj.* 奇异的,奇迹般的,<口语>极佳的

enrichment /inˈritʃmənt/ *n.* 丰富,富足,充实

bestow /biˈstəu/ *v.* 赠给,赐予,给予

 参考译文【Suggested Translation】

人 与 自 然

从地球上人类出现开始,人与自然之间的密切关系也随之诞生,而且这种关系每一世纪都比以前变得更为明智而深远。因此,我们求助于自然,并把自然视为人类的最年长和最有影响力的老师。从某一种观点来看,自然曾经一度是我们的监工,现在却变为我们的奴仆。但从另一种观点来看,自然一直是我们的最忠实的朋友、导师和启发者。这种和谐紧密的关系,如果仅仅是少数人的特权,而大多数人并不能享有,那便会在人们心目中引发一种神秘和情趣。但是事实上,这种亲密关系是被天下所有的人共同享有的,这就使得这和谐紧密的关系失去神秘感和情趣。对于少数人来讲,这种关系在每个时代都充满了

奇妙和美好；对于多数人来讲，这种关系只是理所当然的一件事。天空照耀着每一个人，但是只有在少数人的心目中具有一种变化多端的壮丽，他们在每一个午夜的天空都能看到一种蕴含着创造性的能力的庄严肃穆之美，无论那种景象重复多少次，都不会使那种美模糊不清。如果星辰一千年才照耀一次大地，人们将怀着敬畏尊崇的心情凝视那种美景，而那种美景如果夜夜在全世界的上空出现，不但不会减损，反而更为增加它的奇妙。同样，基于相同的原因，我们对于夏日天空的那种由浮云聚散飘忽所形成的一日之间千变万化的纤巧秀丽或壮丽动人的景色，也都漠然置之。海洋的神秘、恐怖和韵律，有助于医疗疲惫心灵和烦躁精神的森林所具有的奥妙和慑人魂魄的魔力；在其幽深之处保有光与大气之奥秘的山峦所呈现的庄严肃穆之美；从不模仿或重复、永远以一种出人意料的新鲜的美丽来冲击人类想像力的风景变幻无穷——谁能感受到这些奇异景物的全部力量，或者能从它们那里得到它们所赐予的健康、快乐和丰美呢？◆

Who Moved My Cheese?*

"Who moved my cheese?" is a story about change that takes place in a Maze where four amusing characters look for "Cheese" — cheese being a metaphor for what we want to have in life, whether it is a job, a relationship, money, a big house, freedom, health, recognition, spiritual peace, or even an activity like jogging or golf.

Each of us has our own idea of what Cheese is, and we pursue it because we believe it makes us happy. If we get it, we often become attached to it. And if we lose it, or it's

---

   *　作者斯宾塞·约翰逊(Spencer Johnson)，美国南加州大学心理学学士、皇家外科医学院的医学博士，哈佛医学院和 Mayo 诊所的实习医生。他是全球知名的思想先锋、演说家和畅销书作家。他的许多观点，使成千上万的人发现了生活中的简单真理，从而使人们的生活更健康、更成功、更轻松。其畅销书《谁动了我的奶酪？》提供了在工作或生活中处理变化的绝妙方法，已被翻译成 26 种语言，全球销量已经超过了 2000 万册。本文节录的是该书最为精华的部分。

taken away, it can be traumatic.

The "Maze" in the story represents where you spend time looking for what you want. It can be the organization you work in, the community you live in, or the relationships you have in your life.

...

In the story you will see that the two mice do better when they are faced with change because they keep things simple, while the two little people's complex brains and human emotions complicate things. It is not that mice are smarter. We all know people are more intelligent than mice.

However, as you watch what the four characters do, and realize both the mice and the little people represent parts of ourselves — the simple and the complex — you can see it would be to our advantage to do the simple things that work when things change.

The Story of WHO MOVED MY CHEESE? (Extracted)

Having cheese makes you happy.

The more important your cheese is to you, the more you want to hold on to it.

If you do not change you can become extinct.

What would you do if you weren't afraid?

Smell the cheese often so you know when it is getting old.

Movement in a new direction helps you find new cheese.

When you move beyond your fear, you feel free.

Imagining myself enjoying new cheese, even before I find it, leads me to find it.

The quicker you let go of old cheese, the sooner you find new cheese.

It is safer to search in the Maze than remain in a cheese-less situation.

Old beliefs do not lead you to new cheese.

When you see that you can find and enjoy new cheese you can change course.

Noticing small changes early helps you to adapt to the bigger changes that are to come.

THE HANDWRITING ON THE WALL

Change Happens — They keep moving the cheese

Anticipate Change — Get ready for the cheese to move

Monitor Change — Smell the cheese so you know when it is getting old

Adapt To Change Quickly — The quicker you let go of old cheese, the sooner you can enjoy new cheese

Change — Move with the cheese

Enjoy Change — Savor the adventure and enjoy the taste of new cheese

Be ready to change quickly and enjoy it again

They keep moving the cheese

Move With The Cheese And Enjoy It! ✳

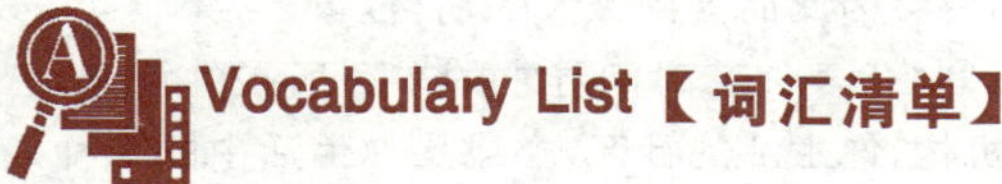 **Vocabulary List 【词汇清单】**

maze /meiz/ *n.* 迷津,迷宫

character /ˈkærɪktə/ *n.* 角色,人物

metaphor /ˈmetəfə/ *n.* ＜修辞＞隐喻,暗喻

jogging /ˈdʒɔgiŋ/ *n.* 慢跑,慢步长跑(锻炼)

attach /əˈtætʃ/ *v.* 使喜爱,使依恋(to)

traumatic /trɔːˈmætik/ *adj.* (精神、心灵)受创伤的

complex /ˈkɔmpleks/ *adj.* 复杂的,难解的

extinct /iksˈtiŋkt/ *adj.* 灭绝的,绝迹的;＜引申＞被淘汰的

course /kɔːs/ *n.* 道路,路线;行动方向

adapt to：使（自己）适应（新的或变化了的情况）（oneself）
anticipate /æn'tisipeit/ *v.* 预见，预料，预言
monitor /'mɔnitə/ *v.* 监视，监控，跟踪检测
savor /'seivə/ *v.* 品尝，尝试

参考译文【Suggested Translation】

谁动了我的奶酪？

《谁动了我的奶酪》所讲的是一个关于"变化"的故事。故事发生在一个迷宫之中，有四个可爱的小生灵在迷宫里寻找他们的奶酪。故事里的"奶酪"是对我们在现实生活中所追求目标的一种比喻，它可以是一份工作，一种人际关系，可以是金钱，一幢豪宅，还可以是自由、健康、社会的认可和老板的赏识。它可以是一种精神上的宁静，甚至还可以是一项运动，如慢跑、高尔夫球等等。

我们每个人的内心都有自己想要的"奶酪"，我们追寻它，想要得到它，因为我们相信，它会带给我们幸福和快乐。然而一旦我们得到了自己梦寐以求的奶酪，又常常会对它产生依赖心理，甚至会成为它的附庸；这时如果我们忽然失去了它，或者它被人拿走了，我们将会因此而受到极大的伤害。

故事里的"迷宫"代表你花时间寻求的东西所在的地方，它可以是你效力的机构，你生活的社区，亦或是你生活中的某种人际关系。

……

在故事里，你会发现，当面对变化时两只小老鼠做得比两个小矮人更好，因为他们总是把事情简单化；而两个小矮人所具有的复杂的脑筋和人类的情感，却总是把事情变得复杂化。这并不是说老鼠比人更聪明，我们都知道人类更具智慧。

当你观察故事中四个角色的行为时，你会发现，其实老鼠和小矮人代表我们自身的不同方面——简单的一面和复杂的一面。当事物发生变化时，或许简单行事会给我们带来许多的便

利和益处。

"谁动了我的奶酪?"的故事(精华摘录)

拥有奶酪,就拥有幸福。

奶酪对你越重要,你就越想抓住它。

如果你不改变,你就会被淘汰。

如果你无所畏惧,你会怎样做呢?

经常闻一闻你的奶酪,你就会知道,它什么时候开始变质。

朝新的方向前进,你就会发现新的奶酪。

当你超越了自己的恐惧时,你就会感到轻松自在。

在我发现奶酪之前,想像我正在享受奶酪,这会帮我找到新的奶酪。

越早放弃旧的奶酪,你就会越早发现新的奶酪。

在迷宫中搜寻比停留在没有奶酪的地方更安全。

陈旧的信念不会帮助你找到新的奶酪。

当你发现你会找到新的奶酪并且能够享用它时,你就会改变你的路线。

尽早注意细小的变化,这将有助于你适应即将来临的更大的变化。

奶酪墙上的话:

变化总是在发生——他们总是不断地拿走你的奶酪。

预见变化——随时做好奶酪被拿走的准备。

追踪变化——经常闻一闻你的奶酪,以便知道它们什么时候开始变质。

尽快适应变化——越早放弃旧的奶酪,你就会越早享用到新的奶酪。

改变——随着奶酪的变化而变化。

享受变化!——尝试冒险,去享受新奶酪的美味!

做好迅速变化的准备,不断地享受变化!

记住:他们仍会不断地拿走你的奶酪。

随着奶酪的变化而变化,并享受变化! ◆

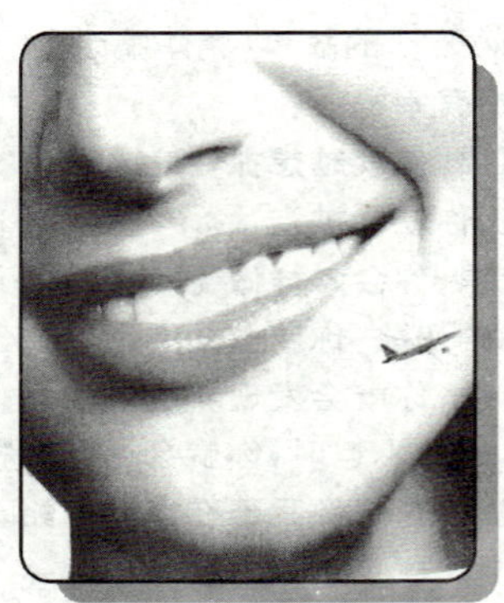

The Smile[*]

I was sure that I was to be killed. I became terribly nervous. I fumbled in my pockets to see if there were any cigarettes, which had escaped their search. I found one and because of my shaking hands, I could barely get it to my lips. But I had no matches, they had taken those. I looked through the bars at my jailer. He did not make eye contact with me. I called out to him, "Have you got a light?" He

---

* 作者安东尼·圣艾修伯里（Antoinede Saint-Exupery, 1900—1944），法国著名作家，其代表作《小王子》成为 20 世纪的儿童文学经典，被译成 100 余种语言，在世界各地的销量超过 5 亿册。圣艾修伯里生前是一名飞行员，被视为法国的民族英雄。二战期间，流亡异国的他在写作之余，以资深飞行员的身份参加法军机队，与德军作战；之前他也曾参加西班牙内战打击法西斯分子，他根据那次被俘的经历写了一篇精彩的故事——《微笑》。1944 年 7 月 31 日，他驾驶一架战机从科西嘉岛的盟军基地起飞，在执行最后一次飞行侦察任务中失踪于地中海上，从此不知生死，成为历史悬案。

looked at me, shrugged and came over to light my cigarette. As he came close and lit the match, his eyes inadvertently locked with mine. At that moment, I smiled. I don't know why I did that. Perhaps it was nervousness, perhaps it was because, when you get very close, one to another, it is very hard not to smile. In any case, I smiled. In that instant, it was as though a spark jumped across the gap between our two hearts, our two human souls. I know he didn't want to, but my smile leaped through the bars and generated a smile on his lips, too. He lit my cigarette but stayed near, looking at me directly in the eyes and continuing to smile.

I kept smiling at him, now aware of him as a person and not just a jailer. And his looking at me seemed to have a new dimension too.

"Do you have kids?" he asked.

"Yes, here, here."

I took out my wallet and nervously fumbled for the pictures of my family. He, too, took out the pictures of his family and began to talk about his plans and hopes for them. My eyes filled with tears. I said that I feared that I'd never see my family again, never have the chance to see them grow up. Tears came to his eyes, too. Suddenly, without another word, he unlocked my cell and silently led me out. Out of the jail, quietly and by back routes, out of the town. There, at the edge of town, he released me. And without another word, he turned back toward the town.

My life was saved by a smile. Yes, the smile — the unaffected, unplanned, natural connection between people. I really believe that if that part of you and that part of me could recognize each other, we wouldn't be enemies. We couldn't hate or envy or fear. ✽

Vocabulary List【词汇清单】

fumble /ˈfʌmbl/ *v.* 摸索,搜寻

barely /ˈbɛəli/ *adv.* 仅仅,刚刚,几乎不能

bar /bɑː/ *n.* 横杠,横木;＜复数＞监牢之栅

jailer /ˈdʒeilə/ *n.* 看守监狱的人,狱卒

make eye contact with：和…目光接触

shrug /ʃrʌg/ *v.* （为表示冷漠、无奈等）耸肩

inadvertently /ˌinədˈvəːtəntli/ *adv.* 无意地,偶然地

spark /spɑːk/ *n.* 火花,火星,闪光

leap /liːp/ *v.* 跳,跳跃,跳过

generate /ˈdʒenəreit/ *v.* 产生,发生

dimension /diˈmenʃən/ *n.* 维,度,方面

cell /sel/ *n.* （监狱或寺院的）单人房间

release /riˈliːs/ *v.* 释放,豁免

unaffected /ˈʌnəˈfektid/ *adj.* 不造作的,自然的,真挚的

参考译文【Suggested Translation】

微　笑

想到自己明天就没命了,我不禁陷入极端的惶恐。翻遍了口袋,我终于找到一支没被他们搜走的香烟,但是我的手紧张得不停发抖,连将烟送进嘴里都成问题,而我的火柴也在搜身时被拿走了。我透过铁栏望着外面的警卫,他并没有注意到我在看他,我叫了他一声:"能跟你借个火吗?"他转头望着我,耸了耸肩,然后走了过来,点燃我的香烟。当他帮我点火时,他的目光无意中与我的相接触,这时我突然冲着他微笑。我不知道自己为何有这般反应,或许是过于紧张,或许是当你如此靠近另一个人,你很难不对他微笑。不管是何理由,我对他笑了。就在那一刹那,这抹微笑如同火花一般,打破了我们心灵之间的隔

阁。受到了我的感染，他的嘴角不自觉地也现出了笑容，虽然我知道他原无此意。他点完火后并没立刻离开，两眼盯着我瞧，脸上仍带着微笑。

我也以笑容回应，仿佛他是个朋友，而不是一个看守我的警卫。他看我的眼神也少了当初的那股凶气。

"你有小孩吗？"他开口问道。

"有，你看。"

我拿出皮夹，手忙脚乱地翻出了我的全家福照片。他也掏出了照片，并且开始讲述他对家人的期望与计划。这时候我眼中沁满了泪水，我说我害怕再也见不到家人了。我害怕没机会看着孩子们长大。他听了也流下两行眼泪。突然间，他二话不说地打开了牢门，悄悄地带我从后面的小路逃离了监狱，出了小镇，就在小镇的边上，他放了我，之后便转身往回走，不曾留下一句话。

一个微笑居然能救自己一条命。是的，微笑是人与人之间最自然最真挚的沟通方式。如果我们能用心灵去认识彼此，世间便不会有结怨成仇的憾事，恨意、妒嫉、恐惧也会不复存在。◆

第 011 篇

Love[*]

Among the more curious questions that can be asked about love is this：when one feels romantic love, does he feel it in breaks, with interruptions or changes, or does he feel it continuously, without interruption or change?

Poetry and song seduce one into thinking love continues without interruption. "Love is not love which alters when it al-

---

　　* 作者佚名。爱作为人类特有的情感，在人的心理上能产生一种巨大的内驱力。有人说："爱是惟一的理性行为。"也有人说："爱是惟一不受理性控制的事情。"此言彼语，莫衷一是。而且，"爱"和"永恒"两个字动辄就被粘贴在一起。本文独辟蹊径，从实然的角度揭示在更多的时候，爱并非永恒不变的。或许我们听过"Love is blind"（爱是盲目的），而这篇文章也许会让我们自问：为什么我们不能爱得理性呢？其实，让我们不妨从"今朝有酒今朝醉"的所谓"洒脱"中解脱，当爱已经接近"同心圆"的边界，在中间留一段距离，把爱放在理性的距离上，从中品尝另一种幸福。

teration finds," wrote Shakespeare in one of his famous sonnets. Love is "an ever-fixed mark that looks on tempests and is never shaken,"he continued. And Elizabeth Barret Browning wrote of her constancy to her husband Robert in such lines as this: "What I do and what I dream include thee." Some of the greatest operas also praise the ever-lasting love by some heroes and heroines dying for it.

In reality, love probably goes on with breaks and interruptions. First, it is diffcult to suppose that one can experience anything continuously. Sleep interrupts wakefulness, and sleep itself is interrupted by dreams and nightmares. The feeling one has for his lover during wakefulness may be blotted out or intensified by sleep. In either case, the feeling changes. When one is awake, he cannot fix his eyes or his attention constantly on a single object. He must blink, if nothing else. More likely he will look to something else for variety or from necessity. His mind may turn to the stock market or he may become fascinated by the operation of a pile driver on his way to work. His focus for much of his day is on work. As he closes the door to his office, his thoughts may turn to his love, but sitting at his desk, his eyes fix on the print and figures there.

Pain and pleasure, either one, can distract a lover from concentrating on his love. Pain calls everything to itself. One can forget one's love for a period even over a stubbed toe. The pleasure of too much food or drink can be totally absorbing. The pleasure even of one's lover may become boring periodically. Often the greatest distraction is oneself. At times the preoccupation with self, the worry over self, the development of self, the delight in self admit no other thought.

Lovely as love might be, one can neither live nor love

continuously. At best, a lover can only echo the words of the poet Ernest Dowson, and say, "I have been faithful to thee in my fashion." ✳

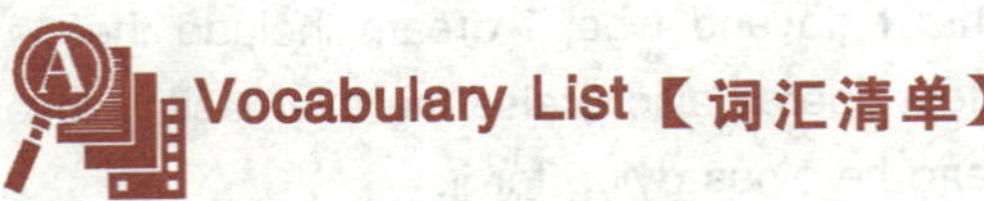

Vocabulary List【词汇清单】

curious /ˈkjuəriəs/ *adj.* 新奇的,古怪的

interruption /ˌintəˈrʌpʃən/ *n.* 中止,中断,暂停

continuously /kənˈtinjuəsli/ *adv.* 持续地,连续不断地

seduce /siˈdjuːs/ *v.* 引诱,诱惑,诱使

Shakespeare /ˈʃeikspiə/ (全名 William Shakespeare)威廉·莎士比亚(1564—1616,英国文艺复兴时期著名的戏剧家、诗人)

sonnet /ˈsɔnit/ *n.* 十四行诗(一种由十四行组成的诗歌形式,通常有一种传统的押韵形式)

tempest /ˈtempist/ *n.* 大风暴,暴风雨

Elizabeth Barret Browning /iˈlizəbəθ ˈbærit ˈbrauniŋ/ 伊丽莎白·芭蕾特·勃朗宁(1806—1861,英国女诗人)

thee /ðiː/ *pron.* <古>汝,你,你自己

nightmare /ˈnaitmɛə/ *n.* 恶梦,梦魇

blot out:遮掩,遮蔽

intensify /inˈtensifai/ *v.* 使增强,使加强;使加剧

blink /bliŋk/ *v.* 眨眼睛,眯眼看

fascinate /ˈfæsineit/ *v.* 迷住,使着迷

distract /disˈtrækt/ *v.* 使分心,转移(注意力)

stub /stʌb/ *v.* 踢碰,偶然碰撞(脚趾或腿)

periodically /ˌpiəriˈɔdikəli/ *adv.* 定期地,间歇地

preoccupation /pri(ː)ˌɔkjuˈpeiʃən/ *n.* 专心,入神,全神贯注

echo /ˈekəu/ *n.* 回声,回音

Ernest Dowson /ˈəːnist ˈdausən/ 欧内斯特·道森(1867—1900,英国颓废派诗人)

 参考译文【Suggested Translation】

爱 情

有关爱情的各种稀奇古怪的问题中，有一个是这样的：当一个人感受浪漫爱情时，他是时断时续或有所变化地感受呢，还是永恒不变地畅游其中？

诗与歌总是诱人相信爱情永恒不变，没有什么中断。莎士比亚在他一首著名的十四行诗中写道："爱不是真爱，如果对方转弯你就调头……爱情是引导航向的灯塔，无论面临何种暴风疾雨也不会动摇。"伊丽莎白·芭蕾特·勃朗宁曾以这样的诗句描述她对丈夫的忠贞不渝："我所做的一切以及我的梦想都不能没有你。"一些伟大的歌剧也颂扬为爱情而殉身的男女主角的永恒爱情。

实际上，爱情很可能间断性地发展：首先，很难想像人们能持续不变地经历任何事情。睡眠中断清醒，而睡眠本身又被美梦和噩梦所搅扰。一个人在清醒时对其爱人的感情也许会被睡眠所遮掩或者在酣睡之中变得更加浓烈了。不管在哪种情况下，感情都发生了变化。当一个人在清醒时，不可能老是盯着某一物体。他至少会眨巴眨巴眼睛；为了寻求变化或出于必要，他十之八九会注意到别的事物。他的心思可能会转向股票市场，或他在上班途中对打桩机的操作感到新奇不已。大多数时候他将注意力放在工作上。当关上办公室门时，他也许会想到爱人，而当他坐到办公桌旁时，他又会全神贯注于文字和数据了。

痛苦与快乐，都会使情侣不能专注于爱情。痛苦使人忘却其他一切而只有痛苦的感受。就连一只撞伤的脚趾头也能让人把爱情暂放一边。吃吃喝喝带来的快乐可令人陶醉。甚至幸福的爱情有时候也会索然无味。通常最大的干扰来自自己。有时对自我的专注，对个人担忧和发展的考虑，对快乐的投入，使人们无暇顾及其他事情。

爱情诚然可爱，但一个人既不可能拥有永恒的生命，也不可能拥有不变的爱情。处于最佳心境的情侣也只能随声附和诗人欧内斯特·道森说的那句话："我以我的方式忠实于你。"◆

Hope Is the Thing with Feathers*

Hope is the thing with feathers
That perches in the soul,

And sings the tune without the words,

And never stops at all.

The sweetest in the gale is heard;

---

　　* 作者艾米莉·迪金森(Emily Dickinson,1830—1886),美国文学史上最著名的诗人之一,被 20 世纪"意象派"诗人尊崇为先驱者。她珠辉玉丽般的独特诗句,凝聚着深厚的情感和创造性的智慧。迪金森几乎一生都是在她的出生地生活,不到 30 岁就开始深居简出,过着隐士般的生活,并且终身未嫁。她的生存方式虽然视野有限,可是她却怡然自得。1886 年迪金森去世后,她妹妹在她的写字台里发现了一千多首诗歌(生前只发表七首),这些诗歌后来被视为美国(乃至世界)现代诗歌的奠基作品。本诗语言不事雕琢,灵动飘逸,是艾米莉·迪金森的代表作之一。

And sore must be the storm
That could abash the little bird
That kept so many warm.

I've heard it in the chillest land,
And on the strangest sea；
Yet, never, in extremity,
It asked a crumb of me. ✳

 ## Vocabulary List【词汇清单】

perch /pəːtʃ/ *v.* 栖息，暂歇，休憩
gale /geil/ *n.* 大风；＜古＞微风
sore /sɔː/ *n.* 痛处，伤心事
abash /ə'bæʃ/ *v.* 使不安，使窘迫
extremity /iks'tremiti/ *n.* 极度，极端；（in）绝境，险境
crumb /krʌm/ *n.* 碎屑，少许，少量

 ## 参考译文【Suggested Translation】

希望是长着羽翼的东西

希望是长着羽翼的东西，
在人的心灵停栖，
唱着没有歌词的曲调，
永远歌声不息。

微风里听歌歌声最甜，
它为千万人送去温暖，
最怕狂猛的暴风骤雨，
会使得小鸟局促不安。

无论天涯海角，僻壤荒丘，
到处有它歌声啁啾；
哪怕山穷水尽，末路绝境，
它也从不向我索求。◆

●Make hay while the sun shines.（趁热打铁。）

●Good health is over wealth.（健康是最大的财富。）

●Judge not from appearances.（人不可貌相。）

●One false move may lose the game.（一着不慎，满盘皆输。）

The Story of Life*

Sometimes people come into your life and you come to realize that they were meant to be there, to serve some sort of purpose, teach you a lesson, or to help you figure out who you are or who you want to become. You never know who these people may be (possibly your roommate, neigh-

---

* 作者佚名。"生活需要耐得住寂寞，精神空虚只能侵蚀脆弱的心灵。生活需要理想——一种巨大的精神力量，她能穿透铁壁铜墙，实现自己的向往；如一瓶醇酒，疲惫之时，闻一闻飘香，浑身充满力量。生活需要调色板，呆板的黑白色需要她；不时的渲染，只是一点的浓重一笔，便能令黑夜缀上几颗繁星，于嫩草中找到几滴鲜红。我们在用青春经营着人生，用时空维系着生命；生活作为载体，不经意间已令我们失去了很多；只为了那心动的一瞥，去苦苦追寻幻象中的安琪儿，为一次的失败而迷失了自我。我们应该用知识充实自己，用爱留住短暂的青春，在生活中过着平凡的生活，书写着不平凡的人生……"是啊，生活的故事如潺潺溪水，如汩汩泉流，讲不尽，说不完。我们每个人都是自己生活的主角。本文句句机警，将生活的故事娓娓道来，相信你读罢更会有非同一般的感受。

bor, co-worker, long-lost friend, lover, or even a complete stranger), but when you lock eyes with them, you know in an instant that they will affect your life in some profound way.

And sometimes things happen to you that may seem horrible, painful, and unfair at first, but in reflection you find that without overcoming those obstacles you would have never realized your potential, strength, willpower or heart. Everything happens for a reason. Nothing happens by chance or by means of good luck. Illness, injury, love, brilliant achievements, and sheer stupidity all occur to test the limits of your soul. Without these small tests, whatever they may be, life would be like a smoothly paved, straight, flat road to nowhere. It would be safe and comfortable, but dull and utterly pointless.

The people you meet who affect your life, and the success and downfalls you experience, help to create who you are and who you become. Even the bad experiences can be learned from. In fact, they are probably the most poignant and important ones. If someone hurts you, betrays you, or breaks your heart, forgive them, for they have helped you learn about trust and the importance of being cautious when you open your heart. If someone loves you, love them back unconditionally, not only because they love you, but because in a way, they are teaching you to love and how to open your heart and eyes to things. Make every day count. Appreciate every moment and take from those moments everything that you possibly can, for you may never be able to experience it again. Talk to people that you have never talked to before, and actually listen. Let yourself fall in love, break free, and set your sights high. Hold your head up because you have every right to. Tell yourself you are a great individual and believe in yourself, for if you don't believe in yourself, it will be hard for others to believe in you.

You can make of your life anything your wish. Create your own life and then go out and live it with absolutely no regrets. Most importantly (！！！), if you LOVE someone tell him or her, for you never know what tomorrow may have in store. ✽

 ## Vocabulary List【词汇清单】

figure out：发现，领会

co-worker /'kəu'wɜːkə/ *n.*　共同工作的人，同事

long-lost /'lɔŋ'lɔst/ *adj.*　长时间未联系的，长时间未见面的

lock eyes with：锁定目光，定睛凝视

profound /prə'faund/ *adj.*　深远的，深邃的，深刻的

obstacle /'ɔbstəkl/ *n.*　障碍，妨碍，阻碍

willpower /'wilpauə/ *n.*　意志力，毅力

stupidity /stjuː'piditi/ *n.*　愚蠢，鲁钝；愚蠢的想法，愚行

pave /peiv/ *v.*　筑路，铺路面

utterly /'ʌtəli/ *adv.*　绝对地，完全地，彻底地

downfall /'daunfɔːl/ *n.*　垮台，挫败，失败

poignant /'pɔinənt/ *adj.*　深刻的，深切的，深深打动人心的

betray /bi'trei/ *v.*　背叛，出卖

cautious /'kɔːʃəs/ *adj.*　细心的，谨慎的

unconditionally /'ʌnkən'diʃənəli/ *adv.*　无条件地，绝对地

absolutely /'æbsəluːtli/ *adv.*　绝对地，确实地，完全地

 ## 参考译文【Suggested Translation】

生 活 的 故 事

有时候，某些人走进了你的生活，而你便会意识到他们就应当出现，出现是为了某种目的，为了给你一个教训，或者为

了帮助你弄清你是谁或者你想成为什么样的人。你无从知道这些人会是谁（也许是你的同屋、邻居、同事、久违的朋友、爱人，甚至是一个完全陌生的人），但是当你定睛凝视他们的时候，顷刻间你便知道他们会以某种深刻的方式影响你的生活。

并且，有时候发生在你身上的事情乍看起来可怕、痛苦，或者不公平，但是细想一下你便会发现如果不是克服这些障碍，你永远也不会意识到自己的潜能、力量、毅力或者内心。凡事皆事出有因。无事出于偶然或侥幸。疾病、伤害、爱情、辉煌的成就和十足的蠢行都会出现在你的生活之中来检验你灵魂的深度。没有这些点点滴滴的考验，不管它是什么，生活将会像一条平坦笔直的道路，一味伸展，而没有目的地。虽然说安全舒适，但是却单调乏味，毫无意义。

你所遇到影响你生活的人，你经历的成功与挫败，都有助于塑造你，造就你。就连那些不幸的经历，你也能从中汲取教训。事实上，它们可能是你最深切最重要的人生阅历。如果某人伤害了你，背叛了你，或者让你心碎不已，原谅他们，因为是他们让你认识到什么是责任，认识到当你敞开心扉时仍然需要保持一份警惕的重要性。如果有人爱你，那么无条件地去爱他们吧，不仅仅因为他们爱你，还因为在某种意义上，他们在教你去爱，教你如何敞开心胸，教你睁大眼睛去感受世间万物。让每一天都充满意义吧。珍惜每一刻并尽己所能地从每时每刻汲取所需，因为你可能永远无法再有这种经历。去和你以前从未交谈过的人聊一聊，并且仔细聆听。让自己陷入情网，让自己跳出情网，让自己看得更高更远。昂起你的头，因为你有充分的权利去正视一切。告诉自己并且相信自己是个了不起的人，因为如果你不自信，别人便难以信任你。

你能够随心所欲安排自己的生活。去创造你自己的生活，要活得无怨无悔。最最重要的是，如果你爱某人，告诉他或她，因为你无从知道明天会发生什么。◆

Night*

Night has fallen over the country. Through the trees rises the red moon, and the stars are scarcely seen. In the vast shadow of night the coolness and the dews descend. I sit at the open window to enjoy them; and hear only the voice of the summer wind. Like black hulks, the shadows of the great trees ride at anchor on the billowy sea of grass. I cannot see the red and blue flowers, but I know that they are

---

　　* 作者纳撒尼尔·霍桑（Nathaniel Hawthorne，1804—1864），美国 19 世纪影响最大的浪漫主义小说家和心理小说家，其作品被称为"心理罗曼史"，曾匿名发表长篇小说《范肖》，后陆续出版短篇小说集《古宅青苔》、《雪影》等，逐渐得到重视和好评。霍桑的代表作《红字》内容深刻，构思新颖，手法独特，标志着美国长篇小说创作上的一个重大突破，被誉为 19 世纪美国文学中最优秀的长篇小说之一；后来又分别出版了"两部罗曼史"，即《带有七个尖角阁的房子》和《福谷传奇》。霍桑对当时美国社会道德沦丧和资产阶级的伪善不满，但是他又不想从根本上改变不合理的社会制度，只谋求社会道德的自我改进和完善。

there. Far away in the meadow gleams the silver Charles. The tramp of horses' hoofs sounds from the wooden bridge. Then all is still save the continuous wind of the summer night. Sometimes I know not if it be the wind or the sound of the neighboring sea. The village clock strikes; and I feel that I am not alone.

How different it is in the city! It is late, and the crowd is gone. You step out upon the balcony, and lie in the very bosom of the cool, dewy night as if you folded her garments about you. Beneath lies the public walk with trees, like a fathomless, black gulf, into whose silent darkness the spirit plunges, and floats away with some beloved spirit clasped in its embrace. The lamps are still burning up and down the long street. People go by with grotesque shadows, now foreshortened, and now lengthening away into the darkness and vanishing, while a new one springs up behind the walker, and seems to pass him revolving like the sail of a windmill. The iron gates of the park shut with a jangling clang. There are footsteps and loud voices; — a tumult; — a drunken brawl; — an alarm of fire; — then silence again. And now at length the city is asleep, and we can see the night. The belated moon looks over the rooftops and finds no one to welcome her. The moonlight is broken. It lies here and there in the squares, and the opening of the streets — angular like blocks of white marble. ✳

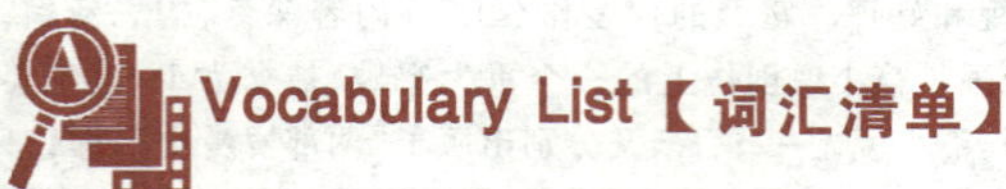

Vocabulary List 【词汇清单】

scarcely /ˈskɛəsli/ *adv.* 几乎不,简直不

dew /djuː/ *n.* 露水,露珠

descend /di'send/ *v.* 下降,下来

hulk /hʌlk/ *n.* ＜复数＞渡船,仓库船

anchor /'æŋkə/ *n.* 锚,锚状物

billowy /'biləui/ *adj.* 波涛汹涌的,惊涛骇浪的

meadow /'medəu/ *n.* 草地,牧场

gleam /gli:m/ *v.* 闪烁,隐约闪光

hoof /hu:f/ *n.* （牛,马等）蹄,足

balcony /'bælkəni/ *n.* 阳台,眺台

bosom /'buzəm/ *n.* 胸,衣服之胸襟;内心

garment /'ga:mənt/ *n.* 衣服,服装

fathomless /'fæðəmlis/ *adj.* 深不可测的,无法估量的

gulf /gʌlf/ *n.* （比 bay 大的）海湾

plunge /plʌndʒ/ *v.* 投入,陷入

clasp /'kla:sp/ *v.* 紧抱,扣紧,（藤等）紧紧缠绕

embrace /im'breis/ *v.* 拥抱,围绕,包含

grotesque /grəu'tesk/ *adj.* 奇异的,怪异的,风格各异的

foreshorten /fɔ:'ʃɔ:tn/ *v.* ＜绘画＞透视缩短（在绘画透视中,
　　如一只手臂向前伸出,从对面看去,则显得很短了）

vanish /'væniʃ/ *v.* 消失,消散

jangle /'dʒæŋgl/ *v.* 发出尖锐的声音

tumult /'tju:mʌlt/ *n.* 喧闹,骚动,纷乱

brawl /brɔ:l/ *n.* 吵嚷,大吵大闹

belated /bi'leitid/ *adj.* 迟的,迟到的,延误的

angular /'æŋgjulə/ *adj.* 有棱角的,生硬的

marble /'ma:bl/ *n.* 大理石,大理岩

 参考译文【Suggested Translation】

夜

夜幕已经笼罩着乡间。一轮红月正从树林后面徐徐升起,天
上几乎见不到星星。在这苍茫的夜色中,寒气与露水降下

来了。我坐在敞开的窗前欣赏着这夜色，耳边只听见那夏天的风声。大树的阴影像黑色的大船停泊在波浪起伏的茫茫草海上。虽然我见不到红色和蓝色的花朵，但是我知道它们在哪儿。远处的草地上，银色的查尔斯河闪闪发光。木桥那边传来了踢嗒踢嗒的马蹄声。接着，万物俱寂，只留下夏夜不断的风声。有时，我丝毫辨别不出它究竟是风声，还是邻近的海涛声。村子里的时钟敲起来了，于是我觉得并不孤单。

　　城市的夜晚是那样的不同呵！夜深了，人群已经散去。你走到阳台上，躺在凉爽和露水弥漫的夜幕中，仿佛你用它作为外衣裹住了你的身子。阳台下面是栽着树木的人行道，像一条深不可测的黑色的海湾，飘忽的精灵就投入了这漆黑沉静的海湾，拥抱着某个所爱的精灵随波荡漾而去。长长的街道上，街灯依然到处亮着。人们从灯下走过，拖曳着各种各样奇形怪状的影子，影子时而缩短，时而伸长，最后消失在黑暗之中；同时，一个新的影子又突然出现在那个行路人的身后，这影子好似风车上的翼板一样，转到他身体的前方去了。公园的铁门当啷一声关上，耳边可以听到脚步声和响亮的说话声；——一阵喧闹；——一阵酒醉后的吵嚷声；——一阵火灾的报警声；——接着，寂静如初。于是，城市终于沉睡，我们终于能够看到夜的景色。姗姗来迟的月亮从屋顶后面探出脸来，发觉没有人在欢迎她。破碎的月光东一块，西一块，撒落在各个广场上和各条大街的开阔处——像一块块白色的大理石一样棱角分明。◆

（蒋美陆　译）

Lady First[*]

For a long period before the 1960s, women were considered to be the weaker sex, just as Shakespeare said in Hamlet：

"Frailty, thy name is women."

In contrast, men were regarded the stronger and the dominant sex. In this light man should undertake the duty to adopt a protective attitude toward the so-called weaker sex.

This implied that men should help women on and off with

---

　　* 作者佚名。"弱者,你的名字是女人!"大文豪莎士比亚一语惊人。这句相对局限性的名言,却是对当时社会妇女地位的真实写照。半个千年过去了,妇女的社会地位今非昔比,但境况依然不容乐观,很多情况下她们依然承受着"弱者"之名,尤其是当面对战争、灾难、疾病的时候。而"女士优先"这种风俗到底是对女性的一种礼遇和尊敬,还是对女性的一种轻蔑和藐视?从根本上来说,女性的地位很大程度上取决于她们自己怎样看待自己。女人是否是弱者,不应该由别人来定义,这个命题,需要她们自己来判断。

their coats, light their cigarettes, open the doors for them to get on and off the wagon, train, bus, etc. Or to enter the houses. Have you ever seen the movie "Titanic"? Well, when the ship was sinking, it was the women who had the right to get on the lifeboats first, just because men had the responsibility for taking care of and protecting women!

This could lead to the conclusion that the custom "Lady First" was developed out of respect in appearance, but in fact it was kind of looking down upon women in nature.

In the 1960s, women began to challenge this tradition. Just as one lady put it, "Historically, men should walk on the outside of the pavement so as to prevent the lady's dress from being spoilt by mud splashed by a carriage. Today a man is supposed to walk on the outside side. A man should walk where he wants to. So should a woman. If out of love and respect, he actually wants to take the blows, he should walk on the inside, because that's where muggers are hiding these days."

This shows that to treat a woman as inferior just because she is a female is not only insulting but also out of step with contemporary American culture.

Women may go to the restaurants Dutch treat. They may refuse such words as chairman, businessmen, policeman ... Instead they prefer chairperson, businessperson, police or cop ... just to show that they are equal in every respect with male! ✱

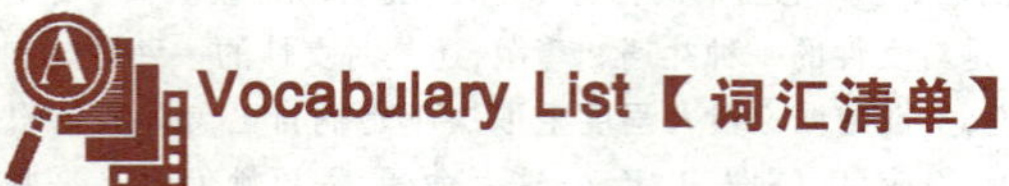

Vocabulary List 【词汇清单】

Hamlet /ˈhæmlit/ 《哈姆雷特》(莎士比亚著名悲剧的剧名)

frailty /'freilti/ *n.* 软弱,脆弱

thy /ðai/ *adj.* ＜古＞你的

dominant /'dɔminənt/ *adj.* 支配的,统治的

adopt /ə'dɔpt/ *v.* 采纳(观点、意见),采取(态度,习惯做法等)

wagon /'wægən/ *n.* 四轮马车

look down upon：轻视,看不起

historically /his'tɔrikəli/ *adv.* 历史地,以往地

pavement /'peivmənt/ *n.* ＜英＞人行道(= ＜美＞sidewalk)

spoil /spɔil/ *v.* 损坏,破坏

splash /splæʃ/ *v.* 溅泼,飞溅,溅湿

mugger /'mʌgə/ *n.* 从背后袭击以行劫的强盗

inferior /in'fiəriə/ *adj.* (位置)较低的,下级的,下等的

contemporary /kən'tempərəri/ *adj.* 当代的,现代的

cop /kɔp/ *n.* ＜美俚＞警察,便衣警察

 **参考译文【Suggested Translation】**

女士优先

在 20 世纪 60 年代之前很长的一段时间里,女子一直被认为是"弱者",正如莎士比亚在其剧本《哈姆雷特》中所说:

"弱者,你的名字是女人!"

与之相反,男子则被视为"强者"或"统治者"。鉴于此,男子就有义务采取一切措施保护所谓的弱者。

这也就意味着当女子穿大衣、脱大衣时男子要帮助;意味着男人要为她们点烟;意味着当女子上下车(马车、火车、汽车……)或者进门时男子要帮忙开门。看过电影《泰坦尼克号》吗? 当轮船正在下沉的时候,首先登上救生艇的是女子。为什么呢? 就因为男子汉有义务照顾和保护她们!

由此便可以得出这样的结论:"女士优先"这种风俗表面上出于尊敬;而实质上是出于对女性的轻视!

　　从上世纪 60 年代起，妇女们开始对这一传统发起挑战。正如一位女士所说："以往，人们认为男子汉应该走在人行道的外侧，这样一来万一有马车路过溅起泥浆时，他会首先'接招'，不至于玷污女士的衣裙。今天的男子汉们仍然沿袭以往的做法，走在人行道的外侧。其实他们应该爱走哪儿就走哪儿，女人也一样。现在的男士们要是真的尊敬女人、真的怜香惜玉，他们倒是应该走在人行道内侧，因为今天的抢劫犯最爱躲藏的地方就是那儿。"

　　这表明，今天还拿女性当"弱者"的看法或者做法不仅仅是对女性的一种"侮辱"，更是与现代美国文化格格不入的"老土"的行为。

　　因此，女士们上餐馆时会实行 AA 制（各付各的）。对于带有性别色彩的词语她们也会抵制，例如 chairman（主席）、businessman（商人）、policeman（警察）……，改用一些中性的词汇，如 chairperson、businessperson、police 或 cop……。总之，她们要证明男子在社会生活的各个方面是平等的。◆

● Observation is the best teacher.（观察是最好的老师。）

● Rome was not built in a day.（冰冻三尺，非一日之寒。）

● It is no use crying over spilt milk.（覆水难收。）

● Nature is the true law.（天行有常，不为尧存，不为桀亡。）

A Better Tomorrow[*]

People often wonder why historians go to so much trouble to preserve millions of books, documents and records of the past. Why do we have libraries? What good are these documents and the history books? Why do we record and save the actions of men, the negotiations of statesmen and the campaigns of armies?

Because, sometimes, the voice of experience can cause us to stop, look and listen. And because, sometimes, past records, correctly interpreted, can give us warning of what to

---

* 作者赫伯特·克拉克·胡佛（Herbert Clark Hoover, 1874—1964），美国政治家，第 31 任总统。值得一提的是，胡佛毕业于斯坦福大学，1898 年曾来到中国，在开平煤矿工作过，后自己开了公司，以其雄厚财产为后盾逐步步入政界。1928 年他接受共和党总统候选人的提名获胜。其上台后，正赶上世界性的经济危机，美国经济坠入深渊，这使他原来的希望依靠美国科学潜力来开辟一个"新时代"的愿望破灭。尽管他进行了不少努力，但危机一天天加重，终无力回天。

do and what not to do.

If we are ever to create enduring peace, we must seek its origins in human experience and in the record of human idealism. From the story of the fortitude, courage and devotion of men and women, we create the inspirations of youth. From stories of the Christian martyrs, right down to Budapest's heroic martyrs of today, history records the suffering, the self-denial, the devotion and the heroic deeds of men. Surely from these records there can come help to mankind in our confusions and perplexities, and in our yearnings for peace.

The supreme purpose of history is a better world. History gives a warning to those who would promote war. History brings inspiration to those who seek peace. In short, history helps us learn. Yesterday's records can keep us from repeating yesterday's mistakes. And from the pieces of mosaic assembled by historians come the great murals which represent the progress of mankind. ✳

Ⓐ Vocabulary List 【词汇清单】

preserve /pri'zə:v/ *v.* 保存,保藏

negotiation /ni͵gəuʃi'eiʃən/ *n.* 谈判,协商,协议

campaign /kæm'pein/ *n.* <军>战役,征战

interpret /in'tə:prit/ *v.* 解释,说明

idealism /ai'diəlizəm/ *n.* 理想主义,理想观念

fortitude /'fɔ:titju:d/ *n.* 坚忍不拔,刚毅

inspiration /͵inspə'reiʃən/ *n.* 鼓舞,鼓励,灵感

Christian /'kristʃən/ *n.* 基督教徒 *adj.* 基督教义的

martyr /'ma:tə/ *n.* 烈士,牺牲者,殉教者

Budapest /'bju:də'pest/ 布达佩斯(匈牙利首府)

self-denial /ˈselfdiˈnaiəl/ *n.*　自我克制，自我牺牲
perplexity /pəˈpleksiti/ *n.*　困惑，窘困
supreme /sju(ː)ˈpriːm/ *adj.*　（地位，权力）至高的，无上的
mosaic /məˈzeiik/ *n.*　马赛克，镶嵌图案（图像）
assemble /əˈsembl/ *v.*　集合，聚集，装配
mural /ˈmjuərəl/ *n.*　壁饰，壁画

参考译文【Suggested Translation】

一个更好的明天

人们常常心怀疑虑，为什么历史学家要费尽周折地保存数以百万计的过去的书籍、文献和记录。我们为什么要有图书馆呢？这些文献和史书有何用处呢？我们为什么要记载并保存人类的行为、政治家的决议和军队的征战呢？

因为，有时候经验之音能促使我们停步、观察和倾听。也因为有时候过去的记载经过正确的诠释，可以给我们一种警示，告诉我们何事可做、何事不可做。

如果我们想要创造持久的和平，我们必须从人类经验以及人类追求理想和记录之中去探索其渊源。从男性和女性刚毅、勇敢和奉献的故事之中，我们创造了青春的灵感。远自基督教殉道者的故事，近至布达佩斯的当代英勇烈士，历史记载着人类的一切苦难、克己、忠诚和英勇的事迹。当然，那些记载一定会对处于困惑、茫然和渴望和平的人们有所助益。

历史的终极目的是实现一个更加美好的世界。历史对那些力主战争的人加以警告，对于那些追寻和平的人予以启示。简而言之，历史帮助我们学习。昨日的记载可以促使我们避免重犯昨日的错误。而这些由历史学家所汇集的镶嵌图案艺术品，将会逐渐成为表现人类进步的伟大壁画。◆

The Watch[*]

I look around me and the room has changed imperceptibly and overtly. There are elephants on thin legs lining the walls, the people around me have become giant insects, my watch melts and slowly drips from my wrist. A Dalinian dream? A Kafkaesque nightmare? The breeze of surrealism blows through my hair; an existential whirlwind captures my imagination.

In the images of these two great creators, I see reflections of beautiful and insatiable imaginations, completely undisciplined, unbounded; yet full of the magic and power of

---

　　* 作者罗曼·阿特舒勒（Roman Altshuler），美国罗得岛州（Rhode Island）普罗维登斯市（Providence）某中型公立高中的学生。本文是这位小作者递交给哈佛大学的自我陈述，其构思奇特，新颖别致，个性鲜明，围绕"调整世界，使之适合我们的思想"而进行了一次生动有趣的想像之旅。本文最终博得哈佛大学录取委员会的首肯，使得罗曼本人如愿跨进哈佛大学这所世界顶尖学府，而该文也被视为哈佛大学录取学生的经典陈述之一。

the artists' visions. These images are not as true as photographs, but they are a hundred times more honest. I, too, often find myself misrepresenting the world. In the midst of a truly dreary lecture I sometimes force wakefulness upon myself by images of what I am learning, and instead of seeing my teacher carrying on about the military campaigns of the Civil War, I see muskets blazing against raised flags.

More often, I see my life as an adventure; romanticized, idealized, exhilarating. Instead of seeing a boring test of memory, I see a test of will; instead of a debate, I see a battle of wits; instead of seeing the photographic image of life, I see the existential and intoxicating war of man against Fate itself. In these images I am sometimes challenged by faceless opponents, sometimes I am climbing a mountain. Perhaps I am fighting a bull or jumping on rooftops.

At times I question the benefits of reinventing the world to suit my fancy. It is true, of course, that everyone does this. Even the strictest of thinkers cannot avoid letting their own vision of the world show through in their works. Dali and Kafka are not exceptions, they are extremes. Why are we all so eager to get away from reality? I find that I, like many others, often don't seem to fuly belong. But of course I do belong, this is my world as much as anyone else's. I try to solve this contradiction between the perceived and the real by altering the world ever so slightly — a horse-drawn carriage instead of a car, a prize-winning essay rather than another homework assignment — so that it finds its place around me.

A simple solution indeed. We do not change ourselves to fit the world, but change the world to fit within us. A simple act of wish fulfillment, and all is done. And, of course, to melt a watch with the mind is far better than to enslave the intellect within the watch like a genie in a bottle. Freedom to think requires only so little, and to adjust the world to one's thought is ever more noble than adjusting thought to the world. ✳

Vocabulary List【词汇清单】

imperceptibly /ˌimpəˈseptəbli/ *adv.* 感觉不到地，微妙地，渐进地

overtly /ˈəuvəːtli/ *adv.* 公开地，明显地

Dalinian /daːˈliːniən/ *adj.* 达利式的，达利风格的

Kafkaesque /ˌkaːfkaːˈesk/ *adj.* 卡夫卡的，卡夫卡（作品）风格的

surrealism /səˈriəlizəm/ *n.* 超现实主义

existential /ˌegzisˈtenʃəl/ *adj.* 存在的，表示存在的，存在主义的

whirlwind /ˈwəːlwind/ *n.* 旋风

insatiable /inˈseiʃiəbl/ *adj.* 不知足的，贪得无厌的

misrepresent /ˈmisˌrepriˈzent/ *v.* 歪曲报导，误述，误传

in the midst of：在…当中，正当…之时

musket /ˈmʌskit/ *n.* 毛瑟枪，滑膛枪（一种旧式步枪，用于 16 世纪后期到 18 世纪）

romanticize /rəˈmæntisaiz/ *v.* 使浪漫化，使传奇化

exhilarate /igˈziləreit/ *v.* 使高兴，使振奋，提神

intoxicate /inˈtɔksikeit/ *v.* （酒类）使醉；使陶醉，使痴迷

rooftop /ˈruːftɔp/ *n.* ＜美＞屋顶，房顶

reinvent /ˌriːinˈvent/ *v.* 重新创造，再发明

Dali /ˈdaːliː/ （全名 Salvador Dali）萨尔瓦多·达利（1904—1989，西班牙超现实主义画家，以其色彩艳丽的个人风格和精细地描绘在画布上的怪诞画像的令人不安的说明而闻名）

Kafka /ˈkaːfkaː/ （全名 Franz Kafka）弗朗兹·卡夫卡（1883—1924，奥地利作家，其许多作品都涉及到荒诞离奇的异化世界里忧心忡忡的个人）

contradiction /ˌkɔntrəˈdikʃən/ *n.* 矛盾，自相矛盾

perceive /pəˈsiːv/ *v.*　知觉,感觉,认识
fulfillment /fulˈfilmənt/ *n.*　实现,成就,达成
enslave /inˈsleiv/ *v.*　使成为奴隶,支配,束缚
genie /ˈdʒiːni/ *n.*　(＝jinni)穆斯林传说中的鬼怪或神灵(能化
　　为人形或兽形,影响人的事务)

 参考译文【Suggested Translation】

手　表

我环顾周围,房间发生的变化微妙却又明显。墙壁上排列满了长着细腿的大象,我四周的人都已变成了巨大的昆虫,我的手表熔化了,从我的手腕上慢慢地往下滴落。难道是达利式的梦? 或者是卡夫卡式的噩梦? 超现实主义的微风撩动着我的头发;存在主义的旋风俘获了我的想像力。

从这两位伟大创作者笔下的形象之中,我看到了其反射出的美丽的和永不满足的想像力,全然不守成规、狂放不羁,然而又充满了艺术家洞察力的神奇和力量。这些形象不如照片那么真实,但是又比照片可信一百倍。我也常常发现自己曲解了这个世界。在听那些着实乏味枯燥的讲演时,我有时对正在学习的东西打开想像之门,使自己保持清醒;我所看到的并不是老师继续讲的美国内战中的战役,而是看到高举的旗帜下步枪在射击。

更多的时候,我把自己的生命视为一次冒险,极富传奇色彩,而且又理想化,令人激动振奋。在我眼中,令人厌倦的记忆力测试变成了对于意志力的检验;辩论变成了智慧之战;生活的画卷变成了人类与命运之神对抗的存在主义的、令人痴迷的战争。在这些画面里,有时我会遭遇无形的敌手的挑战,有时我又在登山。或许我正在和一头公牛鏖战,或许正在屋顶上跳来蹦去。

我时常会想,如果世界变为我想像的模样,将会有什么裨益。当然,每个人都确实这么想过。即使最严谨的思想家也会不可避免地在自己的作品中表现出他们对这个世界的设想。达利和卡夫卡也不例外,他们是极端的情况。为何我们都如此渴

望逃离现实？我发现自己像许多人一样，经常看起来不太属于这个世界。但是当然我又是属于这个世界的，因为这个世界是我的，就像它也是其他任何人的一样。我试图通过对这个世界作出细微的变动来解决感知与真实之间的矛盾——马车代替了小轿车，获奖的散文代替了家庭作业——以便世界在我身边找到自己的位置。

　　这真是个简单的解决办法。我们并不是改变自己来适应这个世界，相反，我们改变世界，以让它适应我们。就靠简单的心愿之旅，一切都可以做到。当然，用意识熔化手表远比被手表束缚住才智好得多，后者就像精灵被瓶子困住手脚一样。思想的自由并不要求太多；调整世界，使之适合我们的思想，要比调整自己的思想使之适合世界高贵得多。◆

（张颖 译）

● If you venture nothing, you will have nothing. （不入虎穴，焉得虎子。）

● The end justifies the means. （只要目的正当，可以不择手段。）

● Out of sight, out of mind. （眼不见，心不烦。）

● Good medicine for health tastes bitter to the mouth. （良药苦口利于病。）

True Nobility[*]

In a calm sea every man is a pilot.

But all sunshine without shade, all pleasure without

---

  * 作者欧内斯特·米勒·海明威（Ernest Miller Hemingway, 1899—1961），蜚声世界文坛的美国现代著名小说家，"迷惘的一代"（The Lost Generation）的代表人物。他生于乡村医生家庭，从小喜欢钓鱼、打猎、音乐和绘画，曾作为红十字会车队司机参加第一次世界大战，以后长期担任驻欧记者，并曾以记者身份参加第二次世界大战和西班牙内战。他在20年代创作的长篇小说《太阳照样升起》和《永别了，武器》成为表现美国"迷惘的一代"的主要代表作。30、40年代他转而塑造摆脱迷惘、悲观，为人民利益而英勇战斗和无畏牺牲的反法西斯战士形象，作品有剧本《第五纵队》、长篇小说《丧钟为谁而鸣》。50年代后，他以"宁折不弯"为主题发表短篇小说《打不败的人》和《五万大洋》。1953年，海明威发表中篇小说《老人与海》，塑造了以桑提亚哥为代表的"可以把他消灭，但就是打不败他"的"硬汉"性格，其文体之简洁，寓意之幽远，代表了海明威的创作风格的极致和创作成就的巅峰，他也因此获得了1953年的普利策奖和1954年的诺贝尔文学奖。文学上的卓越成就与英雄神话般的人生传奇星光互织，使他成为和马克·吐温一样的明星式大作家。1961年，海明威因不堪病痛折磨而饮弹自尽

pain, is not life at all. Take the lot of the happiest — it is a tangled yarn. Bereavements and blessings, one following another, make us sad and blessed by turns. Even death itself makes life more loving. Men come closest to their true selves in the sober moments of life, under the shadows of sorrow and loss.

In the affairs of life or of business, it is not intellect that tells so much as character, not brains so much as heart, not genius so much as self-control, patience, and discipline, regulated by judgment.

I have always believed that the man who has begun to live more seriously within begins to live more simply without. In an age of extravagance and waste, I wish I could show to the world how few the real wants of humanity are.

To regret one's errors to the point of not repeating them is true repentance. There is nothing noble in being superior to some other man. The true nobility is in being superior to your previous self. ✻

Vocabulary List 【词汇清单】

pilot /ˈpailət/ *n.* 舵手,领航员

tangled /ˈtæŋgəld/ *adj.* 缠结的,纠缠的

yarn /jaːn/ *n.* 纱线,纤维(线)

bereavement /biˈriːvmənt/ *n.* 夺去,失去,丧失亲人(之痛)

sober /ˈsəubə/ *adj.* 清醒的,未醉的;冷静的,严肃的

genius /ˈdʒiːnjəs/ *n.* 天资,天分,天赋

discipline /ˈdisiplin/ *n.* 训练,磨练;自制,自控

extravagance /iksˈtrævigəns/ *n.* 放肆,浪费,挥霍无度

humanity /hju(ː)ˈmæniti/ *n.* 人性;人(们),人类

repentance /riˈpentəns/ *n.* 悔恨,悔改

superior /sju(ː)ˈpiəriə/ *adj.* 胜过的，优越的（to）
previous /ˈpriːvjəs/ *adj.* 先前的，以前的，从前的

参考译文【Suggested Translation】

真 正 的 高 贵

在风平浪静的海面上，每一个人都可以成为领航员。

但是，假如只有阳光而没有阴影，只有欢乐而没有痛苦，那就全然不是人生。就拿最幸福的人来说吧——他们的命运是一团纠缠的纱线。丧亲之痛和神恩赐福此起彼伏，让我们悲欢交替。甚至连死亡本身都让人生更为可爱。人们在生命的庄严时刻，在哀伤和丧亲的阴影之下，最接近真实的自我。

在生活或事业的各种事务之中，才智的效用远不如性格，头脑的效用远不如心性，天资远不如由判断力所约束的自制、耐心与教养。

我一向认为，内心开始生活得更为严谨的人，他外在的生活会开始变得更为简朴。在一个奢侈浪费的时代，但愿我能够向世人表明：人类真正的需求是多么的稀少。

反思自己的过错，以至于不重蹈覆辙才是真正的悔悟。比他人优越并无任何高贵之处。真正的高贵在于超越过去的自我。◆

A Mother's Letter to the World*

Dear World：

My son starts school today. It's going to be strange and new to him for a while. And I wish you would sort of treat him gently.

You see, up to now, he's been king of the roost. He's been boss of the back yard. I have always been around to repair his wounds, and to soothe his feelings.

But now — things are going to be different.

This morning, he's going to walk down the front steps, wave his hand and start on his great adventure that will probably include wars and tragedy and sorrow. To live his life in

---

　　* 作者安妮·斯通（Anne Stone），生平不详。母爱是伞，为你遮风挡雨；是衣，为你送去温暖；是灯，为你送去光明；是光，照亮你的心灵。本文是一封饱含情愫的书信，语言平实自然，却凝结着一位母亲对自己孩子的挚爱之情，读来让人感动不已。

the world he has to live in will require faith and love and courage.

So, World, I wish you would sort of take him by his young hand and teach him the things he will have to know. Teach him — but gently, if you can. Teach him that for every scoundrel, there is a hero; that for every crooked politician there is a dedicated leader; that for every enemy there is a friend. Teach him the wonders of books. Give him quiet time to ponder the eternal mystery of birds in the sky, bees in the sun, and flowers on the green hill. Teach him it is far more honorable to fail than to cheat. Teach him to have faith in his own ideas, even if everyone else tells him they are wrong. Teach him to sell his brawn and brains to the highest bidder, but never to put a price on his heart and soul. Teach him to close his ears to a howling mob... and to stand and fight if he thinks he's right. Teach him gently, World, but don't coddle him, because only the test of fire makes fine steel.

This is a big order, World, but see what you can do. He's such a nice little fellow. ✳

 **Vocabulary List 【词汇清单】**

sort of：稍微,有点,有几分

roost /ruːst/ *n.* 栖木,栖息处;卧室(可泛指家)

soothe /suːθ/ *v.* 安慰,抚慰,慰藉

adventure /əd'ventʃə/ *n.* 冒险,探险(活动)

scoundrel /'skaundrəl/ *n.* 无赖,流氓,恶棍

crooked /'krukid/ *adj.* 不正直(正派)的,不诚实的,欺诈的

ponder /'pɔndə/ *v.* 默想,深思,仔细考虑

eternal /i(ː)'təːnl/ *adj.* 无穷尽的,永存的,永恒的

honorable /'ɔnərəbl/ *adj.* 高尚的,光荣的,值得尊敬的

brawn /brɔːn/ *n.* 肌肉的力量，机质，体力
bidder /'bidə/ *n.* （拍卖时的）出价人；投标人
howl /haul/ *v.* 嚎叫，咆哮
mob /mɔb/ *n.* 群氓，匪帮，一群暴徒，乌合之众
coddle /'kɔdl/ *v.* 娇养，溺爱

参考译文【Suggested Translation】

一位母亲写给世界的信

亲爱的世界：

我的儿子今天要开始上学读书了。一时之间，他会感觉陌生而又新鲜。而我希望你能待他温柔一些。

你明白，到现在为止，他一直是家中的小皇帝；一直是后院的王者。我一直在他身旁，忙着为他治疗伤口，并慰藉他的心情。

但是现在———一切都将不同了。

今天清晨，他就要走下前门的楼梯，冲我挥挥手，开始他的伟大的历险征程，其间或许有争斗、不幸或者伤痛。要在这个世界上生存度日，他需要信念、爱心和勇气。

所以，世界啊，我希望你能够时不时握住他稚嫩的小手，教育他所应当知晓的事情。教育他吧——而如果可能的话，温柔一些。教他知道，每有恶人之地，必有豪杰所在；每有奸诈小人，必有献身义士；每见一敌人，必有一友在侧。教他感受书本的神奇魅力。给他时间静思大自然中亘古绵传之奥秘：空中的飞鸟，日光里的蜜蜂，青山上的簇簇繁花。教他知道，失败远比欺骗更为光荣；教他坚定自我的信念，哪怕人人予以否认；教他可以最高价付出自己的精力和智慧，但绝不可出卖良心和灵魂；教他置群氓的喧嚣于度外……并在自觉正确之时挺身而战。温柔地教导他吧，世界，但是不要放纵他。因为只有烈火的考验才能炼出真钢。

这一要求甚高，世界，但是请尽你所能。他是一个如此可爱的小家伙。◆

（《英语沙龙》如风 译）

A to Z *

Avoid negative people, places, things and habits.

Believe in yourself.

Consider things from every angle.

Don't give up and don't give in.

Enrich your life today. Yesterday is history. Tomorrow is mystery.

Family and friends are hidden treasures. Seek them and enjoy their riches.

Give more than you planned to.

Hang on to your dreams.

Ignore those who try do discourage you.

---

　　* 作者佚名。26 个字母,26 条叮嘱,26 项准则,揭示的是一个人安身立命的玄机,蕴含的是无穷无尽的智慧！它是箴言的积木,它是睿语的贴板,它是警句的拼图！不妨敞开你的心扉,让这智慧的丝丝的甘霖滋润和浸透你的心田……

Just do it.

Keep trying no matter how hard it seems. It will get easier.

Live well, love lots, and laugh often.

Make it happen.

Never lie, cheat or steal. Always strike a fair deal.

Open your eyes and see things as they really are.

Practice makes perfect.

Quitters never win and winners never quit.

Read, study and learn about everything important in your life.

Stop procrastinating.

Take control of your own destiny.

Understand yourself in order to better understand others.

Visualize it.

Want it more than anything.

Xcellerate (accelerate) your efforts.

You are unique. Nothing can replace YOU.

Zero in your target, and go for it! ✸

Vocabulary List 【词汇清单】

angle /ˈæŋgl/ *n.* （考虑问题的）角度,方面

give up：放弃,停止

give in：投降,屈服,认输

enrich /inˈritʃ/ *v.* 使丰富,使充实

discourage /disˈkʌridʒ/ *v.* 使泄气,使沮丧

quitter /ˈkwitə/ *n.* ＜美＞轻易放弃工作（或职务）的人,半途而废者,懦夫

procrastinate /prəuˈkræstineit/ *v.* （经常性地）拖延,耽搁,延误

destiny /ˈdestini/ *n.* 命运,定数,天命

visualize /ˈvizjuəlaiz/ *v.* 想像,设想

accelerate /ək'seləreit/ *v.* 加速，加快

参考译文【Suggested Translation】

从 A 到 Z

勿 交是非之人，远离是非之地，勿染不良习惯。

相信你自己。

全方位思考问题。

不要放弃，不要屈服。

充实今天的生活，昨日已成过去，明天还是未知数。

家人和朋友是隐藏的宝藏。努力发掘，共享财富。

给予更多，不必计较。

追逐梦想（矢志不渝）。

忽视那些试图使你气馁之人。

说做就做。

无论事情看上去多么困难也要坚持不懈；事情即会变得容易。

善待生活，热爱一切，并且经常开怀大笑。

让思想变成现实。

决不撒谎、欺骗或偷窃。坚守公平交易之道。

睁大眼睛，看清事情真相。

多练自然熟（熟能生巧）。

退缩者永远不会胜利，胜利者永远不会退缩。

点点滴滴都重要，处处留心皆学问。

不要拖拖拉拉。

掌握你自己的命运。

理解自我以便更好地理解他人。

发挥想像力。

急需之物最重要。

加倍努力。

你举世无双，无人可以替代。

从"零"开始，勇往直前！◢　　　　　　　　（《英语沙龙》陆恩 译）

Successful English Learning[*]

Research in the field of language indicates that there are many things you can do to become a successful learner. Curiosity about language and culture, daily study, and the commitment to use English in every possible situation while in an English-speaking environment, are very important conditions for success.

1. Be clear and realistic about your goals. Your sense of success will depend on your needs for English and whether or not you meet your needs. It is not just a question of measured progress. If you need conversational fluency, notetaking skills will not meet your needs. If you must learn to write effec-

---

* 作者佚名。现今，无数的人正在苦苦寻觅学习英语的有效方法，可是学习有法，但无常法，贵在得法，只有适合于自己的方法才是好方法。面对英语这块"难啃的骨头"，你找到适合自己的方法了吗？

tive business letters, informal conversation with current slang will not help you achieve your goal.

Know what your goals are. Do you need English for occasional speaking situations, for travel or entertaining English-speaking visitors? Do you want to improve comprehension in both written and spoken English? Do you need to write English for professional purpose? Are you preparing for a university career in English? If so, your goals must include proficiency in all skill areas.

Learning a foreign language is an inexact process. Very few people learn to use a foreign language as well as a native speaker does. Fortunately, very few people need to learn English like a native English speaker in every skill area. Be realistic and aware of your goals. There are many reasons to learn English, and your reasons are your own goals.

2. Be realistic about the length of time it takes to learn a language. Programs which promise overnight success are simply not being honest. Language learning is a cumulative process. You will experience bursts of accomplishment as well blocks and delays in progress. You will notice improvement at different speeds in each skill area. Many students progress more quickly in passive skill areas (reading and grammar analysis) than in active and complex skill areas (speaking, notetaking during a lecture). If you are beginning level student whose goal is proficiency, a typical program may include at least nine months of intensive English study. If your study program is short-term and your goals include improvement and review rather than proficiency you may realise some progress in two or more weeks.

3. Be aware of your learning style. If you know that you learn more quickly when you listen to an English statement a

few times before writing it, or if you know that seeing a picture or graphic representation of a word or expression helps you to remember the word, then develop study habits which use the most effective techniques for you. Excellent instructors who know that students must be involved in active learning will created active learning experiences to connect you with the language.

4. Learn something about "language learning". Remember that language is a complex system of meaningful sounds organised with a series of rules (grammar). Every student has to study enough pronunciation, grammar and sentence structure to understand this! It is also true that language is a form of behaviour involving the human need to communicate and to be understood. Language learning involves motivation, emotion, a sense of self, and a set of cultural beliefs. Language is much more than sound and words and grammar. As you learn a new language, you will produce a "series of successive approximations", meaning that each attempt at a new language will bring closer to effective communication. Language learning requires that you make mistakes. Do not be afraid of a language or afraid of making errors. Develop an abiity to relax; "playing" with a new language is an improtant part of learning.

5. Take responsibility for your own learning. A good instructor is half the equation for successful language learning. Take charge of your learning; participate actively in your program. Look for opportunities to use your new language in any of many new environments. Be willing to make mistakes and learn from these mistakes. Focus on your goals, your study habits, and your willingness to "learn to learn". Enjoy the process! Find ihside yourself the reasons you want to learn,

and determine ways to evaluate your success for yourself. ✳

Vocabulary List【词汇清单】

indicate /'indikeit/ v. 显示,表明

curiosity /ˌkjuəri'ɔsiti/ n. 求知欲,好奇心

environment /in'vaiərənmənt/ n. 环境,四周,外界

fluency /'flu(ː)ənsi/ n. 流利,流畅

slang /slæŋ/ n. 俚语,行话

occasional /ə'keiʒnl/ adj. 偶然发生的,偶尔的

proficiency /prə'fiʃənsi/ n. 熟练,精通

inexact /ˌinig'zækt/ adj. 不精确的,不准确的

cumulative /'kjuːmjulətiv/ adj. 累积的,(数量、大小等)渐增的

passive /'pæsiv/ adj. 被动的,消极的

intensive /in'tensiv/ adj. 集中的,集约的;加强的,强化的

representation /ˌreprizen'teiʃən/ n. 表现,表示;画像,肖像

technique /tek'niːk/ n. 技术,技巧,技能

pronunciation /prəˌnʌnsi'eiʃən/ n. 发音,发音法

successive /sək'sesiv/ adj. 接连的,依次的,相继的

approximation /əˌprɔksi'meiʃən/ n. 接近,靠近,近似

participate /paː'tisipeit/ v. 参加,参与(某项活动、事业)

evaluate /i'væljueit/ v. 估价,评价,评估

参考译文【Suggested Translation】

英语学习成功之道

语言领域的研究显示,要想成为一个成功的学习者,你有许多事情可做。对于语言和文化的好奇、日常学习以及处于一个英语环境之中,自觉地在每个可能的场合中使用英语,这些

都是迈向成功的重要条件。

　　1. 目标明确而现实。成功的感觉依赖于你对英语的需要以及你是否满足了这些需要。这不仅仅是一个衡量学习进度的问题。如果你想要流利地对话，笔记技巧不会满足你的需要。如果你一定要学会起草给人印象深刻的商务信函，非正式的、包含日常俚语的对话不能帮你实现目标。

　　要知道你的目标是什么。你学英语是为了应付偶而的说话场合、用于旅行中还是为接待说英语的客人？你想在英语写作和口语的理解方面取得进步吗？你因为职业原因而需要用到英语写作吗？你正准备在大学谋求一份有关英语的职业吗？如果是这样，你的目标一定要包括精通英语的所有技能。

　　学习一门外语是一个非精确的过程。很少有人能学会和外国当地人一样使用英语。所幸的是，也很少有人需要像外国当地人一样学习英语的每一种技能。你的目标必须明确而现实。学英语的原因有许多，依据原因确定你自己的目标。

　　2. 安排学习语言的时间长短要实事求是。承诺一夜成功的培训纯属无稽之谈。语言学习是一个不断积累的过程。在学习进展中，你会突飞猛进，也会经历阻碍和拖延。对于每一种技能，你会发现进步的速度也不尽相同。许多学生在被动的技能训练（阅读和语法分析）中进步更快，而在主动并且复杂的技能训练（说、记课堂笔记）中则进步较慢。如果你是初级阶段的学生，你的目标是熟练，典型的培训则可能包括至少 9 个月的英语强化学习。如果你的学习班是短期性质，你的目标是复习与提高，而不是熟练，你在两个或两个以上的星期内就能取得一些进步。

　　3. 注意你的学习风格。如果你觉得在多次倾听一个英语陈述后写下它将有助于你更快地把握它；或者如果你觉得通过观看某个单词或短语的图示能帮你加强记忆，那么你就要培养这些能帮助你最有效提高的良好学习习惯。深知学生需要主动投入学习的优秀老师，就会努力营造积极的学习实践，使你和语言紧紧联结在一起。

　　4. 掌握学习语言的技巧。要记住，语言是一个按规则（语法）组织起来的具有意义的声音的复杂系统。每一个学生必须通过学习足够的发音、语法和句子结构知识来理解它。语言也是人类用来进行交流和表达自己的一种行为形式。语言学习包括动机、情感、自我感觉和文化理念。语言的意义远不止于声音、词汇和语法。当你学习一门新语言时，你会产生一系列连续性的共鸣，也就意味着，对一种新语言的每一次尝试，都会让你感觉距离有效交流更近一步。语言学习容许你犯错误，不要害怕学习语言或者害怕犯错误。培养一种放松的心态，将学习融入乐趣，这在学习一门新的外语过程中是非常重要的。

5. 对自己的学习负责。有好的老师就是语言学习成功的一半。要管理好自己的学习，积极参与你的培训课程。在任何可能的新环境中寻求使用新语言的机会。乐于犯错误并学会从这些错误中吸取教训；关注你的目标、你的学习习惯以及对"学会学习"的追求。享受这一过程吧！寻找你想要学习的内在动因并为自己找出评价成功的方式。◆

● A fall into a pit, a gain in your wit.（吃一堑，长一智。）

● The world is but a little place, after all.（海内存知己，天涯若比邻。）

● Patience is the best remedy.（忍耐是良药。）

● Heaven never helps the man who will not act.（自己不动，叫天何用。）

Science and Art*

I beg leave to thank you for the extremely kind and appreciative manner in which you have received the toast of Science. It is the more grateful to me to hear that toast proposed in an assembly of this kind, because I have noticed of late years a great and growing tendency among those who

---

　　* 作者托马斯·亨利·赫胥黎（Thomas Henry Huxley, 1825—1895），英国近代杰出的博物学家、科学家和教育家。他是英国第一部初等教育法案的起草人之一，在英国的国民教育和科学教育中发挥了重要作用。他的主要著作有《科学与教育》、《科学与文化》、《在哪里能找到一种自由教育》、《论科学和艺术与教育的关系》、《现实的和理想的大学》等，猛烈抨击了古典人文主义教育的狭隘性，大力阐述科学教育的重要性。尤其可贵的是，他把人文科学、社会科学和自然科学摆在同等重要的位置，克服了当时教育界出现的或重古典教育或重科学教育的倾向，强调进行全面的和谐教育。正是在赫胥黎及其同时代人的倡导下，科学教育开始受到人们的重视，进入了学校的大门，从而打破了传统的古典教育一统天下的局面，奠定了科学教育的地位。

were once jestingly said to have been born in a pre-scientific age to look upon science as an invading and aggressive force, which if it had its own way would oust from the universe all other pursuits. I think there are many persons who look upon this new birth of our times as a sort of monster rising out of the sea of modern thought with the purpose of devouring the Andromeda of art. And now and then a Perseus, equipped with the shoes of swiftness of the ready writer, with the cap of invisibility of the editorial article, and it may be with the Medusahead of vituperation, shows himself ready to try conclusions with the scientific dragon. Sir, I hope that Perseus will think better of it; first, for his own sake, because the creature is hard of head, strong of jaw, and for some time past has shown a great capacity for going over and through whatever comes in his way; and secondly, for the sake of justice, for I assure you, of my own personal knowledge that if left alone, the creature is a very debonair and gentle monster. As for the Andromeda of art, he has the tenderest respect for that lady, and desires nothing more than to see her happily settled and annually producing a flock of such charming children as those we see about us.

But putting parables aside, I am unable to understand how any one with a knowledge of mankind can imagine that the growth of science can threaten the development of art in any of its forms. If I understand the matter at all, science and art are the obverse and reverse of Nature's medal; the one expressing the external order of things, in terms of feeling, the other in terms of thought. When men no longer love nor hate; when suffering causes no pity, and the tale of great deeds ceases to thrill, when the lily of the field shall seem no longer more beautifully arrayed than Solomon in all his glory, and the awe has vanished from the snow-capped peak and deep ra-vine, then indeed science may have the world to itself, but it will not be because the monster has devoured the art, but be-cause one side of human nature is dead, and because men have lost the half of their ancient and present attributes. ✳

Vocabulary List【词汇清单】

appreciative /ə'pri:ʃjətiv/ *adj.* 欣赏的,有欣赏力的;有鉴赏力的,有赏识力的

toast /təust/ *n.* 敬酒,祝酒,祝酒词

assembly /ə'sembli/ *n.* 集会,会议

tendency /'tendənsi/ *n.* 趋势,倾向

jestingly /'dʒestiŋli/ *adv.* 开玩笑地,嘲弄地

invade /in'veid/ *v.* 侵略,入侵,侵犯

aggressive /ə'gresiv/ *adj.* 侵略的,侵犯的,挑衅的

oust /aust/ *v.* 驱逐,撵走

devour /di'vauə/ *v.* 贪婪地吃,狼吞虎咽,吞噬

Andromeda /æn'drɔmidə/ <希腊神话>安德洛墨达(埃塞俄比亚公主,被珀修斯从海怪手中救出并与她结婚)

Perseus /'pə:sju:s/ <希腊神话>珀修斯(宙斯与达那厄所生之子,杀死蛇发女怪美杜莎、后又从海怪掌下救出安德洛墨达的英雄)

swiftness /'swiftnis/ *n.* 迅速,敏捷

invisibility /inˌvizə'biliti/ *n.* 看不见,无形,隐形

editorial /ˌedi'tɔ:riəl/ *adj.* 社论(性)的,评论(性)的

Medusahead /mi'dju:zə/ <希腊神话>美杜莎之脑(美杜莎,三名戈尔工(Gorgon)之一,被珀修斯所杀)

vituperation /viˌtju:pə'reiʃən/ *n.* 谩骂,辱骂,斥责,训斥

assure /ə'ʃuə/ *v.* 使确信(某事),使信服,向…保证

debonair /ˌdebə'nɛə/ *adj.* 亲切的,友好的,和蔼(可亲)的

parable /'pærəbl/ *n.* (道德说教性的)寓言;比喻

obverse /ˈɔbvəːs/ *n.*　正面,前面

reverse /riˈvəːs/ *n.*　背面,反面

medal /ˈmedl/ *n.*　奖章,奖牌,勋章;作为宗教象征的圆牌

cease /siːs/ *v.*　停止,中止

thrill /θril/ *v.*　(使)极度兴奋,(使)激动得发抖

array /əˈrei/ *v.*　装扮,打扮

Solomon /ˈsɔləmən/ *n.*　<圣经>所罗门(古代以色列国王,大卫的儿子和继承者,以智慧著称)

vanish /ˈvæniʃ/ *v.*　消失,消散

snow-capped /ˈsnəukæpt/ *adj.*　(山、树等)被冰雪覆盖的

ravine /rəˈviːn/ *n.*　沟壑,深谷

参考译文【Suggested Translation】

科 学 和 艺 术

请允许我感谢各位以极其友好与欣赏的态度,听取了为科学而作的祝酒词。今天能在这样的会上听到这个祝酒辞,更使我激动不已。因为近些年来我注意到,一种日益强大的、将科学视为一股侵略势力的倾向,已经出现在那些被戏称为生于前科学时代的人们中间。他们以为,如果任由科学随心所欲的话,就必会把其他行业从宇宙中清除出去。我想,现在有许多人都认为这个当代的新生事物出自现代思潮的洪水猛兽,它想要吞噬艺术之神安德洛墨达。于是,一位珀修斯就会时不时出现。他脚蹬令人文思泉涌的"追风靴",头戴重量级社评的"隐形盔",也许还长着装满谩骂之辞的"美杜莎之脑",摆出了欲与科学猛兽一决胜负的阵势。诸位,我希望这位珀修斯三思而后行。首先,是要为自己着想。因为怪兽头坚颌硬,而且一段日子以来,它在冲破任何障碍方面已经大显神威。其次,是要为公正着想。因为我向诸位保证,据我看来,如果不去惹这头怪兽的话,它是非常温文尔雅的。至于艺术之神安德洛墨达,它对那位女士非常恭敬,而且别无他求,只盼望她幸福地安家落户,年年生

育一大群惹人喜爱的儿女，就像我们在自己周围所看到的孩子们一般。

　　但是，如果撇开上述比喻不谈，我实在难以理解，一个具有人类知识的人，怎么能够认为科学的进步竟会威胁到任何艺术形式的发展。如果我理解不错的话，那么科学和艺术代表了自然这枚圣牌的正反两面。一个是以感情来表达事物的永恒的秩序，另一个则是以思想来表述。当人们心中不再有爱恨存在；当苦难不再引起人们同情，英雄们的丰功伟绩不再激动人心；当田野里的野百合不能再与至尊荣耀的所罗门相媲美，白雪皑皑的山峰和深不可测的幽谷不再使人惊叹敬畏，到那时，科学确实有可能独占整个世界，但这并不是因为科学怪兽吞噬了艺术，而应归咎于人类天性的一个方面已经死去，人类丧失了古往今来所拥有的天性的那一半。◆

● Honesty is the best policy.（做人以诚信为本。）

● Pleasure comes through toil.（苦尽甘来。）

● Tomorrow never comes.（我生待明日，万事成蹉跎。）

● A good beginning is half done.（良好的开端是成功的一半。）

Tactics for Job-hunt Success[*]

If you're finding it tough to land a job, try expanding your job-hunting plan to include the following tactics：

Set your target. While you should always keep your options open to compromise, you should also be sure to target exactly what you want in a job. A specific job hunt will be more efficient than a haphazard one.

Schedule ample interviews. Use every possible method to get interviews — answering ads, using search firms, con-

---

　　* 作者佚名。有这样的说法：“求职难,难于上青天！”虽然语气稍显戏谑,却从一个侧面反映出求职的艰辛。而新世纪的职场中,容不得我们逃避、胆怯、犹豫、怠惰、投机和蒙混过关——找工作这一关,倘挺不过去,严重地说——前途无望。有时候,工作就像永不消散的生存雾霭中的小路,有时需要人们倾注全心去探寻。然而,“Nothing is impossible to a willing heart.（心之所愿,无事不成）”只要你认为你行,辅之以适当的技巧,好的工作和职位会接踵而至！

tacting companies directly, surfing the Web, and networking. Even if a job is not perfect for you, every interview can be approached as a positive experience.

Follow up! Even if someone does not hire you, write them a thank-you note for the interview. Then, some weeks later, send another brief letter to explain that you still have not found the perfect position and that you will be available to interview again if the original position you applied for — or any other position, for that matter — is open. Do this with every position you interview for, and you may just catch a break!

Make it your full-time job. You can't find a job by looking sporadically. You have to make time for it. If you're unemployed and looking, devote as much time as you would to a full-time job. If you have a job while you're looking, figure out an organized schedule to maximize your searching time.

Network vertically. In the research phase of your job hunt, talk to people who are on a level above you in your desired industry. They'll have some insights that people at your own level won't have, and will be in a good position to hire you or recommend you to be hired.

Keep your spirits up. Looking for a job is one of the toughest things you will ever have to do. Maintain your confidence, stay persistently, and think positively, and eventually you will get a job that suits you. ✽

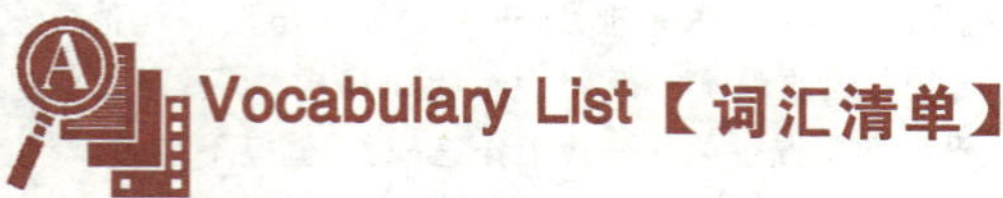

Vocabulary List 【词汇清单】

tactics /ˈtæktiks/ *n.* 策略，手法（尤指熟练的方法）
land /lænd/ *v.* ＜口语＞等到，赢得，获得
option /ˈɔpʃən/ *n.* 选择（权），挑选

compromise /ˈkɔmprəmaiz/ *n.* 妥协,和解,折衷

haphazard /ˈhæpˈhæzəd/ *adj.* 偶然的,非计划的,随意的

ample /ˈæmpl/ *adj.* 充足的,充裕的;足够的,充分的

approach /əˈprəutʃ/ *v.* 靠近,接近;着手,看待

original /əˈridʒənl/ *adj.* 原先的,最初的

sporadically /spəˈrædikəli/ *adv.* 零星地,分散地

figure out：＜美＞预料,打算;制定

maximize /ˈmæksimaiz/ *v.* 使增加(或扩大)到最大限度

vertically /ˈvəːtikəli/ *adv.* 垂直地,纵向地

insight /ˈinsait/ *n.* 洞察力,视野,见识

recommend /ˌrekəˈmend/ *v.* 推荐,介绍

maintain /menˈtein/ *v.* 保持,维持

persistently /pəˈsistəntli/ *adv.* 坚持地,持续地

 ## 参考译文【Suggested Translation】

求 职 胜 略

假如你觉得找工作是一件棘手的事情,那么不妨扩展你的求职计划,并纳入以下策略：

设定目标。尽管你应当永远给你的选择留有妥协的余地,你也应该确切知道你到底想从某份工作中获得什么。明确而具体地寻找工作要比漫无目的地碰运气有效得多。

安排尽量多的面谈。尽可能利用一切办法去争取面试机会——回复招聘广告,利用搜寻公司,直接与公司联系,网上搜索,运用各种关系网,等等。即使某份工作对你不是最为理想的,但是每次面谈都可以是一次有积极意义的经历。

再接再厉！即便别人没有雇用你,给他们写张致谢便笺,感谢他为你安排了一次面试机会。那么,数周之后,如果你原来申请的职位——或者与之相关的某职位——尚无人选落实,你不妨再寄去一封简短的信说你还未找到理想的职位,如果有机会再面试一次将随传随到。你每次应聘面试求职都应这样,没准

儿你就会抓住一个机会。

　　把找工作当成全职工作。你时断时续地找,不可能找到一份理想的工作,你必须去花时间去找。如果你失业了想再找份新工作,尽可能多地付出时间就像你在做全职工作一样。如果你已有工作,但还想找新的机会,制定一个有序的计划,尽可能多地安排时间去搜寻。

　　纵向网罗关系。在找工作的研究阶段,找机会去和你渴望进入的行业中比你高一层次的人物交谈,他们会有你这个层次人物所不具备的视野,会有能力雇用你或将你推荐给其他雇主。

　　心情愉快,充满希望。找工作是你必须做的最为棘手的事情之一。保持自信,坚持不懈,态度乐观,而最终你会找到适合你的工作的。◆

◉Example is better than percept.（说一遍,不如做一遍。）

◉Where there is a will, there is a way.（有志者,事竟成。）

◉The fox knew too much, that's how he lost his tail.（机关算尽太聪明,反误了卿卿性命。）

◉It is better to die when life is a disgrace.（宁为玉碎,不为瓦全。）

Ambition[*]

It is not difficult to imagine a world short of ambition. It would probably be a kinder world：without demands, without abrasions, without disappointments. People would have time for reflection. Such work as they did would not be for themselves but for the collective. Competition would never enter in. Conflict would be eliminated, tension become a thing of the past. The stress of creation would be at an end. Art would no longer be troubling, but purely celebratory in its

---

＊ 作者约瑟夫・爱泼斯坦(Joseph Epstein,1937—　　)，美国著名社会评论家和散文家，从 1975 年起担任《美国学者》杂志(American Scholar) 的主编，曾编撰许多有关美国社会、文化和教育的论著。抱负是什么？抱负是高尚的行为成长的萌芽。托・富勒说："伟大的抱负造就伟大的人。"斯蒂文生说："抱负永远是一种欢乐，是一种如地产一般可靠的财产。"朗费罗说："我的抱负就是我惟一的朋友。"高尔斯华绥说："我饮的是抱负酒，服的是幻想药，所以我会永远朝气蓬勃。"……那么，你的抱负观又是怎样的呢？相信本文会给你或多或少的启示。

functions. The family would become superfluous as a social unit, with all its former power for bringing about neurosis drained away. Longevity would be increased, for fewer people would die of heart attack or stroke caused by tumultuous endeavor. Anxiety would be extinct. Time would stretch on and on, with ambition long departed from the human heart.

Ah, how unrelievedly boring life would be!

There is a strong view that holds that success is a myth, and ambition therefore a sham. Does this mean that success does not really exist? That achievement is at bottom empty? That the efforts of men and women are of no significance alongside the force of movements and events? Now not all success, obviously, is worth esteeming, nor all ambition worth cultivating. Which are and which are not is something one soon enough learns on one's own. But even the most cynical secretly admit that success exists; that achievement counts for a great deal; and that the true myth is that the actions of men and women are useless. To believe otherwise is to take on a point of view that is likely to be deranging. It is, in its implications, to remove all motive for competence, interest in attainment, and regard for posterity.

We do not choose to be born. We do not choose our parents. We do not choose our historical epoch, the country of our birth or the immediate circumstances of our upbringing. We do not, most of us, choose to die; nor do we choose the time or conditions of our death. But within all this realm of choicelessness, we do choose how we shall live: courageously or in cowardice, honorably or dishonorably, with purpose or in drift. We decide what is important and what is trivial in life. We decide that what makes us significant is either what we do or what we refuse to do. But no matter how indifferent the universe may be to our choices and decisions, these choices and decisions are ours to make. We decide. We choose. And as we decide and choose, so are our lives formed. In the end, forming our own destiny is what ambition is about. ✳

 ## Vocabulary List【词汇清单】

shear /ʃiə/ *v.* 剪去,剪掉(毛发等)

abrasion /əˈbreiʒən/ *n.* (皮肤等的)擦伤;<喻>摩擦,磨耗

collectivity /ˌkəlekˈtiviti/ *n.* 集体,总体,团体

eliminate /iˈlimineit/ *v.* 除掉,排除,除去,消除

celebratory /səˈlebrətəri/ *adj.* 庆祝的,欢庆的

superfluous /sju(ː)ˈpəːfluəs/ *adj.* 多余的,不必要的

neurosis /njuəˈrəusis/ *n.* <医>神经机能病,神经(官能)症

stroke /strəuk/ *n.* (疾病的)突然发作(尤指中风)

tumultuous /tjuːˈmʌltjuəs/ *adj.* 喧闹的,吵闹的,喧嚣的;纷乱的,混乱的

endeavor /inˈdevə/ *n.* 努力,尽力,力争

unrelievedly /ˌʌnriˈliːvidli/ *adv.* 未减轻地,未缓和地;彻头彻尾地,完完全全地

myth /miθ/ *n.* 神话,虚构的故事

sham /ʃæm/ *n.* <古>欺骗,骗局

cynical /ˈsinikəl/ *adj.* 玩世不恭的,愤世嫉俗的

derange /diˈreindʒ/ *v.* 打乱(安排或行动),混乱,使混乱

posterity /posˈteriti/ *n.* 子孙,后裔,后世(与 ancestry 相对)

epoch /ˈiːpɔk/ *n.* (新)纪元,(新)时代,(新)时期

upbringing /ˈʌpˌbriŋiŋ/ *n.* 教养,抚育,培养

realm /relm/ *n.* 领域,范围

courageously /kəˈreidʒəsli/ *adv.* 勇敢地,无畏地

cowardice /ˈkauədis/ *n.* 懦弱,胆怯,胆小(in)

参考译文【Suggested Translation】

抱　负

一个缺乏抱负的世界将会怎样，这是不难想像的。或许，这将是一个更加友爱的世界：没有渴求，没有摩擦，没有失望。人们将会有时间进行反思。他们所从事的工作将不是为了他们自身，而是为了整个集体。竞争永远不会介入，冲突将被消除，人们的紧张关系将成为过往云烟。创造的重压将得以终结，艺术将不再惹人讨厌，其功能将是纯粹的庆典。作为社会单位的家庭，因失去了原有的导致精神病痛的力量而将荡然无存。人的寿命将更长，因为由激烈拼争而引起的心脏病和中风死亡将愈加减少。焦虑将会消失。由于抱负早已告别人心，时间将得以无限伸延。

啊，人生将变得多么乏味无聊！

有一种盛行的观点认为，成功是一种神话，因此抱负亦属虚幻。这是不是说成功不会真正存在？成就本质上是一场空？在诸多运动和事件的力量相形之下，世上男男女女的努力微不足道？显然，并非所有的成功都值得景仰，并非所有的抱负都值得栽培。对于值得和不值得的选择，一个人自然而然很快就会学会。但是即使最为愤世嫉俗的人暗地里也承认，成功确实存在，成就的意义举足轻重，而把世上男男女女的努力说成徒劳无功才真正是无稽之谈。不相信成功的存在，就等于接纳了一种很可能造成混乱的观点。这种观点的本意是一笔勾销所有提高能力的动机、求取业绩的兴趣和对子孙后代的关注。

我们无法选择出生。我们无法选择父母。我们无法选择出生的历史时期与国家，以及成长的周遭环境。我们——我们中的大部分——无法选择死亡，也无法选择死亡的时间与条件。但是在这少有选择余地的领域之内，我们确实可以选择如何生活：是勇敢无畏还是战战兢兢，是光明磊落还是厚颜无耻，是目标坚定还是得过且过。我们决定生活中哪些事情至关重要，哪些无足轻重。由于我们作着决定，因此我们做些什么，或者拒绝做些什么,就显示出我们的重要性。但是不管世界对我们的选择和决定多么漠不关心,这些选择和决定是由我们作出的。我们作出决定;我们进行选择。在我们作出决定和选择的过程中,我们的生活得以形成。总而言之,构筑我们的命运是抱负的真意所在。◆

●Hope for the best, but prepare for the worst. (抱最好的期望,做最坏的打算。)

●All good things come to an end. (天下没有不散的筵席。)

●Please the eye and plague the heart. (贪图一时快活,必然留下隐患。)

●Experience is the father of wisdom and memory the mother. (经验是智慧之父,记忆是智慧之母。)

To —*

One word is too often profaned
For me to profane it,
One feeling too falsely disdain'd
For thee to disdain it;

---

  * 作者波西·比希·雪莱（Percy Bysshe Shelley，1792—1822），英国杰出的民主主义诗人，其作品热情而富哲理思辨，诗风自由不羁，常任天上地下、时间空间、神怪精灵往来变幻驰骋，又惯用梦幻象征手法和远古神话题材。其代表作有长诗《仙后麦布》（1813）、抒情故事诗《伊斯兰的反叛》（1818）、政治诗《暴政的行列》（1819）、政治诗《自由颂》（1820）和表现革命热情及胜利信念的《西风颂》（1819），以及取材于古希腊神话，表现人民反暴政胜利后瞻望空想社会主义前景的代表诗剧《解放了的普罗米修斯》（1819）等。雪莱浪漫主义理想的终极目标就是创造一个人人享有自由幸福的新世界。他设想自己是日夜飞翔的天使、飘浮蓝空的云朵、翱翔太空的云雀，乃至深秋季节的西风，是新世界理想的传播者、歌颂者、号召者。他以美丽的语言、丰富的想像描绘了这个新世界的绚丽画面，而且豪迈地预言："如果冬天已经来临，春天还会远吗？"因此，雪莱被恩格斯赞誉为"天才的预言家"。

One hope is too like despair
For prudence to smother,
And pity from thee more dear
Than that from another.

I can give not what men call love;
But wilt thou accept not
The worship the heart lifts above
And the Heavens reject not, —
The desire of the moth for star,
Of the night for the morrow,
The devotion to something afar
From the sphere of our sorrow? ✳

 **Vocabulary List【词汇清单】**

profane /prəˈfein/ *v.* 亵渎,玷污,污损

falsely /ˈfɔːlsli/ *adv.* 谬误地,错误地,不正确地

disdain /disˈdein/ *v.* 玷污(名声),败坏(声誉);鄙视,蔑视,轻视

thee /ðiː/ *pron.* ＜古＞汝,你

prudence /ˈpruːdəns/ *n.* 谨慎,慎重,深谋远虑

smother /ˈsmʌðə/ *v.* 压抑,压制,扼杀

wilt /wilt/ *v. aux.* ＜古＞will 的第二人称单数现在时陈述语气（与 thou 连用）

thou /ðau/ *n.* ＜古＞汝,你(尤在文学、礼拜或祈祷文献中用于指代所强调之人)

reject /riˈdʒekt/ *v.* 拒绝(接受、同意等),否认,排斥

moth /mɔθ/ *n.* 蛾子,飞蛾

morrow /ˈmɔrəu/ *n.* ＜诗或古＞早晨,次日,翌日

afar /əˈfaː/ *adv.* ＜诗或古＞从远处,在远处,遥远地

sphere /sfiə/ *n.* 领域,范围

给——

有一个字常被人滥用，
我不想再滥用它；
有一种感情不被看重，
你岂能再轻视它？
有一种希望太像绝望，
慎重也无法压碎；
只求怜悯起自你心上，
对我就万分珍贵。

我奉献的不能叫爱情，
它只算得是崇拜，
连上天对它都肯垂青，——
想你该不致见外？
这有如飞蛾向往星天，
暗夜想拥抱天明，
怎能不让悲惨的尘寰
对遥远事物倾心？◨

（查良铮 译）

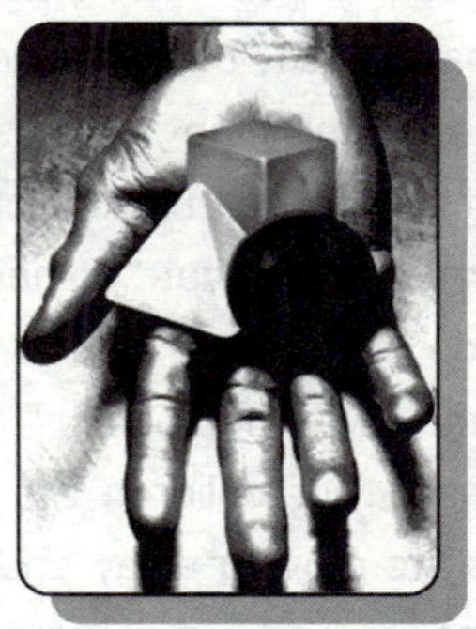

Learn to Live in the Present Moment*

To a large degree, the measure of our peace of mind is determined by how much we are able to live in the present moment. Irrespective of what happened yesterday or last year, and what may or may not happen tomorrow, the present moment is where you are — always!

Without question, many of us have mastered the neurotic art of spending much of our lives worrying about a variety of things — all at once. We allow past problems and future concerns to dominate our present moments, so much so that we end up anxious, frustrated, depressed, and hopeless. On

---

   * 作者理查德·卡里森（Richard Carison），生平不详。世界上有三种人：一种生活在过去，一种生活在将来，一种生活在现在。你是哪一种人呢？不过，不知你发现没有，我们当中的许多人都试图活在另一个时候，另一个地方，甚或另一个人的世界里。这样的人整日殚精竭虑，冥思苦想，却终无所获。那么，何不赶快回到此时此刻，切莫错失了生活！

the flip side, we also postpone our gratification, our stated priorities, and our happiness, often convincing ourselves that "someday" will be better than today. Unfortunately, the same mental dynamics that tell us to look toward the future will only repeat themselves so that "someday" never actually arrives. John Lennon once said, "Life is what's happening while we're busy making other plans." When we're busy making "other plans", our children are busy growing up, and people we love are moving away and dying, our bodies are getting out of shape, and our dreams are slipping away. In short, we miss out on life.

Many people live as if life were a dress rehearsal for some later date. It isn't. In fact, no one has a guarantee that he or she will be here tomorrow. Now is the only time we have, and the only time that we have any control over. When our attention is in the present moment, we push fear from our minds. Fear is the concern over events that might happen in the future — we won't have enough money, our children will get into trouble, we will get old and die, whatever.

To combat fear, the best strategy is to learn to bring your attention back to the present. Mark Twain said, "I have been through some terrible things in my life, some of which actually happened." I don't think I can say it any better. Practice keeping your attention on the here and now. Your efforts will pay great dividends. ✻

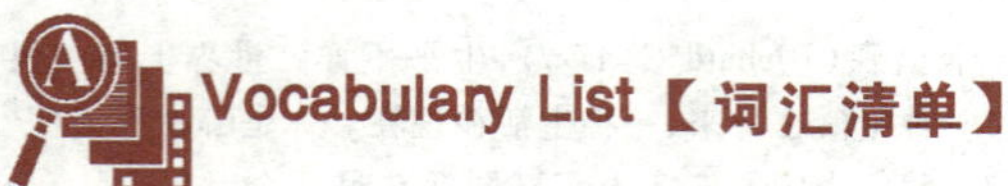

Vocabulary List【词汇清单】

irrespective /ˌiris'pektiv/ *adj.* （of）不管,不顾,不论
neurotic /njuə'rɔtik/ *adj.* 神经（机能）病的,神经官能症的

dominate /ˈdɔmineit/ *v.* 统治,支配,控制,主宰

gratification /ˌɡrætifiˈkeiʃən/ *n.* 满足,满意;喜悦之情,满足感

priority /praiˈɔriti/ *n.* 优先(考虑的事),在先

dynamic /daiˈnæmik/ *n.* (尤指政治的、社会的或心理上的)动力,驱动力

John Lennon /dʒɔn ˈlenən/ 约翰·列农(1940—1980,英国音乐家和作曲家,"披头士乐队"的成员之一)

rehearsal /riˈhəːsəl/ *n.* 彩排,排练,预演

guarantee /ˌɡærənˈtiː/ *n.* 保证,担保

combat /kəmˈbæt/ *v.* 搏斗,战斗,反抗,力图摆脱

dividend /ˈdividend/ *n.* 股利,红利;额外津贴;<引申>意外的收获、利益或好处

 ## 参考译文【Suggested Translation】

学会生活在此时此刻

在很大程度上,衡量我们内心是否平和决定于我们是否能够生活在此时此刻。无论昨天或者去年发生了什么,无论明天可能发生或者不发生什么,现实才始终是你的所在之处。

毋庸置疑,我们当中的许多人已经掌握了一种神经过敏的艺术,也就是把我们的生活虚度在为各种各样事情的烦恼焦虑之中——并且是同时为许多事情忧心忡忡。我们听任过去的问题和未来的忧虑支配我们的现实生活,以至于我们整日心烦意乱,灰心丧气,情绪低落,甚至于悲观绝望。而在另一方面,我们又推延我们的满足之情,推延我们应该首要考虑的事情,以及推延我们的幸福感,并且常常说服我们自己"有一天"将会比今天更好。不幸的是,如此告诉我们期待未来的精神冲动只会周而复始地重复,以至于"有一天"永远不会真正到来。约翰·列农曾经说过:"生活就是当我们忙于制定其他计划的时候所发生的事情。"当我们忙于制定"其他计划"的时候,我们的孩子正在迅

速长大，我们所爱的人离开了甚至于将要去世了，我们的体型开始走样了，而我们的梦想也在悄然逝去。简而言之，我们错失了生活。

许多人的生活似乎是未来某一天的彩排。绝非如此。实际上，没有人能够保证他或者她明天还会活着。现在是我们惟一所拥有的时间，并且也是我们惟一能够掌握的时间。当我们把注意力放在此时此刻，我们就会将恐惧置之脑后。恐惧就是我们为将来可能发生的事情而过于担忧——我们不会有足够多的金钱，我们的孩子会招惹麻烦，我们会变老，会死去。

要想战胜恐惧，最好的策略是学会将你的注意力带回到此时此刻。马克·吐温说过："在生活中，我经历过一些骇人的事情，其中有些的确发生过。"我想我讲不出比这更精辟到位的话。不断地将你的注意力集中于此情此景、此时此刻，你的付出终究会有充裕的回报。◆

(《英语沙龙》忆玫 译)

●To err is human. （人非圣贤，孰能无过。）

●Still water run deep. （静水流深。）

●It is easy to be wise after the event. （事后诸葛亮好当。）

●Fact speak louder than words. （事实胜于雄辩。）

The Telephone[*]

When A. G. Bell first invented the telephone, it was a communication tool. Little did he know that he had created an object of emotional significance.

You know those cute toy telephones with colorful push buttons that make happy noises. Those plastic imitations are supposed to let little Junior copy parental behavior, but little Junior wants the real thing. He wants to hold, bang, push, chew on and talk into the real telephone. You cannot simply buy him off with a little baby toy.

Then little Junior grows up. He is busy, successful and important. Or at least he hopes to appear so. What better

---

　　* 作者佚名。电话从无到有，从有到普及，从有线到无线，福兮？祸兮？佩戴金银珠宝可以显示身份和地位，那么拥有电话也可以如此吗？很多时候，电话给我们生活带来的影响已经远远超出了其作为交流工具本身。我们是现代科技的无可争议的受益者，可是如果这些文明成果没有被善加利用，我们很有可能会成为其受害者呢！

way to feel like a top man than to close a business deal over his cell phone while grabbing his morning cup of Espresso at Starbucks.

There is also that fashionable lady at the cafe. Throughout lunch, her little cell phone in its designer jacket has beeped at least three times, signaling her popularity. Each time, she seemed to enjoy an intimate conversation spiced with little private jokes while you waited in vain for that cellular beep to announce to the world your importance.

Admittedly, not everyone declares social status or personal popularity through the telephone. For many, telephones are practical tools for accessing family, friends and business associates. There are also a few like me who dread the phone. In my youth, I had believed that the more calls I received, the more important and popular I was. Now older, busier and hopefully wiser, there is nothing I detest more than telephone calls. I had beautiful dreams shattered by the shrill summons of the phone, hard-earned coffee breaks dissolved by friendly but unwanted interruptions and even urgent bathroom runs painfully delayed. Having been haunted and hounded by the telephone for many years, I can now ignore its insistent jangle. In fact, I can even with a clear conscience flick the receiver off its hook and slip into blissful dreamland. ✳

Vocabulary List 【词汇清单】

A. G . Bell /ei dʒiː bel/（全名 Alexander Graham Bell）亚历山大·格雷姆·贝尔（1847—1922，苏格兰裔美籍电话发明者，1876 年他用其装置第一次进行了电传导讲话声音的表演）

emotional /iˈməuʃənl/ *adj.* 感情（上）的，情绪（上）的

cute /kjuːt/ *adj.*　<美国口语>伶俐的,乖巧的;娇小可爱的,漂亮的,迷人的

imitation /ˌimiˈteiʃən/ *n.*　仿制品,模仿品,复制品

parental /pəˈrentl/ *adj.*　父母的,属于或有关父母的

bang /bæŋ/ *v.*　敲击,猛敲

buy off：收买,(用钱物)打发

Espresso /eˈspresəu/ *n.*　<意大利>蒸泡咖啡,浓缩咖啡(一种用蒸气加压煮出的咖啡)

Starbucks /ˈstaːbʌks/ *n.*　星巴克(1987 年诞生于美国西雅图,现已发展成全球最大的一流精制咖啡零售商、咖啡加工厂及连锁咖啡店品牌)

beep /biːp/ *v.*　嘟嘟响,发出嘟嘟声

intimate /ˈintimət/ *adj.*　亲密的,亲昵的,亲近的

spice /spais/ *v.*　加香料于;使增添趣味

cellular /ˈseljulə/ *adj.*　蜂窝电话的,手机的

admittedly /ədˈmitidli/ *adv.*　公认地,确定无疑地

access /ˈækses/ *v.*　接通,联络

associate /əˈsəuʃiit/ *n.*　朋友,伙伴,合作者

dread /dred/ *v.*　害怕,恐惧,畏惧

detest /diˈtest/ *v.*　讨厌,厌恶,憎恶

shatter /ˈʃætə/ *v.*　毁坏,粉碎,

shrill /ʃril/ *adj.*　尖声的,伴有尖声的

dissolve /diˈzɔlv/ *v.*　使瓦解,使消失,使消散,使化为泡影

interruption /ˌintəˈrʌpʃən/ *n.*　打断,中断,打扰

haunt /hɔːnt/ *v.*　常找…作伴,追逐;(思想、回忆等)萦绕,(疾病等)缠住

hound /haund/ *v.*　追赶,追逐,追逼

jangle /ˈdʒæŋgl/ *n.*　刺耳的声音,不和谐的铃声

conscience /ˈkɔnʃəns/ *n.*　良心,道德心;意识,内在思想(或感情)

flick /flik/ *v.*　弹掉,轻轻拂去(off)

blissful /ˈblisful/ *adj.*　幸福的,极其快乐的

参考译文【Suggested Translation】

电　话

贝尔发明电话的时候，是为了当作交流工具，却未料到他创造的是一个具有相当情感意义的东西。

你知道那些可爱的玩具电话，其颜色鲜艳的按钮可发出快乐的声音。那些塑料的模仿品是要让小孩模仿父母的动作，但是小家伙要的是真东西。他要真正的电话来握、敲、推、咬和讲，你实在无法用一个小小的婴儿玩具来打发他。

而后，小孩长大了。他成为忙碌、成功和重要的人物，至少他希望看上去如此。为了显示自己的出类拔萃，除了一边在手机里完成交易，一边在星巴克赶着喝早晨那杯意式浓缩咖啡之外，还有更好的方式吗？

此外，坐在咖啡厅里那位走在时代前端的女孩，午餐时，她放在名牌外套里的手机至少已经响了三回，显示她的受欢迎度。每一次，她似乎总带着掺和情趣的笑话小声地亲密交谈，而你却徒然地等待着手机信号来向世界宣扬你的成就。

但无可否认，并不是每个人都通过电话来显耀身份地位或者名望。对于很多人来讲，电话只是用来联系亲朋好友以及商业伙伴的实用工具。也有一些人跟我一样对电话抱有恐惧感。在我年轻的时候，我是认为接到的电话越多，就表示我越重要和越受欢迎。而现在变得更成熟些、忙碌些和有智慧些，我最为讨厌的就是听到电话铃响了。我的美梦曾经被电话尖锐刺耳的召唤声破坏殆尽；辛辛苦苦获得的休息时间因为友好但不受欢迎的打岔而化为泡影；甚至要急着上厕所而强忍着痛楚而被扣留。多年以来被电话所缠绕和穷追不舍，现在我已经可以不理会它无休的刺耳响声。事实上，我甚至可以坦然的把话筒拿开，溜进幸福美妙的梦乡。◆

Privacy as Border *

There are quite a few questions that are supposed never to be asked about. It is impolite or rude even to mention them in a conversation. These topics include one's age, income, marriage, religious belief and political position as well as any other fields of privacy. In order to understand the American or western idea of a personal concept of privacy, one may think of the concept of "territory". As well known, a nation has borders or boundaries with other countries and everything within

---

* 作者佚名。隐私权(The Right to Privacy)的理论产生于美国。一般认为,构成隐私权有两个要件:一是"私",二是"隐"。前者指纯粹是个人的,与公共利益、群体利益无关的事情,这是隐私权的本质所在;后者则是指某个事物、某个信息不为人知的事实状态。因此,隐私权是自然人享有的对其个人的,与公共利益无关的个人信息、私人生活和私有领域进行支配的权利。作为一项人身权,只要权利人没有言明放弃自己的禁止权,任何人均无权泄露和公开与此相关的信息和内容。那么,从社会这个更广泛的意义上讲,隐私又包括哪些内容呢?

the border belongs to the nation alone and no one else.

One's home — one's castle

Is one able to enter another country without a passport — a permit from another? Absolutely not. It is the same for one's home.

If one enters someone else's home without asking for permission, he is likely to be charged with trespassing or even burglary. Inside the house everything is within the territory of the owner, no one else. A bedroom is his or her castle. No one may visit it without permission.

Inside the room — confidential

No one has the right to open a closet, desk or drawer in the room — these are something secret in the host or hostess' castle. On top of the desk there may be letters, business papers or exercise books, these too are within the owner's territory. Never touch them or read them! Similarly never read over one's shoulder when he or she is reading something! You don't want to behave like a spy, do you? Anything one is reading is his or her private property. Don't invade it!

Income — a top secret

In the United States, one's income is the top secret. Never even try to ask any questions about it! Avoid asking for dishonor. In the same way, it is impolite to inquire about one's property or the cost of some articles. You may say how cool something is, but never ask about the price.

Age — taboo for everyone

Age is considered a taboo, especially for the ladies. They hate any topics about age, simply because they hate to get old, because they want to stay young forever! They are very sensitive to questions like: "When were you born?" or "Do you have artificial teeth?" Never make any comment like

"You have grey hair", otherwise the males and females alike will beat you black and blue.

Religion — sensitive

Religion is what one believes in personally. It is totally a personal matter. Never ask, "Why do you worship as a Christian", it is none of your business. Everyone has the freedom to believe as they choose in belief.

Politics — big men's affairs

Politics is a sensitive topic too. It's completely of personal opinion. There is no argument about taste, anyway. Besides, such questions as "Do you believe Israel will accept the conditions for peace talks?" should be on the agenda of those "big men", not for a "nobody" like you and me. ✲

# Vocabulary List 【词汇清单】

territory /ˈteritəri/ *n.* 领土，领地；<美>（按某种目的划定的）区域

boundary /ˈbaundəri/ *n.* 边界，分界线

trespass /ˈtrespəs/ *v.* 非法侵入，未经许可进入私人土地；<法律>（非法）侵害，侵入私宅

burglary /ˈbəːgləri/ *n.* 入室行窃，夜盗行为

confidential /ˌkɔnfiˈdenʃəl/ *adj.* 机密的，秘密的

invade /inˈveid/ *v.* 侵略，侵入，侵犯

dishonor /disˈɔnə/ *n.* 不名誉，不光彩；羞耻，丢脸（的事、行为）

taboo /təˈbuː/ *n.* <宗教>（社会习俗或传统方面的）禁忌，禁讳

Israel /ˈizreiəl/ *n.* 以色列（西南亚的一个国家，位于地中海东岸，1948 年 5 月 14 日在联合国推荐下建国，耶路撒冷是其首都。此后，以色列与其阿拉伯邻国的不和睦导致了许多战争。在国际社会的斡旋下，巴以双方开始寻找政治解决的途径。国际社会先后提出了一系列和平方案，但均遭沙龙政府

拒绝。2003 年,联合国、美国、欧盟和俄罗斯中东问题四方正式公布并启动了实现巴以和平的中东"路线图"计划。但因以色列坚持其强硬政策,巴以冲突再起,"路线图"计划被搁浅至今。)

参考译文【Suggested Translation】

隐 私 如 国 境

有一些话题在谈话中永远不要涉及,提一提都是无礼、甚或粗鲁的行为。这些话题包括一个人的年龄、收入、婚姻状况、宗教信仰、政治立场以及其他个人领域的事物。为了理解美国以及其他西方国家有关个人隐私的观念,我们不妨从"领土"这个概念说起。众所周知,一国总以边境或边界与他国为界,而之内的一切事物仅属于该国所有,别国不得侵犯。

住宅——个人城堡

假如没有护照(进入一国的许可证),任何人能够进入他国吗?绝不可能。同理,进入他人住宅也必须得到许可。

如果未经允许就闯进别人家里,轻则告你"擅闯民宅",重则告你"入室行窃"。同样,家里的一切都是主人领土上的财产,他人不得擅动。而卧室简直就是他或她的"城堡"——未经允许不得参观。

室内——保密

任何人都无权乱翻他人室内的衣柜、书桌或者抽屉——这些是主人城堡里的秘密!书桌上也许有信件、商务文函或练习本——这些也是他人境内的财产。千万别碰它们,也别拿来读。同样,当别人在阅读什么的时候,千万不要站在别人后面"偷"看!你不想成为一个间谍,是吧?别人正在阅读的一切都是他的私人财产,千万不要侵犯!

收入——最高机密

在美国,个人收入是最高机密。你甚至不要试图去打听有关的问题,不要自讨没趣!同样,询问他人的财产或某件物品的价格也是不礼貌的。你可以说某样东西多么多么酷，但就是别问价格！

年龄——个人禁忌

年龄是一个非常忌讳的问题，对于女士尤其如此。她们讨厌任何与年龄有关的话题，只因为她们害怕衰老，总想永葆青春！她们对和年龄有关的问题十分敏感，诸如"您什么时候出生的?"或者"您戴假牙吗?"。千万不要说"您的头发都白了"一类的话，否则人家会把你揍得鼻青脸肿！

宗教——敏感的话题

宗教纯粹属于个人信仰，其完全是个人的事情。千万别问"您为什么信仰基督教"之类的话，这不关你的事。再者说，人人都有信仰自由。

政治——大人物的事

政治也是一个敏感的话题。它完全属于个人看法，无论如何也没什么好争论的。更何况，诸如"您认为以色列会接受和谈条件吗?"之类的问题是"大人物"们关心的事，不是你我这样的"无名小卒"该管的。◆

● It never rains but it pours. （不鸣则已，一鸣惊人。）

● All work and no play makes Jack a dull boy. （只会用功不玩耍，聪明孩子也变傻。）

● The early bird catches the worm. （捷足先登。）

● Do as you would be done by. （己所不欲，勿施于人。）

Of Studies*

Studies serve for delight, for ornament, and for ability. Their chief use for delight, is in privateness and retiring; for ornament, is in discourse; and for ability, is in the judgment and disposition of business. For expert men can execute, and perhaps judge of particulars, one by one; but the general counsels, and the plots and marshalling of affairs, come best from those that are learned. To spend too much time in studies is sloth; to use them too much for ornament, is

---

* 作者弗兰西斯·培根（Francis Bacon，1561—1626），英国著名的唯物主义哲学家和科学家，第一个提出"知识就是力量"，在文艺复兴时期的巨人中被尊称为哲学史和科学史上划时代的人物。马克思称培根是"英国唯物主义和整个现代实验科学的真正始祖"，罗素则尊称他为"给科学研究程序进行逻辑组织化的先驱"。培根的处女作《论说随笔文集》表现了自己对于人生、对于社会的种种现象、种种问题的独到的见解与鞭辟入里的议论，其中名言警句俯仰皆是，深受广大读者的欢迎。本文是该文集最著名的篇章之一。

affectation; to make jugment wholly by their rules, is the humour of a scholar. They perfect nature, and are perfected by experience: for natural abilities are like natural plants, that need pruning by study; and studies themselves do give forth directions too much at large, except they be bounded in by experience. Crafty men contemn studies, simple men admire them, and wise men use them; for they teach not their own use; but that is a wisdom without them, and above them, won by observation. Read not to contradict and confute; nor to believe and take for granted; nor to find talk and discourse; but to weigh and consider. Some books are to be tasted, others to be swallowed, and some few to be chewed and digested; that is, some books are to be read only in parts; others to be read, but not curiously; and some few to be read wholly, and with diligence and attention. Some books also may be read by deputy, and extracts made of them by others; but that would be only in the less important arguments, and the meaner sort of books, else distilled books are, like common distilled waters, flashy things.

Reading maketh a full man; conference a ready man; and writing an exact man. And therefore, if a man write little, he had need have a great memory; if he confer little, he had need have a present wit; and if he read little, he had need have much cunning, to seem to know that he doth not. Histories make men wise; poets witty; the mathematics subtitle; natural philosophy deep; moral grave; logic and rhetoric able to contend. Abeunt studia in mores. Nay there is no stand or impediment in the wit, but may be wrought out by fit studies: like as diseases of the body may have appropriate exercises. Bowling is good for the stone and reins: shooting for the lungs and breast; gentle walking for the stomach; riding for the head; and the like. So if a man's wit be wandering, let him study the mathematics; for in demonstrations, if his wit be called away never so little, he must begin again. If his wit be not apt to distinguish or find differences, let him study the Schoolmen; for they are cymini sectores. If he be not apt to beat over matters, and to call up one thing to prove and illustrate another, let him study the lawyers' cases. So every defect of the mind may have a special receipt. ✳

Vocabulary List 【词汇清单】

ornament /ˈɔːnəmənt/ *n.* 装饰, 修饰

discourse /ˈdiskɔːs/ *n.* 交谈, 谈话; 演讲, 演说

disposition /ˌdispəˈziʃən/ *n.* 部署, 安排; (事务的)处理, 处置

marshal /ˈmaːʃəl/ *v.* 排列, 安排, 整理

sloth /sləuθ/ *n.* 怠惰, 懒散

prune /pruːn/ *v.* 修剪(树枝等), 删节

crafty /ˈkraːfti/ *adj.* 狡猾的, 狡诈的, 诡计多端的

contemn /kənˈtem/ *v.* 轻视, 轻蔑, 藐视, 蔑视

confute /kənˈfjuːt/ *v.* 驳斥, 驳倒(某人、论据等), 辩驳

swallow /ˈswɔləu/ *v.* 吞下, 咽下

distilled /disˈtild/ *adj.* 蒸馏; <引申>(精华)被提取出来

confer /kənˈfəː/ *v.* 讨论, 磋商, 商讨, 交换意见

doth /dʌθ/ (= does) <古> do 的第三人称单数现在时的陈述
语气(主要用于助动词用法)

subtle /ˈsʌtl/ *adj.* 敏锐的, 明察的, 精细的

rhetoric /ˈretərik/ *n.* 修辞学, 修辞技巧

Abeunt studia in mores: <拉丁文>凡有所学, 皆成性格。

nay /nei/ *adv.* <书>不仅如此, 而且, 甚至

impediment /imˈpedimənt/ *n.* <罕用>妨碍, 阻碍, 障碍

wrought /rɔːt/ *v.* <古>work 的一种过去式和过去分词

reins /reinz/ *n.* <古>肾脏; 腰部

be apt to: 易于…, 倾向于…

cymini sectores: <拉丁文>过分讲究细节的人

receipt /riˈsiːt/ *n.* （recipe 的旧体）处方，药方

 参考译文【Suggested Translation】

谈 读 书

读书足以怡情，足以博彩，足以长才。其怡情也，最见于独处幽居之时；其博彩也，最见于高谈阔论之中；其长才也，最见于处世判事之际。练达之士虽能分别处理细事或一一判别枝节，然纵观统筹、全局策划，则舍好学深思者莫属。读书费时过多易惰，文采藻饰太盛则矫，全凭条文断事乃学究故态。读书补天然之不足，经验又补读书之不足，盖天生才干犹如自然花草，读书然后知如何修剪移接；而书中所示，如不以经验范之，则又大而无当。有一技之长者鄙读书，无知者羡读书，唯明智之士用读书，然书并不以用处告人，用书之智不在书中，而在书外，全凭观察得之。读书时不可存心诘难作者，不可尽信书上所言，亦不可只为寻章摘句，而应推敲细思。书有可浅尝者，有可吞食者，少数则须咀嚼消化。换言之，有只须读其部分者，有只须大体涉猎者，少数则须全读，读时须全神贯注，孜孜不倦。书亦可请人代读，取其所作摘要，但只限题材较次或价值不高者，否则书经提炼犹如水经蒸馏、淡而无味矣。

读书使人充实，讨论使人机智，笔记使人准确。因此不常作笔记者须记忆特强，不常讨论者须天生聪颖，不常读书者须欺世有术，始能无知而显有知。读史使人明智，读诗使人灵秀，数学使人周密，科学使人深刻，伦理学使人庄重，逻辑修辞之学使人善辩：凡有所学，皆成性格。人之才智但有滞碍，无不可读适当之书使之顺畅，一如身体百病，皆可借相宜之运动除之。滚球利睾肾，射箭利胸肺，慢步利肠胃，骑术利头脑，诸如此类。如智力不集中，可令读数学，盖演题须全神贯注，稍有分散即须重演；如不能辨异，可令读经院哲学，盖是辈皆吹毛求疵之人；如不善求同，不善以一物阐证另一物，可令读律师之案卷。如此头脑中凡有缺陷，皆有特药可医。◆

（王佐良 译）

The Urgency*

June 24

If a man is ever going to abmit that he belongs to the earth, not the other way round, it probably will be in late June. Then it is that life surpasses man's affairs with incredible urgency and outreaches him in every direction. Even the farmer, on whom we all depend for the substance of existence, knows then that the best he can do is cooperate with wind and weather, soil and seed. The incalculable energy of chlorophyll, the green leaf itself, dominates the earth, and the root in the soil is the inescapable fact. Even the roadside weed ignores man's legislation.

---

　　* 作者赫尔·波兰德（Hal Borland, 1900—1978），美国著名作家和诗人。本文体裁属于日记体散文，描绘的是初夏时节自然界的动植物繁衍生息之时一片欣欣向荣的景象。"本文尤其着重写只有短暂生命的小生物抓紧时机完成其生命历程的紧迫性，使人不禁对生命珍惜、时光宝贵产生震撼感。"（陈文伯语）

The urgency is everywhere. Grass blankets the earth, reaching for the sun, spreads its roots, flowers and comes to seed. The forest widens its canopy, strengthens its boles, nurtures its seedlings, ripens its perpetuating nuts. The birds nest and hatch their fledglings. The beetle and the bee are busy at the grassroot and the blossom, and the butterfly lays eggs that will hatch and crawl and eat and pupate and take to the air once more. Fish spawn and meadow voles harvest the wild meadows, and owls and foxes feed their young. Dragonflies and swallows and nighthawks seine the air where the minute winged creatures flit out their minute life spans.

And man, who glibly calls the earth his own, neither powers the leaf nor energizes the fragile wing. Man participates, but his dominance is limited. It is the urgency of life, or growth, that rules. Late June and early Summer are the ultimate, unarguable proof. ✽

Vocabulary List 【词汇清单】

surpass /səˈpaːs/ *v.* （数量、程度等）超越,超过,胜过

outreach /autˈriːtʃ/ *v.* 超出…范围,胜过,占…上风

incalculable /inˈkælkjuləbl/ *adj.* 数不清的,数不胜数的,无数的,极大的

chlorophyll /ˈklɔrəfil/ *n.* ＜生化＞叶绿素（在植物体内能够吸收太阳光以促进其生长的一种绿色物质）

dominate /ˈdɔmineit/ *v.* 统治,支配,主宰

inescapable /ˌiniˈeskeipəbl/ *adj.* 不可避免的,无法规避的,逃避不了的,必然（发生）的

canopy /ˈkænəpi/ *n.* （床或宝座上的）顶盖,天篷,华盖

bole /bəul/ *n.* 树干,主干

nurture /ˈnəːtʃə/ *v.* 养育,给与营养物,滋养

perpetuate /pəˈpetʃueit/ *v.* 使永久存在,使不朽

fledgling /'fledʒliŋ/ *n.* 刚生羽毛（或刚会飞）的小鸟，雏鸟，幼鸟

crawl /krɔːl/ *n.* （虫、蚁等）爬行，蠕动，缓慢的行进

pupate /'pjuːpeit/ *v.* ＜昆＞化蛹，变成蛹

spawn /spɔːn/ *v.* （鱼等）产卵

vole /vəul/ *n.* ＜动物＞田鼠，仓鼠

owl /aul/ *n.* ＜动物＞猫头鹰，枭

nighthawk /'naithɔːk/ *n.* ＜动物＞夜鹰

seine /sein/ *v.* 用围网（拉网）捕鱼或打捞

flit /flit/ *v.* （鸟、蝙蝠等）轻快地飞过，掠过

life span ：某种生物可预期的最长寿命；平均生命期

glibly /'glibli/ *adv.* 圆滑地，随便地；油嘴滑舌地，油腔滑调地

 ## 参考译文【Suggested Translation】

紧 迫 性

6 月 24 日

如果一个人愿意承认他是属于地球的而不是地球属于他，那很可能就是在 6 月份的晚些时候。这个时候，自然生机那种只争朝夕的精神比起人类事务来真是紧迫得令人难人置信，在各方面都胜人类一筹。就连农民（我们依靠他们生产的东西维持生存）也知道这时候最好是能顺应风雨天候，照料土壤种子。主宰着大地的是叶绿素无法估算的能源以及绿叶本身，土壤中有根的存在，这是自不待言的。即使是路边的野草也都冲破人为的制约蔓生开来。

那种只争朝夕的紧迫感无处不在。草如绿毯，铺满大地，一直伸向太阳；它四处伸延根须，开花结籽。森林拓展其华盖，强固其主干，给其秧苗输送养分，并使长了许久的坚果渐趋成熟。鸟雀筑巢并孵化雏鸟。甲虫在草根旁奔忙，蜜蜂在花丛中飞逐。蝴蝶则在产卵，将来孵出的小虫从爬行、吃食、化蛹到振翅飞舞再经历一次循环。鱼儿也在产卵，田鼠则在野生的牧场上采获食物。猫头鹰和狐狸给它们的幼仔喂食。蜻蜓、燕子和夜鹰在天空中像围网似地捕食，而极小的有翼动物在空中轻快地飞来

飞去，顷刻间其短暂的生命便结束了。

　　然而，人类扬言地球属于他们，可是既不能给叶片以能量又不能给脆弱的翅膀以力量。人类只是参与其中，而其主导地位是有限的。驾御一切的是生命或生长只争朝夕的紧迫性。6 月份晚些时候的初夏时节从根本上无可争辩地证明了这一点。◆

●All that ends well is well. （结果好则一切皆好。）

●Every advantage has its disadvantage. （凡事有利必有弊。）

●We shall never have friends if we expect to find them without fault. （欲求完美无缺的朋友必然成为孤家寡人。）

●Life is not all roses. （人生并不是康庄大道。）

The Happy Door[*]

Happiness is like a pebble dropped into a pool to set in motion an ever-widening circle of ripples. As Stevenson has said, being happy is a duty.

There is no exact definition of the word happiness. Happy people are happy for all sorts of reasons. The key is not wealth or physical well-being, since we find beggars, invalids and so-called failures who are extremely happy.

Being happy is a sort of unexpected dividend. But sta-

---

　　* 作者米尔德里德·克拉姆(Mildred Cram)，生平不详。快乐，是人真实的、相对的感觉。它反映人在物质上或精神上的一种满足，一种愉悦的心情。它既有人的本性一面，也有人的情操成分。现实生活中，快乐的确是很难有统一标准的。有的人认为很平常的事，对于其他人来说则是快乐的；有的人认为很快乐的事，对于另一些人来说则是痛苦的；有的人其实已经很快乐，可他还认为不快乐而四处寻求快乐；有的人非常痛苦没有快乐但他却从痛苦中去感悟快乐。"宠辱莫惊，闲看庭前花开花落；去留无意，漫随天外云卷云舒。"笑对生活，知足常乐；享受快乐，顺其自然。你打开你的快乐之门了么？

ying happy is an accomplishment, a triumph of soul and character. It is not selfish to strive for it. It is, indeed, a duty to ourselves and others.

Being unhappy is like an infectious disease; it causes people to shrink away from the sufferer. He soon finds himself alone, miserable and embittered. There is, however, a cure so simple as to seem, at first glance, ridiculous: If you don't feel happy, pretend to be!

It works. Before long you will find that instead of repelling people, you attract them. You discover how deeply rewarding it is to be the center of wider and wider circles of good will.

Then the make-believe becomes a reality. You possess the secret of peace of mind, and can forget yourself in being of service to others.

Being happy, once it is realized as a duty and established as a habit, opens doors into unimaginable gardens thronged with grateful friends. ✳

 ## Vocabulary List 【词汇清单】

pebble /'pebl/ *n.* 小圆石，小鹅卵石

ripple /'ripl/ *n.* （水、草等）呈波状起伏，波纹

Stevenson /'stiːvnsn/ （全名 Robert Louis Balfour Stevenson）罗伯特·路易斯·鲍尔福·斯蒂文生（1850—1894，苏格兰小说家、诗人和随笔作家）

well-being /'wel'biːiŋ/ *n.* 幸福，福利，健康欢乐

invalid /in'vælid/ *n.* 病弱者，久病衰弱者

strive /straiv/ *v.* 努力，奋斗，力争（for）

embitter /im'bitə/ *v.* （使）难受，（使）怨恨，（使）愁眉不展

ridiculous /ri'dikjuləs/ *adj.* 可笑的，荒谬的

repel /ri'pel/ *v.* 使厌恶，使反感，使不愉快

unimaginable /ˌʌni'mædʒinəbl/ *adj.* 无法想像的，想像不到

的,不可思议的
throng /θrɔŋ/ *v.* 拥挤,挤满,群集(with)
grateful /ˈgreitful/ *adj.* 感谢的,感激的,致谢意的

 **参考译文【Suggested Translation 】**

快 乐 之 门

快乐好似掷入池塘里的一枚鹅卵石,会激起不断扩散的一圈圈涟漪。正如斯蒂文生所说:"快乐是一种责任。"

快乐这个字眼并没有确切的定义。快乐的人可以因种种理由而快乐。其关键并非在于财富或健康,因为我们可以发现有些乞丐、病弱的人和所谓的失败者却极其快乐。

快乐是一种意料不到的收益。而能保持快乐则是一项成就,也是灵魂与品性的胜利。努力追求快乐算不上是自私。事实上,追求快乐不仅是对我们自己,也是对别人的一种责任。

闷闷不乐就像是一种传染病;染上这种疾病的人大家都避之如蛇蝎。这种人很快就会发现自己感到孤单、痛苦和难过。然而,有一种很简单的治疗方法,乍看起来似乎荒谬可笑,那就是:如果你觉得不快乐,就假装快乐吧!

这个方法很有效的。不久你就会发现自己非但不会使人反感,反而还能吸引别人。你会发现,能够成为广结善缘的中心人物是多么值得的事。

于是,原本装扮的快乐就变成了真正的快乐。你会拥有心境平和的秘诀而又能忘情于服务他人。

一旦快乐被认作一种责任履行并成为一种习惯的时候,它就会开启大门,引领我们进入无法想像的花园中,里边云集着满怀感激的朋友。◆

Farewell to the Highlands,
farewell to the North,
The birthplace of valour,
the country of worth;
Wherever I wander, wherever I rove,
The hills of the Highlands for ever I love!

Farewell to the mountains
high cover'd with snow!
Farewell to the straths
and green valleys below!
Farewell to the forests
and wild hanging woods!
Farewell to the torrents
and loud-pouring floods!

My heart's in the Highlands,
my heart is not here;
My heart's in the Highlands
a-chasing the deer,
A-chasing the wild deer,
and following the roe,
My heart's in the Highlands wherever I go. ✳

Vocabulary List【词汇清单】

highland /'hailənd/ *n.* 高地,高原
roe /rəu/ *n.* 野狍(鹿的一种)
farewell /'fɛə'wel/ *interj.* 再见！再会！　*n.* 告别,辞别
valour /'vælə/ *n.* (美语亦可拼作 valor)勇气,英勇
strath /'stræθ/ *n.* 老谷底,宽平河谷

valley /'væli/ *n.* 山谷，溪谷；流域
torrent /'tɔrənt/ *n.* 急流，洪流，湍流

 参考译文【Suggested Translation】

我的心呀在高原

我的心呀在高原，
这儿没有我的心；
我的心呀在高原，
追逐着那鹿儿，
追逐着那野鹿，跟踪着那野狍——
我的心呀在高原，无论我人在哪儿！

再会吧，我的高原，
再会吧，我的北国，
你是勇士的沃土，
美德的故乡；
无论我到哪儿流浪；无论我
漂泊到何方，
高原的群山我永不相忘！

再会吧，白雪皑皑的山峰！
再会吧，青翠的山谷与河滩！
再会吧，枝条横斜的森林！
再会吧，汹涌咆哮的洪水与河流！

我的心呀在高原，这儿没有我的心；
我的心呀在高原，
追逐着那鹿儿，
追逐着那野鹿，跟踪着那野狍——
我的心呀在高原，无论我人在哪儿！ ◈

The Road to Success *

It is well that young men should begin at the beginning and occupy the most subordinate positions. Many of the leading businessmen of Pittsburgh had a serious responsibility thrust upon them at the very threshold of their career. They were introduced to the broom, and spent the first hours of their business lives sweeping out the office. I notice we have janitors and janitresses now in offices, and our young

---

　　* 作者安德鲁·卡内基（Andrew Carnegie，1835—1919），美国著名的钢铁大王，"美国梦"的典型，是美国人耳熟能详的成功典范。他生于苏格兰，幼时家贫，所受教育不多，后自学成才，并靠个人奋斗兴办铁路，开采石油，建造钢铁厂，终于成为亿万富翁。卡内基发迹后，俨然成为美国人心目中的英雄和个人奋斗的楷模。他频频应邀发表谈话，宣传企业成功之道。作为一位不曾挪用公司一分钱的慈善家，他致力于用金钱的力量变革社会。晚年热心于图书馆事业和其他慈善事业，曾捐巨款在贫困地区兴建近千所公共图书馆。本文节选自 1885 年他对柯里商业学院毕业生的讲话，这次讲话是他最杰出的代表作之一。

men unfortunately miss that salutary branch of a business education. But if by chance the professional sweeper is absent any morning the boy who has the genius of the future partner in him will not hesitate to try his hand at the broom. The other day a fond fashionable mother in Michigan asked a young man whether he had ever seen a young lady sweep in a room so grandly as her Priscilla. He said no, he never had, and the mother was gratified beyond measure, but then said he, after a pause, "What I should like to see her do is sweep out a room." It does not hurt the newest comer to sweep out the office if necessary. I was one of those sweepers myself.

Assuming that you have all obtained employment and are fairly started, my advice to you is "aim high." I would not give a fig for the young man who does not already see himself the partner or the head of an important firm. Do not rest content for a moment in your thoughts as head clerk, or foreman, or general manager in any concern, no matter how extensive. Say to yourself, "My place is at the top." Be king in your dreams.

And here is the prime condition of success, the great secret: concentrate your energy, thought, and capital exclusively upon the business in which you are engaged. Having begun in one line, resolve to fight it out on that line, to lead in it, adopt every improvement, have the best machinery, and know the most about it.

The concerns which fail are those which have scattered their capital, which means that they have scattered their brains also. They have investments in this, or that, or the other, here, there, and everywhere. "Don't put all your eggs in one basket." is all wrong. I tell you "put all your eggs in one basket, and then watch that basket." Look round you and take notice, men who do that not often fail. It is easy to watch and carry the one basket. It is trying to carry too many baskets that breaks most eggs in this country. He who carries three baskets must put one on his head, which is apt to tumble and trip him up. One fault of the American businessman is lack of concentration.

To summarize what I have said: Aim for the highest, never enter a bar room; do not touch liquor, or if at all only at meals; never speculate; never indorse beyond your surplus cash fund; make the firm's interest yours; break orders always to save owners; concentrate; put all your eggs in one basket, and watch that basket; expenditure always within revenue; lastly be not impatient, for as Emerson says, "no one can cheat you out of ultimate success but yourselves." ✳

 **Vocabulary List【词汇清单】**

subordinate /səˈbɔːdineit/ *adj.* 次要的，下级的

Pittsburgh /ˈpitsbəːg/ 匹兹堡（美国东北部重工业城市）

threshold /ˈθreʃhəuld/ *n.* 入门，开始，开端

broom /bruːm/ *n.* 扫帚

janitor /ˈdʒænitə/ *n.* 看门人；房屋管理员（负责做日常修理工作等）

janitress /ˈdʒænitris/ *n.* 女看门人；女房屋管理员

salutary /ˈsæljutəri/ *adj.* 有益健康的，有益的

absent /ˈæbsənt/ *adj.* 缺席的，不在的，不在场的

hesitate /ˈheziteit/ *v.* 犹豫，迟疑（to）

fashionable /ˈfæʃnəbl/ *adj.* （赶）时髦的，（追求）流行的

Michigan /ˈmiʃigən/ 密歇根州（一译"密执安"）（美国州名）

gratify /ˈgrætiˌfai/ *v.* 使愉快，使高兴，使满意

clerk /ˈklə:k/ *n.* 职员，雇员

foreman /ˈfɔ:mən/ *n.* 工头，领班

extensive /iks'tensiv/ *adj.* 广泛的，广阔的，广大的

prime /praim/ *adj.* 首要的，主要的；基础的，基本的

exclusively /iks'klu:sivli/ *adv.* 独有地，独占地；专用地，专有地

resolve /ri'zɔlv/ *v.* 下决心，决定（to）

adopt /ə'dɔpt/ *v.* 采用，采纳，采取（某种态度、习惯做法等）

machinery /mə'ʃi:nəri/ *n.* <总称>机器，机器设备

scatter /ˈskætə/ *v.* 使分散，使散开

be apt to：往往，易于，动辄

tumble /ˈtʌmbl/ *v.* 跌倒，摔交，摔倒

trip sb. up：绊了一下，绊跌

concentration /ˌkɔnsən'treiʃən/ *n.* （密切）注意，专心，专注

summarize /ˈsʌməraiz/ *v.* 总结，概述

speculate /ˈspekjuleit/ *v.* 投机，做投机买卖

indorse /in'dɔ:s/ *v.* <商>（＝endorse）背书，在（文件）背面签名

surplus /ˈsə:pləs/ *adj.* 多余的，剩余的，过剩的

expenditure /iks'penditʃə/ *n.* （金钱、时间等的）花费，消耗，支出

revenue /ˈrevinju:/ *n.* 收入，收益

ultimate /ˈʌltimit/ *adj.* 最后的，最终的，终极的

 参考译文【Suggested Translation】

成 功 之 路

年轻人应该从头开始，从基层做起，这是一件很好的事情。匹兹堡有很多出类拔萃的企业家在创业之初，都承担过一项重要职责：他们手握扫帚，在清扫办公室中度过了创业生涯的最初时光。我注意到，我们的办公室现在都配置了工友，这使得我们的年轻人很不幸地失去了企业教育中一个有益的环节。但是，假如某一天早晨，专职的清洁工凑巧没来，那么某位具有未

来合伙人潜质的小伙子就会毫不犹豫地拿起扫帚。有一天，密歇根有一位溺爱孩子并且非常时髦的母亲问一个年轻人，是否见过有哪个年轻女士像她的女儿普里茜拉那样潇洒地在屋子里扫地。年轻人回答说从未见过，那位母亲乐不可支。可是年轻人停了一下又说，"我想看到的是她在屋子外面打扫。"如有必要，让新来的员工在办公室外面进行打扫对他们并没有什么坏处。我自己就曾经是那些扫地人之中的一员。

假如你获得录用并拥有一个良好开端时，我对你的忠告是："确立远大目标。"对于那些尚未把自己看成大公司未来的合伙人或者老板的年轻人，我是无话可说的。无论公司规模有多大，在思想上永远不要满足于充当这家公司的首席职员、领班或者总经理。要告诉自己："我的位置在最高层。"在你的梦想之中，你是王者之王。

获取成功的基本条件与重大秘密是：把你的精力、思想和资本完全集中于你所从事的事业上。开始投身于哪一行，就要决心在这一行做出一番事业，做这一行的领导人物，采纳每一点改进，采用最好的设备，尽力通晓专业知识。

失败的企业就是那些分散了资金，同时也意味着分散了精力的企业。它们投资于这方面，那方面，这里，那里，到处都有投资。"不要把所有的鸡蛋放在同一个篮子里"这句话大错特错了。我要告诉你们的是"把所有的鸡蛋都放在同一个篮子里，然后看紧它。"观察周围，谨慎留意，做到了这一点，你就往往不会失败。照管和携带一个篮子是很容易的。就是因为人们总是试图提很多的篮子，从而打破了这个国家大部分的鸡蛋。一次提着三个篮子的人，就得把一个篮子顶在头上，这个篮子很容易就会掉下来并把他绊倒。美国企业家的缺点之一就是缺乏专注之心。

我所说的话归纳起来就是：要目标远大；不要涉足酒吧；不要酗酒，除非仅在用餐时喝一点；不要做投机买卖；不要签署支付超过储备的现金利润的款项；把企业的利益看成是你自己的；只有基于救助货主的目的才能取消定单；要专心致志；要把所有的鸡蛋放在同一个篮子里，并且将它看管好；支出永远要小于收入；最后，不要不耐烦，因为正如爱默生所说："除了你自己之外，没有人能够哄骗你脱离最终的成功。"◆

Eyes Can Speak[*]

Much meaning can be conveyed, clearly, with our eyes, so it is often said that eyes can speak.

Do you have such kind of experience? In a bus you may look at a stranger, but not too long. And if he is sensing that he is being stared at, he may feel uncomfortable.

The same in daily life. If you are looked at for more than necessary, you will look at yourself up and down, to see if there is anything wrong with you. If nothing goes wrong, you will feel angry toward other's stare with you that way. Eyes do speak, right?

* 作者佚名。眼睛——心灵之窗！而且，你相信吗？眼睛还会说话呢！有的眼神，令人久久难以忘怀；有的眼神，令人豁然开朗；有的眼神，令人心旷神怡；有的眼神，令人暇想连连；有的眼神，给人一种很温暖的感觉……不仅如此，在我们的社会交往中，目光接触还真的有一些说法呢！看看本文是怎么说的吧……

Looking too long at someone may seem to be rude and aggressive. But things are different when it comes to stare at the opposite sex. If a man glances at a woman for more than 10 seconds and refuses to avert his gaze, his intentions are obvious, that is, he wishes to attract her attention, to make her understand that he is admiring her.

However, the normal eye contact for two people engaged in conversation is that the speaker will only look at the listener from time to time, in order to make sure that the listener does pay attention to what the former is speaking. As for the listener, he will to a certain extent look continuously at the speaker, to tell him that he is attentive.

If a speaker looks at you continuously when speaking, as if he tries to dominate you, you will feel disconcerted. A poor liar usually exposes himself by looking too long at the victim, since he believes in the false idea that to look straight in the eye is a sign of honest communication. Quite the contrary.

In fact, continuous eye contact is confined to lovers only, who will enjoy looking at each other tenderly for a long time, to show affection that words cannot express.

Evidently, eye contact should be done according to the relationship between two people and the specific situation. ✳

Vocabulary List 【词汇清单】

convey /kən'vei/ *v.* 传递,传达(感情、思想等)

stare /stɛə/ *v.* 盯,凝视,目不转睛地看(at)

aggressive /ə'gresiv/ *adj.* 侵犯的,好寻衅的;(行为等)过分的,放肆的

glance /glaːns/ *v.* 瞥,很快看一下(at)

avert /ə'vəːt/ *v.* 避开,转移(目光、思想等)

intention /in'tenʃən/ *n.* 目的,意图
engage /in'geidʒ/ *v.* 从事于,致力于,忙于(in)
to a certain extent：在一定程度上
continuously /kən'tinjuəsli/ *adv.* 持续地,不间断地
dominate /'dɔmineit/ *v.* 支配,控制,主宰
disconcert /ˌdiskən'səːt/ *v.* 使困窘,使不安,使仓皇失措
victim /'viktim/ *n.* 受骗者,被骗者
confine /kən'fain/ *v.* 保持在…限度内,限制
tenderly /'tendəli/ *adv.* 温和地,柔和地,温柔地
affection /ə'fekʃən/ *n.* 爱慕,钟爱

 参考译文【Suggested Translation】

眼 睛 会 说 话

我们的眼睛能够明确地传达许许多多的意思,所以难怪有人说"眼睛会说话"。

你有过类似的体验吗? 在一辆公共汽车上,你或许会看一个陌生人,但是时间不能太久。如果他感觉到有人在盯着他看,他就会感到不自在。

日常生活中同样如此。假如别人盯着我们看的时间过长,我们就会将自己从上到下扫视一下,看看自己是否有什么地方不对劲。假如没有什么事儿,我们会对这种注视方式感到几分气愤和反感。眼睛确实会说话,不是吗?

盯着一个人看的时间太久会给人以鲁莽和侵犯他人隐私的感觉。可是,假如这种事发生在异性之间,情况就不同了。如果一个男子注视一个女子的时间超过 10 秒钟,而且还不想移开他的目光,那他的意思就很明显了:他想吸引她的注意力,想让她体会到他对她倾慕不已。

然而,平时生活中进行正常交谈时的目光接触是这样的:说话者只是偶尔看一眼听者,为的是确认一下他是否在专心听自己讲话。而对于听者,他应当时不时地瞥一眼说话人,告诉他自

己一直在专心致志地听着。

　　如果说话者讲话时直愣愣地瞪着你，好像要吃了你似的，你就会觉得无所适从。有些功夫不到家的撒谎者往往不自觉地露了馅，正是由于他们注视别人的时间太久了，还自以为这么做是诚实沟通的表现呢，事实上却恰恰相反！

　　实际上，长时间的目光接触仅仅限于情人之间。他们喜欢相互温柔地凝视对方许久许久，表达言语无法传递的柔情蜜意。

　　显而易见，目光接触要看双方的关系和依据特定场合而定。

◉ We should never remember the benefits we have offered nor forget the favor received. (自己的好事别去提，别人的恩惠要铭记。)

◉ He is not fit to command others that cannot command himself. (正人先正己。)

◉ There is no general rule without some exception. (任何法规均有例外。)

◉ A sound mind in a sound body. (健全的精神寓于健康的身体。)

第 035 篇

Relish the Moment*

Tucked away in our subconsciousness is an idyllic vision. We see ourselves on a long trip that spans the continent. We are traveling by train. Out the windows, we drink in the passing scene of cars on nearby highways, of children waving at a crossing, of cattle grazing on a distant hillside, of smoke pouring from a power plant, of row upon row of corn and wheat, of flatlands and valleys, of mountains and rolling hillsides, of city skylines and village halls.

But uppermost in our minds is the final destination. On a certain day at a certain hour, we will pull into the station.

　＊ 作者罗伯特·J·黑斯廷斯（Robert J. Hastings），生平不详。生活在哪里？答案其实已很明确：生活只能在现在。"Tomorrow never comes.（明天永远不会来到）"有时候，当你做着将来的美梦或者为过去的某件事情而后悔不已时，你惟一拥有的现在却从你手中溜走了。因而，珍视现在吧！抓住现在吧！品味现在吧！

Bands will be playing and flags waving. Once we get there, so many wonderful dreams will come true and the pieces of our lives will fit together like a completed jigsaw puzle. How restlessly we pace the aisles, damning the minutes for loitering — waiting, waiting, waiting for the station.

"When we reach the station, that will be it!" we cry. "When I'm 18." "When I buy a new 450SL Mercedes Benz!" "When I put the last kid through college." "When I have paid off the mortgage!" "When I get a promotion." "When I reach the age of retirement, I shall live happily ever after!"

Sooner or later, we must realize there is no station, no one place to arrive at once and for all. The true joy of life is the trip. The station is only a dream. It constantly outdistances us.

"Relish the moment" is a good motto, especially when coupled with Psalm 118:24: "This is the day which the Lord hath made; we will rejoice and be glad in it." It isn't the burdens of today that drive men mad. It is the regrets over yesterday and the fear of tomorrow. Regret and fear are twin thieves who rob us of today.

So stop pacing the aisles and counting the miles. Instead, climb more mountains, eat more ice cream, go barefoot more often, swim more rivers, watch more sunsets, laugh more, cry less. Life must be lived as we go along. The station will come soon enough. ✳

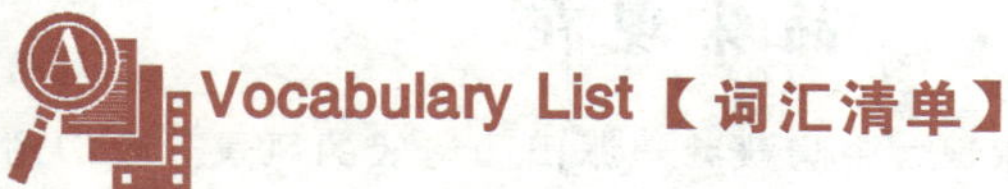

Vocabulary List 【词汇清单】

tuck /tʌk/ v. 折起,卷起;把…放入隐蔽的地点,使隐藏
subconsciousness /ˌsʌbˈkɔnʃəsnis/ n. 下意识,潜意识

idyllic /iˈdilik/ *adj.* 田园短诗（或散文）的；描写牧人（或乡村）生活的；生动逼真的

span /spæn/ *v.* 跨越，横跨

graze /greiz/ *v.* 啃食（生长着的草、牧草等），吃（田野里的）草

flatland /ˈflætˌlænd/ *n.* 平地，平原地区

uppermost /ˈʌpəməust/ *adj.* （＝upmost）最上的，最高的，最主要的

band /bænd/ *n.* 乐队，乐团

jigsaw puzzle：＜美＞拼板玩具，拼图玩具

restlessly /ˈrestlisli/ *adv.* 不安地，焦虑地，烦躁地

aisle /ail/ *n.* 通道，走廊

damn /dæm/ *v.* 诅咒，咒骂

loiter /ˈlɔitə/ *v.* 消磨时光（常与 about 连用）；虚度（时光）

Mercedes Benz：梅赛德斯—奔驰牌汽车（一种高档豪华汽车，以设计精巧、做工精细、质量优良而闻名于世界）

mortgage /ˈmɔːgidʒ/ *n.* 抵押，抵押契据，抵押单

outdistance /autˈdistəns/ *v.* （在竞赛中）领先；大大超过，胜过

motto /ˈmɔtəu/ *n.* 格言，座右铭，箴言

Psalm /saːm/ *n.* （基督教《圣经》中的）《诗篇》（亦作 Book of Psalms）

Lord /lɔːd/ *n.* （the）上帝，耶稣

rejoice /riˈdʒɔis/ *v.* 欣喜，高兴（常与 at, in, over 连用）

barefoot /ˈbɛəfut/ *adv.* 赤脚地，不穿鞋袜地

 ## 参考译文【Suggested Translation】

品 味 现 在

在我们的潜意识之中隐藏着一派田园诗般的风景。我们仿佛处在一次横跨大陆的迢迢旅途之中。我们乘着火车，领略着窗外流动的景色：附近高速公路上驰骋的汽车、十字路口处

挥手的孩童、远处山坡上吃草的牛群、不断从电厂排放出的烟尘、一片一片的玉米和小麦、平原和山谷、群山和绵延的丘陵、天空衬托下城市的轮廓，以及乡间的庄园宅第。

可是我们心中想得最多的却是最后的目的地。在某一天的某一时刻，我们将会抵达进站。迎接我们的将是演奏的乐队和飘舞的彩旗。一旦到了那儿，多少美妙的梦将成为现实，我们的生活也将变得完整，好像一幅拼好了的拼图。可是我们现在在车厢过道里烦躁不安地踱来踱去，咒骂火车的磨磨蹭蹭。我们等待着，等待着，等待着火车进站的时刻。

"当我们到站的时候，一切就都好了！"我们呼喊着。"当我到18岁的时候。""当我有了一辆新的450SL奔驰轿车的时候！""当我供最小的孩子念完大学的时候。""当我偿清抵押贷款的时候！""当我升官晋职的时候。""当我到了退休的时候，从此就可以过上幸福的生活啦！"

可是我们迟早会认识到人生之旅并没有什么车站，也没有什么能够"一到永逸"的地方。生活的真正乐趣在于旅行的过程，而车站仅仅是个梦，它总是遥遥领先于我们。

"品味现在"是一句很好的箴言，尤其是当它与《圣经·诗篇》中第118章第24行的一段话相映衬的时候，更是如此："今日乃主所创造；生活在今日我们将欢欣、高兴。"真正让人发疯的不是今天的负担，而是对昨天的悔恨及对明天的恐惧。悔恨和恐惧是一对孪生窃贼，将今天从我们身边偷走。

那么就停止在车厢过道里徘徊吧，别总惦记着你距离车站还有多远。何不换一种活法，去攀爬更多的高山，多吃点冰淇淋解解馋，经常光着脚闲游漫步，在更多的河流里游弋，多多欣赏夕阳西下，多点欢笑，少些泪花。生活要过得自自然然，该怎样就怎样。那么车站就会很快到达。◆

On Motes and Beams *

It is curious that our own offenses should seem so much less heinous than the offenses of others. I suppose the reason is that we know all the circumstances that have occasioned them and so manage to excuse in ourselves what we cannot excuse in others. We turn our attention away from our own defects, and when we are forced by untoward events to consider them, find it easy to condone them. For all I know we are right to do this; they are part of us and we must ac-

---

* 作者威廉·萨默赛特·毛姆(William Somerset Maugham, 1874—1965),20 世纪英国最伟大的作家之一,其一生创作颇丰,1897 年出版了第一部小说《兰贝斯的莉莎》;1915 年出版其不朽的巨著《人性的枷锁》;此后又有无数作品问世。他出于高度的爱国主义热情,曾经替英国军事情报局第六处(MI 6)工作的历史,却鲜为人知,而他则是该处早期最有传奇色彩的成员之一。后来,他根据当间谍的经历,创作了极有影响的间谍小说《艾兴顿》,"艾兴顿"已经成为世界间谍小说的一个典型人物。总之,毛姆脍炙人口的作品像他的名字一样,一直都在世界各地广为流传。

cept the good and bad in ourselves together.

But when we come to judge others, it is not by ourselves as we really are that we judge them, but by an image that we have formed of ourselves from which we have left out everything that offends our vanity or would discredit us in the eyes of the world. To take a trivial instance: how scornful we are when we catch someone out telling a lie; but who can say that he has never told not one, but a hundred?

There is not much to choose between men. They are all a hotchpotch of greatness and littleness, of virtue and vice, of nobility and baseness. Some have more strength of character, or more opportunity, and so in one direction or another give their instincts freer play, but potentially they are the same. For my part, I do not think I am any better or any worse than most people, but I know that if I set down every action in my life and every thought that has crossed my mind, the world would consider me a monster of depravity. The knowledge that these reveries are common to all men should inspire one with tolerance to oneself as well as to others. It is well also if they enable us to look upon our fellows, even the most eminent and respectable, with humor, and if they lead us to take ourselves not too seriously. ✳

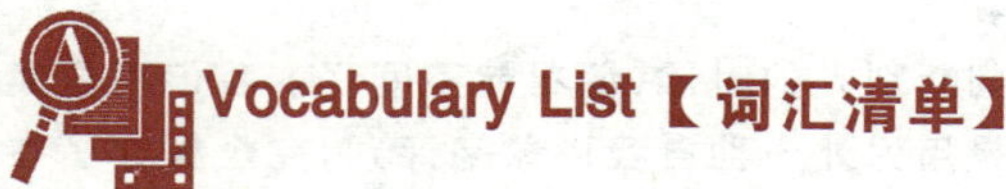

Vocabulary List 【词汇清单】

curious /ˈkjuəriəs/ *adj.* 好奇的, 奇怪的

heinous /ˈheinəs/ *adj.* 极可恨的, 极可恶的, 极坏的

circumstance /ˈsəːkəmstəns/ *n.* （伴随的）情况, 境况, 境遇

untoward /ʌnˈtəuəd/ *adj.* 不顺利的, 不幸的, 麻烦的

condone /kənˈdəun/ *v.* 原谅, 宽恕, 饶恕

vanity /ˈvæniti/ *n.* 虚荣, 虚荣心

discredit /dis'kredit/ *v.* 损害…的信誉（或名誉、名声），使丧失名誉（或名声），使丢脸

trivial /'triviəl/ *adj.* 平凡的，平常的

scornful /'skɔːnful/ *adj.* 轻蔑的，藐视的

hotchpotch /'hɔtʃpɔtʃ/ *n.* （＝hodgepodge）（肉菜合煮的）什锦菜，大杂烩，混合物

vice /vais/ *n.* 罪恶，恶习

depravity /di'præviti/ *n.* 堕落，腐化，腐败

revery /'revəri/ *n.* （＝reverie）梦幻，幻想，白日梦

tolerance /'tɔlərəns/ *n.* 容忍，宽容，宽恕

eminent /'eminənt/ *adj.* 杰出的，卓越的，著名的，优秀的

respectable /ris'pektəbl/ *adj.* 值得尊敬的，可敬的

 参考译文【Suggested Translation】

微 尘 与 栋 梁

让人好奇的是，和别人的过错比起来，我们自身的过错往往不是那样的可恨。我想，其原因应该是我们知晓一切导致过错出现的情况，因此，能够设法谅解自己犯的一些不允许他人犯的过错。我们对自己的缺点不甚关注，即便是深陷困境而不得不正视它们的时候，我们也会很容易就宽恕自己。据我所知，我们这样做是正确的。缺点是我们自身的一部分，我们必须接纳自己的好和坏。

但是当我们判断别人的时候，情况就不同了。我们不是通过真实的自我而是用另外一种自我形象来评判，完全摒弃了在任何世人眼中，会伤害到自己的虚荣或者体面的东西。举一个小例子来说：当觉察到别人说谎时，我们是多么地轻蔑藐视啊！但是又有谁能够说自己从未说过谎？也许还不止一百次呢！

人和人之间没什么大的差别。他们皆是伟大与渺小，善良与邪恶，高尚与低俗的混合体。虽然有的人性格比较坚毅，机会也比较多，因而在这个或者那个方面，能够更自由地发挥自己的

禀赋，但是人类的潜能却都是相同的。对于我来说，我认为自己并不比大多数人更好或者更差，但是我知道，假如我记下我生命中每一次举动和每一个掠过我脑海的想法的话，世界就会将我视为一个邪恶的怪物。每个人都会有这样的怪念头，这样的认识应当能够启发我们宽容自己，也宽容他人。同时，假如因此使我们以幽默的态度看待他人，即使是对天下最优秀最令人尊敬的人，而且假如我们也不太较真的话，那也是很有裨益的。◆

◎Like tree, like fruit.（羊毛出在羊身上。）

◎Four eyes see more than two.（集思广益。）

◎Books and friends should be few but good.（读书如交友，应求少而精。）

◎To know oneself is true progress.（人贵自知。）

A Leap in Thought[*]

You've had a problem, you've thought about it till you were tired, forgotten it and perhaps slept on it, and then flash! When you weren't thinking about it suddenly the answer has come to you, as a gift from the gods.

Of course all ideas don't come like that, but the interesting thing is that so many do, particularly the most important ones. They burst into the mind, glowing with the heat of creation. How they do it is a mystery. Psychology does not yet understand even the ordinary processes of conscious

---

* 作者兰斯洛特·怀特(Lancelot Whyte)，生于 1896 年，是英国著名物理学家，同时又是卓有成就的社会学家，本文选自其名篇《妙想从何而来?》(Where Do Those Bright Ideas Come From?)。独创性思维是发现问题和创造性地解决问题的思维，它不仅能揭示客观事物的本质特征和内部规律，而且能产生新颖的、前所未有的思维成果，是智力高度发展的表现。那么，它是从何而来的呢? 请跟随作者的思路去看一看吧……

thought, but the emergence of new ideas by a "leap in thought" is particularly intriguing, because they must have come from somewhere. For the moment let us assume that they come from the "unconscious". This is reasonable, for the psychologists use this term to describe mental processes which are unknown to the subject, and creative thought consists precisely in what was unknown becoming known.

It seems that all truly creative activity depends in some degree on these signals from the unconscious, and the more highly intuitive the person, the sharper and more dramatic the signals become.

But growth requires a seed, and the heart of the creative process lies in the production of the original fertile nucleus from which growth can proceed. This initial step in all creation consists in the establishment of a new unity from disparate elements, of order out of disorder, of shape from what was formless. The mind achieves this by the plastic reshaping, so as to form a new unit, of a selection of the separate elements derived from experience and stored in memory. Intuitions arise from richly unified experience.

This process of the establishment of new form must occur in pattern of nervous activity in the brain, lying below the threshold of consciousness, which interact and combine to form more comprehensive patterns. Experimental physiology has not yet identified this process, for its methods are as yet insufficiently refined, but it may be significant that a quarter of the total bodily consumption of energy during sleep goes to the brain, even when the sense organs are at rest, to maintain the activity of ten thousand million brain cells. These cells, acting together as a single organ, achieve the miracle of the production of new patterns of thought. No calculating machine can do that, for such machines can "only do what we know how to design them to do", and these formative brain processes obey laws which are still unknown.

Can any practical conclusions be drawn from the experience of genius? Is there an art of thought for the ordinary person? Certainly there is no single road to success; in the world of the imagination each has to find his own way to use his own gift. ✳

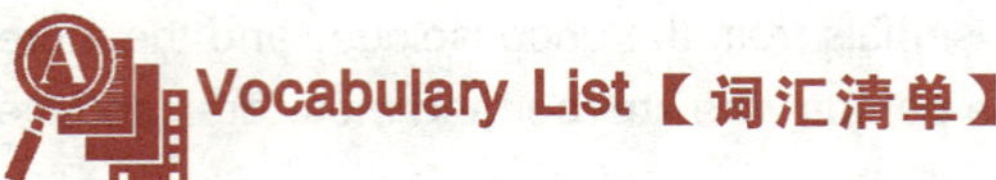

Vocabulary List【词汇清单】

psychology /saiˈkɔlədʒi/ *n.* 心理学（研究心理过程和行为的科学）

intrigue /inˈtriːg/ *v.* 引起…的兴趣或好奇,强烈地吸引住,迷住

precisely /priˈsaisli/ *adv.* 精确地,明白地,确实如此

intuitive /inˈtju(ː)itiv/ *adj.* 与直觉（或直观）有关的,有直觉力的

fertile /ˈfəːtail/ *adj.* 多产的,带来丰产的,利于生产的

nucleus /ˈnjuːkliəs/ *n.* <生物>细胞核,胚胎

disparate /ˈdispərit/ *adj.* 全异的,（性质）截然不同的,无联系的

derive /diˈraiv/ *v.* 得到,取得,获得（from）

threshold /ˈθreʃhəuld/ *n.* <心理>阈限,范围,界限

physiology /ˌfiziˈɔlədʒi/ *n.* 生理学（对有生命的有机体及其组成部分的功能进行的生物学研究）

insufficiently /ˌinsəˈfiʃəntli/ *adv.* 不足地,不够地,不充分地

formative /ˈfɔːmətiv/ *adj.* 使成形的,有助于形成或发展的

参考译文【Suggested Translation】

思 维 的 飞 跃

遇到了一个难题,为其绞尽脑汁,直至精疲力竭,将它置之脑后,或许带着疑虑进入梦乡。然而,忽然之间灵光一闪!

当你没在思考这一问题时,答案如同天赐神助一般,突然出现在你的脑子里。

当然,并非所有的妙想都是这样得来,可有趣的是,许多想法,特别是那些至关重要的想法都是这样产生的。它们倏忽之间闯入脑海,散发着独创的光热。它们的形成过程是一个谜。心理学迄今甚至连普通的有意识思维过程都没有研究清楚,但是依靠"思想的火花"产生创见的现象还是让人特别感兴趣,因为这种创见必定有个出处。我们暂且假定它们来自于"潜意识"。这也是有道理的,因为心理学家们利用这个术语来描述对于未知研究对象的心理过程,而创造性思维正是在于认清未曾认识到的东西。

在某种程度上,所有真正的创造性活动似乎都取决于这些来自潜意识的信号,并且,一个人的直觉愈加强烈,这些信号就愈加鲜明,愈加富有戏剧性。

可是萌芽生长需要种子,而创造过程的核心也在于形成最初的丰实的胚胎,使成长得以进行。所有创造的第一步,均在于把没有联系的因素重新结合,将无序变成有序,将无形变成有形。要做到这一点,大脑就要选择从经验中得到的或者存储于记忆之中的互无关联的因素,并加以整理重塑,以形成新的统一体。直觉来源于丰富的系统化的经验。

这种新形式的形成过程只能出现在大脑神经活动模式之中,处于意识范围的开端,相互作用又相互融合,而形成更加复杂的模式。实验生理学还无法识别这一过程,原因是其实验方法仍不够完善。可或许值得注意的是,人在睡眠的时候,尽管感觉器官处于休息状态,但是所有体能消耗的四分之一却用于大脑,以维持其上百亿个脑细胞的活动。这些共同运作的脑细胞创造了产生思维新模式的奇迹。计算机不能做到这一点,因为它们"只能按照我们的设计力所能及的方式运行",而那些具有建构能力的大脑活动过程遵循的却是我们所未知的规律。

从天才们的经验中,我们能得到任何实际的结论吗?有没有适用于普通人的思维艺术?成功之路不止一条。在一个提倡想像力的世界中,每个人都要找到发挥自己天分的道路。◆

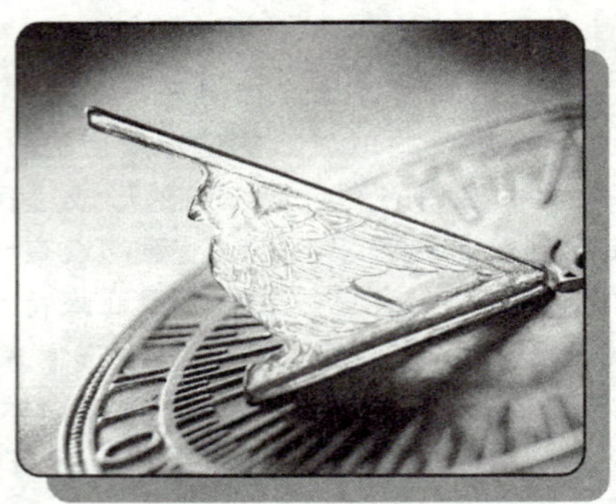

Our Family Creed *

They are the principles on which my wife and I have tried to bring up our family. They are the principles in which my father believed and by which he governed his life. They are the principles, many of them, which I learned at my mother's knee.

They point the way to usefulness and happiness in life, to courage and peace in death.

If they mean to you what they mean to me, they may perhaps be helpful also to our sons for their guidance and inspi-

---

＊ 作者约翰·戴维森·洛克菲勒（John Davison Rockefeller, 1874—1960），美国著名工业家和慈善家，石油大亨老约翰·洛克菲勒之子，笃信基督教，创办了以他名字命名的基金会，秉承"在全世界造福人类"的宗旨，曾捐赠联合国总部用地。洛克菲勒的创业史在美国早期富豪中颇具代表性：异常冷静、精明，富有远见，凭借独有的魄力和手段，一步步建立起庞大的商业帝国。洛克菲勒曾经这样说道："如果把我剥得一文不名丢在沙漠的中央，只要一行驼队经过——我就可以重建整个王朝。"

ration.

Let me state them:

I believe in the supreme worth of the individual and in his right to life, liberty and the pursuit of happiness.

I believe that every right implies a responsibility; every opportunity, an obligation; every possession, a duty.

I believe that the law was made for man and not man for the law; that government is the servant of the people and not their master.

I believe in the dignity of labor, whether with head or hand; that the world owes no man a living but that it owes every man an opportunity to make a living.

I believe that thrift is essential to well-ordered living and that economy is a prime requisite of a sound financial structure, whether in government, business or personal affairs.

I believe that truth and justice are fundamental to an enduring social order.

I believe in the sacredness of a promise, that a man's word should be as good as his bond, that character — not wealth or power or position — is of supreme worth.

I believe that the rendering of useful service is the common duty of mankind and that only in the purifying fire of sacrifice is the dross of selfishness consumed and the greatness of the human soul set free.

I believe in an all-wise and all-loving God, named by whatever name, and that the individual's highest fulfillment, greatest happiness and widest usefulness are to be found in living in harmony with His will.

I believe that love is the greatest thing in the world; that it alone can overcome hate; that right can and will triumph over might.

These are the principles, however formulated, for which all good men and women throughout the world, irrespective of race or creed, education, social position or occupation, are standing, and for which many of them are suffering and dying.

These are the principles upon which alone a new world recognizing the brotherhood of man and the fatherhood of God can be established. ✳

 # Vocabulary List【词汇清单】

creed /kriːd/ *n.* 信条,信念,教义

principle /ˈprinsəpl/ *n.* 行为的准则(尤指正确的规则),原则

govern /ˈgʌvən/ *v.* 指导,支配,决定,左右

guidance /ˈgaidəns/ *n.* 引导,指导

pursuit /pəˈsjuːt/ *n.* 追赶,追求,追踪

imply /imˈplai/ *v.* 包含,含有;暗指,含有…的意思

obligation /ˌɔbliˈgeiʃən/ *n.* 义务,职责

possession /pəˈzeʃən/ *n.* 拥有,占有

dignity /ˈdigniti/ *n.* 尊贵,高贵,荣誉

thrift /θrift/ *n.* 节俭,节约

essential /iˈsenʃəl/ *adj.* 基本的,基础的;首要的,主要的

economy /iˈkɔnəmi/ *n.* 节俭,节约

requisite /ˈrekwizit/ *n.* 需要,需求,必需品

fundamental /ˌfʌndəˈmentl/ *adj.* 基础的,根本的,实质的

sacredness /ˈseikridnis/ *n.* 神圣,神圣不可侵犯

render /ˈrendə/ *v.* 付出,给予,提供

purify /ˈpjuərifai/ *v.* 使洁净,使纯净;精炼,提纯

dross /drɔs/ *n.* 渣滓,杂质

fulfillment /fulˈfilmənt/ *n.* 满足(要求、愿望等),实现(渴望、期望等)

in harmony with:和…和谐一致,与…相协调

overcome /ˌəuvə'kʌm/ *v.* 战胜，征服，克服

triumph /'traiəmf/ *v.* 征服，击败，战胜（over）

formulate /'fɔːmjuleit/ *v.* 系统地阐述（或提出）（理论、计划等）

irrespective /ˌiris'pektiv/ *adj.* 不管，不考虑，不论（of）

brotherhood /'brʌðəhud/ *n.* 兄弟（般的）关系

fatherhood /'faːðəhud/ *n.* 父亲的身份（或资格）

 **参考译文【Suggested Translation】**

家 族 的 信 条

　　这些是我妻子和我在教育培养我们子女时尽力倚靠的信条，这些是我父亲所笃信并以之规范其生活的信条，这些信条中的大部分是我从母亲的膝下秉承而来的。

　　这些信条指明了人们如何幸福而有所作为地生活，也指明了人们如何勇敢而安详地对待死亡。

　　如果这些信条对于诸位的意义如同它们对于我的意义，那么它们或许可以有效地指导和鼓舞我们的子女们。

　　让我将这些信条陈述如下：

　　我相信，个人拥有至上的价值，拥有生存、自由和追求幸福的权利。

　　我相信，每一项权利都必然蕴含着一种责任，每一个机遇都必然蕴含着一种义务，每一种获得都必然蕴含着一种职责。

　　我相信，法律为人所制定，而非人为法律而生，政府是人民的仆人，而非人民的主人。

　　我相信，不管体力劳动抑或脑力劳动都是高尚的，世界不会让人不劳而获，但却会给每个人一次谋生的机会。

　　我相信，不管是在政府、商业还是个人事务中，勤俭节约都是合理安排生活之基本要素，而经济适用是健全的金融机制之主要需求。

　　我相信，真理与正义是任何一个长治久安的社会秩序之基

石。

我相信，承诺是神圣的；并且，假如人的言语和契约同样可靠，那么这种品质——而非财富、权势与身份地位——就具有至高无上的价值。

我相信，人类共同的职责是有助益地服务社会，只有在自我牺牲的炼火之中，自私的渣滓才会被焚为灰烬，人类灵魂中的伟大情操才会获得自由。

我相信，有一位无所不知、大慈大悲的上帝存在——尽管人们对他的称呼各不相同——人们能在和他的意志和谐相处的过程中得到最高的满足感、最大的幸福感，以及最广博的成就感。

我相信，爱是这个世界上最伟大的事物，只有爱才能够战胜仇恨，而正义能够而且必定击败强权。

无论怎样表述，以上就是这些信条——全世界所有不计种族、信仰、教育程度、社会地位或职业的善良的男男女女们所赞同的信条——而且正是为了这些信条，他们中的许多人正在忍受苦痛，甚至即将死去。

只有凭借这些信条，人类才能建立起人人如手足、上帝如慈父的新世界。◈

Mother's Day and Father's Day[*]

People in the United States honor their parents with two special days: Mother's Day, on the second Sunday in May, and Father's Day, on the third Sunday in June.

Mother's Day was proclaimed a day for national observance by President Woodrow Wilson in 1915. Ann Jarvis from Grafton, West Virginia, had started the idea to have a day to honor mothers. She was the one who chose the second Sunday in May and also began the custom of wearing a carnation.

---

* 作者佚名。每年 5 月的第二个星期日,你是否给母亲献上了一点你的心意? 因为那一天是母亲节;每年 6 月的第三个星期日,你是否给父亲送上了一份你的祝福? 因为那一天是父亲节。我们的父母赐予我们生命,养育我们长大。更重要的是,他们对于我们世界观、人生观和价值观的塑造起着决定性的作用。让我们对他们永存感怀之心,而不只是在母亲节和父亲节才想到他们。事实上,母亲节和父亲节是从美国传过来的,那美国人又是怎样开始这两个节日的呢?

In 1909, Mrs. Dodd from Spokane, Washington, thought of the idea of a day to honor fathers. She wanted to honor her own father, William Smart. After her mother died, he had the responsibility of raising a family of five sons and a daughter. In 1910, the first Father's Day was observed in Spokane. Senator Margaret Chase Smith helped to establish Father's Day as a national commemorative day, in 1972.

These days are set aside to show love and respect for parents. They raise their children and educate them to be responsible citizens. They give love and care.

These two special days are celebrated in many different ways. On Mother's Day people wear carnations. A red one symbolizes a living mother. A white one shows that the mother is dead. Many people attend religious services to honor parents. It is also a day when people whose parents are dead visit the cemetery. On these days families get together at home, as well as in restaurants. They often have outdoor barbecues for Father's Day. These are days of fun and good feelings and memories.

Another tradition is to give cards and gifts. Children make them in school. Many people make their own presents. These are valued more than the ones bought in stores. It is not the value of the gift that is important, but it is "the thought that counts". Greeting card stores, florists, candy makers, bakeries, telephone companies, and other stores do a lot of business during these holidays. ✳

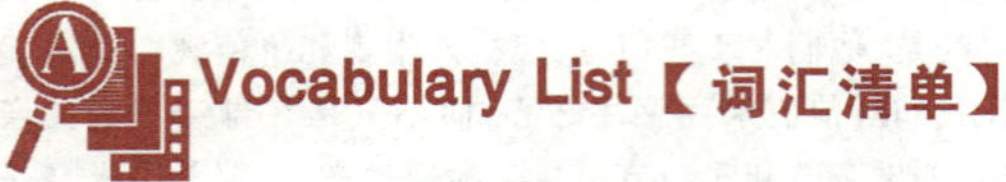

Vocabulary List 【词汇清单】

honor /ˈɔnə/ v. 尊敬，尊重，对…表示敬意

proclaim /prəˈkleim/ *v.*　正式宣布，宣告

observance /əbˈzɔːvəns/ *n.*　（法律、习俗、规章等的）遵守，奉行；习惯，惯例

Woodrow Wilson /ˈwudrəu wilsn/　伍德罗·威尔逊（1856—1924，美国第 28 任总统，民主党人）

Virginia /vəˈdʒinjə/　弗吉尼亚州（美国州名）

Spokane /spəuˈkæn/　斯波坎（美国华盛顿州城市）

responsibility /risˌpɔnsəˈbiliti/ *n.*　责任，职责

senator /ˈsenətə/ *n.*　参议员，上议院成员

commemorative /kəˈmemərətiv/ *adj.*　纪念（性）的

carnation /kɑːˈneiʃən/ *n.*　＜植物＞康乃馨，麝香石竹

symbolize /ˈsimbəlaiz/ *v.*　象征，代表

cemetery /ˈsemitri/ *n.*　公墓，墓地

barbecue /ˈbɑːbikjuː/ *n.*　＜美＞吃烤肉的宴会或野餐

value /ˈvæljuː/ *v.*　重视，珍视，把…看得高于…

 **参考译文【Suggested Translation】**

母亲节与父亲节

美国人以两个特殊的日子向他们的父母表示敬意：这就是每年 5 月份第二个星期日的母亲节和 6 月份第三个星期日的父亲节。

母亲节作为一个全国性的节日是伍德罗·威尔逊总统于 1915 年宣布的。西弗吉尼亚州格拉弗顿区的安·贾维斯女士首先想到应该有一个特殊的日子向母亲致以敬意。是她选择了五月份的第二个星期日，也是由她开始了佩戴康乃馨的习俗。

1909 年，华盛顿州斯波坎市的多德夫人想到应该为父亲设置一个特殊日子以示敬意。她想向自己的父亲——威廉姆·斯马特表示感激之情。她母亲去世之后，是父亲担起了养活五子一女的责任。1910 年，第一个父亲节在斯波坎市诞生。参议员玛格丽特·切斯·史密斯于 1972 年帮助把父亲节推广成为全

国性节日。

这两天是儿女向父母表示一片爱心和敬重之情的日子。父母们把孩子们带大，教育他们成为有责任感的公民，并给予他们爱心和关怀。

人们用各种形式来庆贺这两个特殊的日子。在母亲节那天，人们佩戴康乃馨。佩戴红色康乃馨表示母亲依然健在，佩戴白色康乃馨则表示母亲已经去世。许多人参加宗教仪式以向父母致意，或者去公墓缅怀逝去的父母。在这两天，家家都会聚在餐馆或家中。人们也常在父亲节那天举办露天烧烤聚会。这是充满欢歌笑语、美好情感和无限回忆的日子。

另一个传统习俗是赠送卡片和礼物。孩子们在学校亲手制作，许多成年人也自制礼物。这些亲手制作的礼物比那些花钱买来的更有价值。礼物的贵贱并不重要，"重要的是对父母的拳拳之心"。贺卡屋、花店、糖果店、面包房、电话公司，以及许多其他商店在节日里会大做生意。◆

（《英语沙龙》天昊 译）

●Don't count your chickens before they are hatched.（鸡蛋未孵出之前不算数；切莫过于乐观。）

●He who makes constant complaint gets little compassion.（经常诉苦，没人同情。）

●Too much praise is a burden.（过多夸奖，反成负担。）

●Look before you leap.（三思而后行。）

Expressing One's Individuality*

A most curious and useful thing to realize is that one never knows the impression one is creating on other people. One may often guess pretty accurately whether it is good, bad, or indifferent — some people render it unnecessary for one to guess, they practically inform one — but that is not what I mean. I mean much more than that. I mean that one has one's self no mental picture corresponding to the mental picture which one's personality leaves in the minds of one's friends. Has it ever struck you that there is a mysterious individual going around, walking the streets, calling at houses for

---

　　* 作者阿诺德·本涅特（Arnold Bennett，1867—1931），20 世纪初期英国现实主义文学家，其主要作品有《五镇的安娜》、《老妇人的故事》、《克莱汉格》三部曲、《怪人》及其续篇《摄政者》、《里程碑》（剧本）和《伟大的冒险》等。本涅特受左拉和巴尔扎克的影响较深，善于描写平凡的生活琐事，在平淡无奇中揭示生活中的诗意。他认为作家不应成为生活的评论者或辩护者，而应观察和记录人生，因此他的写作风格带有自然主义的倾向。

tea, chatting, laughing, grumbling, arguing, and that all your friends know him and have long since added him up and come to a definite conclusion about him — without saying more than a chance, cautious word to you; and that that person is you? Supposing that you came into a drawing-room where you were having tea, do you think you would recognize yourself as an individuality? I think not. You would be apt to say to yourself as guests do when disturbed in drawing-rooms by other guests: "Who's this chap? Seems rather queer. I hope he won't be a bore." And your first telling would be slightly hostile. Why, even when you meet yourself in an un-suspected mirror in the very clothes that you have put on that very day and that you know by heart, you are almost always shocked by the realization that you are you. And now and then, when you have gone to the glass to arrange your hair in the full sobriety of early morning, have you not looked on an absolute stranger, and has not that stranger piqued your curiosity? And if it is thus with precise external details of form, colour, and movement, what may it not be with the vague complex effect of the mental and moral individuality?

A man honestly tries to make a good impression. What is the result? The result merely is that his friends, in the privacy of their minds, set him down as a man who tries to make a good impression. If much depends on the result of a single interview, or a couple of interviews, a man may conceivably force another to accept an impression of himself which he would like to convey. But if the receiver of the impression is to have time at his disposal, then the giver of the impression may just as well sit down and put his hands in his pockets, for nothing that he can do will modify or influence in any way the impression that he will ultimately give. The real impress is, in the end, given unconsciously, not consciously; and further, it is received unconsciously, not consciously. It depends partly on both persons. And it is immutably fixed beforehand. There can be no final deception. . . ✳

 **Vocabulary List 【词汇清单】**

individuality /ˌindiˌvidjuˈæliti/ *n.* 个性，个人的特征（性格、人格、品格）

accurately /ˈækjuritli/ *adv.* 精确地，准确地

practically /ˈpræktikəli/ *adv.* 实际上，事实上；＜口语＞几乎，简直

corresponding /ˌkɔrisˈpɔndiŋ/ *adj.* 相当的，对应的，一致的

mysterious /misˈtiəriəs/ *adj.* 神秘的，不可思议的

grumble /ˈgrʌmbl/ *v.* 抱怨，鸣不平

cautious /ˈkɔːʃəs/ *adj.* 谨慎的，慎重的，警惕的

be apt to：往往，易于，有…的倾向

chap /tʃæp/ *n.* ＜口语＞家伙；男孩，小伙子

queer /kwiə/ *adj.* ＜口语＞奇怪的，（性情）古怪的

unsuspected /ˈʌnsəsˈpektid/ *adj.* 未被预料到的，出乎意料的

realization /ˌriəlaiˈzeiʃən/ *n.* 认清，觉悟，真正了解

sobriety /səuˈbraiəti/ *n.* 清醒，平静，冷静

pique /piːk/ *v.* 激发，激起

vague /veig/ *adj.* 模糊的，不清楚的，不确切的

conceivably /kənˈsiːvəbli/ *adv.* 可想像地，想得到地，大概

convey /kənˈvei/ *v.* 表达，传达，传递

at one's disposal：由某人作主，供某人随便使用，由某人自行支配

immutably /iˈmjuːtəbli/ *adv.* 永不变地，不可改变地

deception /diˈsepʃən/ *n.* 欺骗，蒙蔽（的行为或手段）

参考译文【Suggested Translation】

个 性 的 表 达

一件认识起来很奇特却很受益的事情是，一个人常常不晓得别人对他的印象是什么。是好呢，是坏呢，还是不好不坏，这些倒是能够十分准确地猜测出来——有些人甚至没有必要让你去猜测，他们实质上就讲给你听了——但是我想要说的不是这个。我想要说的远不止这个。我想要说的是，一个人头脑中对自己的印象和他本人在他朋友们头脑中的印象，往往很不一致。你曾经想到过这样的事情吗？——世界上有那么一个诡异的人，到处跑来跑去，上街访友，又说又笑，口出怨言，大发议论，他的朋友都对他很熟悉，对他早已知根知底，对他的看法早有定论——但是除了偶尔且谨慎的只言片语以外，平时却很少对你透露。而那个人就是你自己。比如，你走进一家客厅去喝茶，你敢说你就能认得这个人就是你自己吗？我看不一定。很可能，你也会像客厅里的客人那样，当你难以忍受其他客人的骚扰时心里就盘算说："这是哪个家伙，真是怪异。但愿他少讨人嫌。"你的第一个反应就是略带敌意。甚至就连你突然在一面镜子前面遇到了你自己，穿的衣服也正是你心里记得很清楚的那天的服装，怎么样，你还是会因为认出了你是你这件事而感到吃惊。还有当你有时候到镜子前去整理头发时，尽管是在最清醒的大清早，你不是也好像瞥见一个完全陌生的人吗？而且这个陌生人还让你颇为好奇呢。如果说连形式颜色动作这类外观准确的细节都是这样，那么对于像心智和道德这种不易把握的复杂印象又将怎样呢？

有的人真心实意地去努力制造一个好印象。但是结果如何呢？不过是被他的朋友们在内心深处认为他是一个刻意给人留下好印象的人。如果一切只凭着单独地会一次面或者见几次面，——这个人倒是很可能迫使另一个人接受他本人希望造成的某种印象。但是如果接受印象的人有足够的时间来自由支配，那么印象的给予者就干脆束手静坐了，因为他的所有招数都丝毫改变不了或者影响不了他最终所造成的印象。总之，真正的印象是无意而不是刻意造成的。进而，它也是无意而不是刻意被接受的。它的形成要依靠双方，而且是事先就已经确定的，最终的欺骗是不可能的……◈

◉No one can call back yesterday.（昨日不会重现。）

◉Far from eye, far from heart.（眼不见，心不烦。）

◉An eye for an eye and a tooth for a tooth.（以眼还眼，以牙还牙。）

◉You cannot eat your cake and have it.（鱼肉熊掌，不可得兼。）

If*

f you can keep your head when all about you

Are losing theirs and blaming it on you；

If you can trust yourself when all men doubt you，

---

　　* 作者卢迪亚·吉卜林（Rudyard Kipling，1865—1936），英国著名作家，他长期生活在印度，作品大多取材于生活在印度的英国殖民者的家庭生活，书中的人物多是生活在中下层的普通人，很能引起读者的兴趣和共鸣。这使得他在 19 世纪 90 年代的英国声名显赫，成为家喻户晓的人物。其代表作有儿童故事《丛林故事》、《丛林故事续篇》，游记《从大海到大海》，自传体散文《关于我本人的某些事》等。"这位世界名作家的作品以观察入微、想像独特、气概雄浑、叙述卓越见长"，1907 年获得诺贝尔文学奖。《如果》是他当时写给自己 12 岁的儿子的一首诗，是其脍炙人口诗歌的代表作。怎样才能称得上是一个真正的人？恐怕千人千论，标准无法统一。吉卜林却凭手中妙笔，勾勒出一幅毕加索式的立体画，使人生种种境遇，跃然纸上。短短的一首诗，语言质朴，风格简约，平平淡淡中蕴含着深邃的哲理，如一杯清茶，在心田里留下几缕清香，令人久久回味。这首诗历来备受推崇，而且吉卜林本人曾经这样说道："如果你在每天清晨读一遍这首诗，你将成为高尚的人；如果你在每天晚上读一遍这首诗，你将成为圣洁的人。"

But make allowance for their doubting too;
If you can wait and not be tired by waiting,
Or, being lied about, don't deal in lies,
Or, being hated, don't give way to hating,
And yet don't look too good, nor talk too wise;

If you can dream — and not make dreams your master;
If you can think — and not make thoughts your aim;
If you can meet with triumph and disaster
And treat those two impostors just the same;
If you can bear to hear the truth you've spoken
Twisted by knaves to make a trap for fools,
Or watch the things you gave your life to broken,
And stoop and build 'em up with worn-out tools;

If you can make one heap of all your winnings
And risk it all on one turn of pitch-and-toss,
And lose, and start again at your beginnings
And never breathe a word about your loss;
If you can force your heart and nerve and sinew
To serve your turn long after they are gone,
And so hold on when there is nothing in you
Except the Will which says to them: "Hold on!"

If you can talk with crowds and keep your virtue,
Or walk with kings — nor lose the common touch;
If neither foes nor loving friends can hurt you;
If all men count with you, but none too much,
If you can fill the unforgiving minute
With sixty seconds' worth of distance run —
Yours is the Earth and everything that's in it,

And — which is more — you'll be a Man, my son! ❋

Vocabulary List 【词汇清单】

blame /bleim/ *v.* 责备,谴责,指责

allowance /ə'lauəns/ *n.* 宽容,允许,许可(限度)

triumph /'traiəmf/ *n.* 凯旋,胜利,成功

impostor /im'pɔstə/ *n.* 冒名顶替者,招摇撞骗者

twist /twist/ *v.* 拧,扭曲,搓,捻

knave /neiv/ *n.* 流氓,无赖,恶棍

trap /træp/ *n.* (捕捉野兽的)陷阱;圈套,诡计

stoop /stuːp/ *v.* 弯腰,屈服,堕落

heap /hiːp/ *n.* 堆,大量,许多

pitch-and-toss /pitʃ-ænd-tɔs/ *n.* 掷硬币游戏(瞄准目标投掷钱币的游戏)

sinew /'sinjuː/ *n.* 肌肉,精力,体力

virtue /'vəːtjuː/ *n.* 德行,美德

foe /fəu/ *n.* 反对者,敌人

参考译文【Suggested Translation】

如　　果

如果在众人六神无主之时,
你能镇定自若而不是人云亦云;
如果在被众人猜忌怀疑之日,
你能自信如常而不去枉加辩论;
如果你能够等待,却不因此而厌烦,
或者被人欺骗,却不以血还血,
或者被人所恨,却不以牙还牙,
同时,依然不愠不火,谈吐不凡。

如果你有梦想，又能不迷失自我；

如果你有神思，又不致走火入魔；

如果在成功之中能不忘形于色，

而在灾难之后也勇于咀嚼苦果；

如果听到自己说出的奥妙，被无赖

歪曲成面目全非的魔术而不生怨艾；

如果看到自己追求的美好，受天灾

破灭为一摊零碎的瓦砾，也不说放弃；

如果你辛苦劳作，已是功成名就，

为了新目标你依旧冒险一搏，哪怕功名成乌有；

即使惨遭失败，也仍要从头开始，

而丝毫不去计较个人得失；

如果你的整个身心已经灰飞烟灭，

而你驱使其留下的德行能流芳万世；

那么坚持到底吧——即使你的内心已经空无一物，

只能听到意志的呼唤："坚持！"

如果你跟村夫交谈而不离谦恭之态，

和王侯散步而不露谄媚之颜；

如果你的敌手和挚友都无法伤害你，

如果所有人都指望你，却无人全心全意；

如果你肯花六十秒钟进行短程跑，

去填满生命中无情的每一分钟，

那么你就可以拥有整个世界及其万物，

更重要的是，你就是个真正的男子汉了，我的孩子！◈

（文美惠 译）

True and False Simplicity *

Simplicity is an uprightness of soul that has no reference to self; it is different from sincerity, and it is a still higher virtue. We see many people who are sincere, without being simple; they only wish to pass for what they are, and they are unwilling to appear what they are not; they are always thinking of themselves, measuring their words, and recalling their thoughts, and reviewing their actions, from the fear that they have done too much or too little. These persons are sincere, but they are not simple; they are not at ease with oth-

---

* 作者弗朗索瓦·费奈隆（Francois Fénelon，1651—1715），法国著名神学家和作家，曾任主教。本文贯穿着一种"回归真实自我"的意象，文思缜密，说理透彻，将真实的纯朴和虚假的纯朴进行了详明的对比。而且，仔细体味就会发觉：作者眼中的"真实的纯朴"和中国传统的"中庸之道"（中者天下之正道，庸者天下之定理，不偏之为中，不易之为庸）在某种程度上还有异曲同工之妙呢！

ers, and others are not at ease with them; they are not free, ingenuous, natural; we prefer people who are less correct, less perfect, and who are less artificial. This is the decision of man, and it is the judgment of God, who would not have us so occupied with ourselves, and thus, as it were, always arranging our features in a mirror.

To be wholly occupied with others, never to look within, is the state of blindness of those who are entirely engrossed by what is present and addressed to their sense; this is the very reverse of simplicity. To be absorbed in self and in whatever engages us, whether we are laboring for our fellow beings or for God — to be wise in our own eyes reserved, and full of ourselves, troubled at the least thing that disturbs our self-complacency, is the opposite extreme. This is false wisdom, which, with all its glory, is but little less absurd than that folly, which pursues only pleasure. The one is intoxicated with all it sees around it; the other with all that it imagines it has within; but it is delirium in both. To be absorbed in the contemplation of our own minds is really worse than to be engrossed by outward things, because it appears like wisdom and yet is not, we do not think of curing it, we pride ourselves upon it, we approve of it, it gives us an unnatural strength, it is a sort of frenzy, we are not conscious of it, we are dying, and we think ourselves in health.

Simplicity consists in a just medium, in which we are neither too much excited, nor too composed. The soul is not carried away by outward things, so that it cannot make all necessary reflections; neither does it make those continual references to self, that a jealous sense of its own excellence multiplies to infinity. That freedom of the soul, which looks straight onward in its path, losing no time to reason upon its steps, to study them, or to contemplate those that it has already taken, is true simplicity. ✳

Vocabulary List【词汇清单】

simplicity /sim'plisiti/ *n.* 纯朴,朴素,朴实

uprightness /'ʌpraitnis/ *n.* 公正,正直,诚实

sincerity /sin'seriti/ *n.* 真诚,诚实,真挚

at ease with：对…感到放松(自在、无拘束)

ingenuous /in'dʒenjuəs/ *adj.* 坦率的,正直的,朴实的

artificial /ˌaːti'fiʃəl/ *adj.* 不自然的,做作的,娇揉造作的

wholly /'həulli/ *adv.* 完全地,十足地

engross /in'grəus/ *v.* 使全神贯注,使聚精会神,吸引(注意)

self-complacency /'self kəm'pleisnsi/ *n.* 自满,自以为是,沾沾自喜

absurd /əb'səːd/ *adj.* 荒谬的,荒唐的,愚蠢可笑的

intoxicated /in'tɔksikeitid/ *adj.* 陶醉的,沉迷的,如痴如醉的

delirium /di'liriəm/ *n.* 精神混乱,神智不清

contemplation /ˌkɔntem'pleiʃən/ *n.* 沉思,深思,冥想

frenzy /'frenzi/ *n.* 暴怒,狂乱

medium /'miːdiəm/ *n.* 中庸,适度,适中

composed /kəm'pəuzd/ *adj.* 镇静自若的,沉着冷静的

reflection /ri'flekʃən/ *n.* 深思熟虑,内省,反省

infinity /in'finiti/ *n.* 无限,无穷无尽(to)

参考译文【Suggested Translation】

真正的纯朴与虚假的纯朴

朴是无私的灵魂中一种正直的品质;它与真诚不同,是一种更高层次的品德。我们看到,许多人真诚,但并不单纯;

他们只是希望以本来面目示人；他们总是在想着自己，说话时斟字酌句，思考时一再反省，行动时再三审视，因为他们总是担心做得过多或者过少。这些人是真诚的，但他们并不纯朴；与人相处之时，他们总是难以放松，同样，别人对他们也十分拘谨；他们不随意、不率直、不自然；我们更喜欢偶尔犯点错误、不那么完美、不那么做作的人们。人类是如此判断的，上帝也如此认为。上帝不愿让我们如此沉湎于自我，而正如整日对着镜子整理自己的容颜。

　　另外一种人处于盲目状态，他们完全专注于他人而从不自省。他们所有的注意力都集中于眼前的事物以及感觉到的一切；这与纯朴恰恰相反。无论在为人类还是为上帝效力，假如我们总是全神贯注于自己，我们就走向了另外一个极端——自以为聪明含蓄，非常自我；自命不凡稍受打击就觉得心烦意乱。这不是真正的智慧；尽管看上去值得夸耀，其实与那些仅仅追求享乐的傻念头同样荒谬。一些人沉迷于其所见到的事物而乐不可支，另一些人则沉迷于自己的幻想而欣喜若狂；但是这两者都是虚幻不实的。沉迷于自己的幻想之中比专注于外界事物更为糟糕，因为这种情况虽然很不明智，可是看起来却很英明，以至于人们非但不会想法去改正，反而会引以为荣。人们赞同这种行为，它带给我们一种怪异的力量，那是一种癫狂，我们却感知不到——我们已经命在旦夕，却还以为自己十分健康。

　　纯朴在于中庸。我们既不会对其过度兴奋，也不会过于镇静。灵魂不会受外物迷惑以至于无力做必要的内省；也不会时刻以自我为中心，以至于对自己的所谓美好品质无穷无尽地患得患失。真正的纯朴，是一种灵魂的自由——它直视道路的前方，不会浪费时间仔细权衡自己脚下的步伐，也不会再去沉思已经走过的道路。◆

Last Letters Home from an American Soldier Who Died in Iraq[*]

To my son, Cecil,

Just a quick note preface before I start in earnest. When I wrote this you were 8, still a little boy. In 2002, I was called to active duty in the Marine Corps in the War on Terrorism. On the 11th of September 2001 when America was attacked, I knew that I would eventually have to go and I was filled with a deep sense of sadness. That night as you and Keiko were asleep, I looked at your little faces and couldn't help but fight the tears. I knew it would be hard for you be-

---

* 作者詹姆斯·考雷(James Cawley)，美国派往伊拉克参加反恐战争的一名普通士兵。"父爱，是一杯苦咖啡。只有真正理解了那种深厚的感觉，才知道父爱真的是那么含蓄，那么深沉。"本文是詹姆斯·考雷写给自己至亲至爱家人的绝笔家书，文字虽然朴实无华，但是却情真意切、感人至深，将父爱之情淋漓演绎。

cause I had a similar experience. When I was a little boy aged 6, my Dad, your Grandpa Cawley, was sent to Vietnam during the War there. I remember how much I missed him, too. But now unfortunately I have come to realise just how rough it must have been for Grandpa to be away from his children for a year. Thinking about this, I wanted to put my thoughts and feelings down for you and your sister. I am so sorry that I had to leave for such a long time. There is no place I would rather be than with you and Keiko. You two are the lights of my life. I have known no greater joy than in the few years since you two were born. I hope to have many more years with you. If this doesn't happen, then know that I love you more than words can express. If for some reason I don't make it home, I will need you to take care of your little sister and your Mom. You will be the Man of the Cawley family. Be good my son and God will watch over you as he has me. I will be waiting impatiently for the time when we can all be together again.

All my love, Dad

(Two days after Cawley's death, his last letter arrived at his family's home in Utah, written on the packaging of an MRE Meal Ready to Eat, the US military's frontline ration. It consisted of a message in Japanese to his wife and his final words to his children.)

Dear Cecil and Keiko,

Hi little guys. How are you? Daddy is fine. I miss you. Send me a letter okay. It will make me very happy. I am proud of you. You are such good kids. I will see you again.

Love, Daddy ✳

Vocabulary List【词汇清单】

Iraq /iˈrɑːk/ 伊拉克（西南亚国家，首都巴格达）

preface /ˈprefis/ n. 开端，序幕，开始

in earnest：郑重其事地，正经地

the Marine Corps：海军陆战队

terrorism /ˈterərizəm/ n. 恐怖主义，恐怖行为

eventually /iˈventʃuəli/ adv. 最后，终于

Vietnam /ˈvjetˈnæm/ n. 越南（亚洲国家）

unfortunately /ʌnˈfɔːtʃənitli/ adv. 不幸地，倒霉地

impatiently /imˈpeiʃəntli/ adv. 不耐烦地，焦急地，渴望地

Utah /ˈjuːtɑː/ 犹他州（美国州名）

MRE：（＝ Meals Ready to Eat）快餐，即食便餐

frontline ration：（食品等）前线供给，前线配给

consist of：由…组成，包括…

参考译文【Suggested Translation】

一名在伊拉克阵亡美军士兵的最后家书

给 儿子塞西尔：

在正式开始之前我先简单说几句吧。当我写这封信时，你才 8 岁，还是一个小男孩。2002 年，在反恐战争中，我被征召去海军陆战队服役。2001 年 9 月 11 日美国遭受恐怖袭击时，我便知道我终究是要走的，为此我感到深深的悲哀。那天晚上，当你和惠子熟睡的时候，我看着你们的小脸蛋，强忍着泪水。我知道随之而来的生活对你们是会很艰难的，因为我也有过类似的经历。当我还是一个 6 岁孩子的时候，我爸爸，也就是你们的爷爷考利，被派往越南参加那里的战争。我还记得当时我也是多么地想念他。然而不幸的是，现在我开始体会到，你的爷爷离开自己的孩子们一年之久，那是多么难受的事情。一想到这些，

我便打算把我的想法和感受给你和你妹妹写下来。我非常难过不得不离开这么长时间。除了与你和惠子在一起，我哪儿也不愿意去。你们俩是我生命中的光芒。你们俩来到这个世界后的这几年，是我生命中最快乐的时光。我希望还可以和你们一起度过更多的岁月。如果不能如愿，我希望你们知道我对你们的爱是无法用语言来表达的。如果因故我不能再回到家里，我需要你来照顾你的妹妹和妈妈。你将是考利家族的男人。乖一点，我的孩子，如果上帝将我收回，他会照看你的。我会急切地等待着我们全家重新相聚的那一天。

　　我全部的爱，爸爸

　　（在考利阵亡之后两天，他最后的家书到达了他在犹他州的家。信是写在美国前线士兵配给的快餐包装纸上的。信中有用日文写给妻子的留言，以及给孩子们的绝笔。）

亲爱的塞西尔和惠子：

　　嗨，小家伙们。你们好吗？爸爸很好。我想念你们。给我来封信好吗？那会让我非常开心的。我因你们而自豪。你们都是这么好的孩子。我会与你们重新相聚的。

　　爱你们的，爸爸 ◈

（飞象 译）

第 044 篇

Jimmy Carter's Nobel Lecture（Ⅰ）*

Your Majesties, Members of the Norwegian Nobel Committee, Excellencies, Ladies and Gentlemen,

It is with a deep sense of gratitude that I accept this prize. I am grateful to my wife Rosalynn, to my colleagues at

---

    * 作者詹姆斯·厄尔·卡特（James Earl Carter，1924——　），习称吉米·卡特（Jimmy Carter），美国第 39 任总统，在其任期内，与中国达成了正式建立外交关系的协议。卡特在埃及与以色列的和谈并签署戴维营协议中也起到了重要作用。1975 年出版自传《为什么不是最好的？》，以后又陆续写了《一个与其人民一样诚实的政府》（1977）和《保持信心，一个总统的回忆录》（1982）。1990 年 7 月 4 日获费城自由勋章。1995 年 1 月 10 日获得 1994 年度联合国教科文组织设立的费利克斯·乌弗埃—博瓦尼和平奖。1997 年 11 月，印度英·甘地纪念基金会授予他 1997 年度英·甘地奖，以奖励他为全球和平、裁军和发展所作的贡献。1998 年 12 月 10 日，获 1998 年度联合国人权奖。2002 年 10 月 11 日，挪威诺贝尔委员会在奥斯陆宣布将 2002 年诺贝尔和平奖授予他，以表彰他数十年来为寻求和平解决国际冲突所作出的不懈努力。

the Carter Center, and to many others who continue to seek an end to violence and suffering throughout the world.

Most Nobel laureates have carried out our work in safety, but there are others who have acted with great personal courage. None has provided more vivid reminders of the dangers of peacemaking than two of my friends, Anwar Sadat and Yitzak Rabin, who gave their lives for the cause of peace in the Middle East.

Like these two heroes, my first chosen career was in the military, as a submarine officer. My shipmates and I realized that we had to be ready to fight if combat was forced upon us, and we were prepared to give our lives to defend our nation and its principles. At the same time, we always prayed fervently that our readiness would ensure that there would be no war.

Later, as President and as Commander-in-Chief of our armed forces, I was one of those who bore the sobering responsibility of maintaining global stability during the height of the Cold War, as the world's two superpowers confronted each other.

The world has changed greatly since I left the White House. Now there is only one superpower, with unprecedented military and economic strength. The coming budget for American armaments will be greater than those of the next fifteen nations combined, and there are troops from the United States in many countries throughout the world.

But instead of entering a millennium of peace, the world is now, in many ways, a more dangerous place. The greater ease of travel and communication has not been matched by equal understanding and mutual respect. There is a plethora of civil wars, within which an overwhelming portion of the casualties are unarmed civilians who have no ability to defend themselves. And recent appalling acts of terrorism have reminded us that no nations, even superpowers, are invulnerable.

It is clear that global challenges must be met with an emphasis on peace, in harmony with others, with strong alliances and international consensus. Imperfect as it may be, there is no doubt that this can best be done through the United Nations.

We must remember that today there are at least eight nuclear powers on earth, and three of them are threatening to their neighbors in areas of great international tension. For powerful countries to adopt a principle of preventive war may well set an example that can have catastrophic consequences.

If we accept the premise that the United Nations is the best avenue for the maintenance of peace, then the carefully considered decisions of the United Nations Security Council must be enforced. All too often, the alternative has proven to be uncontrollable violence and expanding spheres of hostility. (To be continued) ✻

Vocabulary List 【词汇清单】

Majesty /ˈmædʒisti/ *n.* 陛下（对于国王、女王、皇帝、皇后等的尊称）

Norwegian /nɔːˈwiːdʒən/ *adj.* 挪威的，挪威人的

Excellency /ˈeksələnsi/ *n.* 阁下（大使主教总督等职位高的人的尊称）

gratitude /ˈɡrætitjuːd/ *n.* 感激，感恩

laureate /ˈlɔːriit/ *n.* 桂冠诗人；获得荣誉者

reminder /ri'maində/ *n.* 提醒者，助人记忆的事物

Anwar Sadat /'ænwɔː sə'dæt/ 安瓦尔·萨达特（1918—1981，埃及前总统，对收复埃及全部领土、推动中东和平进程做出杰出贡献，于 1981 年 10 月 6 日被极端势力组织分子刺杀身亡）

Yitzak Rabin /i'zæk 'raːbiːn/ 伊扎克·拉宾（1922—1995，以色列军事家和政治领袖，曾出任总理，为中东和平进程取得突破性进展做出杰出贡献，于 1995 年 11 月 4 日被以色列极右势力所暗杀）

submarine /ˌsʌbmə'riːn/ *n.* 潜水艇

fervently /'fəːvəntli/ *adv.* 热心地，热烈地

commander-in-chief /kə'maːndə-in-tʃiːf/ *n.* 总司令，指挥官

sobering /'səubəriŋ/ *adj.* 使清醒的，使冷静的

superpower /ˌsjuːpə'pauə/ *n.* 超级大国，极有力量和影响力的国家（尤指在一国际权力集团中控制着其盟国或附属国的核大国）

unprecedented /ʌn'presidəntid/ *adj.* 史无前例的，空前的

armament /'aːməmənt/ *n.* （常用复数）（一国的）武装力量，军队，武装，军备

millennium /mi'leniəm/ *n.* 一千年（的期间）；太平盛世，黄金时代

plethora /'pleθərə/ *n.* 太多，过多，过剩

overwhelming /ˌəuvə'welmiŋ/ *adj.* 压倒性的，势不可挡的

casualty /'kæʒjuəlti/ *n.* 伤亡（人数），伤亡人员，死难者

civilian /si'viljən/ *n.* 平民，老百姓（与军警相对而言）

appalling /ə'pɔːliŋ/ *adj.* 令人毛骨悚然的，令人震惊的

invulnerable /in'vʌlnərəbl/ *adj.* 不易受伤的，刀枪不入的，无懈可击的

alliance /ə'laiəns/ *n.* 同盟，联盟

consensus /kən'sensəs/ *n.* 大多数人的意见；一致同意（尤指意见的一致）

preventive /pri'ventiv/ *adj.* 预防的，防止的

catastrophic /ˌkætə'strɔfik/ *adj.* 灾难性的，毁灭性的

premise /'premis/ *n.* 假定,(逻辑)前提
maintenance /'meintinəns/ *n.* 保持,维持
sphere /sfiə/ *n.* 范围,区域,领域

 参考译文【Suggested Translation】

吉米·卡特的诺贝尔和平奖受奖演说(一)

敬的国王夫妇、挪威诺贝尔和平奖委员会委员、大使阁下、女士们、先生们:

　　我怀着一种深挚的感激之情接受这一奖项。我要感谢我的妻子罗莎琳、我在卡特中心的同事们和许多其他继续寻求终结全世界暴力和苦难的人们。

　　大多数诺贝尔和平奖获得者可以安全地从事我们的工作,可是也有一些人在工作中表现出巨大的个人勇气。最为清楚地提醒我们缔造和平的危险的是我的两个朋友——安瓦尔·萨达特和伊扎克·拉宾,他们为中东的和平事业献出了自己的生命。

　　和这两位英雄一样,我首先选定的职业是在军队做一名潜水艇军官。我的战友和我认识到假如战争强加于我们,我们必须准备战斗,为捍卫祖国及其原则而献出我们的生命。与此同时,我们总在热诚地祈祷,我们的准备可以确保战争不会爆发。

　　后来,作为总统和武装部队的总司令,我承担着在冷战高峰时期世界两个超级大国相互敌视状态下维护全球稳定的重大责任。

　　自从我离开白宫以来,世界已经发生了巨大变化。现在世界上仅剩下一个超级大国,其拥有史无前例的军事和经济实力。美国来年的军事预算将超过位居其后的 15 国的总和,而且美军驻扎在全世界许许多多的国家。

　　但是,我们并未进入一个和平的新千年。在许多方面,现在的世界反而是一个更加危险的地方。旅行和通讯的极大便利并未带来同样的理解和相互尊重。世界上依然有很多内战,绝大部分内战的死难者是那些手无寸铁而又无力自卫的平民。而新

近发生的骇人听闻的恐怖主义行动提醒我们，没有一个国家能够幸免，甚至是超级大国。

显然，全球性的挑战必须以强调和平的重要性、和他国和睦相处与结成稳固的联盟和国际共识的手段来应对。尽管联合国并不完美，但是无疑通过它可以最好地应对这种挑战。

我们必须牢记，今天的地球上至少有 8 个拥有核武器的国家，其中的 3 个正在充满国际紧张局势的地区威胁着它们的邻国。对于强国来讲，采取先发制人的战争原则将会树立具有灾难性后果的先例。

假如我们接受联合国是最好的维护和平的途径这一前提，那么联合国安理会经过审慎考虑后的决议就必须得以贯彻执行。历史一再证明，其他的选择将带来难以掌控的暴力并扩大敌对的范围。（未完待续）◈

◉ A little knowledge is a dangerous thing.（一知半解，自欺欺人。）

◉ A good book is the best of friends, the same today and forever.（一本好书，相伴一生。）

◉ He who does not advance loses ground.（逆水行舟，不进则退。）

◉ When in Rome, do as the Romans do.（入国问禁，入乡随俗。）

Jimmy Carter's Nobel Lecture（Ⅱ）

I am not here as a public offcial, but as a citizen of a troubled world who finds hope in a growing consensus that the generally accepted goals of society are peace, freedom, human rights, environmental quality, the alleviation of suffering, and the rule of law.

During the past decades, the international community, usually under the auspices of the United Nations, has struggled to negotiate global standards that can help us achieve these essential goals. They include: the abolition of land mines and chemical weapons; an end to the testing, proliferation, and further deployment of nuclear warheads; constraints on global warming; prohibition of the death penalty, at least for children; and an international crimial court to deter and to punish war crimes and genocide. Those agreements already adopted must be fully implemented, and others should be pursued aggressively.

Despite theological differences, all great religions share common commitments that define our ideal secular relationships. I am convinced that Christians, Muslims, Buddhists, Hindus, Jews, and others can embrace each other in a common effort to alleviate human suffering and to espouse peace.

At the beginning of this new millennium I was asked to discuss, here in Oslo, the greatest challenge that the world faces. Among all the possible choices, I decided that the most serious and universal problem is the growing chasm between the richest and poorest people on earth. Citizens of the ten wealthiest countries are now seventy-five times richer than those who live in the ten poorest ones, and the separation is increasing every year, not only between nations but also within them. The results of this disparity are root causes of most of the world's unresolved problems, including starvation, illitaracy, environmental degradation, violent conflict, and unnecessary illnesses that range from Guinea worm to HIV/ AIDS. But tragically, in the industrialized world there is a terrible absence of understanding or concern about those who are enduring lives of despair and hopelessness. We have not yet made the commitment to share with others an appreciable part of our excessive wealth. This is a potentially rewarding burden that we should all be willing to assume.

Ladies and gentlemen,

War may sometimes be a necessary evil. But no matter how necessary, it is always an evil, never a good. We will not learn how to live together in peace by killing each other's children. The bond of our common humanity is stronger than the divisiveness of our fears and prejudices. God gives us the capacity for choice. We can choose to alleviate suffering.

We can choose to work together for peace. We can make these changes — and we must. Thank you. ✻

# Vocabulary List 【词汇清单】

alleviation /əˌliːviˈeiʃən/ *n.* （苦痛的）减轻，缓和

auspice /ˈɔːspis/ *n.* 吉兆；（复数）保护，赞助，主办

abolition /ˌæbəuˈliʃən/ *n.* 废除，废止，消除

proliferation /prəuˌlifəˈreiʃən/ *n.* 扩散，增加，激增

constraint /kənˈstreint/ *n.* 限制，约束，制约

genocide /ˈdʒenəsaid/ *n.* 种族灭绝（的行动计划）；灭绝种族的屠杀

implement /ˈimplimənt/ *v.* 执行，完成（任务等）；履行（诺言、契约等）

aggressively /əˈgresivli/ *adv.* 积极地，进取地

commitment /kəˈmitmənt/ *n.* 许诺，承诺，承担（义务）

Chrisitian /ˈkristʃən/ *n.* 基督教徒

Muslim /ˈmuslim/ *n.* 回教徒，伊斯兰教徒

Buddhist /ˈbudist/ *n.* 佛教徒

Hindu /ˈhinˈduː/ *n.* 印度教教徒（或信仰者）

Jew /dʒuː/ *n.* 犹太教徒

espouse /isˈpauz/ *v.* （对事业、主义等）信奉，拥护，支持，提倡

Oslo /ˈɔzləu/ 奥斯陆（挪威首都）

chasm /ˈkæzəm/ *n.* 深沟，裂缝

disparity /disˈpæriti/ *n.* 差异，差别，悬殊

unresolved /ˈʌnriˈzɔlvd/ *adj.* 未解决的；未解答的，未弄清的

starvation /staːˈveiʃən/ *n.* 饥饿，饿死

illiteracy /iˈlitərəsi/ *n.* 文盲，未受教育，不能读或写

degradation /ˌdegrəˈdeiʃən/ *n.* 恶化；降级，退化

Guinea worm：＜动物＞龙线虫（一种寄生虫）

HIV：（＝Human Immunodeficiency Virus）人体免疫缺损病毒，艾滋病病毒

AIDS：（= Acquired Immune Deficiency Syndrome）艾滋病，获得
  性免疫缺损综合症
appreciable /əˈpriːʃəbl/ *adj.* 可估计的，少许的
prejudice /ˈpredʒudis/ *n.* 偏见，成见
divisiveness /diˈvaisivnis/ *n.* 分裂，分歧，不和

参考译文【Suggested Translation】

吉米·卡特的诺贝尔和平奖受奖演说（二）

我并不是作为一名政府官员，而是作为一个动乱世界的公民来到这里，并在日益增长的共识中发现了希望，即全社会普遍接受的目标是和平、自由、人权、环境质量、减轻痛苦和法治。

在过去的几十年当中，通常是在联合国的主持之下，国际社会竭力商议能够帮助我们实现这些基本目标的全球标准，包括：消除地雷和化学武器，终止试验、扩散和进一步部署核弹头，控制全球变暖，废除死刑、至少是针对儿童的死刑，建立阻止和惩罚战争罪犯和种族屠杀的国际刑事法院。这些已被通过的决议必须得到彻底的实施，对于其他协议也应孜孜以求。

尽管存在神学上的分歧，但是所有伟大的宗教都拥有明确我们理想的世俗关系的共同承诺。我坚信，基督教徒、穆斯林、佛教徒、印度教徒、犹太教徒和其他教派能够在减轻人类苦难和拥护和平的共同努力中相互拥抱。

在新千年伊始，我曾被要求在奥斯陆这里讨论世界所面临的最大挑战。在所有可能的选择中，我认为最严重和最普遍的问题是地球上最富有的人和最贫穷的人之间日益增长的鸿沟。现在，最富有的 10 个国家的公民要比最贫困的 10 个国家的公民富 75 倍，这种差别每年都在加大，不仅在国家之间，而且在一国的富人和穷人之间。这种差距是导致世界上大多数未解决问题的根源，包括饥饿、文盲、环境恶化、暴力冲突和从龙线虫病到艾滋病的一系列原可避免的疾病。而悲惨的是，工业化国家对

那些正在遭受绝望和痛苦的人们却极不理解和关心。我们并未做出将我们多余财富的一部分与他人分享的承诺，而这却是一个我们所有人都应该承担的具有巨大回报的责任。

女士们，先生们：

有时候，战争也许是一个必要的恶魔。但是，不管多么必要，它终究永远是一个恶魔，而绝非福音。我们不可能通过杀戮对方的孩子而学会怎样和平地一起生活。我们共同的人性联结远远大于我们的恐惧和偏见造成的分歧。上帝给予我们选择的能力。我们能够选择减轻痛苦！我们能够选择一道为和平而工作！我们能够做出这些改变——我们必须这样做！谢谢大家。

◆

● God helps those who help themselves. （自助者天助。）

● Adversity leads to prosperity. （穷则思变。）

● We can't judge a person by what he says but by what he does. （判断一人，不听其言而要看其行。）

● Fortune favors those who use their judgement. （机遇偏爱善断之人。）

A Visit to an American Court[*]

In America, courtroom proceedings are generally open to the public and can, within strict guidelines, be reported on in newspapers and on radio and television. We use the word "allegation" and its verb form "allege" to indicate that charges brought against a person have not been proven. Cameras are also generally barred from courtrooms to protect the identities of the jurors, unless special permission is given by the judge. A jury, by the way, consists of from six to twelve ordinary citizens who are chosen by lottery to hear a case and decide, under instructions from the judge, on

---

* 作者罗伯特·艾博(Robert Abel),生平不详。"情理道理,明辨法理;谁是谁非,法断是非"。作为社会关系的调整器,法律在当今社会的作用日益显著和加强。当然,中西的法律制度在诸多方面迥然不同。在美国的法庭上,法官既不对案件的事实认定负责,也不对适用法律负责,而是由陪审团来认定案件事实并判定被告人是否有罪……

whether the persons being tried are guilty or innocent. In some cases which attract widespread public interest, permission is given to televise the proceedings if and only if the television cameras never photograph the members of the jury.

An exception to the rule of open proceedings are the proceedings of a Grand Jury. Grand Jury proceedings are always secret. In this instance, a jury is convened not to judge a defendant guilty or not guilty but to decide if sufficient evidence is on hand to bring charges against someone and begin a public trial. The secrecy of the grand jury proceedings is considered necessary to protect the integrity of the testimony and the evidence which may be brought forward later in a public trial. The secrecy prevents any future jury members from having formed an opinion about the case before the facts are known; and it protects the reputations of people who may have been wrongfully or unnecessarily accused of a crime. The fundamental rule of American legal practice is that a person accused of a crime is innocent until proven guilty. The people accusing or prosecuting the defendant must prove through facts and testimony that the person is guilty "beyond a reasonable doubt." ✳

 **Vocabulary List 【词汇清单】**

proceeding /prə'siːdiŋ/ *n.* （复数）诉讼程序

guideline /'gaidlain/ *n.* （常用复数）准则，指导方针

allegation /ˌæli'geiʃən/ *n.* ＜法律＞（尤指有待证实的）指控，（提不出证据的）辩解

charge /tʃaːdʒ/ *n.* 指控，控告，控诉

bar /baː/ *v.* （用法律手段）阻止或禁止

juror /'dʒuərə/ *n.* ＜法律＞陪审员

permission /pəˈmiʃən/ *n.* 允许,许可,准许

jury /ˈdʒuəri/ *n.* ＜法律＞陪审团(尤指受法律的传唤,在宣誓后,就提交给法院的案子予以听证并给出裁定的团体)

lottery /ˈlɔtəri/ *n.* 抽签(法)

convene /kənˈviːn/ *v.* 召集,集合,集会

integrity /inˈtegriti/ *n.* 完整,完全

testimony /ˈtestiməni/ *n.* 证言,口供,证据

wrongfully /ˈrɔŋfuli/ *adv.* 犯法地,非法地违法地

accuse /əˈkjuːz/ *v.* 指控,控告,控诉(of)

prosecute /ˈprɔsikjuːt/ *v.* 对…提起公诉,告发,检举

 参考译文【Suggested Translation】

到美国法庭看一看

在美国,法庭的诉讼程序一般是公之于众的,并且依照严格的规定,可以让报纸、广播和电视等传媒进行报道。我们使用 allegation"无充分证据的指控"一词(其动词形式是 allege)表明对某人的指控尚未得到证实。除非获取法官的特别许可,法庭上一般禁止摄影拍照以保护陪审员的身份。让我顺便解释一下陪审团:一个陪审团通常由 6 名至 12 名普通公民组成。这些成员用抽签法选定,到法庭听讼,并在法官的指导下决定被指控的人有罪还是无罪。一些能吸引广大公众兴趣的案子,准许用电视播放整个过程,但绝对不能将电视镜头瞄向陪审团的成员。

大陪审团的诉讼程序并不遵循公开诉讼程序的规定,大陪审团的诉讼程序总是保密的。在这种情形中,一个陪审团召集起来并非去判断一位被指控的人有罪还是无罪,而是决定是否已收集到充足的证据来指控某人并着手准备公开审讯。大陪审团的诉讼程序的保密性对保证证词和证据的完整性是必要的,因为证词和证据在日后的公开审判中会公之于众。保守秘密能使日后的陪审员不致在事实水落石出前就对案件形成自己的意见,也能保护那些遭到错误指控或无端指控的人的声誉。美国

法律最基本的原则是受到犯罪指控的人在最后被证实为有罪之前是无罪的。控告或起诉被告的人必须提供充足的事实和证词证明被告"不容置疑"地有罪。◆

◉Every minute counts.（分秒必争。）

◉Tit for tat is fair play.（人不犯我，我不犯人；人若犯我，我必犯人。）

◉Never say die.（永不言败。）

◉Fear always springs from ignorance.（恐惧源于无知。）

The Man and the Opportunity*

The lack of opportunity is ever the excuse of a weak, vacillating mind. Opportunities! Every life is full of them.

Every lesson in school or college is an opportunity. Every examination is a chance in life. Every business transaction is

---

* 作者奥里森·斯维特·马登（Orison Swett Marden，1848—1924），美国家喻户晓的成功学励志大师，美国的《成功》杂志创办人。他出生于美国新罕布什尔州的桑顿乔森林地区一块贫瘠的土地上，3 岁丧母，7 岁时父亲也去世了。为了生存，小小年纪的他就给人打工，受尽了苦难的折磨。正是有了这些经历，马登才决心要通过自己的奋斗摆脱贫困，最终他成功了。后来他总结出成功的经验之一就是：贫穷是我们努力奋斗最有利的出发点，贫穷是最大的财富。马登一生写了大量鼓舞人心的著作，包括《一生的资本》、《思考与成功》、《伟大的励志书》、《成功的品质》、《高贵的个性》等等，"内容都是激励兴奋年轻人的文字，为文鞭辟入理，剀切详明，令人百读不厌"（林语堂语），在整个世界广为传诵，影响了一代又一代渴望奋斗和成功的年轻人。

an opportunity — an opportunity to be polite, an opportunity to be manly, an opportunity to be honest, an opportunity to make friends. Every proof of confidence in you is a great opportunity. Every responsibility thrust upon your strength and your honor is priceless. Existence is the privilege of effort, and when that privilege is met like a man, opportunities to succeed along the line of your aptitude will come faster than you can use them.

Young men and women, why do you stand here all the day idle? Was the land all occupied before you were born? Has the earth ceased to yield its increase? Are the seats all taken? The positions all filled? The chances all gone? Are the resources of your country fully developed? Are the secrets of nature all mastered? Is there no way in which you can utilize these passing moments to improve yourself or benefit another? Don't wait for your opportunity. Make it, make it as Napoleon made his in a hundred "impossible" situations. Make it, as all leaders of men, in war and in peace, have made their chances of success. Make it, as every man must, who would accomplish anything worth the effort. Golden opportunities are nothing to laziness, but industry makes the commonest chances golden. ✻

Vocabulary List 【词汇清单】

vacillating /ˈvæsileitiŋ/ *adj.* 动摇的，犹豫不决的

transaction /trænˈzækʃən/ *n.* 交易；事务，事项

proof /pruːf/ *n.* 试验，考验，测验

priceless /ˈpraislis/ *adj.* 无价的，贵重的，无法估价的

priviledge /ˈprivilidʒ/ *n.* （尤指某些个人、集团或阶层所享有的）特权；优惠，特殊的荣幸

aptitude /'æptitjuːd/ *n.* 才能,才干,天资
cease /siːs/ *v.* 结束,停止,终止
yield /jiːld/ *v.* 生产,产出(自然作物)
utilize /'juːtilaiz/ *v.* 使用,利用
industry /'indəstri/ *n.* 勤劳,勤奋,勤勉

 参考译文【Suggested Translation】

人 与 机 会

意 志脆弱优柔寡断的人,总是以缺乏机会作为借口。机会!在每个人的生活当中,无处不在!

　　学校里的每一节课都是一次机会。每一场考试都是人生的契机。每一次商务往来都是一次机会——一次礼貌待人的机会,一次果敢行事的机会,一次诚实守信的机会,一次广交朋友的机会。每一份对你的信任,对你都是一次莫大的机会。基于你的才干和声望而寄予你的每一份责任,都是无价的。生存是奋斗赋予的特权,而当你如男子汉一般邂逅那份殊荣时,一个个发挥你聪明才智、助你获取成功的机会便会接踵而至,令你应接不暇。

　　年轻人啊,为何你们整日裹足不前而虚掷光阴?难道在你们出生之前,每一寸土地都已被他人所占据?难道地球已不再繁衍生息?难道所有的席位都已另有归属?所有的职位都已人满为患?所有的机会都一去不返?难道你国内的资源都已开发殆尽?难道大自然的奥秘都已了如指掌?难道你无法抓住这些转瞬即逝的时机来改善自我或者造福他人?切莫株守机会。去创造它,正如拿破仑在无数次"绝"境中创造自己逢生的机会一样。去创造它,正如战争或者和平年代的领袖们创造他们取得胜利的机会那样。去创造它,人人必须如此,任何人都能获得应有的回报。对于懒惰来讲,天赐良机也会化为乌有;对于勤奋而言,即使是微不足道的机会,也会变得金光闪闪! ◆

The Daffodils[*]

I wander'd lonely as a cloud
That floats on high o'er vales and hills,
When all at once I saw a crowd,
A host, of golden daffodils;
Beside the lake, beneath the trees,

---

　　* 作者威廉·华兹华斯(William Wordsworth,1770—1850),英国浪漫主义诗歌的主要奠基人和魁首,也是莎士比亚和弥尔顿以后英国最著名的浪漫主义诗人,"湖畔派"的代表人物,1843 年被宫廷封为"桂冠诗人"。他曾说:"诗是从平静中回想的情绪发生的。"《水仙》是 1804 年诗人回忆两年前见到一片水仙花的情景而写下的一首诗。对于这首诗,华兹华斯本人曾说:"对于人,对于自然,对于人生,在静寂的冥想中,我常常在眼前看到几多伴着好感的悲伤和雅悦的情操的美丽幻影。"因而,这首诗既是一幅奇丽的风景画,绘出了水仙的迷人光彩和妩媚风姿,也写出由水仙形成的令人陶醉的美景给诗人孤寂的心灵带来的慰藉。诗中多用比喻和拟人手法描写水仙的景象,生动、形象、活泼、优美;其中又融入了诗人浓郁的情感,因而景中有情,景因情而有了活力。

Fluttering and dancing in the breeze.

Continuous as the stars that shine
And twinkle on the Milky Way,
They stretch'd in never-ending line
Along the margin of a bay：
Ten thousand saw I at a glance,
Tossing their heads in sprightly dance.

The waves beside them danced；but they
Out-did the sparkling waves in glee：
A poet could not but be gay,
In such a jocund company!
I gazed — and gazed — but little thought
What wealth the show to me had brought：

For oft, when on my couch I lie
In vacant or in pensive mood,
They flash upon that inward eye
Which is the bliss of solitude；
And then my heart with pleasure fills,
And dances with the daffodils. ✳

Vocabulary List 【词汇清单】

daffodil /ˈdæfədil/ *n.* 水仙花

float /fləut/ *v.* 浮动,飘流

o'er = over

vale /veil/ *n.* ＜古＞谷,山谷

a host of：大群,众多,许多

flutter /ˈflʌtə/ *v.* 迅速而无规则地挥动,飘动

breeze /briːz/ *n.* 和风,微风

twinkle /ˈtwiŋkl/ *v.* (星星等)闪烁,闪耀,闪光

the Milky Way：银河

stretch /stretʃ/ *v.* 拉伸,伸展,伸长

never-ending /ˈnevə-ˈendiŋ/ *adj.* 无止境的,不断的

margin /ˈmɑːdʒin/ *n.* (湖、池等的)边缘,边沿

bay /bei/ *n.* 湾,海湾

glance /glɑːns/ *n.* 一瞥,匆匆一看

toss /tɔs/ *v.* 摇荡,摇摆

sprightly /ˈspraitli/ *adj.* 轻快的,活泼的

out-do /autˈduː/ *v.* 超过,胜过

sparkling /ˈspɑːkliŋ/ *adj.* 闪烁的,闪闪发光的

glee /gliː/ *n.* 欢喜,高兴

gay /gei/ *adj.* 欢快的,轻松的

jocund /ˈdʒɔkənd/ *adj.* 欢乐的,愉快的

company /ˈkʌmpəni/ *n.* 陪伴,陪同

gaze /geiz/ *v.* 注视,凝视

oft /ɔːft/ *adv.* <诗歌用语>经常(相当于 often)

couch /kautʃ/ *n.* <文学>床榻,睡椅

vacant /ˈveikənt/ *adj.* 头脑空虚的,神情茫然的

pensive /ˈpensiv/ *adj.* 沉思的,深思的

flash /flæʃ/ *v.* 闪光,闪现

inward /ˈinwəd/ *adj.* 内在的,内心的

bliss /blis/ *n.* 福佑,天赐之福

solitude /ˈsɔlitjuːd/ *n.* 孤独,孤单

 **参考译文【Suggested Translation】**

水 仙

我孤独地漫游,像一朵云
在山丘和谷地上飘荡,

忽然间我看见一群
金色的水仙花迎春开放，
在树荫下，在湖水边，
迎着微风起舞翩翩。

连绵不绝，如繁星灿烂，
在银河里闪闪发光，
它们沿着湖湾的边缘
延伸成无穷无尽的一行；
我一眼看见了一万朵，
在欢舞之中起伏颠簸。

粼粼波光也在跳着舞，
水仙的欢欣却胜过水波；
与这样快活的伴侣为伍，
诗人怎能不满心欢乐！
我久久凝望，却想像不到
这奇景赋予我多少财宝，——

每当我躺在床上不眠，
或心神空茫，或默默沉思，
它们常在心灵中闪现，
那是孤独之中的福祉；
于是我的心便涨满幸福，
和水仙一同翩翩起舞。◆

（飞白 译）

Man Will Prevail*

I feel that this award was not made to me as a man, but to my work — a life's work in the agony and sweat of the human spirit, not for glory and least of all for profit, but to create out of the materials of the human spirit something which did not exist before. So this award is only mine in trust.

---

　　* 作者威廉·福克纳(William Faulkner,1897—1962),美国现代以描写南方的历史、风俗、人情为主要题材的"南方文学"流派的代表性作家,"因为他对当代美国小说做出了强有力的和艺术上无与伦比的贡献",1949 年荣获诺贝尔文学奖。此外,1951 年他又获得全国图书奖,1955、1963 年两次荣获普利策奖,其代表作有《我弥留之际》、《八月之光》、《寓言》、《老人》等。他后期最重要的作品是《村子》、《小镇》、《大宅》,这三部小说被称作"斯诺普斯三部曲"。福克纳在西方文坛被称为"现代的经典作家",其作品被认为表现了"时代的精神",题材广阔,规模宏大,人物众多,描写了两百年来美国南方社会的变迁和各种人物地位的浮沉及其精神面貌的变化。本文是他在接受诺贝尔文学奖时发表的一篇简短而重要的演说,表达了对于人类未来的坚定信念。

It will not be diffcult to find a dedication for the money part of it commensurate with the purpose and significance of its origin. But I would like to do the same with the acclaim too, by using this moment as a pinnacle from which I might be listened to by the young men and women already dedicated to the same anguish and travail, among whom is already that one who will some day stand here where I am standing.

Our tragedy today is a general and universal physical fear so long sustained by now that we can even bear it. There are no longer problems of the spirit. There is only the question: When will I be blown up? Because of this, the young man or woman writing today has forgotten the problems of the human heart in conflict with itself which alone can make good writing because only that is worth writing about, worth the agony and the sweat.

He must learn them again. He must teach himself that the basest of all things is to be afraid; and, teaching himself that, forget it forever, leaving no room in his workshop for anything but the old verities and truths of the heart, the old universal truths lacking which any story is ephemeral and doomed — love and honor and pity and pride and compassion and sacrifice. Until he does so, he labors under a curse. He writes not of love but of lust, of defeats in which nobody loses anything of value, of victories whthout hope and, worst of all, without pity or compassion. His griefs grieve on no universal bones, leaving no scars. He writes not of the heart but of the glands.

Until he relearns these things, he will write as though he stood among and watched the end of man. I decline to accept the end of man. It is easy enough to say that man is immortal simply because he will endure: that when the last ding-dong of doom has clanged and faded from the last worthless rock hanging tideless in the last red and dying evening, that even then there will still be one more sound: that of his puny inexhaustible voice, still talking. I refuse to accept this. I believe that man will not merely endure: he will prevail. He is immortal, not because he alone among creatures has an inexhaustible voice, but because he has a soul, a spirit capable of compassion and sacrfice and endurance. The poet's, the writer's duty is to write about these things. It is his privilege to help man endure by lifting his heart, by reminding him of the courage and honor and hope and pride and compassion and pity and sacrifice which have been the glory of his past. The poet's voice need not merely be the record of man, it can be one of the props, the pillars to help him endure and prevail. ❋

Vocabulary List 【词汇清单】

dedication /ˌdediˈkeiʃən/ *n.* 奉献,供奉

commensurate /kəˈmenʃərit/ *adj.* 相称的,相当的,适当的

significance /sigˈnifikəns/ *n.* 意义,旨趣,重要性

acclaim /əˈkleim/ *n.* 鼓掌欢迎,欢呼,喝采;<引申>得到的荣誉

pinnacle /ˈpinəkl/ *n.* 顶点,顶峰,极点

anguish /ˈæŋgwiʃ/ *n.* 极度痛苦,苦恼,悲痛

travail /ˈtræveil/ *n.* 艰苦(的工作),辛苦,劳苦

sustain /səsˈtein/ *v.* 忍耐,忍受,承受

blow up: (使)爆炸,炸毁,毁掉

verity /ˈveriti/ *n.* 真理,真实的事物(尤指持久的真理)

ephemeral /iˈfemərəl/ *adj.* (生命)短暂的,瞬息的,昙花一现的

doom /duːm/ *v.* 命定,注定(尤指厄运或劫数不可避免的破坏

　　或毁灭）

compassion /kəmˈpæʃən/ *n.* 同情,怜悯

sacrifice /ˈsækrifais/ *n.* 牺牲,献身

under a curse：被诅咒,被咒骂(labor under a curse 意思是"劳动不会有成果,徒劳无功")

lust /lʌst/ *n.* 欲望,贪欲;强烈的性欲

grief /griːf/ *n.* 悲痛,悲伤,不幸(下文的 grieve 是其动词形式)

scar /skaː/ *n.* 伤疤,伤痕,疤痕

immortal /iˈmɔːtl/ *adj.* 不朽的,永恒的,流芳百世的

ding-dong /ˈdiŋˈdɔŋ/ *n.* ＜拟声词＞丁当(声),丁冬(声)(ding-dong of doom 意思是"丧钟声")

clang /klæŋ/ *v.* 丁当响,铿锵作响

tideless /ˈtaidlis/ *adj.* 无潮的,平潮的

puny /ˈpjuːni/ *adj.* 小的,弱的,细微的

inexhaustible /ˌinigˈzɔːstəbl/ *adj.* 无穷无尽的,取之不尽、用之不竭的

prop /prɔp/ *n.* 支柱,支持物,后盾

pillar /ˈpilə/ *n.* 柱子,柱形物,栋梁

prevail /priˈveil/ *v.* 获胜,优胜,成功

参考译文【Suggested Translation】

人 类 必 胜

　　我觉得这不是对于我个人的奖励,而是对于我的事业的奖励——这是一项在人类精神备受折磨和煎熬的过程中进行的毕生事业,既不为名,更不为利,而是要以人类精神为原材料而创造出前所未有的东西。因而,这一奖励只是交由我代管而已。对于其中的奖金部分,我将寻找符合这种奖励创设的宗旨和意义的方式将其捐献,这是不难做到的。而对于我所得到的荣誉,我也想作出同样的处理,那就是利用这个被视为成就顶峰的时刻,让已经献身于同一种痛苦而艰巨事业的青年男女作

家们听我讲几句话。在他们中间，有人迟早会站在我此刻所站立的地方。

我们当今的悲剧是一种普遍性的、全球性的生理恐惧。这种恐惧由来已久，以至于到现在我们竟能忍受下去。精神上的问题已不再存在。人们所关切的问题只是：我们何时会被炸得粉身碎骨？正是如此，今天从事写作的青年男女们已经忘了人类的内心冲突问题。然而，只有写这类问题才能写出好作品，因为只有这类问题才值得去写，才值得作家们为其呕心沥血。

作家必须重新认识这些问题。他必须使自己明白，所有事物中最可鄙的事情莫过于恐惧；而且，他必须在明白这个道理之后永远忘掉恐惧。在他的工作室里，只允许有心灵中亘古不变的真理——爱、荣誉、怜悯、自尊、同情和奉献，这些都是古老而普遍的真理，假如缺少这些，任何故事都只能昙花一现，注定要泯灭。除非他这样做，否则他的劳动就如同置于魔咒的掌控之下，徒劳无益：他所写的就不会是爱，而是欲；他所写的失败是没有人失去有价值的东西的失败；他所写的胜利是没有希望、甚至于没有怜悯和同情的胜利；他所写的悲哀不是普遍的悲哀，不会留下切肤之痛；他写的不是人的心灵，而人的分泌组织——腺。

除非他重新认识这些事物，否则他写作时就只不过像站在人群之中瞧着人类走向末日。我拒绝接受人类会有末日的观点。之所以说人类不朽，只不过因为人类能够永久延续下去，只不过因为即使世界末日的最后的丧钟丁当敲响了，并从夕阳残照、海潮退尽的最后一块微不足道的礁石上消逝了，甚至那时还会听到一个声音，那就是人类微弱无力却不绝如缕的话语声，说这样的话太容易了。我不接受这样的说法。我相信人类不仅仅会延续下去，而且必胜。人类之不朽，不是因为在生物界唯独人有无穷无尽的话语，而是因为人有灵魂，有同情心，有牺牲和忍耐精神。而写出这些正是诗人和作家的职责。他的殊荣就是使人类的心灵得到升华，使人类回忆起曾经引以为荣的勇气、荣誉、希望、自尊、同情、怜悯和牺牲精神，从而帮助人类继续生存。诗人的声音不只是人类的记录，它还能成为帮助人类持久生存并且走向胜利的支柱和栋梁。◆

An October Sunrise[*]

I was up the next morning before the October sunrise, and away through the wild and the woodland. The rising of the sun was noble in the cold and warmth of it; peeping down the spread of light, he raised his shoulder heavily over the edge of Gray Mountain and wavering length of upland. Beneath his gaze the dew-fogs dipped and crept to the hollow places, then stole away in line and column, holding skirts and clinging subtly at the sheltering corners where rock hung over grassland, while the brave lines of the hills came

---

  * 作者理查德·D·布莱克默（Richard D. Blackmore，1825—1900），英国著名作家，曾出版几本诗集和小说，其中最有名的小说是《洛娜·杜恩》（Lorna Doone）。本文中，作者为我们展现了一幅清丽爽约的画面：乍寒的清晨、辽远的旷野、层叠的丛林、辉煌的日出、薄薄的晨曦、朦胧的山岗、连绵的高地、湿润的雾气、低低的洼地、横空的悬岩、端庄的峰峦、威严的山谷、蜷伏的洞穴、美丽的花朵、嫩嫩的蓓蕾、跳跃的鸟雀……"万物都将踊跃升腾，在造物主慈爱的光芒中生辉，因为太阳已经升起。"

forth, one beyond other gliding.

The woods arose in folds, like drapery of awakened mountains, stately with a depth of awe, and memory of the tempests. Autumn's mellow hand was upon them, as they owned already, touched with gold and red and olive, and their joy towards the sun was less to a bridegroom than a father.

Yet before the floating impress of the woods could clear itself, suddenly the gladsome light leaped over hill and valley, casting amber, blue, and purple, and a tint of rich red rose, according to the scene they lit on, and the curtain flung around; yet all like a dispelling fear and the cloven hoof of darkness, all on the wings of hope advancing, and proclaiming, "God is here!" Then life and joy sprang reassured from every crouching hollow; every flower and bud and bird had a fluttering sense of them, and all the flashing of God's gaze merged into soft beneficence.

So, perhaps, shall break upon us that eternal morning, when crag and chasm shall be no more, neither hill and valley, nor great unvintaged ocean; when glory shall not scare happiness, neither happiness envy glory; but all things shall arise, and shine in the light of the Father's countenance, because itself is risen. ✳

Ⓐ Vocabulary List 【词汇清单】

woodland /'wudlənd/ *n.* 林地,树林,森林

peep /piːp/ *v.* 初现,慢慢出现,隐约显现

waver /'weivə/ *v.* 波动,起伏

creep /kriːp/ *v.* 爬行,匍匐(而行),爬动

subtly /'sʌtli/ *adv.* 微细地,隐约地

drapery /'dreipəri/ *n.* (供装饰用的)织物,帷帐,帷帘

awe /ɔ:/ *n.* 敬畏，畏惧

tempest /'tempist/ *n.* 大风暴，暴风雨

mellow /'meləu/ *adj.* （水果）甜熟的；（酒）醇香的；（颜色）柔美的，（光线）柔和的，（声音）圆润的

gladsome /'glædsəm/ *adj.* 可喜的，令人高兴的，使人喜悦的

amber /'æmbə/ *adj.* 琥珀（的），琥珀（色）的

tint /tint/ *n.* 淡色，浅色；色彩，色泽

dispel /dis'pel/ *v.* 驱散，驱逐；（使）消除，（使）消散

cloven /'kləuvn/ *adj.* 分开的，裂开的

proclaim /prə'kleim/ *v.* 正式宣布，宣告，公布

crouch /'krautʃ/ *v.* 蜷缩，蹲伏，弯身

flutter /'flʌtə/ *v.* （轻微地）抖动，颤动，摆动

beneficence /bi'nevələns/ *v.* 慈善，捐赠

crag /kræg/ *n.* 危崖，峭壁

unvintaged /ʌn'vintidʒd/ *adj.* ＜古＞广阔的，浩瀚无边的

countenance /'kauntinəns/ *n.* 面容，面貌，脸色

 **参考译文【Suggested Translation】**

十 月 的 日 出

第二天凌晨，在十月的太阳升起之前，我已经起身，并穿过旷野和丛林。十月的清晨乍寒还暖，日出的景象是很壮观的。透过一片晨曦，朝日从朦胧的山岗和起伏连绵的高地边际，沉重地抬起肩头。在它的逼视下，蒙蒙的雾气向下沉降，落到洼地里去，接着化成一丝丝一缕缕，悄悄地飘去了，而在草地之上悬岩之下的那些隐蔽角落里，雾气却还在引裾徘徊，而群山的雄姿却在接二连三地涌现。

树木层层叠叠，宛若披在刚被唤醒的山峦的斗篷，端庄威严，唤起狂风暴雨的回忆。秋季的成熟的手已经在抚摸它们了，它们顺从秋季的到来，染上了金黄、丹红和橄榄绿。它们对朝日所怀的一片喜悦，像是奉献给一个新郎的，但更像是奉献给一位

尊长的。

　　然而，在树林的缥渺的印象逝去之前，突然那欢悦的晨光跃过峰峦和山谷；光线所及，把照到的景致和撒开的帷幕分别染成青色、紫色、琥珀色和富丽的红玫瑰色。而所有的一切都同样在驱散恐惧和黑暗的魔影；所有的一切都展开希望的翅膀，向前飞翔，并大声宣告"上帝来到这里！"于是生命和欢乐从每一个蜷伏的洞穴里信心十足地欣然跃出；一切花朵、蓓蕾和鸟雀都感到了生命和欢乐而抖动起来；上帝炯炯的目光全部融入温柔的恩泽。

　　也许，那永恒的晨光就会这样降临人间，那时不再有险崖沟壑，不再有峰峦山谷，也不再有浩瀚而无际的海洋；那时荣耀不会吓走幸福，幸福也不会忌妒荣耀；万物都将踊跃升腾，在造物主慈爱的光芒中生辉，因为太阳已经升起。◆

（周嘉栋 译）

●Time cures all things.（时间是医治一切创伤的良药。）

●Friends agree best at distance.（保持距离，友谊常青。）

●An ounce of prevention is worth a pound of cure.（预防为主，治疗为辅。）

●Lookers-on see more than players.（当局者迷，旁观者清。）

The Art of Living[*]

The art of living is to know when to hold fast and when to let go. For life is a paradox：It enjoins us to cling to its many gifts even while it ordains their eventual relinquishment. The rabbis of old put it this way："A man comes to this world with his fist clenched, but when he dies, his hand is open."

Surely we ought to hold fast to life, for it is wondrous, and full of a beauty that breaks through every pore of God's own earth. We know that this is so, but all too often we recognize this truth only in our backward glance when we re-

---

＊作者约翰·博因顿·普里斯特利（John Boynton Priestley, 1894—1984），英国著名小说家、剧作家和散文家，曾就读于英国剑桥三一学院（Trinity Hall），其代表作有小说《好伙伴》（The Good Companions）、《天使人行道》（Angel Pavement），剧本有《危险的角落》（Dangerous Corner）、《我曾到过那里》（I Have Been There Before）和《菩提树》（The Linden Tree）等，以具有喜剧意味的形式讲述社会各阶层的人生故事，进而展现英国广大地区的生活百态。

member what was and then suddenly realize that it is no more.

We remember a beauty that faded, a love that waned. But we remember with far greater pain that we did not see that beauty when it flowered, that we failed to respond with love when it was tendered.

A recent experience re-taught me this truth. I was hospitalized flollowing a severe heart attack and had been in intensive care for several days. It was not a pleasant place.

One morning, I had to have some additional tests. The required machines were located in a building at the opposite end of the hospital, so I had to be wheeled across the courtyard on a gurney.

As we emerged from our unit, the sunlight hit me. That's all there was to my experience. Just the light of the sun. And yet how beautiful it was — how warming, how sparking, how brilliant! I looked to see whether anyone else relished the sun's golden glow, but everyone was hurrying to and fro, most with eyes fixed on the ground. Then I remembered how often I, too, had been indifferent to the grandeur of each day, too preoccupied with petty and sometimes even mean concerns to respond from that experience is really as commonplace as was the experience itself: life's gifts are precious — but we are too heedless of them.

Here then is the first pole of life's paradoxical demands on us: Never too busy for the wonder and the awe of life. Be reverent before each dawning day. Embrace each hour. Seize each golden minute.

Hold fast to life ... but not so fast that you cannot let go. This is the second side of life's coin, the opposite pole of its paradox: we must accept our losses, and learn how to let go.

This is not an easy lesson to learn, especially when we are young and think that the world is ours to command, that whatever we desire with the full force of our passionate being can, nay, will, be ours. But then life moves along to confront us with realities, and slowly but surely this truth dawns upon us.

At every stage of life we sustain losses — and grow in the process. We begin our independent lives only when we emerge from the womb and lose its protective shelter. We enter a progression of schools, then we leave our mothers and fathers and our childhood homes. We get married and have children and then have to let them go. We confront the death of our parents and our spouses. We face the gradual or not so gradual waning of our strength. And ultimately, as the parable of the open and closed hand suggests, we must confront the inevitability of our own demise, losing ourselves as it were, all that we were or dreamed to be. ✳

 ## Vocabulary List 【词汇清单】

paradox /ˈpærədɔks/ *n.* 悖论,自相矛盾（下文的 paradoxical 是其形容词形式）

enjoin /inˈdʒɔin/ *v.* 吩咐,命令,嘱咐

cling to：牢牢抓住,坚持不放;怀念,依恋

ordain /ɔːˈdein/ *v.* 注定,规定（不容更改地预先安排）

relinquishment /riˈliŋkwiʃmənt/ *n.* 离开,放弃,抛却

rabbi /ˈræbai/ *n.* ＜犹太教＞拉比（意为"先生"、"夫子",系犹太人对师长和有学识者的尊称）

clench /klentʃ/ *v.* 紧攥在一起,紧握（拳头）

wondrous /ˈwʌndrəs/ *adj.* (= wonderful) 令人惊奇的,奇妙的,奇异的

pore /pɔː/ *n.* （岩石或其他物质的）孔隙，微孔

wane /wein/ *v.* 衰落，衰退，消逝

hospitalize /ˈhɔspitlaiz/ *v.* 入院治疗，使住院就医

gurney /ˈgəːni/ *n.* 盖尼式床，（医院内运送病人等用的）轮床

relish /ˈreliʃ/ *v.* 喜好，乐于，玩味

to and fro：来回地，往复地

grandeur /ˈgrændʒə/ *n.* 庄严，高尚，伟大

preoccupied /pri(ː)ˈɔkjupaid/ *adj.* 全神贯注的，出神的

commonplace /ˈkɔmənpleis/ *adj.* 平常的，平凡的，平淡无奇的

heedless /ˈhiːdlis/ *adj.* 掉以轻心的，漫不经心的

pole /pəul/ *n.* （南、北）极，极（点）；磁极，电极

reverent /ˈrevərənt/ *adj.* 恭敬的，虔诚的

passionate /ˈpæʃənit/ *adj.* 激情洋溢的，充满热情的

womb /wuːm/ *n.* ＜医＞子宫；孕育任何事物的场所

inevitability /inˌevitəˈbiliti/ *n.* 不可避免，无法规避，必然（性）

demise /diˈmaiz/ *n.* （尤指帝王）死亡，逝世

参考译文【Suggested Translation】

生 活 的 艺 术

生活的艺术是要知晓何时取得与何时放弃。因为生活自身便是一个矛盾：它一方面劝诫我们要珍惜它的诸多恩赐，同时最后又注定将其统统收回。在古时候，犹太教的教士们曾这样说过："一个人来到这个世界上的时候，他的手是紧握成拳的；但是当他离开这个世界的时候，他的手掌是张开的。"

当然，我们应该紧紧抓住生活，因为它奇妙无比，并且饱含渗透每一寸土地的美感。纵然我们明白这一点，可是往往只是在我们回首从前忆起往事，而后忽然发觉已经物是人非之时，才会对此颇有感触。

我们记得已经凋落的美，已经消褪的爱。可是，我们的回忆却满是痛苦：我们没有在美丽绽放之时看到它，没有在爱意缱绻

之时以爱去回应。

　　最近，我的一次经历让我再一次认识到这一真理。在一次严重的心脏病发作之后，我住进医院接受治疗，在特别护理区住了好几天。那可不是什么让人感到愉快的地方。

　　有一天早晨，我不得不再做一些检测，检测的器械在医院对面尽头的一幢大楼上，因此我不得不躺在轮床上让人推着从院子里经过。

　　当我们从病房里出来的时候，阳光照射在我身上。这便是我当时所感受到的一切。仅仅是太阳的光芒；可是那阳光多么美妙啊——那样温暖，那样耀眼，那样灿烂！我四下张望，想看看是否还有人在品味这金灿灿的阳光，可是每个人都是行色匆匆，大多数眼睛紧盯着地面。这时候，我回想起对于每一天的阳光我也是常常漠不关心，只关注琐碎甚至于毫无意义的小事，而忽视了对于司空见惯的经历做出反应；生活的馈赠是珍贵的——但是我们却忽略了它们。

　　那么，这就是生活对于我们相互矛盾的要求的一极：永远不要由于过度忙碌而忽视生活的奇妙和庄严。要对即将到来的每一天虔诚恭敬。拥抱每一个小时。抓住珍贵的每一分钟。

　　抓住生活……可是不要抓得太紧，以至于你无法放弃。这是生活如硬币似的另一面，也就是其矛盾的另一极：我们必须接受失去，并且学会放弃。

　　要学会这一课，并非易事，尤其是当我们年轻气盛之时，因为那时我们认为自己是世界的主宰，认为我们以充满激情的躯体中的力量去渴求的东西最终是我们的。可是，随之而来的生活将现实摆在我们面前，然后我们也将明白这一道理。

　　在人生的每个阶段，我们都会有所失去——并在此过程中成长。我们只有在离开母体并且失去其庇护之时才开始我们独立的生活。我们进入各级学校就读，然后我们离开了父母和幼时生活过的故乡。我们结婚生子，然后又放飞子女。我们要面对父母和配偶的离世。我们要面对我们自身或快或慢的衰弱。最后，就像张开和闭合的手一样，我们必须面对我们自己的死亡，失去原有的自我，失去我们所有的一切或者我们所梦想的一切。◆

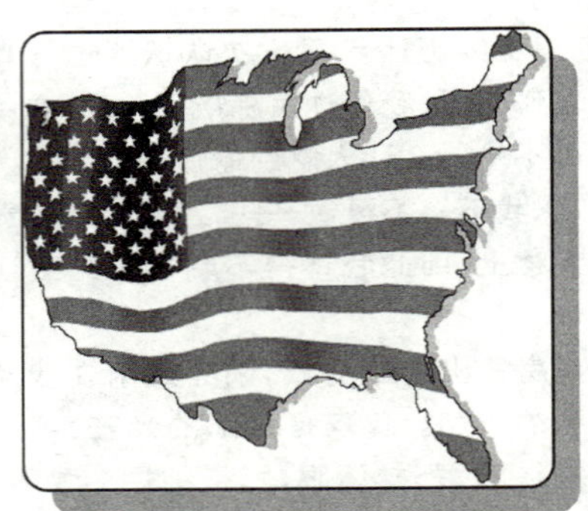

The American Character*

Most Americans have great vigor and enthusiasm. They prefer to discipline themselves rather than be disciplined by others. They pride themselves on their independence, their right to make up their own minds. They are prepared to take the initiative, even when there is a risk in doing

---

　　* 作者佚名。每个民族都有其独特的性格，人们常常谈及英国人的矜持、法国人的浪漫、日本女子的柔顺等等，同样，美国人的性格也有其明显特点。众所周知，美国的最早移民是来自英国的清教徒，他们为了逃避英政府的压迫而背井离乡，最后定居在北美大陆。他们认为自己是新时代的圣徒，肩负着神圣使命，要离开旧世界去开辟在美洲的人间乐土，一个新的以色列。清教徒（Puritan）一词原是他们的反对者为讽刺他们生造出来的，说他们自诩比别人圣洁、纯净。这个词的意思是"would-be purifier"，即"人间清洁工"。但是清教徒骄傲地接受了这个绰号。他们生活俭朴、严格自律，以此取悦并荣耀全能的上帝。这可以被视为美国人性格的发端和渊源。此后，随着社会变迁，他们逐渐形成了这样的性格特征：待人热情、开朗大方、易于接近、独立进取、讲求实际、格外看重成功的价值等等。

so. They have courage and do not give in easily. They will take any sort of job anywhere rather than be unemployed. They do not care to be looked after by the government. The average American changes his or her job nine or ten times during his or her working life.

Americans have a warmth and friendliness which is less superficial than many foreigners think. They are considered sentimental. When on ceremonial occasions they see a flag, or attend parades celebrating America's glorious past, tears may come to their eyes. Reunions with family and friends tend to be emotional, too. They like to dress correctly, even if "correctly" means flamboyantly. They love to boast, though often with tongue in cheek. They can laugh at themselves and their country, and they can be very self-critical, while remaining always intensely patriotic. They have a wide knowledge of everyday things, and a keen interest in their particular city and state. Foreigners sometimes complain, however, that they have little interest in or knowledge of the outside world.

The Americans have a passion for grandeur. Their skyscrapers, bridges and dams often have a splendor which matches in beauty and scale the country's natural wonders. Is the sole aim of most Americans to make money and possess luxuries which could be called excessive? The majority of Americans would certainly deny this, though most feel proud to amass wealth and possessions through hard work. In the USA, about 90% of the population is well enough off to expect a brighter future. The USA still has one of the highest standards of living in the world, although, at the present time, 10% are below what the Government considers to be the "poverty line." While these underprivileged people receive help from the Government, they have no high hopes for their future. It is from this "underclass," and those who take advantage of it, that most of the violence springs, which is one of the least pleasant aspects of American society. Americans are beginning to realize that this terrible problem of poverty is their problem and not just the Government's. It has been said that the individual American is generous, but that the American nation is hard.

The USA is reputed to be a classless society. There is certainly not much social snobbery or job snobbery. The manual worker is usually quite at ease in any company. This is partly explained by the fact that people of all income groups go together to the same schools. Americans are far more race-conscious than they are class-conscious. ✳

Vocabulary List【词汇清单】

vigor /'vigə/ *n.* 精力,活力,生命力

discipline /'disiplin/ *v.* 使守纪律,训导,管制

independence /ˌindi'pendəns/ *n.* 独立,自主,自立

initiative /i'niʃiətiv/ *n.* 主动,积极性,首创精神

superficial /ˌsjuːpə'fiʃəl/ *adj.* 表面的,肤浅的,浅薄的

sentimental /ˌsenti'mentl/ *adj.* 感伤的,多愁善感的

ceremonial /ˌseri'məunjəl/ *adj.* 典礼的,仪式的

parade /pə'reid/ *n.* 游行,游行队伍

glorious /'glɔːriəs/ *adj.* 光荣的,荣耀的

emotional /i'məuʃənl/ *adj.* 易动感情的,易激动的

flamboyantly /flæm'bɔiəntli/ *adv.* 过分华丽(艳丽)地,奢侈浮华地

intensely /in'tensli/ *adv.* 强烈地,极度地

patriotic /ˌpeitri'ɔtik/ *adj.* 爱国(主义)的,有爱国心的

skyscraper /ˈskaiˌskreipə/ *n.*　＜美＞摩天大楼

splendor /ˈsplendə/ *n.*　光彩,光辉;壮丽,壮观

sole /səul/ *adj.*　单独的,惟一的

excessive /ikˈsesiv/ *adj.*　过多的,过分的,过度的

amass /əˈmæs/ *v.*　（尤指财富）积累,积聚

underprivileged /ˌʌndəˈprivilidʒd/ *adj.*　（因贫穷、受歧视而）
　　被剥夺基本社会权益的

snobbery /ˈsnɔbəri/ *n.*　势利,势利性格（或行为等）

 ## 参考译文【Suggested Translation】

美国人的性格

大多数的美国人精力充沛,热情高涨。他们宁愿自律,而不愿受制于人。他们为能独立行事、为有权做出自己的决定而感到自豪。他们做事会采取主动,即使这样做要冒风险,也在所不惜。他们有勇气,不会轻易屈服。他们愿意到任何地方干任何工作,也不愿意失业。他们不想得到政府的照顾。普通美国人一生中换九到十次工作。

美国人热情友好,其友好程度要比许多外国人所想的更真实一些。人们认为美国人易动感情。在典礼上看到国旗,或者参加庆祝美国光荣历史的游行时,美国人可能会热泪盈眶。与家人团圆或与朋友相聚时,他们也会十分激动。他们喜欢穿着得体,即使"得体"无异于奢华炫耀。他们喜欢自吹自擂,尽管多数情况下只不过是说说而已。他们有时会嘲笑自己、嘲笑自己的国家,有时候甚至极为自责,然而他们始终有着强烈的爱国之心。他们对日常事情所知甚广,对自己所在的城市和州深为关切。然而,有时候外国人却抱怨说,美国人对外部世界漠不关心,一无所知。

美国人酷爱豪华的气派。他们的摩天大楼、桥梁和水坝往往气势壮观,与美国的自然奇观之壮美和恢宏相得益彰。赚钱和拥有称得上过多的奢侈品,是不是大多数美国人惟一的目标?

多数美国人肯定会予以否认，虽然他们对通过辛勤劳动积攒钱财引以为豪。在美国，90% 左右的人们生活富足，可以期盼更美好的未来。美国的生活水平世界上依然名列前茅，尽管现在还有 10% 左右的人处在政府认为的"贫困线"以下。这些生活水平低下的人们虽然得到政府的救助，但是他们对未来不抱多大希望。正是这个"社会下层阶级"以及利用这个阶层的人引发了社会上的大多数暴乱，使之成为美国社会中最令人不快的一面。美国人开始意识到，这个非常严重的问题是他们自身的问题，而不仅仅是政府的问题。有这样的说法：美国人作为个人是慷慨的，但美国作为一个民族则是吝啬的。

人们普遍认为，美国是个没有阶级的社会。的确，美国人对社会地位或不同工作没有什么势利眼。体力劳动者在任何场合通常都相当自在。收入档次不同的人上同一所学校，这个事实多少说明了这一点。与其说美国人有阶级意识，倒不如说他们有种族意识。◆

◉Let bygones be bygones. （过去的就让它过去吧；既往不咎。）

◉The first step is the only difficulty. （迈出第一步是最艰难的。）

◉Genius is nothing but labor and diligence. （天才不过是勤奋而已。）

◉Diamond cuts diamond. （强中自有强中手。）

The Pleasure of Reading[*]

All the wisdom of the ages, all the stories that have delighted mankind for centuries, are easily and cheaply available to all of us within the covers of books but we must know how to avail ourselves of this treasure and how to get the most from it. The most unfortunate people in the world are those who have never discovered how satisfying it is to read good books.

I am most interested in people, in them and finding out about them. Some of the most remarkable people I've met

---

* 作者佚名。"在今天这个时代,人的智力发展在越来越大的程度上取决于他是否善于在知识的浩瀚的海洋里辨明方向,是否善于利用知识的仓库——书籍。"(苏霍姆林斯基)"知识是使人类快乐的主要因素。"(罗素)而获取知识的主要途径就是读书。书读得越多,对人生百味便体会得愈浓,愈烈,愈切。很多时候,读书之乐,是一种知识传承,是一种思维享受,是一种情感升华。

existed only in a writer's imagination, then on the pages of his book, and then, again, in my imagination. I've found in books new friends, new societies, new words.

If I am interested in people, others are interested not so much in who as in how. Who in the books includes everybody from science fiction superman two hundred centuries in the future all the way back to the first figures in history. How covers everything from the ingenious explanations of Sherlock Holmes to the discoveries of science and ways of teaching manner to children.

Reading is pleasure of the mind, which means that it is a little like a sport: your eagerness and knowledge and quickness make you a good reader. Reading is fun, not because the writer is telling you something, but because it makes your mind work. Your own imagination works along with the author's or even goes beyond his. Your experience, compared with his, brings you to the same or different conclusions, and your ideas develop as you understand his.

Every book stands by itself, like a one-family house, but books in a library are like houses in a city. Although they are separate, together they all add up to something, they are connected with each other and with other cities. The same ideas, or related ones, turn up in different places; the human problems that repeat themselves in life repeat themselves in literature, but with different solutions according to different writings at different times. Books influence each other; they link the past, the present and the future and have their own generations, like families. Wherever you start reading you connect yourself with one of the families of ideas, and in the long run, you not only find out about the world and the people in it; you find out about yourself, too.

Reading can only be fun if you expect it to be. If you concentrate on books somebody tells you you "ought" to read, you probably won't have fun. But if you put down a book you don't like and try another till you find one that means something to you, and then relax with it, you will almost certainly have a good time — and if you become, as a result of reading, better, wiser, kinder, or more gentle, you won't have suffered during the process. ✳

 ## Vocabulary List【词汇清单】

available /əˈveiləbl/ *adj.* 可得到的，可达到的；便于使用的，便利的（to）

cover /ˈkʌvə/ *n.* （图书、杂志的）封皮，封面

avail oneself of：利用（尤指机会、提议等）

unfortunate /ʌnˈfɔːtʃənit/ *adj.* 不幸运的，时运不济的

ingenious /inˈdʒiːnjəs/ *adj.* 机灵的，机智的；巧妙的，有独创性的

Sherlock Holmes /ˈʃɔːlɔk ˈhəumz/ 谢洛克·福尔摩斯（柯南道尔小说中虚构的英国侦探）

add up to：加起来共计（等于）；（总起来）意味着

turn up：出现；被发现，被找到

literature /ˈlitəritʃə/ *n.* 文学，文学作品

 ## 参考译文【Suggested Translation】

读 书 之 乐

人类世世代代全部的聪明才智，几百年来愉悦人们的所有故事，都可以轻易而实惠地从书中获得。可是，我们必须要

懂得如何利用这一宝藏，进而获得最大收益。世界上最不幸的人就是那些从未体会到阅读佳作是多么令人心满意足的人。

我对人很感兴趣，对他们个人以及发掘他们同样兴趣十足。我所碰到的一些卓越的人物只能到作家的想像之中去寻找，然后又体现在作家的作品中，最后又出现在我的想像之中。我在书中结识了新朋友，拓展了社会知识，也学到了新的语言。

如果说我是对人感兴趣，那么其他人的兴趣则是关注"怎样"而不是"谁"的问题。书中的"谁"所包括的人物可谓丰富多彩，不仅有科幻小说中描写的两万年之后的超人，还可以追溯到人类历史的开端。而书中的"怎样"所记录的事情也是千奇百怪，从对福尔摩斯侦探故事的巧妙叙述到科学发现以及管教孩子的方法。

读书是一种思维享受，也就是说有点像体育运动。善于读书的人需要强烈的求知欲、丰富的知识和敏捷的反应。读书之所以是一种乐趣，并不在于作者告诉你什么，而是由于读书使你积极思考。在作者的引导之下，你的想像任意驰骋，甚至超越作者的想像。对比作者的经历，你会得出自己的结论，也许相同，也许相悖，而随着你对作者思想的逐步理解，你也会变得越来越深刻。

每一部书都独立存在，犹如独门独户的房子。而图书馆中的书籍则像城市中的建筑。尽管它们各成一体，但是却共同构成一个整体。不仅它们之间相互关联，而且也与其他城市相互联系。相同或者相关的看法在不同的地方出现。文学作品中反映的就是人们生活中经常出现的事情，但是在不同时期作者的处理方式却大相径庭。书籍之间也相互影响，它们传承过去，体现现在，预测未来，相互联系，代代相传，形成各个家族。不管你从何处读起，都会有一种观点与你的相符。从长远来看，你不仅从书中了解世界，体验别人的生活，你也会认识你自己。

只有你诚心读书，阅读才会成为一种乐趣。假如你读的是别人认为"该"读的书，你很有可能觉得索然无味。假如你放下自己不喜欢的书，另试一本，直到发现自己觉得有意义的书，然后心情轻松地读下去，你肯定会感到心情畅快。假如你因阅读而变得更为高尚、聪明、善良、文雅，那读书的过程就不再是一种负担了。◆

A Knack of Wal-Mart's Success[*]

How did a peddler of cheap shirts and fishing rods become the mightiest corporation in America? The short version of Wal-Mart's rise to glory goes something like this: In 1979 it racked up a billion dollars in sales. By 1993 it did that much business in a week; by 2001 it could do it in a day.

It's a stunning tale — one that propelled Wal-Mart from rural Arkansas, where it was founded in 1962, to the top of the Fortune 500 this year. Sam Walton, Wal-Mart's founder, pushed sales growth relentlessly while squeezing costs with sophisticated information technology. He exhorted employees

---

    * 作者凯特·墨菲(Cait Murphy),《财富》杂志的知名编辑。至今,沃尔玛已连续三年荣登"《财富》500 强"榜首,其近年来的迅速发展引起举世关注。沃尔玛的企业文化精髓是"尊重个人、服务顾客、追求卓越",这三条原则是其成功的根本。本文从一个侧面揭示了商业帝国沃尔玛迅速崛起的历史,或许会对今天的我们有一定的借鉴意义。

to sell better with the "ten-foot rule" (greet customers if they are that close). He was, in other words, an early evangelist for the first commandment of today's economy: Service rules. Wal-Mart, in fact, is the first service company to rise to the top of the Fortune 500. When Fortune first published its list of the largest companies in America in 1995, Wal-Mart didn't even exist. That year General Motors was America's biggest company, and in every year that followed, either GM or another mighty industrial, Exxon, was NO. 1.

Wal-Mart's achievement caps a bigger economic shift — from producing goods to providing services. Manufacturing's share of U. S. employment peaked in 1953, at 35%. It has been declining steadily since. In the decade that will end in 2010, the Bureau of Lador Statistics figures that goods-producing industries will create 1.3 million new jobs, compared to 20 million for service industries. To look at it another way, today there are about four times as many people working in service jobs as in other kinds of jobs. And even within manufacturing, services are an increasingly large share of operations.

As America got richer consumption got more complicated. With more income to throw around, people started spending more on services — movies and travel, mortgages to buy houses, insurance to protect those houses, the occasional decadent weekend at a luxury hotel. Economists call this a shift in the demand pattern; Fortune calls it the main reason that 64 of this year's top 100 are service companies. Over the next few years, only three of the ten fastest-growing occupations (software engineers, nurses, and computer support) pay middle-class salaries. The rest could be called, well, Wal-Mart kinds of jobs — cashiers, retail assistants, food service, and so on. In short, the service economy is delivering more good jobs than ever before. ✳

Vocabulary List【词汇清单】

knack /næk/ *n.* 窍门,诀窍;谋略,策略

peddler /ˈpedlə/ *n.* （沿街叫卖的）商贩,（挨户兜售的）小贩

mighty /ˈmaiti/ *adj.* 强有力的,强大的

rack up：＜俚＞获胜,积累,得（分）

stunning /ˈstʌniŋ/ *adj.* 使人晕倒（或吃惊）的;＜口语＞极其
   漂亮的,极其出色的

propel /prəˈpel/ *v.* 推进,推进

Arkansas /ˈɑːkənsɔː/ 阿肯色州（美国中南部的州）

squeeze /skwiːz/ *v.* 压缩,挤榨

sophisticated /səˈfistikeitid/ *adj.* （机械等）高级的,尖端的

exhort /igˈzɔːt/ *v.* 规劝,劝告;激励,鼓励（做应当或该做的事）

evangelist /iˈvændʒilist/ *n.* 福音传教士

commandment /kəˈmɑːndmənt/ *n.* 训令,戒律;＜圣经＞摩
   西十诫中的任何一诫

cap /kæp/ *v.* 做得更好（用更好的事物来接续）,超过,胜过

peak /piːk/ *v.* （使）达到最高点,（使）达到高峰

manufacture /ˌmænjuˈfæktʃə/ *n.* （大规模）制造,加工;制造业

complicated /ˈkɔmplikeitid/ *adj.* （结构）复杂的,难弄的

decadent /ˈdekədənt/ *adj.* 颓废的,堕落的;自我放纵的

retail /riˈteil/ *n.* 零售　*adj.* （从事）零售的

参考译文【Suggested Translation】

沃尔玛发迹妙诀

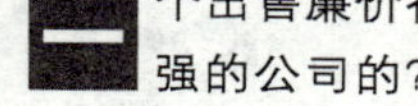

一个出售廉价衬衣和钓鱼竿的商贩是如何成为美国实力最
强的公司的? 沃尔玛百货公司的发迹史可以浓缩为以下

三个阶段：1979 年它全年的销售额为 10 亿美元；到 1993 年，一周就能达到这个数额；在 2001 年仅需一天之功。

这是一个惊人的传奇故事——这家 1962 年始创于阿肯色州乡村地区的沃尔玛百货公司在今年一跃登上了《财富》500 强的榜首。公司创始人萨姆·沃尔顿一面千方百计提高销售额，一面以先进的信息技术降低成本。他以严格的"10 英尺规则"（向在这距离之内的顾客致意）鼓励员工提高销售业绩。换句话说，他是当今经济戒律——服务规则——的第一位传道者。事实上，沃尔玛百货公司是第一个跃居《财富》500 强榜首的服务业公司。1955 年，当《财富》杂志第一次公布美国最大公司的排名时，沃尔玛甚至尚未问世。那一年，通用汽车公司是美国最大的公司，此后不是通用汽车公司就是另一个大公司——埃克森公司独占鳌头。

沃尔玛的成就还标志着一个更重要的经济转变——从生产商品向提供服务的转变。1953 年美国制造业的就业人数占总就业人数的比例达到历史最高点——35％，从此就开始逐年下降。根据劳工统计局的数据，到 2010 年底的未来 10 年间，制造业将创造 130 万个就业机会，而服务业创造的就业机会将高达 2000 万个。换一个角度看，今天在服务业中工作的人数大约是其他行业的 4 倍。即使在制造业中，服务在业务经营中所占的比例也越来越大。

随着美国人富裕程度的日益增高，消费也变得越来越复杂。人们开始把更多的钱花在接受服务方面——看电影、旅游、抵押贷款买房、为房屋保险、偶尔到豪华饭店度个奢侈的周末。经济学家称这种现象为需求变化；《财富》杂志则认为这是本年度评出的 100 家最大公司中有 64 家是服务业公司的主要原因。在未来几年中，10 种发展最快的职业中只有 3 种（软件工程、护士和电脑支持）能够提供中等收入，其余都可称作沃尔玛式的职业——收银员、售货员、食品服务，以及诸如此类的职业。总之，同过去相比，服务业正在提供更多相当不错的就业机会。◆

（孙钰 译）

第 055 篇

Gettysburg Address*

Fourscore and seven years ago, our fathers brought forth upon this continent a new nation, conceived in liberty, and dedicated to the proposition that all men are created equal.

Now, we are engaged in a great civil war, testing wheth-

---

* 作者亚伯拉罕·林肯（Abraham Lincoln，1809—1865），美国第 16 任总统，领导了拯救联邦和结束奴隶制度的斗争,是美国伟大的民主主义政治家。尽管他只接受过极其有限的初级教育,担任公职的经验也很少,然而,他那敏锐的洞察力和深厚的人道主义意识使他成为美国历史上最伟大的总统。不幸的是,林肯于 1865 年 4 月 15 日在华盛顿福特剧院遇刺身亡。由于林肯在美国历史上所起的进步作用,人们称赞他为"新时代国家统治者的楷模"。本文是 1863 年 11 月 19 日林肯在宾西法尼亚州葛底斯堡国家烈士公墓落成典礼上发表的演讲。尽管这篇演讲只有 10 个句子,不足 300 字,但是却被后人评价为"一次完美无缺的演讲",其讲稿是"一篇誉满全球的演说词"。这次演讲的手稿现珍藏于美国国会图书馆,讲辞被铸成金字文,放在牛津大学,作为英语演讲的最高典范。

er that nation, or any nation so conceived and so dedicated, can long endure. We are met on a great battlefield of that war. We have come to dedicate a portion of that field as a final resting-place for those who here gave their lives that that nation might live. It is altogether fitting and proper that we should do this.

But, in a larger sense, we cannot dedicate — we cannot consecrate — we cannot hallow — this ground. The brave men, living and dead, who struggled here, have consecrated it far above our power to add or detract. The world will little note nor long remember what we say here, but it can never forget what they did here. It is for us, the living, rather, to be dedicated here to the unfinished work which they who fought here have thus far so nobly advanced. It is rather for us to be here dedicated to the great task remaining before us — that from these honored dead we take increased devotion to that cause for which they gave the last full measure of devotion; that we here highly resolve that these dead shall not have died in vain; that this nation, under God, shall have a new birth of freedom; and that government of the people, by the people, and for the people, shall not perish from the earth. ✳

Vocabulary List 【词汇清单】

Gettysburg /ˈɡetizˌbəːɡ/ 葛底斯堡（美国城市，曾是美国南北战争的重要战场）

fourscore /ˈfɔːˈskɔː/ *n.* *adj.* 八十（的），二十的四倍

bring forth：产生，引起，提出

conceive /kənˈsiːv/ *v.* 怀（孕）；构思出（主意、计划等）；持有（见解）

dedicate /ˈdediˌkeit/ *v.* 奉献,献(身),致力于
proposition /ˌprɔpəˈziʃən/ *n.* 主张,提议,建议
consecrate /ˈkɔnsikreit/ *v.* 使神圣,奉为神圣
hallow /ˈhæləu/ *v.* 使神圣,视为神圣
detract /diˈtrækt/ *v.* 贬低,毁损,减损(名誉、价值等)
honor /ˈɔnə/ *v.* 尊敬,尊重;对…表示敬意,给…以荣誉
perish /ˈperiʃ/ *v.* 毁灭,灭亡;消亡,消失

 ## 参考译文【Suggested Translation】

葛底斯堡演说

十七年前,我们的先辈们在这个大陆上创立了一个新的国家,她孕育于自由的理念之中,奉行一切人生来平等的原则。

现在,我们正在进行一场伟大的内战,以考验这个国家,或者任何一个孕育于自由和奉行上述原则的国家是否能够长久存在下去。我们在这场战争中的一个伟大战场上集会。我们来到这里,就是要把这个战场的一部分奉献给那些为了国家的生存而捐躯的人们,使其成为他们最后的安息之所。我们这样做是完全应该而且是非常恰当的。

但是,从更广泛的意义上来说,这块土地我们不能够奉献,不能够圣化,不能够神化。那些曾在这里战斗过的勇士们,活着的和死去的,已经把这块土地圣化了,这远不是我们微薄的力量所能增减的。我们今天在这里所说的话,全世界不大会注意,也不会长久地记住,但是勇士们在这里的丰功伟绩,全世界却永远不会忘记。毋宁说,倒是我们这些还活着的人,应该在这里把自己奉献给勇士们已经如此崇高地向前推进但尚未完成的事业。倒是我们应该在这里把自己奉献于仍然留在我们面前的伟大任务——我们要从这些光荣的牺牲者身上汲取更多的献身精神,来完成他们已经完全彻底为之献身的事业;我们要在这里下定最大的决心,不让这些烈士们白白牺牲;我们要使国家在上帝福佑下得到自由的新生,要使这个民有、民治、民享的政府永世长存。◆

The Love of Beauty *

The love of beauty is an essential part of all healthy human nature. It is a moral quality. The absence of it is not an assured ground of condemnation, but the presence of it is an invariable sign of goodness of heart. In proportion to the degree in which it is felt will probably be the degree in which nobleness and beauty of character will be attained.

Natural beauty is an all-pervading presence. The universe is its temple. It unfolds into the numberless flowers of spring. It waves in the branches of trees and the green blades of grass. It haunts the depths of the earth and the

---

* 作者约翰·罗斯金（John Ruskin，1819—1900），英国散文家、批评家和艺术家，其代表作有《时至今日》、《芝麻与百合》、《野橄榄花冠》、《劳动者的力量》等。他的文笔非常优美，色彩绚丽，音调铿锵。罗斯金认为工业资本主义社会过于丑恶，没有艺术，没有美；同时，他又穷其一生为"美"而战斗，在英国被称为"美的使者"达 50 年之久，又被誉为英国社会的"精神导师和先知者"。

sea. It gleams from the hues of the shell and the precious stone. And not only these minute objects but the oceans, the mountains, the clouds, the stars, the rising and the setting sun — all overflow with beauty. This beauty is so precious, and so congenial to our tenderest and noblest feelings, that it is painful to think of the multitude of people living in the midst of it and yet remaining almost blind to it.

All persons should seek to become acquinted with the beauty in nature. There is not a worm we tread upon, nor a leaf that dances merrily as it falls before the autumn winds, but calls for our study and admiration. The power to appreci-ate beauty not merely increases our sources of happiness — it enlarges our moral nature, too. Beauty calms our restless-ness and dispels our cares. Go into the fields or the woods, spend a summer day by the sea or the mountains, and all your little perplexities and anxieties will vanish. Listen to sweet music, and your foolish fears and petty jealousies will pass away. The beauty of the world helps us to seek and find the beauty of goodness. ✳

 **Vocabulary List 【词汇清单】**

condemnation /ˌkɔndemˈneiʃən/ *n.* 谴责,责难,非难

invariable /inˈvɛəriəbl/ *adj.* 不变的,永恒的,恒定的

in proportion to：与…成比例,与…相称

all-pervading /ˌɔːlpəːˈveidiŋ/ *adj.* 遍及的,遍布的,充满的

haunt /hɔːnt/ *v.* 常去,常到,时常出没于(某地)

gleam /gliːm/ *v.* 隐约闪光,闪烁,发出微光

hue /hjuː/ *n.* 色调, 色光,色彩(浓淡)

overflow /ˌəuvəˈfləu/ *v.* 溢出,充满,洋溢

congenial /kənˈdʒiːnjəl/ *adj.* 情趣相投的,情投意合的 ;适合

的,相宜的(to)

multitude /ˈmʌltitjuːd/ *n.* 众多,大量;大群,大批(of)

dispel /disˈpel/ *v.* 消除,消释,使消散,驱散

perplexity /pəˈpleksiti/ *n.* 困惑,窘困,茫然

vanish /ˈvæniʃ/ *v.* 消失,消散,逐渐消逝

jealousy /ˈdʒeləsi/ *n.* 留意的提防,谨慎的戒备,猜忌

参考译文【Suggested Translation】

爱　美

爱美乃是健全人性不可或缺的一部分。它是道德的一种品质。缺乏这种品质并不能作为责难的真正理由,但是拥有这种品质则是心灵美好的永恒标志。品德之高尚与完美所达到的程度可能与爱美的感受程度成正比。

大自然之美无处不在。整个宇宙就是其殿堂。美,在春日百花中绽放;美,在绿叶嫩枝间摇曳;美,在深海幽谷里游弋;美,在奇石与贝壳的缤纷色彩中闪烁。不只是这些细微之物,甚至大洋大川,云朵繁星,日出日落——一切都洋溢着美。这样的美如此珍贵,与我们最温柔、最高尚的情感是如此相宜。然而,想到很多人置身于美,却几乎对它视若无睹,真是令人痛心不已。

所有的人都应该去感知大自然之美。我们所踩过的小虫以及秋风拂掠之际飘落飞舞的树叶,皆值得我们探究与赞赏。具有欣赏美的能力不仅可以使我们快乐的源泉汩汩喷涌——它也可以拓展我们的德性。美,抚平我们心中的不安,也驱散了我们的忧虑。走进田野或树林,在夏日的海滨或山间度过一天的时光,那么你所有微不足道的困惑和焦虑都会烟消云散。倾听美妙的音乐,你那愚蠢的恐惧与琐碎的猜忌都会消逝无踪。世间万物之美总会有助于我们探寻与发现善良之美。◆

The Road Not Taken[*]

Two roads diverged in a yellow wood,
And sorry I could not travel both
And be one traveler, long I stood
And looked down one as far as I could
To where it bent in the undergrowth;

---

* 作者罗伯特·弗罗斯特（Robert Frost, 1874—1963），美国著名诗人，曾以《新罕布夏》、《诗经》、《又一片牧场》等著作四度获得普立策奖，是美国历史上第一个四次获此殊荣的人，被公认为非正式的桂冠诗人，曾应美国总统之邀作客白宫。其著作还包括《孩子的意愿》、《波士顿以北》、《西去的溪流》、《理智的假面具》、《慈悲的假面具》、《林间中地》等。他的许多诗歌反映了人与大自然的贴近，通过自然来表达一种象征意义。《未选择之路》这首诗是弗罗斯特的代表作之一，作于1915年。我们的生活充满了选择，而什么样的选择决定什么样的生活。今天的生活是由三年前我们的选择决定的，而今天我们的抉择将决定我们三年后的生活。进一步讲，人的命运在于选择，而选择的轴心是观念。人的命运不在出身，人的成功不在才能，人的幸福不在物质。人懂得完美，甚至都不在教育；人的成功在于作出选择时的观念——符合时代需求的价值观念、思维方法和意识形态。

Then took the other, as just as fair,
And having perhaps the better claim,
Because it was grassy and wanted wear;
Though as for that the passing there
Had worn them really about the same,

And both that morning equally lay
In leaves no step had trodden black.
Oh, I kept the first for another day!
Yet knowing how way leads on to way,
I doubted if I should ever come back.

I shall be telling this with a sigh
Somewhere ages and ages hence：
Two roads diverged in a wood, and I —
I took the one less traveled by,
And that has made all the difference. ✽

Vocabulary List 【词汇清单】

diverge /daiˈvəːdʒ/ *v.* （道路等）分叉，岔开

long /lɔŋ/ *adv.* 长期地，长久地

bend /bend/ *v.* 拐弯，转向

undergrowth /ˈʌndəɡrəuθ/ *n.* （尤指大树下的）灌木丛

fair /fɛə/ *adj.* 合宜的，合理的

claim /kleim/ *n.* 主张，要求而得到的东西

grassy /ˈɡrɑːsi/ *adj.* 被草覆盖的，长满草的

want wear：缺少（人践踏的）踪迹，意即无人践踏

tread /tred/ *v.* （trodden 是其过去分词形式）行走，踩碎，践踏

hence /hens/ *adv.* 今后，从此

参考译文【Suggested Translation】

未选择之路

从黄树林里分叉两条路，
只可惜我不能都踏行。
我，单独的旅人，伫立良久，
极目眺望一条路的尽头，
看它隐没在丛林深处。

于是我选择了另一条路，
一样平直，也许更值得，
因为青草茵茵，还未被踏过，
若有过往人踪，
路的状况会相差无几。

那天早晨，两条路都覆盖在枯叶下，
没有践踏的污痕：
啊，原先那条路留给另一天吧！
明知一条路会引出另一条路，
我怀疑我是否会回到原处。

在许多许多年以后，在某处，
我会轻轻叹息说：
黄树林里分叉两条路，而我——
我选择了人迹较少的一条，
从而使得一切多么的不同。◈

第058篇

On Leadership*

What is leadership? Its qualities are difficult to define. But they are not so difficult to identify.

Leaders don't force other people to go along with them. They bring them along. Leaders get commitment from others by giving it themselves, by building an environment that encourages creativity, and by operating with honesty and fairness.

Leaders demand much of others, but also give much of themselves. They are ambitious — not only for themselves, but also for those who work with them. They seek to attract,

---

　　* 作者佚名。领导,管理学上的定义是"影响和推动一个群体或多个群体的人们朝某个方向和目标努力的过程"。在实际的工作中,为什么员工会对一个领导者言听计从,而对另一个领导者却很勉强? 其实,这在很大程度上和领导者的素质有关。那么,什么样的领导者可谓成功的表率? 领导能否"制造"? 能否"克隆"? 无数科学家和学者们一直在试图解开"领导"背后的奥秘。

retain and develop other people to their full abilities.

Good leaders aren't "lone rangers". They recognize that an organization's strategies for success require the combined talents and efforts of many people. Leadership is the catalyst for transforming those talents into results.

Leaders know that when there are two opinions on an issue, one is not bound to be wrong. They recognize that hustle and rush are the allies of superficiality. They are open to new ideas, but they explore their ramifications thoroughly.

Successful leaders are emotionally and intellectually oriented to the future — not wedded to the past. They have a hunger to take responsibility, to innovate, and to initiate. They are not content with merely taking care of what's already there. They want to move forward to create something new.

Leaders provide answers as well as direction, offer strenght as well as dedication, and speak from experience as well as understanding of the problems they face and the people they work with.

Leaders are flexible rather than dogmatic. They believe in unity rather than conformity. And they strive to achieve consensus out of conflict.

Leadership is all about getting people consistently to give their best, helping them to grow to their fullest potential, and motivating them to work toward a common good. Leaders make the right things happen when they're supposed to.

A good leader, an effective leader, is one who has respect. Respect is something you have to have in order to get. A leader who has respect for other people at all levels of an organization, for the work they do, and for their abilities, aspirations and needs, will find that respect is returned. And all concerned will be motivated to work together. ✳

Vocabulary List 【词汇清单】

commitment /kə'mitmənt/ *n.* 承诺,许诺,承担义务

retain /ri'tein/ *v.* 保持,保有,保留,留住

ranger /'reindʒə/ *n.* 漫游者,闲荡者;骑兵巡逻队队员;突击队员(lone rangers:源自美国过去一度流行的电视连续剧 The Lone Ranger(孤胆骑警),该剧描述了一个穿红衫戴面具的森林骑警行侠仗义的故事)

catalyst /'kætəlist/ *n.* <化学>催化剂,触媒;刺激(或促进)因素,作为促进因素的人(或物)

hustle /'hʌsl/ *n.* (乱)挤,(硬)推;<美国口语>仓促准备,匆匆做成

superficiality /ˌsjuːpəˌfiʃi'æliti/ *n.* 肤浅,浅薄

ramification /ˌræmifi'keiʃən/ *n.* (众多复杂而又难以预料的)结果,后果

wedded /'wedid/ *adj.* 执着,全力以赴;结合在一起,融为一体(to)

innovate /'inəuveit/ *v.* 改革,革新,变革

initiate /i'niʃieit/ *v.* 发起,创办,创始

dogmatic /dɔg'mætik/ *adj.* 武断的,独断的,固执己见的

consensus /kən'sensəs/ *n.* 大多数人的意见,一致同意(尤指意见的一致),共识

potential /pə'tenʃəl/ *n.* 潜力,潜能(成长、发展或形成的内在能力或才能)

aspiration /ˌæspə'reiʃən/ *n.* 热望,渴望,愿望

参考译文【Suggested Translation】

论 领 导

什么是领导?领导所应具备的品质很难精确界定,但是辨认指陈却并不困难。

　　领导者不会强制他人与自己保持协调一致，而是引导他们跟进。领导者要让别人承担义务，首先自己去承担，并创设一种能够鼓励创造的环境，为人处事诚恳而公正。

　　领导者对别人要求甚多，同时给予别人也很多。他们拥有雄心壮志——不仅为自己，也为和他一起工作的人。他们想方设法吸引人才，留住他们，力求人尽其才。

　　好的领导者不是"独行侠"。他们认识到一个组织要获取成功，其方针在于将许多人的才能和力量联结起来。领导艺术是一种催化剂，将众人的才智转化为业绩。

　　领导者明白，在争论的问题上出现两种意见的时候，并非必然有一种是错误的。他们认识到匆忙草率就会导致肤浅片面。他们对新的设想或建议敞开心胸，但是对于其细节和后果要做精细的探讨。

　　成功的领导者无论是在情感上还是理智上都着眼于未来而不沉迷于过去。他们渴望肩负责任、锐意改革和积极开拓。他们不会满足于仅仅守成，他们要向前进取，要创造新事物。

　　领导者不但给予他人方向性指导，也对问题和要求提供具体解答，不仅示以献身的精神，而且给予行事的力量。他们说话既根据以往的经验，也根据对问题的认识以及对同事的了解。

　　领导者处事灵活而不武断。他们认为与其循规蹈矩不如协调一致。而且他们力求在矛盾冲突中求得意见的统一。

　　领导艺术全然在于使下级工作人员不断地发挥所长，帮助他们最大限度地发掘潜力，推动他们为共同的事业而工作。领导者务必使该办的事情按时完成。

　　一个好的领导者，卓有成效的领导者，善于对人关怀尊重。要得到别人的尊重必须首先尊重别人。领导者对本组织各级人员都会示以尊重，对他们的工作、能力、愿望与需求示以关怀，而他也会发现人家也尊重他关怀他。这样，所有有关人员就都会被激励起来而共同努力工作。◆

Address to the Millennium Summit[*]

Madam President (of Finland),
Mr. President (of Namibia),
Excellencies,
Ladies and Gentelemen,

I am deeply honored to welcome you all.

Never before have the leaders of so many nations come together in a single Assembly. This is a unique event. A unique opportunity. And therefore a unique responsibility.

---

* 作者科菲·安南(Kofy Annan,1938—　),生于加纳,联合国第七任秘书长,也是出身联合国工作人员而当选的第一位秘书长。安南是一位经验丰富的外交家,懂英语、法语和几种非洲语言。他就任秘书长后采取了一系列的措施:通过全面改革方案恢复联合国的活力;加强联合国在发展和维持国际和平与安全方面的传统工作;鼓励并提倡人权、法治以及《联合国宪章》所载的关于平等、容忍和人类尊严的普遍价值观念;恢复公众对联合国的信任,向新的伙伴伸手和套用他的话说,"使联合国更接近人民",等等。2001 年 10 月,安南与联合国同获当年诺贝尔和平奖。

You, ladies and gentlemen, are the leaders to whom the world's peoples have entrusted their destiny. They look to you to protect them from the great dangers of our time; and too ensure that all of them can share in its great achievements.

In an age when human beings have learnt the code of human life, and can transmit their knowledge in seconds from one continent to another, no mother in the world can understand why her child should be left to die of malnutrition or preventable disease. No one can understand why they should be driven from their home, or imprisoned or tortured for expressing their beliefs. No one can understand why the soil their parents tilled has turned to desert, or why their skills have become useless and their family is left hungry.

People know that these challenges cannot be met by one country alone, or by one government alone. Change cannot be held back by frontiers. Human progress has always come from individual and local initiatives, freely devised and then freely adapted elsewhere.

Your job, as political leaders, is to encourage such initiatives. To make sure they are not stifled, and that all your peoples can benefit from them. And to limit, or to compensate for, the adverse effects that change always has, on some people, somewhere.

Your peoples look to you for a common effort to solve their problems. They expect you to work together, as governments. And they expect you to work together with all the other institutions — profit or non-profit, public and private — where human beings join hands to promote their ideas and their interests.

People want to see this happen between neighboring

countries, and among all the countries of each region. But since today's biggest challenges are global, they expect above all that we will work together at the global level, as the United Nations.

My friends, that is why we are here. We are here to strengthen and adapt this great institution, forged 55 years ago in the crucible of war, so that it can do what people expect of it in the new era — an era in which rule of law must prevail. Last month I sent you a Report, produced by a panel of experts, which makes detailed suggestions for strengthening the United Nations in the crucial area of peace and security — the area where people look especially to the State, and where the world's peoples look to the United Nations, to save them "from the scourge of war". Please consider that Report very seriously.

It is not only in that field, however, that the United Nations needs strengthening. We must strengthen it across the whole range of our activities.

We need to decide our priorities. And we must adapt our United Nations, so that in future those priorities are reflected in clear and prompt decisions, leading to real change in people's lives.

That, my friends, is what the peoples expect of us. Let us not disappoint them.

Thank you. ✳

Vocabulary List 【词汇清单】

summit /ˈsʌmit/ *n.* ＜美＞峰会,政府首脑会议,最高级别会议
Finland /ˈfinlənd/ 芬兰(北欧国家)

Namibia /naːˈmibiːə/ 纳米比亚（非洲西南部的一个国家，位于大西洋沿岸）

Excellency /ˈeksələnsi/ *n.* 阁下（对大使、主教、总督等职位高的人的尊称）

Assembly /əˈsembli/ *n.* （特殊目的的）集会，聚会，会议

entrust /inˈtrʌst/ *v.* 委托，托付，交托

destiny /ˈdestini/ *n.* 命运，定数，天命

ensure /inˈʃuə/ *v.* 保证，担保，确保

code /kəud/ *n.* 密码，编码；遗传密码

transmit /trænzˈmit/ *v.* 传达，传导，传递，传播

malnutrition /ˈmælnju(ː)ˈtriʃən/ *n.* 营养失调，营养不良

imprison /imˈprizn/ *v.* 监禁，关押，禁闭

till /til/ *v.* 耕种，耕耘，耕作

adapt /əˈdæpt/ *v.* 使（自己）适合/适应（新的或变化了的情况）（oneself）

stifle /ˈstaifl/ *v.* 使窒息，压制，扼杀

compensate /ˈkɔmpenseit/ *v.* 补偿，抵偿，弥补

adverse /ˈædvəːs/ *adj.* 相反的，对立的；不利的，有害的

crucible /ˈkruːsibl/ *n.* 坩埚，熔炉；＜引申＞磨炼，严酷（严峻）的考验

prevail /priˈveil/ *v.* 胜过，优胜，获胜；流行，盛行，普遍

panel /ˈpænl/ *n.* （选定的）专门小组，专家咨询组

crucial /ˈkruːʃəl/ *adj.* 最重要的，决定性的

scourge /ˈskəːdʒ/ *n.* 灾害，祸患；苦难（或灾祸）的根源

prompt /prɔmpt/ *adj.* 敏捷的，迅速的，果断的

 参考译文【Suggested Translation】

在千年首脑峰会上的演讲

 统女士（芬兰），
总统先生（纳米比亚），

诸位阁下，

女士们，先生们：

在此欢迎诸位，我深感荣幸。

这么多国家的领导人聚集一堂参加同一次大会，这是前所未有的事情。这是一件非比一般的盛事，这是一次极不寻常的机会。因此，诸位负有独特的责任。女士们，先生们，你们是领导者，世界各国人民已经将他们的命运托付于你们。他们期望你们保护他们，不让他们遭受我们这个时代的严重危害；他们期望你们确保他们能够分享我们这个时代所取得的伟大成就。

现今，人类已经破解了生命的密码，并且能够在几秒钟之内将知识从一个大陆传输到另一个大陆。在这样一个时代，世界上没有一个母亲能够理解为什么她的孩子竟然无人救助、死于营养不良或者本来可以预防的疾病。没有一个人能够理解为什么袒露自己信念的人居然被逐出家园，被囚禁牢中，甚至被拷打折磨。没有一个人能够理解为什么他们的父辈辛勤耕耘过的土地变成了荒漠，为什么他们的劳动技能变得毫无用处，为什么他们的家人忍饥挨饿。

大家知道，这些难题单靠一个国家是解决不了的，也不可能单靠一届政府就能解决的。疆土边境不可能阻止变革。人类的进步总是来自于个人和局部的首创精神；这些首创精神是被自由地创造出来，然后经过自由发挥，适用于其他地方。

作为政治领袖，你们的工作就是要鼓励这种首创精神。要确保这种精神不被扼杀，并确保你们的人民都能从中受益。如果在某些地方某些人民身上改种变革产生不利影响，那就要加以限制或者加以弥补。

你们的人民期待着你们共同努力解决他们的问题。他们期望你们代表政府协同工作。并且他们期望你们同所有其他机构——赢利性的和非赢利性的，公共的和私人的——一道工作，携手推广人类的观念，共同促进人类感兴趣的事业。

人们希望看到毗邻的国家以及世界各地所有国家都出现这种合作的局面。但是，因为我们今天遇到的最大挑战是全球性的，所以人们首要希望的是我们代表联合国在全球的范围之内携手合作。

朋友们,这就是我们聚集在一起的原因。我们聚集在这里是为了加强和改进这个伟大的机构——这个伟大的机构是55年前在战争的严峻考验之中经过艰难困苦建立起来的,这个机构能够在法制必胜的新纪元里不辜负人们的期望。上个月,我将专家组所拟的一份报告寄给了你们。报告提出了详细的建议,旨在加强联合国在和平与安全这个关键领域中的作用。在这一领域,人民特别希望其国家,世界人们则指望联合国,将他们从"战争的苦难"中解救出来。敬请认真考虑这个报告。

然而,不仅仅是在上述领域联合国需要加强合作,发挥更大作用。在所有活动范围内,我们都必须加强联合国的作用。

事情的轻重缓急,孰先孰后,我们需要作出决定。我们必须对我们的联合国进行改革,以期在将来需要优先考虑的重大事情在明确而果断的决策中得以体现,并真正给人民的生活带来变化。

朋友们,这就是人民寄予我们的期望。我们不能让人民失望。

谢谢大家。◆

Napoleon to Josephine*

I have your letter, my adorable love. It has filled my heart with joy ... Since I left you I have been sad all the time. My only happiness is near you. I go over endlessly in my thought of your kisses, your tears, your delicious jealousy. The charm of my wonderful Josephine kindles a living, blazing fire in my heart and senses. When shall I be able to pass every minute near you, with nothing to do but to love you and nothing to think of

---

　　* 作者拿破仑·波拿巴（Napoleon Bonaparte,1769—1821）,法兰西第一帝国皇帝,杰出的政治家、军事家,其执政期间对外战争频繁,在和反法同盟的战争中拿破仑率领法国军队取得了辉煌的胜利,多次打败数量上占优势的欧洲各国联军。1815 年 6 月,在滑铁卢被第七次反法同盟打败,被迫退位,并被流放到圣赫勒拿岛。本文是拿破仑于 1796 年 7 月 17 日在麻密罗洛给当时的社会名媛约瑟芬所写的一封情浓语烈的情书。虽然这封赞美诗式的情书结构是散的,思维是散的,表达方式是散的,但是情却是凝结的,爱却是真挚的,堪称情书中的经典之作。

but the pleasure of telling you of it and giving you proof of it? I loved you some time ago; since then I feel that I love you a thousand times better. Ever since I have known you I adore you more every day. That proves how wrong is that saying of La Bruyere "love comes all of a sudden."

Ah, let me see some of your faults; be less beautiful, less graceful, less tender, less good. But never be jealous and never shed tears. Your tears send me out of my mind ... they set my very blood on fire. Believe me that it is utterly impossible for me to have a single thought that is not yours, a single fancy that is not submissive to your will. Rest well. Restore your health. Come back to me and then at any rate before we die we ought to be able to say："We were happy for so very many days!" Millions of kisses even to your dog. ✳

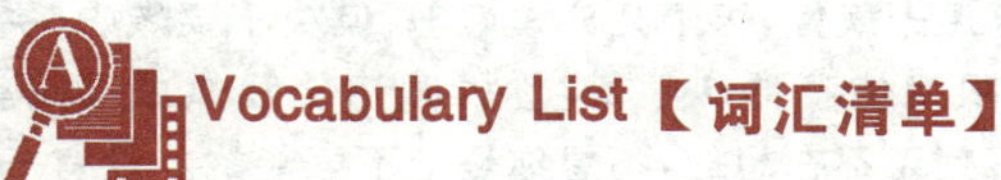

Vocabulary List【词汇清单】

adorable /əˈdɔːrəbl/ *adj.* 值得崇拜的，值得敬慕的；＜口语＞讨人喜欢的，可爱的

jealousy /ˈdʒeləsi/ *n.* 嫉妒；小心谨慎

charm /tʃaːm/ *n.* （女人的）引诱力，魅力；（女子的）妩媚，美色

kindle /ˈkindl/ *v.* 使燃烧，点燃，点（火）；激起（兴趣、感情等）

blaze /ˈbleiz/ *v.* 发（强）光，发亮，闪耀，放光彩

La Bruyere /laː bruːˈjiə/ 拉布吕耶尔（1645—1696，全名 Jean de La Bruyere，法国著名道德家和古典主义散文家，著有《性格论》一书）

graceful /ˈgreisful/ *adj.* 优美的，幽雅的

utterly /ˈʌtəli/ *adv.* 完全地，全然地，彻底地

submissive /səbˈmisiv/ *adj.* 顺从的，柔顺的，服从的

restore /risˈtɔː/ *v.* 恢复（健康、气力等）

参考译文【Suggested Translation】

拿破仑致约瑟芬

我收到了你的信,我崇拜的心上人。你的信使我充满了欢乐……自从与你分手以后,我一直闷闷不乐,愁眉不展。我惟一的幸福就是伴随着你。你的吻给了我无限的遐思和回味,还有你的泪水和甜蜜的嫉妒。我迷人的约瑟芬的魅力就像一团炽热的火在心里燃烧。什么时候我才能在你身旁度过每分每秒,除了爱你什么也不需要做;除了向你倾诉我对你的爱并向你证明爱的那种愉快,什么也不用想了? 我不敢相信不久之前爱上你,自那以后我感到对你的爱更增加了一千倍。自从我与你相识,我一天比一天更崇拜你。这正好证明了拉布吕耶尔所说的"爱,突如其来"多么不切合实际。

　　啊,让我看看你的一些美中不足吧。再少几分甜美,再少几分优雅,再少几分温柔妩媚,再少几分姣好吧;但决不要嫉妒,决不要流泪。你的眼泪使我神魂颠倒,你的眼泪使我热血沸腾。相信我,我每时每刻无不在想你,不想你是绝不可能的。没有一丝意念能够不顺着你的意愿。好好休息,早日康复。回到我的身边,不管怎么说,在我们谢世之前,我们应当能说:"我们曾经有多少个幸福的日子啊!"千百万次吻,甚至吻你的爱犬。◆

Questions Asked in an Interview*

" What can you tell me about yourself?" This is not an invitation to give your life history. The interviewer is looking for clues about your character, qualifications, ambitions, and motivations. The following is a good example of a positive response. "As a college student, I worked in a clothing store part-time and found that I could sell things easily. The sale was important, but for me, it was even more important to make sure that the customer was satisfied. It was not long

---

　　* 作者佚名。从某种意义来说，获得面试机会就意味着已获得招聘单位的初步认可，说明你的基本条件已符合公司和职位的要求。到了面试这个阶段，如何与面试官进行良好沟通就成为重中之重。求职面试同其他社会交往一样，是以语言表达思维、互相沟通的社会行为。虽然面试等应聘环节对语言没有特别的标准和要求，但是良好和娴熟的语言习惯和技巧，无疑是求职面试成功的重要条件。当然造就个人良好的语言习惯和技巧，决非一蹴而就之举，但是通过实例去体会什么是良好的语言习惯和技巧，并在应聘中有意识的加以注意，对提高应聘成功率是很有好处的。

before customers came back to the store and specifically asked for me to help them. "

"Why do you want to work for us?" This is an obvious question and, if you have done your research on the company, you should be able to give a good reason. Organize your reasons into several short sentences that clearly spell out your interest. "You are a leader in the field of electronics. Your company is a Fortune 500 company. "

"Why should I hire you?" Once again, you should not be long winded, but you should provide a summary of your qualifications. Be positive and show that you are capable of doing the job. It can be "Based on the internships that I have participated in and the related part-time experiences I have had, I can do the job. "

"How do you feel about your progress to date?" Never apologize for what you have done. "I think I did well in school. In fact, in a number of courses I received the highest exam scores in the class. " "As an intern for the X Company, I received some of the highest evaluations that had been given in years. "

"What would you like to be doing five years from now?" Know what you can realistically accomplish. "I hope to be the best I can be at my job and because many in this line of work are promoted to area manager, I am planning on that also. "

"What is your greatest weakness?" You cannot avoid this question by saying that you do not have any, everyone has weaknesses. The best approach is to admit your weakness but show that you are working on it and have a plan to overcome it.

"What is your greatest strength?" This is a real opportunity to toot your own horn. Do not brag or get too egotistical, but let the employer know that you believe in yourself and that you know your strengths. "I feel that my strongest asset is my ability to stick to things to get them done. I feel a real sense of accomplishment when I finish a job and it turns out just as I'd planned."

"What goals have you set and how did you meet them?" This question examines your ability to plan ahead and meet your plan with specific actions. "Last year, during a magazine drive to raise money for our band trip, I set my goal at raising 20 percent more than I had the year before. I knew the drive was going to begin in September, so I started contacting people in August. I asked each of my customers from last year to give me the names of one or two new people who might also buy a magazine. I not only met my goal, but I also was the top salesperson on the drive." No matter what question you are asked, answer it honestly and succinctly. Most interviewers are looking for positive statements, well-expressed ideas, persuasiveness, and clear thinking under pressure.

Always maintain eye contact with the interviewer. Show that you are confident by looking straight at the person. Most interviewers greet the applicant with a handshake. Make sure that your clasp is firm. Being jittery about the interview can result in cold, clammy hands, which create a negative impression. Therefore, make sure your hands are warm and dry. Before leaving, try to find out exactly what action will follow the interview and when it will happen. Shake hands as you say good-bye and thank the interviewer for spending time with you. ✳

 Vocabulary List 【词汇清单】

qualification /ˌkwɔlifiˈkeiʃən/ *n.* 资格,资历,(担任某种职务等)必不可少的品质(或技能等)

motivation /məutiˈveiʃən/ *n.* 动机,动力;激发,促动

specifically /spiˈsifikəli/ *adv.* 特定地,明确地

electronics /ilekˈtrɔniks/ *n.* (与动词单数形式连用)电子学(研究电子现象的科学和技术)

internship /ˈintəːnʃip/ *n.* <美>实习医师(职位),实习医师期

brag /bræg/ *v.* 自夸,吹牛,夸夸其谈

egotistical /ˌegəuˈtistikəl/ *adj.* 自我主义的,自高自大的,自负的

succinctly /səkˈsiŋktli/ *adv.* 简洁地,简明地,简短地

persuasiveness /pəˈsweisivnis/ *n.* 劝导性的话语,有说服力的言谈

clasp /klaːsp/ *n.* 握住,紧握,握(手)

jittery /ˈdʒitəri/ *adj.* <美国口语>非常不安的,战战兢兢的,心神不宁的

clammy /ˈklæmi/ *adj.* (触摸起来)湿冷的,冷而粘的

 参考译文【Suggested Translation】

求 职 面 试 题

"关于你自己,你能告诉我些什么?"这一问题并非在请你大谈你的个人历史。雇主是在寻找有关你性格、资历、志向和生活动力的线索。下面是一个积极正面回答的好例子:"大学期间,我曾在一家服装店打工,我发现自己能轻而易举地将东西推销出去。销售固然重要,但对我来说,更重要的是要确保顾客能够满意。不久便有顾客返回那家服装店点名让我为他们服务。"

　　"你为什么想为我们工作?"这个问题是显而易见的。如果你对该公司做过调查研究,你应该能够给出很好的理由。你要将你的理由归结为几句简短的话,清楚地表明你的兴趣。如可答:"你们在电子领域是领头人。你们公司是《财富》杂志评选的 500 强之一。"

　　"为什么我应该聘用你?"同样,你不应长篇大论,而应提供有关你资历的扼要说明。要肯定自己,表明你能胜任此项工作。如答:"根据我参加过的实习和与此相关的打工经历。我能胜任。"

　　"对于你至今所取得的进步你是怎样看的?"绝不要对你以前的所作所为表示内疚。如可答:"我认为我在学校表现不错。事实上,有好几门功课我的成绩居全班第一。""在某公司实习时,我获得了该公司数年来给予其雇员的好几项最高评价。"

　　"今后五年内你想做些什么?"你要清楚你在现实工作中能取得什么样的业绩。如可答:"我希望能在我的职位上尽力做得最好,由于在同一领域工作的许多人都被提为区域负责人,所以我亦有此打算。"

　　"你最大的弱点是什么?"你不应该说你没有任何弱点,以此来回避这个问题;每个人都有弱点。最佳策略是承认你的弱点,但同时表明你在予以改进,并有克服弱点的计划。

　　"你最突出的优点是什么?"这是你"展示自己"的最佳机会,不要吹嘘自己或过于自负,但要让雇主知道你相信自己,你知道自己的优点。如可答:"我认为我最大的优点是能够执着地尽力把事情办好。当做完一件工作而其成果又正合我的预想时,我会有一种真正的成熟感。"

　　"你确定过什么目标,你又是怎样达到那些目标的?"这一问题在考查你预先计划和以具体行动完成计划的能力。你可答:"去年在为我们乐队旅行集资而开展的一家杂志促销活动中,我定下的目标是比我前一年达到的再多 20%。我知道促销将于 9 月份展开,于是我在 8 月份就开始联系客户。我请求我前一年的顾客给我提供一个或两个可能会买杂志的新客户。我不仅达到了目标,还成为促销活动中销售量最高的人员。"总之,不管你在面试中被问到什么问题,回答都要诚实而简明。雇主大都希求明确的陈述，表达良好的想法，有说服力的言谈和压力之下清晰的思路。

　　和雇主要一直保持目光接触。直视对方说明你有自信。面试的雇主大都会与应聘者握握手。要确保你的握手有力量。情绪紧张地来参加面试会使你伸出的手冰冷潮湿，会给雇主留下负面印象。所以，要让你的手温暖干燥。临走之前，争取问问面试后下一步该是什么，何时开始。道别时要握手感谢雇主花时间对你进行面试。◆

● Whatever you do, do with all your might.（不管做什么，都要一心一意。）

● Seek the truth from facts.（实事求是。）

● Constant dripping wears away a stone.（水滴石穿，绳锯木断。）

● Justice has long arms.（天网恢恢，疏而不漏。）

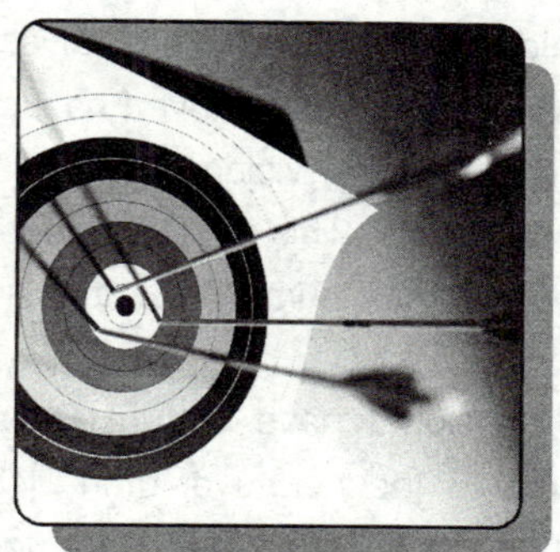

What I Have Lived for[*]

Three passions, simple but overwhelmingly strong, have governed my life: the longing for love, the search for knowledge, and unbearable pity for the suffering of mankind. These passions, like great winds, have blown me hither and thither, in a wayward course, over a deep ocean of anguish, reaching to the very verge of despair.

I have sought love, first, because it brings ecstasy — ecstasy so great that I would often have sacrificed all the rest of my life for a few hours of this joy. I have sought it, next, because it relieves loneliness — that terrible loneliness in

---

* 作者伯特兰·罗素(Bertrand Russell,1872—1970),英国哲学家、数学家、社会学家,也是 20 世纪西方最著名、影响最大的学者和社会活动家之一,其大部分著作都能把理论的深刻性和表达的通俗性结合起来,既有亚里士多德、黑格尔的思辨性,又有伏尔泰、达·芬奇作品的那种文采,其流畅清新的散文在英国文学中也享誉甚高。1950 年,为了"表彰他所写的捍卫人道主义思想和思想自由的多种多样意义重大的作品",罗素被授予诺贝尔文学奖。

which one shivering consciousness looks over the rim of the world into the cold unfathomable lifeless abyss. I have sought it, finally, because in the union of love I have seen, in a mystic miniature, the prefiguring vision of the heaven that saints and poets have imagined. This is what I sought, and though it might seem too good for human life, this is what — at last — I have found.

With equal passion I have sought knowledge. I have wished to understand the hearts of men. I have wished to know why the stars shine. And I have tried to apprehend the Pythagorean power by which number holds away above the flux. A little of this, but not much, I have achieved.

Love and knowledge, so far as they were possible, led upward toward the heavens. But always pity brought me back to earth. Echoes of cries of pain reverberate in my heart. Children in famine, victims tortured by oppressors, helpless old people a hated burden to their sons, and the whole world of loneliness, poverty, and pain make a mockery of what human life should be. I long to alleviate the evil, but I cannot, and I too suffer.

This has been my life. I have found it worth living, and would gladly live it again if the chance were offered me. ✳

Vocabulary List 【词汇清单】

overwhelmingly /ˌəuvə'welmiŋli/ *adv.*　压倒性地，不可抵挡地

unbearable /ʌn'bɛərəbl/ *adj.*　无法忍受的，难以容忍的

hither and thither：到处，各处，四面八方

wayward /'weiwəd/ *adj.* 任性的；反复无常的，难以捉摸的

anguish /'æŋgwiʃ/ *n.* 极度痛苦，悲痛

verge /vəːdʒ/ *n.* 边缘，边界，界限，范围（of）

ecstasy /ˈekstəsi/ *n.*　狂喜,欣喜若狂;陶醉,入迷

relieve /riˈliːv/ *v.*　减轻,缓解,解除(痛苦、忧虑等)

shivering /ˈʃivəriŋ/ *adj.*　颤抖的,颤栗的,哆嗦的

consciousness /ˈkɔnʃəsnis/ *n.*　意识,知觉,感觉,觉悟

rim /rim/ *n.*　(圆形物的)边,边缘(of)

unfathomable /ʌnˈfæðəməbl/ *adj.* 深不可测的;< 比喻 > 神秘莫测的

abyss /əˈbis/ *n.*　深渊,深海;< 神学 >(创世之前的)混沌,洪荒

mystic /ˈmistik/ *adj.*　(= mystical)神秘(主义)的,奥秘的,玄秘的

miniature /ˈminjətʃə/ *n.*　袖珍画,缩图,缩影

prefigure /ˈpriːˈfigə/ *v.*　预想,预示,预测,预兆

saint /seint/ *n.*　圣徒,圣者;虔诚慈善的人

apprehend /ˌæpriˈhend/ *v.*　领悟,领会,理解

Pythagorean /paiˌθægəˈri(ː)ən/ *adj.*　毕达哥拉斯的,毕达哥拉斯学说的(Pythagoras:毕达哥拉斯,公元前 6 世纪希腊哲学家、数学家,认为数是万物之本源,证明了毕达哥拉斯定理的广泛有效性,并被认为是世界上第一位真正的数学家)

flux /flʌks/ *n.*　持续的运动,不断的变化,变迁

reverberate /riˈvəːbəreit/ *v.*　使(声音)回响,使回荡

famine /ˈfæmin/ *n.*　< 古 > 饥饿;饥荒,饥馑

torture /ˈtɔːtʃə/ *v.* 折磨,虐待,使痛苦

oppressor /əˈpresə/ *n.*　压迫者,残酷的统治者,暴君

poverty /ˈpɔvəti/ *n.* 贫穷,贫困

mockery /ˈmɔkəri/ *n.*　嘲笑,嘲弄,奚落

alleviate /əˈliːvieit/ *v.*　减轻(苦痛、疾苦等),使缓和;减少,减小

参考译文【Suggested Translation】

我 为 何 而 生

对爱情的渴望,对知识的探求和对人类苦难不可遏制的同情,是支配我一生的单纯而难以抗拒的三种情感。这些情

感如阵阵飓风，随意地把我吹得飘来荡去，有时吹过深沉痛苦的海洋，直抵绝望的边缘。

　　我曾经追求过爱情，首先是因为爱情可以给我带来狂喜，这种狂喜竟如此强烈，以至于我常常会为了体验几小时爱的欢娱，而宁愿牺牲生命中的其他一切。我曾经追求过爱情，其次是因为爱情可以摆脱孤寂——置身于那可怕的孤独之中，那令人战栗的感觉，有时会掠过世界的边缘，把人带到寒气袭人且没有生命的无底深渊。我曾经追求过爱情，还因为在爱的结合中，我看到了古今圣贤以及诗人们梦想中天堂的神秘缩影。这也正是我所追寻的人生境界。虽然它对一般的人类生活也许太美好了，但这正是我透过爱情最终所找到的。

　　我曾以同样的感情追求知识。我一直渴望去了解人类的心灵，也渴望知道星星为什么会发光，同时我还想理解毕达哥拉斯的力量，通过它的力量，数驾驭了万物的变化。我学到了一点点知识，但仅是皮毛而已。

　　爱情与知识，总是可以把我引领到天堂的境界。可对于人类苦难的同情经常把我带回现实世界。那些痛苦的呼唤经常在我内心深处回响激荡。嗷嗷待哺的孩童，压迫者折磨之下的受害者，给子女造成重负的孤苦无依的老人，以及那充满孤独、贫穷和痛苦的世界，是对人类所应该拥有的生活的无视和嘲弄。我常渴望能尽自己的微薄之力去减轻这不必要的痛苦，但是却无能为力，而我也因此受着痛苦的煎熬。

　　这就是我的生活，我觉得是值得活的。如果有谁再给我一次生活的机会，我将欣然接受这难得的赐予。◆

（《英语沙龙》泰云 译）

第 篇

Cars *

My friend said cars are a pain. What he meant was that his car was a lot of trouble. I suppose he must have bought a "lemon", that is, a car full of problems and not worth its keep.

Not everybody feels the same way about cars. To some, cars are just machines on wheels. These people hunt for the best value. They look for vehicles that are affordable but reliable, gas efficient, comfortable enough, reasonably safe and

---

 * 作者佚名。如果有人要问汽车是什么,那得到的第一个回答肯定是"交通工具",是一种彻底改变了我们生活的交通工具。从 A 点到 B 点,让空间、时间都浓缩——可如果这就是汽车惟一的作用和意义,无法想像已经被机械包围的城市会是多么单调乏味。事实证明,人们对汽车的要求绝不仅仅是代步工具这么简单。当汽车在它发展的过程中被赋予了这样的涵义,那么人们拥有汽车也就不光是拥有了一件物品那样简单。现代汽车的设计在让大家感到越来越美观、舒适的同时,也把更多的涵义呈现在大家面前,比如时尚,比如个性,比如生活。当汽车成为一种生活,我们也有了更多选择不同生活的理由和方式。

not too expensive to repair. In contrast, you have also seen owners who lovingly polished their machines, dressing them in fancy seat covers, and attaching cute little doodads to the windows.

To some, cars are not machines. They are the emotional extensions of their owners. Think about the adrenalin high when one looks at a BMW. The status, speed and wealth identified with the BMW are certainly tempting. Think Jaguar, and we picture the sleek, dangerous, fast and powerful black cat with rippling muscles leaping after its prey. What about the latest hot wheels — the mini-vans and jeeps? They spell outdoors, young, sporty, carefree, cool. Or cute little Smart cars — trendy, city, efficient, modern.

There is also a special class of car owners — the sentimental. To them, modern day vehicles are artistic disasters — tasteless and boring. For them, the only real cars are vintage — those really old-fashion vehicles you see in movies about the days of our great-grandparents. These cars may be antique but not ugly. They are polished to a dazzling shine, with spotless chrome and bright clean tires.

As for me, I shudder at the cost of a new vehicle. So for now, just get me a sturdy used car that can bring me from here to there without breaking down. Besides, I do not have to fret about someone running an initiation scratch on the new paint job. ✳

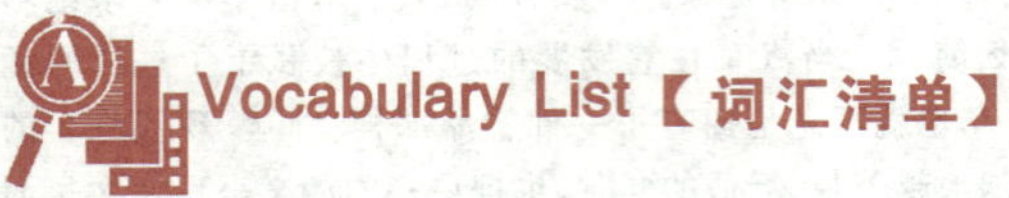

Vocabulary List 【词汇清单】

lemon /ˈlemən/ *n.* 柠檬（树）；＜美＞（非正式用语）次品，劣质品，蹩脚货

affordable /ə'fɔːdəbl/ *adj.* （费用等）买得起的，担负得起的

reasonably /'riːznəbli/ *adv.* 合理地，适度地，相当地

polish /'pɔliʃ/ *v.* 磨光，擦亮，（涂蜡等）打光滑

doodad /'duːdæd/ *n.* ＜美国口语＞小件饰物，小摆设

extension /iks'tenʃən/ *n.* 延长，延伸；扩充，扩展

adrenalin /ə'drenəlin/ *n.* 激动感，紧张感

BMW：（＝Bavarian Motor Works）德国宝马汽车/公司（宝马是驰名世界的汽车企业，也被认为是高档汽车生产业的先导。宝马公司创建于 1916 年，总部设在幕尼黑（Munich）。宝马标志中间的蓝白相间图案，代表蓝天白云和旋转不停的螺旋桨，喻示宝马公司渊源悠久的历史。宝马公司的德文全称是 Bayerische Motor en Werhe AG，BMW 即这三个单词的首位字母缩写。）

Jaguar /'dʒæɡjuə/ 美洲虎，英国轿车的一种名牌产品，其公司创建于 1934 年，总部设在考文垂（Coventry）。商标为一只正在跳跃前扑的"美洲虎"雕塑，矫健勇猛，形神兼备，具有时代感与视觉冲击力，它既代表了公司的名称，又表现出向前奔驰的力量与速度，象征该车如美洲虎一样驰骋于世界各地。

sleek /sliːk/ *adj.* （毛发等）光滑的，有光泽的

ripple /'ripl/ *v.* 波动，飘动，呈波状起伏

mini-van /'minivæn/ *n.* ＜英＞小卡车，小货车

Smart /smaːt/ 戴姆勒—克莱斯勒汽车公司所推出城市轿车的一个品牌，以高品质及运动风格而出众，具有时尚灵动的外观、卓越的动力性能和杰出的环保节能等特点。

trendy /'trendi/ *adj.* ＜口语＞极时髦的，流行的

vintage /'vintidʒ/ *adj.* 古典的，古老而享有声誉的；精选的，最好的

dazzle /'dæzl/ *adj.* （强光或闪光）炫耀，眩目，耀眼

chrome /krəum/ *n.* ＜化学＞铬，铬合金，镀有铬合金的东西

shudder /'ʃʌdə/ *n.* 震颤，战栗，发抖

sturdy /'stəːdi/ *adj.* （构造等）坚固的，结实的，耐用的

fret /fret/ *v.* 烦闷，烦恼；焦躁，焦急

scratch /'skrætʃ/ *n.* 抓痕，刮痕，擦痕

 参考译文【Suggested Translation】

汽　车

我的朋友视汽车为眼中钉，他的意思是他的车子为他添了许多麻烦。我猜想他必定是买了一件"蹩脚货"，也就是一辆问题多多、不值得保留的汽车。

每个人对汽车都有不同的看法。对某些人而言，汽车只不过是装有轮子的机器。这些人会寻找最有价值的汽车。他们所寻找的是购买得起而且也可靠、省油、足够舒适、相当安全，并且维修费用不太高的汽车。相比之下，你也会看到车主温柔的把他们的车子擦亮，并套上特制的椅套，还在车窗上挂上可爱的小饰物。

对有些人而言，汽车不是机器，而是车主情感上的延伸。想想看到一辆宝马车时的兴奋之感，它所带来的对地位、速度和财富的认同的确颇具诱惑。想到美洲虎，就可能想到一只皮毛光滑、危险、快速和肌肉强健有力的黑猫在抓捕猎物。而最近炙手可热的车子——小型车辆和吉普车——又代表什么？它们代表户外、年轻、运动气质、自由自在、独具一格。另外，小巧可爱的 Smart，代表时髦、都市、效率和现代。

此外，还有另一族群的车主，就是怀旧感伤的车主。他们把现代的汽车视为艺术的败类——单调又乏味。对他们而言，古典精致的车辆才真正称得上汽车——就是那些我们可以从祖父辈时代的影片上看到的古董老爷车。这些车虽然古老但并不丑陋，它们已被擦得明亮眩目，并且具有无瑕的铬片和干净亮丽的轮胎。

至于我，想到一辆新汽车的价位就令我颤抖。所以到目前为止，只要给我一辆坚固耐用的、能将我从此地运至彼地而中途又不抛锚的车子即可。除此以外，我也用不着顾虑有人在新漆的车身上刮上划痕。◆

The Lover and the Beloved*

First of all, love is a joint experience between two persons — but the fact that it is a joint experience does not mean that it is a similar experience of the two people involved. There are the lover and the beloved, but these two come from different countries. Often the beloved is only a stimulus for all the stored-up love which has lain quiet within the lover for a long time hitherto. And somehow every lover knows this. He feels in his soul that his love is a solitary thing. He comes to know a new, strange loneliness and it is this knowledge which makes him suffer. So there is only one thing for the lover to do. He must house his love within himself as best he can; he must create for himself a whole new inward world — a world intense and

---

* 作者卡森·麦卡勒斯（Carson McCullers，1917—1967），美国著名的黑人女作家，其年轻时患病导致半身瘫痪，在轮椅上度过余生，本文选自其代表作《伤心咖啡店之歌》（The Ballad of the Sad Cafe）。正如她自己所说："世界上有爱者，也有被爱者，这是截然不同的两类人。"

strange, complete in himself. Let it be added here that this lover about whom we speak need not necessarily be a young man saving for a wedding ring — this lover can be man, woman, child, or indeed any human creature on this earth.

Now, the beloved can also be of any description. The most outlandish people can be the stimulus for love. A man may be a doddering great-grandfather and still love only a strange girl he saw in the streets of Cheehaw one afternoon two decades past. The preacher may love a fallen woman. The beloved may be treacherous, greasy-headed, and given to evil habits. Yes, and the lover may see this as clearly as anyone else — but that does not affect the evolution of his love one whit. A most mediocre person can be the object of a love which is wild, extravagant, and beautiful as the poison lilies in the swamp. A good man may be the stimulus for a love both violent and debased, or a jabbering madman may bring about in the soul of someone a tender and simple idyll. Therefore, the value and quality of any love is determined solely by the lover himself.

It is for this reason that most of us would rather love than be loved. Almost everyone wants to be the lover. And the curt truth is that, in a deep secret way, the state of being beloved is intolerable to many. The beloved fears and hates the lover, and with the best of reasons. For the lover is forever trying to strip bare his beloved. The lover craves any possible relation with the beloved, even if this experience can cause him only pain. ✳

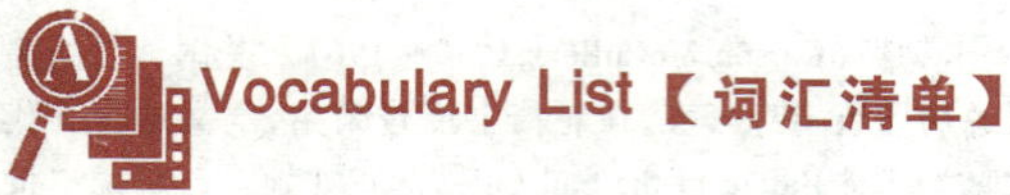

Vocabulary List 【词汇清单】

stimulus /ˈstimjuləs/ *n.* 刺激, 激励, 刺激因素

hitherto /ˌhiðətuː/ *adv.*　迄今,至今,到目前为止

solitary /ˈsɔlitəri/ *adj.*　孤独的,寂寞的,孤寂的

outlandish /autˈlændiʃ/ *adj.*　稀奇古怪的,怪异的,奇异的

doddering /ˈdɔdəriŋ/ *adj.*　蹒跚的,踉跄的,摇晃的

preacher /ˈpriːtʃə/ *n.*　布道者,传教士,牧师

treacherous /ˈtretʃərəs/ *adj.*　背叛的,不可靠的,奸诈的

whit /wit/ *n.*　些微,一点点,丝毫(主要用于否定结构中)

mediocre /ˈmiːdiəukə/ *adj.*　普通的,平凡的

extravagant /iksˈtrævigənt/ *adj.*　放纵的,挥霍的,奢侈浪费的

lily /ˈlili/ *n.*　<植物>百合,百合花,睡莲

swamp /swæmp/ *n.*　沼泽,沼地,湿地

debase /diˈbeis/ *v.*　败坏,贬低,降低(品质、价值等)

jabber /ˈdʒæbə/ *v.*　急促而含糊地说,无意义地讲话

idyll /ˈidil/ *n.*　田园短诗(或散文),牧歌

solely /ˈsəuli/ *adv.*　独自地,单独地;仅仅,只是

curt /kəːt/ *adj.*　(说话、文笔等)简短的,扼要的,简略的

intolerable /inˈtɔlərəbl/ *adj.*　无法忍受的,不能容忍的

crave /kreiv/ *v.*　渴望,热望,非常需要

参考译文【Suggested Translation】

施爱者和被爱者

爱,首先是两个人之间共同的一种经历。但是,这并不意味着相关的两个人的经历是相似的。其中,一方是施爱者,另一方则是被爱者。他们两个来自不同的世界。通常,被爱者只是一个刺激因素,激发起施爱者长期隐藏在心底的爱。而每一位施爱者都明白这一点。在灵魂深处,他感到他的爱是孤独的。他会逐渐地认识到一种新奇而又陌生的孤寂。而且,正是这一认识使他忍受痛苦。因此,施爱者只有惟一一种选择。他必须尽可能地把爱珍藏在心底。他必须自己创造一个全新的内心世界——一个深切、陌生而却完整的世界。需要补充说明的

是，我们谈论的施爱者未必是一个为买结婚戒指而储蓄的年轻人——他可能是男人、女人或者是孩子，甚或是世界上任何一个人。

当然，被爱者也同样可能是任何类型的人。最怪异的人可能会激起爱的涟漪。一位步履蹒跚的曾祖父可能依旧爱恋着二十年前的一个下午在街头见到的一位陌生女郎。一位牧师也许会爱上一个堕落的女人。被爱者也可能奸诈、油头滑脑，而且沉溺于各种恶习。的确，施爱者对此可能像其他人一样了解得一清二楚。但是，这丝毫不影响他的爱情的进展。一个很平凡的人可能成为一个疯狂、放纵而美丽的爱的对象，就像沼泽地里的毒百合；一个善良的人可能激发起一种粗暴而有损人格的爱；或者一个语无伦次的疯子也可能使某个人充满温柔而纯朴的浪漫情怀。因此，任何一种爱的价值和品质只能取决于施爱者本身。

正是基于这一原因，我们当中的大多数人宁愿去爱而不是被人所爱。几乎每个人都想成为爱的给予者。而事实上，对许多人来说，处于被爱的情形在内心深处是难以承受的。被爱者总是害怕进而憎恨施爱者，而这种心理的产生有其充分的理由。因为，施爱者总是在试图不断地使被爱者尊严无存。他总是企盼能够与被爱者建立任何可能的某种关系，即使这一经历结果只能给他招致痛苦。◆

Human Life Like a Poem[*]

I think that, from a biological standpoint, human life almost reads like a poem. It has its own rhythm and beat, its internal cycles of growth and decay. It begins with innocent childhood, followed by awkward adolescence trying awkwardly to adapt itself to mature society, with its young passions and follies, its ideals and ambitions; then it reaches a manhood of intense activities, profiting from experience and

---

* 作者林语堂(1895—1976)，福建龙溪人，原名和乐，后改玉堂，又改语堂，曾获上海圣约翰大学学士学位、美国哈佛大学比较文学硕士学位、德国莱比锡大学语言学博士学位，是一位以英文写作而扬名海外的中国作家，也是集语言学家、哲学家、文学家、旅游家、发明家于一身的知名学者。林语堂因为翻译"幽默"（Humor）一词，以及创办《论语》、《人间世》和《宇宙风》三本杂志，提倡幽默文学，"幽默大师"自此加冕，同时提倡"以自我为中心，以闲适为格调"的小品文，其代表作有《吾国与吾民》、《生活的艺术》、《京华烟云》和《风声鹤唳》等经典英文名著。本文选自其英文名作《生活的重要性》（The Importance of Living）。

learning more about society and human nature; at middle age, there is a slight easing of tension, a mellowing of character like the ripening of fruit or the mellowing of good wine, and the gradual acquiring of a more tolerant, more cynical and at the same time a kindlier view of life; then in the sunset of our life, the endocrine glands decrease their activity, and if we have a true philosophy of old age and have ordered our life pattern according to it, it is for us the age of peace and security and leisure and contentment; finally, life flickers out and one goes into eternal sleep, never to wake up again. One should be able to sense the beauty of this rhythm of life, to appreciate, as we do in grand symphonies, its main theme, its strains of conflict and the final resolution.

The movements of these cycles are very much the same in a normal life, but the music must be provided by the individual himself. In some souls, the discordant note becomes harsher and harsher and finally overwhelms or submerges the main melody. Sometimes the discordant note gains so much power that the music can no longer go on, and the individual shoots himself with a pistol or jumps into a river. But that is because his original leitmotif has been hopelessly over-shadowed through the lack of a good self-education. Otherwise the normal human life runs to its normal end in a kind of dignified movement and procession.

No one can say that a life with childhood, manhood and old age is not a beautiful arrangement; the day has its morning, noon and sunset, and the year has its seasons, and it is good that it is so. There is no good or bad in life, except what is good according to its own season. And if we take this biological view of life and try to live according to the seasons, no one but a conceited fool or an impossible idealist can deny that human life can be lived like a poem. ✲

Vocabulary List 【词汇清单】

biological /ˌbaiə'lɔdʒikəl/ *adj.* 生物学的，与生物学有关的

rhythm /'riðəm/ *n.* 节奏，韵律

decay /di'kei/ *n.* （精力等）衰减，衰退，衰弱

innocent /'inəsnt/ *adj.* 单纯的，天真烂漫的

adolescence /ˌædəu'lesns/ *n.* 青春，青春期（一般指成年以前由 13 至 15 岁的发育期）

awkwardly /'ɔ:kwə:dli/ *adv.* 尴尬地；不熟练地，笨拙地

folly /'fɔli/ *n.* 愚笨，愚蠢（的行为或思想）

mellow /'meləu/ *v.* 使（变）醇香，使（变）成熟，使（变）柔美

endocrine /'endəukrain/ *n.* 内分泌的，内分泌腺的

gland /glænd/ *n.* <解剖学>腺（一个或一群细胞或一个器官，它们能生产出供身体或体腔使用的或者排泄体内废物的分泌液）

flicker /'flikə/ *v.* （如蜡烛在风中）闪烁（不定），闪动，忽隐忽现，明灭不定

symphony /'simfəni/ *n.* <音乐>交响乐，交响曲

discordant /dis'kɔ:dənt/ *adj.* 不和谐的，不协调的，不调和的

harsh /ha:ʃ/ *adj.* （声音）尖得（或粗得）令人不快的，刺耳的

submerge /səb'mə:dʒ/ *v.* 淹没，浸没，遮盖

pistol /'pistl/ *n.* 手枪

leitmotif /'laitməuˌti:f/ *n.* （也作 leitmotiv）<音乐>主导主题，主旋律

over-shadow /ˌəuvə'ʃædəu/ *v.* 对…投上阴影，遮暗，夺去…光彩

dignified /'dignifaid/ *adj.* 有（或表示）尊严的，尊贵的

conceited /kən'si:tid/ *adj.* 自高自大的，骄傲自满的；异想天开的

参考译文【Suggested Translation】

人 生 如 诗

我想，从生物学的观点来说，人生品味起来就像一首诗。它有其自身的韵律和节拍，有其生老病死的内在循环过程。它以天真烂漫的童年为序曲；接着便是青涩的青春期，带着青年人的热情和愚蠢、理想和抱负，羞涩、懵懂地迈向成人的世界；然后便进入一个活力充沛的成年时期，这个时期人们从阅历中获益，对社会及人性也有了更多了解；到中年之时，压力才稍为减轻，人的性格就像熟透的水果或醇厚的美酒一般，更为圆熟，这时候，对人生的态度也逐渐变得更宽容、更随性、更仁慈。此后，便到了我们的迟暮之年，内分泌腺的活动逐渐趋缓。如果我们对年老持一种真正的达观态度，并以此来安排我们的生活方式，那么，这个时期对我们来说，就是安宁、稳定、闲逸和满足的时期；最终，生命的火光摇曳不定，之后人将永远地长眠，不再醒来。人应该能够体会这种人生之韵的美，应该能够像欣赏盛大的交响乐那样，去欣赏人生的主旋律，欣赏它的冲突片断和最后的尾声。

这些循环过程的运动在每个常人的生命中并无二至，但是生命的乐曲须由我们每个人自己来谱写。在有些人的灵魂之中，不和谐的音符变得愈加刺耳，到最后完全盖过或是湮没了生命的主旋律。有时候，这种不和谐的音符会如此强大以至于生命的乐曲不能继续演奏，而使人饮弹自尽或者投河而亡。但那是由于缺乏良好的自我修养，人最初的主旋律就已投上了无望的阴影。否则，一个正常人的生活会以一种尊贵的方式演进而最后得以正常结束。

没有人能够说，由童年、成年和老年组成的人生不是一种完美的安排；就像一天有早晨、中午和晚上，一年有四季，如此存在就是美好的。人生并没有好坏之分，只要符合我们所处的阶段，生活就都是人生的大好时光。而如果我们采纳这种看待人生的生物学观点，并且，尽量依照不同的阶段来生活，那么，除了狂妄自大的蠢人或不可理喻的理想主义者之外，没有人能够否认：人生可以活得像一首诗。◆

Benjamin Franklin*

Franklin's life is full of charming stories which all young men should know — how he peddled ballads in Boston, and stood as the guest of kings in Europe; how he worked his passage as a stowaway to Philadelphia, and rode in the queen's own litter in France; how he walked the streets of Philadelphia, homeless and unknown, with three penny rolls for his breakfast, and dined at the tables of princes, and received his friends in a palace; how he raised a kite from a cow shed, and was showered with all the high degrees the colleges of the world could give; how he was duped by a false friend as a boy, and became the friend of all humanity

---

* 作者埃尔布里奇·斯特雷特·布鲁克斯（Elbridge Streeter Brooks, 1846—1902），生平不详。本文选自其名作《本杰明·富兰克林的真实故事》（The True Story of Benjamin Franklin）。

as a man; how he was made Major General Franklin, only to resign because, as he said, he was no soldier, and yet helped to organize the army that stood before the trained troops of England and Germany.

This poor Boston boy, with scarcely a day's schooling, became master of six languages and never stopped studying; this neglected apprentice tamed the lightning, made his name famous, received degrees and diplomas from colleges in both hemispheres, and became forever remembered as "Doctor Franklin", philosopher, patriot, scientist, philanthropist and statesman. Self-made, self-taught, and self-reared, the candle maker's son gave light to all the world; the street ballad seller set all men singing of liberty; the runaway apprentice became the most sought after man of two continents, and brought his native land to praise and honor him.

He built America, for what our Republic is today is largely due to the prudence, the forethought, the statesmanship, the enterprise, the wisdom, and the ability of Benjamin Franklin. He belongs to the world, but especially does he belong to America. As the nations honored him while living, so the Republic glorifies him when dead, and has enshrined him in the choicest of its niches, the one he regarded as the loftiest — the hearts of the common people, from whom he had sprung and in their hearts Franklin will live forever. ✳

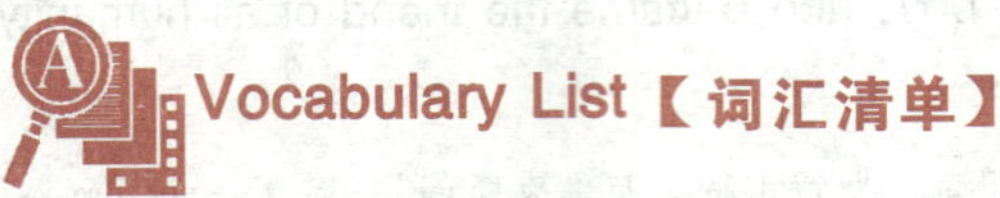

Vocabulary List 【词汇清单】

peddle /'pedl/ *v.* 沿街叫卖，挨户兜售

ballad /'bæləd/ *n.* 民歌，民谣，叙事歌谣（唱本）

stowaway /ˈstəuəwei/ *n.* 偷渡者,无票偷乘者(藏于轮船或其他交通工具内以免付票费的人)

Philadelphia /ˌfiləˈdelfjə/ *n.* 费城(美国宾西法尼亚州东南部港口城市)

litter /ˈlitə/ *n.* (旧时抬要人的)轿,舆

dupe /djuːp/ *v.* 欺骗,诓骗,愚弄

apprentice /əˈprentis/ *n.* 学徒,艺徒,徒弟

diploma /diˈpləumə/ *n.* 奖状,(授予荣誉、特权等的)证书;毕业文凭,毕业证书

hemisphere /ˈhemisfiə/ *n.* (地球的)半球,半球上的国家

patriot /ˈpeitriət/ *n.* 爱国者,爱国主义者

philanthropist /fiˈlænθrəpist/ *n.* (尤指对慈善机构进行捐款的)慈善家

prudence /ˈpruːdəns/ *n.* 谨慎,慎重,审慎,深谋远虑

enterprise /ˈentəpraiz/ *n.* 事业心,进取心,冒险(首创)精神

enshrine /inˈʃrain/ *v.* 把…置于神龛内;把…奉为神圣,祀奉;铭记

choice /tʃɔis/ *adj.* 精选的;(质量等)优良的,上等的

niche /nitʃ/ *n.* 壁龛(墙壁上凹进去的空间,用来放置雕像、花瓶等装饰品)

lofty /ˈlɔfti/ *adj.* (品德)高尚的,崇高的

 ## 参考译文【Suggested Translation】

本杰明·富兰克林

兰克林的一生充满了令人着迷的故事,所有的年轻人都应该知道:他怎样在波士顿街头叫卖叙事歌谣唱本,而后来却成为欧洲各国君主的贵客;他怎样偷偷上船,在船上靠干活抵偿船票才来到费城,而后来却坐进了法国王后的乘舆;他怎样在费城沿街瞎逛,无家可归,没人理睬,仅买得起三便士的面包卷(卷饼)当早饭,而后来却在君王的餐桌前进餐,在宫殿里接待

朋友；他如何从牛棚上放起风筝，而后来却荣获世界上多所名牌大学所能授予的一切最高学位；他在童年时如何被一个虚假的朋友所蒙骗，而后来却成为全人类的朋友；他如何被授予少将军衔，但是他却辞职不干，因为他说他没有军人气度，然而就是他帮助组建了同训练有素的英德联军对阵的联邦军队。

这个波士顿的穷孩子几乎没有上过一天学，后来却掌握了六种语言，并且学习锲而不舍。这个被人忽视的学徒制服了闪电，扬名天下，获得了东西两半球各国大学的学位和证书，成为留芳百世的"富兰克林博士"、哲学家、爱国者、科学家、慈善家和政治家。这个蜡烛制造商的儿子自我奋斗、自学成才、自强自立，给全世界带来了光明；这个叙事歌谣唱本的街头叫卖者让全人类唱起了自由之歌；这个逃亡的学徒成了欧、美两块大陆最令人仰慕的人物，使他的祖国对他赞扬不已、崇敬备至。

他缔造了美国，因为我们的共和国能有今天，在很大程度上归功于本杰明·富兰克林的深谋远虑、远见卓识、治国之术、进取精神、大睿大智和精明能干。他属于全世界，但是他更属于美国。他在世时，各国人民尊敬他；他去世后，共和国同样颂扬他，把他尊奉在最珍贵的壁龛里———一个他视为最崇高的位置——普通老百姓的心中。富兰克林来自于人民，他也将永远活人民的心中。◆

Perseverance*

Napoleon declared, "Victory belongs to the most persevering." Upon careful study we find perseverance depends upon three things — purpose, will, and enthusiasm. He who has a purpose is always concentrating his forces. By the will, the hope and the plan are prevented from evaporating into dreams. Enthusiasm keeps the interest up, and makes the obstacles seem small.

Life is in a sense a battle. The man who thinks to get on by mere smartness and by idling meets failure at last. Perseverance is the master impulse of the firmest souls, and holds

---

* 作者佚名。芸芸众生，有多少执着和勤奋地追求着人生理想的人，都赤诚地燃烧着自己的生命，刻苦地磨砺着自己的灵魂。可是又有多少人在自己将要成功之际退缩和放弃，使自己当初美好的梦想付诸东流，使自己多年的希冀化为泡影。坚持不懈吧！只有这样，幸福才会向我们伸出温暖的双手，我们才能迈向更加华美、峻拔与深沉的人生新境界。

the key to those treasure-houses of knowledge from which the world has drawn its wealth both of wisdom and of moral worth.

Great men never wait for opportunities; they make them. They seize upon whatever is at hand, work out their problem, and master the situation. The greatest thing a man can do in this world is to make the most possible out of the stuff that has been given to him. This is success and there is no other.

One of the important lessons of life is to learn how to get victory out of defeat. It takes courage and stamina, when mortified by humiliating disaster, to seek in the ruins the elements of future conquest. Yet this measures the difference between those who succeed and those who fail. We cannot measure a man by his failures. We must know what use he makes of them. The man who has not fought his way upward and does not bear the scar of desperate conflict does not know the highest meaning of success. ✳

 ## Vocabulary List 【词汇清单】

perseverance /ˌpəːsiːˈviərəns/ *n.* 坚定不移,坚持不懈,持之以恒

Napoleon /nəˈpəuljən/ （全名 Napoleon Bonaparte）拿破仑一世（1769—1821,法国皇帝（1804—1814）,伟大的军事战略家）

enthusiasm /inˈθjuːziæzəm/ *n.* 热情,热心,热忱,激发热情的事物

concentrate /ˈkɔnsəntreit/ *v.* 集中（思想、精力等）,使集中于（或引向）一点

evaporate /iˈvæpəreit/ *v.* （使）蒸发,（使）挥发;（蒸气般）消失,消散

obstacle /ˈɔbstəkl/ *n.* 障碍,妨碍（物）

impulse /ˈimpʌls/ *n.* 刺激,激励;冲力,推动力

stamina /ˈstæminə/ *n.* （对疲劳、疾病、贫困等的）耐力,毅力,持久力

mortify /ˈmɔːtifai/ *v.* 使受辱,损害…自尊心

humiliate /hjuːˈmiliˌeit/ *v.* 使受辱,使丢脸,羞辱,屈辱

conquest /ˈkɔŋkwist/ *n.* 征服,战胜（的行为或过程）

参考译文【Suggested Translation】

坚 持 不 懈

破仑宣称,"胜利属于坚持不懈的人"。经过仔细研究,我们会发现,坚持不懈取决于于三个方面——目标,意志和热情。一个目标明确的人总是能够集中他的精力。有了坚定的决心,就能够避免希望和计划在梦想中化为泡影。而冲天的热情,能够让人永远兴致勃勃,藐视一切艰难险阻。

从某种意义上讲,生活是一场战役。那种妄想凭借小聪明闲混到出人头地的人最终只会落得失败的下场。坚持不懈是那些信念坚定的人主导性的精神动力,其把持着开启那些知识宝库的钥匙,全世界的人都可以从中获取智慧和道德的财富。

伟大的人们从不坐等机会;他们会自行创造。他们会抓住一切手边的机会,解决遇到的难题,并且自己掌控局面。在这个世界上,一个人所能做的最伟大的事情就是,从给予他的有限的机会之中进行最大可能的发掘。这便是成功,仅此而已。

人生最重要的一课,便是学会如何从失败之中迈向成功。身负失败的屈辱和不幸,我们需要勇气和毅力,在失败的废墟中寻找未来获胜的要素。而这恰能衡量出成功者与失败者的不同。我们不能用失败来衡量一个人。我们必须了解他如何利用这些失败。一个不思上进、没有绝望挣扎的伤痕烙在心头的人,无法体会成功的最高意境。◆

Paris: a Romantic Capital[*]

Ah, beautiful Paris. For centuries this city has attracted the admiration of the world. The allure and charm of Paris captivate all who visit there.

Where can you discover the charm of Paris for yourself? Is it in the legacy of all the Fre"nch rulers who worked to

---

　　*　作者佚名。巴黎——浪漫之都,世界著名的繁华大都市之一,是法国的政治中心、文化中心和举世闻名的美食之都。从历史上讲,1789 年 7 月 14 日以前,巴黎一直是法国历代王朝的宫廷所在地。巴黎是文学家、艺术家的摇篮。如果说巴黎的生活场景是莫里哀、雨果、巴尔扎克、大仲马等大文豪的创作源泉,那么塞纳河便是印象主义画派的母亲。在巴黎,大厨师的地位等同于富豪名流,备受尊崇;五星级餐厅傲视群伦,是社会的谈论焦点、观光客的话题;顶级餐厅打出"一生一次奢华"的口号,让人感觉如果不去似乎缺憾无限。咖啡,尤其是喝露天咖啡,在巴黎是全民运动,更是一种悠闲的表征。雄伟庄严的凯旋门和屹立于塞纳河畔的艾菲尔铁塔是巴黎及法国的标志。您不能不去的地方——收藏艺术瑰宝的卢浮宫、美伦美奂的凡尔赛宫、集历史、建筑、文学于一身的巴黎圣母院、可能是世界上最漂亮的大道——香榭丽舍……

beautify their beloved city? Is it in the famous castles, palaces, statues and monuments, such as the Eiffel Tower? Can you find it in the world-class museums, such as the Louvre? Perhaps Paris' allure lies in the zest and style of the Parisians.

When you visit Paris, you don't have to spend all of your time visiting museums and monuments. They are certainly worthy of your time, but ignore them for a day. First take some time to look around and experience life in Paris. You'll find it charming.

Take a stroll along the Seine River. Browse through the art vendors' colorful paintings. Peek through delicate iron gates at the well-kept gardens. Watch closely for the French attention to detail that has made France synonymous with good taste. You will see it in the design of a doorway or arch and in the little fountains and quaint balconies. No matter where you look, you will find everyday objects transformed into works by art.

Spend some time in a quiet park relaxing on an old bench. Lie on your back on the green grass. When you need refreshment, try coffee and pastries at a sidewalk cafe. Strike up a conversation with a Parisian. This isn't always easy, though. With such a large international population living in Paris, ture natives are hard to find these days.

As evening comes to Paris, enchantment rises with the mist over the riverfront. You may hear music from an outdoor concert nearby: classical, jaz, opera or chansons, those French folk songs. Parisians love their music. The starry sky is their auditorium. You can also hear concerts in the chateaux and cathedrals. In Paris the Music never ends.

Don't miss the highlight of Paris evening: eating out.

Parisians are proud of their cuisine. And rightly so; it's world famous. Gourmet dining is one of the indispensable joys of living. You need a special guidebook to help you choose one of the hundreds of excellent restaurants. The capital of France boasts every regional specialty, cheese and wine the country has to offer. If you don't know what to order, ask for the suggested menu. The chef likes to showcase his best dishes there. Remember, you haven't tasted the true flavor of France until you've dined at a French restaurant in Paris.

After your gourmet dinner, take a walking tour of the floodlit monuments. Cross the Pont Neuf, the oldest bridge in the city, to the Ile de la Cite. The most famous landmark of Paris looms up in front of you: the Notre Dame Cathedral (Cathedral of Our Lady). Stand in the square in front of the cathedral. Here, you are standing in the center of France. All distances are measured from the front of Notre Dame. Every road in France leads to her front door. All French kings and leaders have journeyed here to commemorate important occasions and give thanks. Notre Dame is the heart of Paris and the heart of France.

Your visit in Paris has only just begun. You've just started to discover the charm of this old city. May the rest of your journey be unforgettable. When it is time to leave, you will go reluctantly. You will say with the French, "A bientot, Paris, a bientot!" (See you again soon, Paris!) ✳

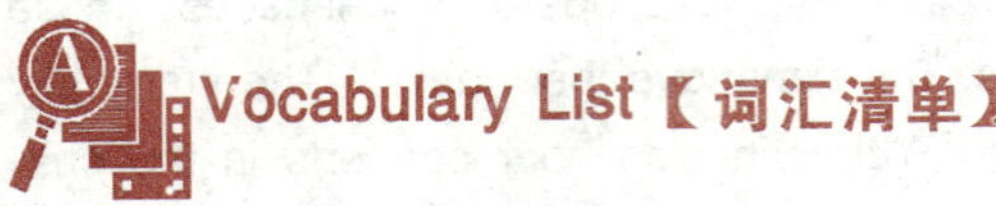

Vocabulary List 【词汇清单】

allure /əˈljuə/ *n.* 诱惑力, 吸引力, 魅力
captivate /ˈkæptiveit/ *v.* （用魅力、美貌、优点等）迷住, 使着

迷,强烈地感染

legacy /ˈlegəsi/ *n.* 遗产,遗赠(祖先、前人或过去相传下来的某种东西)

castle /ˈkaːsl/ *n.* 城堡(多指中世纪贵族的要塞)

monument /ˈmɔnjumənt/ *n.* 纪念碑,纪念馆;遗址,遗迹

the Eiffel Tower：(巴黎)艾菲尔铁塔(由法国工程师艾菲尔为1889年在巴黎举行的世界博览会而设计建造的铁塔)

the Louvre：卢浮宫(巴黎王宫,18世纪起辟为艺术博物馆)

parisian /pəˈrizjən/ *n.* 巴黎人 *adj.* 巴黎的,巴黎式的,巴黎人的

the Seine River：塞纳河(法国北部河流,发源于东部朗格勒高原,注入英吉利海峡,它从罗马时代起就是重要的商业水道)

browse /brauz/ *v.* 浏览,翻阅,随便看看

peek /piːk/ *v.* 偷看,窥视;一瞥,尤指从缝隙(或隐蔽处)看

synonymous /siˈnɔniməs/ *adj.* 同义的,同义词的;等同于…的(with)

arch /aːtʃ/ *n.* 拱门,拱桥,拱洞,拱廊,拱街,拱顶

quaint /kweint/ *adj.* (设计等)灵巧的,精巧的;古雅的,优雅的

balcony /ˈbælkəni/ *n.* 阳台,眺台

pastry /ˈpeistri/ *n.* 面制糕点,有馅的点心(如大馅饼等)

enchantment /inˈtʃaːntmənt/ *n.* 魅力,魔力,吸引力

chanson /ˈʃænsən/ *n.* <法>香颂(11—13世纪的古法语史诗,尤指《罗兰之歌》);<法>歌曲,歌谣,小调

auditorium /ˌɔːdiˈtɔːriəm/ *n.* <美>(供公众集会、演讲等用的)礼堂,大讲堂

chateau /ˈʃætəu/ *n.* (复数形式:chateaux)<法>城堡,别墅

cathedral /kəˈθiːdrəl/ *n.* (泛指)大教堂

cuisine /kwi(ː)ˈziːn/ *n.* 厨房烹调法,烹饪法,烹调风格

gourmet /ˈguəmei/ *n.* <法>美食家,讲究饮食的人,美酒美食品尝家

indispensable /ˌindisˈpensəbl/ *adj.* 不可缺少的,绝对必要的

chef /ʃef/ *n.* <法>(餐馆的)男厨师长,主厨,厨房领班师傅

floodlit /ˈflʌdlit/ *adj.* 用泛光灯(探照灯)照明的

Notre Dame /'nəutrə deim/ *adj.* （巴黎）圣母院（全称 Notre
　　Dame de Paris）
commemorate /kə'meməreit/ *v.* （以某种仪式）纪念，庆祝
reluctantly /ri'lʌktəntli/ *adv.* 不情愿地，勉强地

 **参考译文【Suggested Translation】**

巴黎：浪漫之都

啊，美丽的巴黎！几个世纪以来，这个城市一直受到世人的
倾慕。巴黎的诱惑与魅力令所有到此游玩的人深深着迷。

巴黎之于你，其魅力究竟何在？是在历任的法国统治者美
化他们所钟爱的城市所留下的传统里？还是在那些著名的城
堡、皇宫、雕像和纪念碑，例如艾菲尔铁塔之中？你能否在世界
一流的博物馆，如卢浮宫中找到它？或许巴黎的诱惑力就在于
巴黎人的特殊品味和风格吧。

当你到巴黎游玩时，不必把时间全都花在看博物馆和纪念
碑上面。当然，它们很值得你花些时间，但今天权且忘掉它们
吧。首先到四处看看，体验一下巴黎的生活。你会发现它的迷
人之处。

沿着塞纳河散散步。沿途浏览一下卖美术作品人们色彩缤
纷的绘画，透过那些精致的铁门，可以瞥见里面精心照看的花
园。仔细留心法国人对于细节的独具匠心，这使得法国成为高
雅品位的代名词。而这些在门廊或拱门以及小巧的喷泉和奇妙
的阳台的设计上就可见一斑。无论你向哪里看，你都会发现日
常物品都已变成了艺术品。

花些时间，在一座宁静的公园里的古旧长椅上放松一下，或
躺在青青的草地上休憩一番。想吃点儿点心的时候，就尝尝路
边咖啡馆的咖啡和糕点。找一个巴黎人聊聊天，不过这也不太
容易。在国际人口如此密集的巴黎，如今要找到一个真正的当
地人是很困难的。

傍晚来临之时，随着河岸上升起的雾气，巴黎的魅力也随之

而起。你会听到附近露天音乐会所演奏的乐曲：古典乐、爵士乐、歌剧或是香颂即法国的民歌。巴黎人热爱自己的音乐。繁星点缀的天空，就是他们演奏的大礼堂。你也可以在城堡或教堂里聆听音乐会。在巴黎，音乐是从不会止息的。

别错过了巴黎夜晚的亮点：下馆子。巴黎人对他们的烹饪引以为荣。理应如此，因为它驰名世界。美食本来就是与生活享乐不可分割的。为了帮你从几百所绝佳的餐厅中做选择，你需要一本特别的指南。法国的首都以全国各地的特色风味、乳酪和酒著称于世，如果你不知道要叫什么，就看看推荐的菜谱。大厨喜欢在此将他最拿手的菜作一番展示。请记住，没到巴黎的法国餐厅吃饭之前，都不算尝过真正的法国风味。

在你的晚餐美食之后，可以到一片灯海照耀的纪念碑走一趟。穿过"第九桥"（此城市中最古老的桥），到达"城市之岛"。巴黎最有名的标志性建筑就隐约地呈现在你面前：圣母院。站在教堂前面的广场，在这里，你即处于法国的正中心。所有的距离皆是以圣母院前门开始测算的。法国的每一条道路都通往它的前门。法国所有的国王和统治者都曾经到此来纪念重要的节日或表示感恩。圣母院是巴黎的中心，也是法国的中心。

你的巴黎之旅才刚刚开始呢。你才刚刚开始发现这个古老城市的魅力。祝愿你剩余的旅程将令你难以忘怀。当你该启程回家的时候，你会依依不舍。你将会用法语说道："后会有期，巴黎！"◆

Eulogy for a Dog*

Gentlemen of the jury, the best friend a man has in this world may turn against him and become his enemy. His son or daughter that he has reared with loving care may prove ungrateful.

Those who are nearest and dearest to us, those whom

---

* 作者乔治·格雷厄姆·维斯特（George Graham Vest, 1830—1904），生于美国密苏里州，1879—1903 年间任美国参议员，他是当时美国参议院最有名的演讲家和辩论家。当年，他在密苏里州做律师时，他的当事人状告别人枪杀了自家的狗。这桩关于狗的官司由地方法院一直打到了最高法院。1870 年 9 月，在本案终审时，参议员维斯特在法庭上代表自己的当事人朗诵了一篇名为《狗的颂歌》的辩护词。陪审团和法官们被这篇千古难寻的奇文深深地感动，维斯特便最终赢得了这场诉讼。此案在当时立即引起了轰动，影响面很广，从而成为世界著名的法律案例。同样，维斯特的这篇《狗的颂歌》文辞优美，工于排比，善用对比，将狗对主人最朴素、最纯真、最珍贵的情感表达得淋漓尽致，以其强烈的感染力成为全球养犬爱好者珍爱的经典篇章，长久以来备受推崇，万人争颂，其影响力至今不衰。

we trust with our happiness and our good name, may become traitors to their faith. The money that a man has, he may lose. It flies away from him perhaps when he needs it most. A man's reputation may be sacrificed in a moment of ill-considered action.

The people who are prone to fall on their knees to do us honor when success is with us may be the first to throw the stone of malice when failure settles its cloud upon our heads.

The one absolutely unselfish friend that a man can have in this selfish world, the one that never deserts him and the one that never proves ungrateful or treacherous is his dog.

Gentlemen of the jury, a man's dog stands by him in prosperity and in poverty, in health and in sickness.

He will sleep on the cold ground where the wintry winds blow and the snow drives fiercely, if only he may be near his master's side. He will kiss the hand that has no food to offer, he will lick the wounds and sores that come in encounters with the roughness of the world. He guards the sleep of his pauper master as if he were a prince.

When all other friends desert, he remains. When riches take wings and reputation falls to pieces, he is as constant in his love as the sun in its journey through the heavens.

If fortune drives the master forth an outcast in the world, friendless and homeless, the faithful dog asks no higher privilege than that of accompanying him to guard against danger, to fight against his enemies, and when the last scene of all comes, and death takes the master in its embrace and his body is laid away in the cold ground, no matter if all other friends pursue their way, there by his graveside will the noble dog be found, his head between his paws, his eyes sad but open in alert watchfulness, faithful and true, even to death. ✳

 Vocabulary List【词汇清单】

eulogy /ˈjuːlədʒi/ *n.* 颂词,颂文,歌功颂德的话(或文章)

traitor /ˈtreitə/ *n.* 叛逆者,背叛者

be prone to：有…倾向的,易于…的

malice /ˈmælis/ *n.* 恶意,怨恨;＜法律＞预谋,蓄意犯罪

treacherous /ˈtretʃərəs/ *adj.* 背叛的,不忠的,背信弃义的

wintry /ˈwintri/ *adj.* 寒冷的,风雪交加的

fiercely /ˈfiəsli/ *adv.* 猛烈地,凛冽地,狂暴地

pauper /ˈpɔːpə/ *n.* 靠救济过活的人;穷人,贫民

outcast /ˈautkaːst/ *adj.* 被遗弃的,无家可归的

graveside /ˈgreivˌsaid/ *n.* ＜美＞坟墓边,坟墓旁

watchfulness /ˈwɔtʃfulnis/ *n.* 注意,留心;警惕,戒备

 参考译文【Suggested Translation】

狗 的 颂 歌

陪审团诸君:世上亲如手足的挚友可能会疏远叛离,反目成仇。含辛茹苦的父母面临的也许是儿女的忘恩负义。

　　有些人备受我们尊敬和爱戴,有些人是我们幸福之所依,声誉之所系;即便如此,他们也会背信弃义。人的钱财会失去,而且可能在急需之时偏偏散失殆尽。人的名誉也会因为一时的考虑不周而荡然无存。

　　当胜利与我们同行时,有些人往往向我们俯伏下跪,称颂致敬;但是当风云突变,失败的黑云压顶之时,最先落井下石的或许就是他们。

　　在这个私欲横流的世界上,一个人可能拥有的绝对无私的朋友乃是他的狗。它从不抛弃主人,永不忘恩负义,也永不心怀鬼胎。

　　陪审团诸君:无论在主人富裕之日还是贫困之时,也无论主人健康无恙还是病入膏肓,守卫在他身边的始终是他的狗。

　　只要它能够贴近于主人,它就宁愿蜷伏于冰冷的地面,任寒风刺骨,冰雪袭身。它愿意亲吻主人的手,即便主人并未施与食物。它会舔舐主人在与这个粗暴的世界奋战中留下的伤口和痛处。它守候着睡梦中的赤贫如洗的主人就如同守候着君主王侯一般。

　　当所有的朋友都弃主人而去,唯有它仍留守在主人身旁。即使主人倾家荡产、身败名裂,它依然爱心如常宛若日行中天。

　　一旦主人遭遇不幸被众人抛弃而举目无亲之时,忠贞不渝的狗别无他求,唯以伴随主人抵御危险和抗击敌人为荣。待到主人大限临近,最终被死神攫入怀抱,尸入凉冢,长眠黄泉,任凭其他朋友各奔东西,趴在主人墓旁的仍是这只高尚的狗。它的头伏于双爪之间,警觉地圆睁着抑郁的双眼,尽诚尽职,死而后已。◆

◉Be swift to hear, slow to speak. (听宜敏捷,言宜缓行。)

◉To save time is to lengthen life. (节约时间就是延长生命。)

◉Happy is the man who learns from the misfortunes of others. (吸取他人教训,自己才会走运。)

◉Wise men are silent; fools talk. (智者沉默寡言,愚者滔滔不绝。)

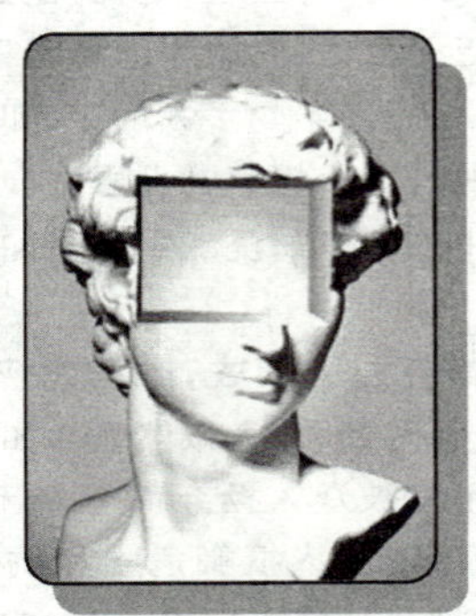

The Reward of Solitary Life*

For me the most interesting thing about a solitary life, and mine has been that for the last twenty years, is that it becomes increasingly rewarding. When I can wake up and watch the sun rise over the ocean, as I do most days, and know that I have an entire day ahead, uninterrupted, in which to write a few pages, take a walk with my dog, lie down in the afternoon for a think (Why does one think better in a horizontal position?), read and listen to music, I am flooded with happiness.

I am lonely only when I am overtired, when I have

---

　　* 作者梅·萨尔顿(May Sarton,1912—1995),生于比利时,4 岁时随其父移民美国,后成为美国著名诗人、小说家和散文家,其很多著作文笔清新俊雅,妙趣横生,令人百读不厌。生活在这纷扰喧嚣的世界,有时真的需要有自己独处的空间。可以放飞自己的心灵,什么都可以想,什么都可以不想。一人独处静美随之而来,清灵随之而来,温馨随之而来;一人独处的时候,贫穷也富有,寂寞也温柔……生活也许本应如此。

worked too long without a break, when for the time being I feel empty and need filling up. And I am lonely sometimes when I come back home after a lecture trip, when I have seen a lot of people and talked a lot, and am full to the brim with experience that needs to be sorted out.

Then for a little while the house feels huge and empty, and I wonder where myself is hiding. It has been recaptured slowly by watering the plants, perhaps, and looking again at each one as though it were a person, by feeding the two cats, by cooking a meal.

It takes a while, as I watch the surf blowing up in fountains at the end of the field, but the moment when the world falls away, and the self emerges again from the deep unconsciousness, bringing back all I have recently experienced to be explored and slowly understood, when I can converse again with my hidden powers, and so grow, and so be rewarded, till death do us part. ✳

Vocabulary List 【词汇清单】

rewarding /ri'wɔːdiŋ/ *adj.* 报答的,有益的,值得做的

uninterrupted /'ʌnˌintə'rʌptid/ *adj.* 不停的,持续的,不间断的,未受干扰的

horizontal /ˌhɔri'zɔntl/ *adj.* 地平线的;与水平面平行的,卧式的

be flooded with: 充满,充斥

brim /brim/ *n.* (杯,碗等)边,边缘(to the brim:充满,满到边缘上)

recapture /ri'kæptʃə/ *v.* 重获,再次捕获;再体验,再体会

surf /səːf/ *n.* 海浪,激浪,拍岸浪

fountain /'fauntin/ *n.* 泉水,喷泉

unconsciousness /ʌn'kɔnʃəsnis/ *n.* <心理>无意识,不知不觉

converse /kən'vəːs/ *v.* <非正式>谈话,会话,交谈(with)

独身生活的回报

对我而言,独身生活中最有趣的——也是我最近20年以来深有体会的——就是它使生活变得越来越有情调了。当我早晨醒来看到太阳从大海上冉冉升起的时候——尽管我几乎每天都是如此——我就知道面前将有没人打搅的整整一天时间了。在这一天里,我可以悠闲地写几页文章,可以带着狗散散步,午后还可以躺下来思考思考问题(为什么平躺的时候更加有利于思考呢?),看看书,听听音乐,心中洋溢着快乐之情。

只有在我过度疲劳的时候,或是在我工作太久而没有休息的时候,或是在我当时觉得空虚因而需要充实的时候,我才会感到孤独。而有时,当我在外地演讲后赶回家的时候,当我和许多人见面并且交谈甚多的时候,当许多经历多得要溢出来,因而需要整理的时候,我才会感到孤独。

那个时候,房子一度让人觉得太大、太空,而我却不知道自我藏身于何处。也许通过给花草浇水,并对其逐一端详,好像端详人一样;也许通过喂那两只猫和做一餐饭,我才能又慢慢捕捉到自我了。

过了一会儿,我看到地平线的尽头海浪如泉水般喷涌,那一刻,世界消逝殆尽了,而自我从深层的无意识中再一次浮现,这才使我想起最近所经历的一切,让我去探究、去慢慢了解。此时,我又能与隐藏的力量交流了,于是我又在成长,并在成长中得到回报,直到死亡将我们分开。◆

Life Is a Game *

Image life as a game in which you are playing some five balls in the air. You name them — work, family, health, friends and spirit, and you're keeping all these balls in the air.

You understand that work is a rubber ball. If you drop it, it will bounce back. But the other four balls are made of glass. If you drop one of these, it will be irrevocably scuffed,

---

* 作者佚名。放眼社会，我们每个人的地位不同，所做的事情轻重不同，责任也不相同，就像是戏中不同的角色一样的繁多。要演好一场人生戏，是一种体现价值人生观的哲学。对于我们每个人每天都在不停演出的一出戏，戏演得好不好，关键在于你是否懂得认识生活，理解生活的意义，找到生活的目标而努力前进，是否懂得享受生活，享受人生。对于这场人生之戏，我们是导演，同时也是演员；而且，我们大多数人正在努力做一个好导演，好演员。本文虽然将生活比作一场游戏，却丝毫没有"游戏人间"的轻薄与浮华，而是用平实的语言将生活的戒条陈列无遗，或许会给读者带来一份昭示和启迪。

marked, damaged or even broken into pieces. They will never be the same. You must learn to strive for balance in your life. How?

Don't undermine your worth by comparing yourself to others. It is because we are different that each of us is special.

Don't set your goals by what other people consider important. Only you know what is best for you.

Don't take for granted the things closest to your heart. Hold on to them as you would to life, for without them, it's meaningless.

Don't give up when you still have something to give. Nothing is really over until the moment you stop trying.

Don't be afraid to admit that you are less than perfect. It is this fragile thread that binds us to each together.

Don't be afraid to encounter risks. It is by taking chances that we learn how to be brave.

Don't shut love out of your life by saying it's impossible to find. The quickest way to receive love is to give it; the fastest way to lose love is to hold it too tightly; and the best way to keep love is to give it wings.

Don't forget, a person's greatest emotional need is to feel appreciated.

Don't be afraid to learn. Knowledge is weightless, a treasure you can always carry easily.

Don't use time or words carelessly. Neither can be retrieved.

Don't let life slip through your fingers by living in the past or in the future. By living your life one day at a time, you live all the days of your life.

Don't run through life so fast that you forget not only

where you've been, but also where you are going.

Life is not a race, but a journey to be enjoyed slowly each step of the way. Yesterday is history, tomorrow is a mystery, and today is a gift. That's why we call it — the present. ✽

Vocabulary List【词汇清单】

irrevocably /i'revəkəbli/ *adv.* 不可变更（或改变）地，无可挽回地

scuff /skʌf/ *v.* 拖着（脚）走；磨损，摩擦

undermine /ʌndə'main/ *v.* 削弱…的基础；暗中破坏

fragile /'frædʒail/ *adj.* 易损（坏）的，脆（弱）的

encounter /in'kauntə/ *v.* 遭遇，遭受，面临（困难、麻烦等）

weightless /'weitlis/ *adj.* 无重量的，不可称量的

treasure /'treʒə/ *n.* 金银财宝，财富

retrieve /ri'triːv/ *v.* 重新得到，重获；挽救，拯救

run through：挥霍，浪费，花光，浪费

参考译文【Suggested Translation】

生活是一场游戏

想像生活就是一场游戏，在这个游戏中，你向空中抛出五个球。你点着它们的名字：工作，家庭，健康，朋友和心境，而你正在让这些球保持在空中。

你明白工作是一个橡胶球。既使你没有接住它，它也会反弹回来。但是其他四个球都是用玻璃制成的。如果你掉落其中一个，它将会无法挽回地留下划痕和缺口，甚或是摔得粉碎。它们永远都不会恢复到原来的样子了。你必须努力学会权衡生活。怎样去做呢？

不要因为和他人比较而使自己的价值逐渐削弱，因为我们每个人都是与众不同的。

不要把目标定在别人所认为重要的事情上，因为只有你才知道什么最适合自己。

不要把什么事情都看作心中最紧要的，并依靠它们去活命，因为它们有时候毫无意义。

不要在你尚可给予的时候放弃，因为没有任何事情会在你尝试之前失败。

不要担心承认你不够完美，因为正是这根脆弱的细线将我们联结在一起。

不要畏惧遭遇冒险，因为这正是使我们学会勇敢的机会。

不要说不可能找到爱就把爱关在生活的门外，因为最快得到爱的方式就是付出爱，最快失去爱的方式就是把爱抓得太紧，而保持爱的最好方式是让它插上翅膀。

不要忘记，一个人最大的情感需求是得到欣赏（赏识）。

不要害怕去学习，因为知识是没有重量，并且总是能够轻易随身携带的财富。

不要轻率地使用时间或者言辞，因为两者都不可能被收回。

不要因生活在过去或者将来而让生命从你的指尖滑过，一天接一天踏实地去生活，那你生活的每一天都是自己的生活。

不要过快地穿越生活而忘记了你身在何处，将向何方。

生活不是跑步比赛，而是沿途每一步都值得慢慢欣赏的旅行。昨天已是历史，明天还是一个谜，而今天则是一份礼物。因此我们称它为"present"。◆

第 072 篇

Globalization[*]

What exactly does globalization mean? Concepts related to globalization include internationalization, "multidomestic marketing", and "multinational or transnational marketing", suggesting that the basic criterion is transactions across national boundaries. In the marketing and strategic management literature, globalization is conceptualized as a means to gain competitive advantage by locating different stages of production in different geographic regions according to the particular region's comparative advantages. This conceptualization focuses only on the economic aspects of

---

＊ 作者佚名。对于当今世界的重大经济问题，或许没有一个话题比"全球化"更具争议了。有人认为它提供了资本、技术、市场等方面的大量机会，但也有人认为，伴随全球化的是经济不平等的加剧，全球化的果实没有被公平地分享。概括地讲，全球化是一柄"双刃剑"。可是，究竟何谓"全球化"？至今人们并没有统一的界定。

globalization; social, cultural and political factors are only considered in the context of achieving economic advantage. Thus, being "culturally sensitive" in global markets is being able to sell one's product with enough ingenuity to avoid possible pitfalls arising from the seller's ignorance of local customs. International marketing textbooks discuss such cultural pitfalls in great detail; however, the cultural contest of globalization is always framed by the economic.

Broader conceptualizations of globalization can be found in other disciplines such as sociology and anthropology. Waters defined globalization as "a social process in which the constraints of geography on social and cultural arrangements recede and in which people become increasingly aware that they are receding." This conceptualization with its much broader scope, allows for the examination of a number of consequences of globalization, not just economic but social, cultural and political ones.

While there are a few different conceptualizations of globalization, researchers seem to be in agreement that there are at least three dimensions of globalization: economic, political and cultural. The economic aspects of globalization stem from the spread of the capitalist world economy and the resulting expansion of gegraphical boundaries for the production and consumption of goods and services. The need for cheap raw materials, cheap labor and new markets saw the expansion of the capitalist world economy from one that was primarily Eurocentric to one that encompassed the entire world. This process was achieved by various means and often involved overcoming political rosistances (frequently through military means) in the new "markets". The political aspects of globalization involved establishing control over markets and raw materials through either the use of direct military power or the establishment of international institutions (through diplomacy) that control such markets. The rise of the nation-state is an example of the political aspect of globalization, although it is argued that advances in telecommunications and information systems and the resulting constructions of institutions that transcend territorial boundaries are making the nation-state obsolete.

If the economic and political aspects of globalization involve material and power exchanges, the cultural of globalization involves the expression of symbols that repressent facts, meanings, beliefs, preferences, tastes and values. In fact, these symbolic exchanges are increasingly displacing economic and political exchanges in the spread of global mass culture. Traditional barriers of language pose no problems to modern means of cultural production such as satellite television and film. However, the new "global culture", despite its manifestations through consumption of global products and symbols in different parts of the globe, is essentially the culture of domimant groups centered in the West.

Thus it is important to realize that despite its "worldwide" connotation, globalization is essentially a Western notion inextricably linked economic development. It is a Western world view which in economic terms defines the world as a market that can be exploited to generate wealth. ✳

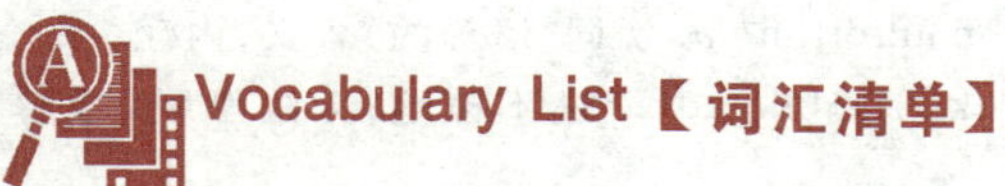

Vocabulary List 【词汇清单】

internationalization /ˌintə(ː)ˌnæʃənlaiˈzeiʃən/ *n.* ＜计＞国际化, 国际共管

multinational /ˌmʌltiˈnæʃənəl/ *adj.* 多国的（属于或涉及两国以上的，在两个以上国家有运营、附属机构或投资的）

transnational /trænsˈnæʃənəl/ *adj.* 超越国界的，跨国的（与多个国家或民族有关的或涉及到多个国家或民族的）

criterion /kraiˈtiəriən/ *n.* （批判、判断的）标准，准则，规范，准绳

conceptualize /kənˈseptjuəlaiz/ *v.* 使有概念，使概念化，形成…的概念（下文的 conceptualization 是其名词形式）

geographic /dʒiəˈgræfik/ *adj.* （亦作 geographical）地区（性）的，（按照）地理学的

ingenuity /ˌindʒiˈnjuːiti/ *n.* 机智，足智多谋；独创性，创造力；巧妙，独出心裁

pitfall /ˈpitfɔːl/ *n.* （捕捉动物的）陷阱；不明显的危险，隐藏的困难

anthropology /ˌænθrəˈpɔlədʒi/ *n.* 人类学（研究人的生物、文化、地理和历史情况相互关系的一门学科）

constraint /kənˈstreint/ *n.* 约束，限制，束缚，制约

dimension /diˈmenʃən/ *n.* 维（数），度（数）；方面，因素

Eurocentric /ˌjuərəuˈsentrik/ *adj.* 以欧洲为中心的，主要与欧洲（或欧洲人）有关的

encompass /inˈkʌmpəs/ *v.* 包围，环绕；包含、包括（某事物）

transcend /trænˈsend/ *v.* 超越，超出

territorial /ˌteriˈtɔːriəl/ *adj.* 领土的，领地的，区域性的

obsolete /ˈɔbsəliːt/ *adj.* （在设计、样式或构造上）陈旧过时的，不再使用的

barrier /ˈbæriə/ *n.* （阻碍通道的）障碍物；障碍，阻碍，隔阂

manifestation /ˌmænifesˈteiʃən/ *n.* 表明，显示，表现形式

dominant /ˈdɔminənt/ *adj.* 主导的，占优势的，支配的

connotation /ˌkɔnəuˈteiʃən/ *n.* （词、语等的）含义，内涵

inextricably /inˈekstrikəbli/ *adv.* 逃不掉地，无法摆脱（或解脱）地

exploit /iksˈplɔit/ *v.* 开发，开采，开拓

参考译文【Suggested Translation】

全 球 化

全球化究竟意味着什么？与全球化相关的概念包括"国际化"，"多国国内营销"，"多国或跨国营销"，这意味着全球化的基本标准是跨越国界的交易。在营销和战略管理文献中，全球化的概念是，根据特定地区的比较优势，确立不同地区生产的不同阶段，从而获得竞争优势的一种手段。这一概念只强调了全球化的经济方面，而社会、文化及政治因素只在取得经济优势的背景下才加以考虑。因此，在全球市场中的"文化敏感"，就是指销售者要尽量避免由于不了解当地风俗习惯而可能遇到的陷阱，要别出心裁地把自己的产品销售出去。尽管国际营销教科书对这类文化陷阱阐述得十分详尽，然而全球化的文化进程总是受经济的制约。

关于全球化更广义的概念可见之于其他诸如社会学和人类学等学科中。沃特斯把全球化定义为"一种社会进程，在此进程中，反映在社会和文化方面在地域上的限制减少了，而且在这一进程中人越来越认识到这种限制正在减少。"具有更为广阔含义的这一概念在考察全球化的后果时，不仅仅包括经济方面的，而且包括社会、文化及政治方面的后果。

尽管全球化有不同的概念，但研究者们似乎一致认为全球化至少有三个层面：经济的，政治和文化的。经济全球化方面起源于资本主义世界经济的扩张以及由此产生了为扩大产品和服务的生产及消费而了出现的地理边界的扩张。对廉价原材料、劳动力和新市场的需要，使得资本主义世界经济从主要以欧洲为中心进而囊括了整个世界。这一全球化进程是通过各种手段来实现的，其中包括克服来自新"市场"的政治对抗（通常通过军事手段）。政治全球化方面包括通过直接动用军事力量或者（通过外交）建立能控制这些市场的国际机构，来达到对市场和原材料的控制。民族国家的兴起就是政治全球化方面的一个例证，尽管也有人认为，电讯及信息系统的进步以及由此建立的超越领土边界的机构正在使得民族国家过时了。

如果说全球化的经济和政治方面涉及物质和权力的交换，全球化的文化方面则指那些代表着事实、意义、信仰、喜好、趣味及价值取向的一系列象征意义的表达。事实上，在全球大众文化的传播中，这些象征意义的交流正日益取代经济和政治方面的交流。传统的语言障碍对诸如卫星电视、电影等现代手段的文化产品并不构成任何问题。然而，新的"全球文化"，尽管它以消费全球产品和在不同地区的象征意义表现出来，其本质仍然是以西方为中心的大国集团的文化。

因此，重要的是要认识到尽管有着"世界范围"的含义，但全球化本质上仍然是一个和经济发展必然联系在一起的西方观念，是一种西方世界观，这种世界观用经济学术语，把世界定义为一个可以开发以便产生财富的市场。◆

- Nothing is to be got without pains but poverty. （世上唯有贫穷可以不劳而获。）
- Time tries all. （路遥知马力，日久见人心。）
- He who makes no mistakes makes nothing. （不犯错误则一事无成。）
- A burden of one's choice is not felt. （爱挑的担子不嫌重。）

第 **073** 篇

Self-control[*]

Self-control is essential to happiness and usefulness. It is the master of all the virtues, and has its root in self-respect. Let a man yield to his impulses and passions, and from that moment he gives up his moral freedom.

It is the self-discipline of a man that enables him to pursue success with superior diligence and sobriety. Many of the great characters in history illustrate this trait. In ordinary life

---

　　* 作者佚名。古希腊哲学家苏格拉底曾说:"自制是一切美德的基础。"在《圣经》中,赞誉之词并不给予那些"攻城掠地"的强者,而是给予那些能"主宰自己灵魂"的十分坚强的人们。"一个不能自制的人并不是损害别人而有利于自己,像一个贪得无厌的人,掠夺别人的财物来饱足自己的私囊那样,而是对人既有损,对己更有害。不自制的最大害处就是不仅毁坏自己的家庭,而且还毁坏自己的身体和灵魂。……每一个人的本分岂不就是把自制看做是一切德行的基础,在自己心里树立起一种自制的美德来吗?有哪个不自制的人能学会任何的好事,或者把它充分的付诸实践呢?有哪个做肉欲奴隶的人会不是在身体和灵魂双方面都处于同样恶劣的情况呢?"

the application is the same. He who would lead must first command himself. The time of test is when everybody is excited or angry, then the well-balanced mind comes to the front.

There is a very special demand for the cultivation of his trait at present. The young men who rush into business with no good education or drill will do poor and feverish work. Endurance is a much better test of character than act of heroism.

A fair amount of self-examination is good. Self-knowledge is a preface to self-control. Too much self-inspection leads to morbidness; too little conducts to careless and hasty action. There are two things which will surely strengthen our self-control. One is attention to conscience; the other is a spirit of good will. The man who would succeed in any great undertaking must hold all his faculties under perfect control; they must be disciplined and drilled until they quickly and cheerfully obey the will. ✽

Vocabulary List 【词汇清单】

yield /jiːld/ *v.* （对外力）屈服，屈从，让步（to）

self-discipline /'self'disiplin/ *n.* 自律，自我约束

superior /sju(ː)'siəriə/ *adj.* （位置）较高的，（在）上面的；（质地、价值等）较好的（to）

sobriety /səu'braiəti/ *n.* 清醒，冷静，稳健

well-balanced /'wel'bælənst/ *adj.* 平衡的，均衡的；神智健全的，明智的

cultivation /ˌkʌlti'veiʃən/ *n.* 耕作，培养；教养

feverish /'fiːvəriʃ/ *adj.* 非常焦虑的，焦躁不安的

endurance /in'djurəns/ *n.* 忍受，坚韧，忍耐（力）

heroism /'herəuizəm/ *n.* 英雄品质（或行为），英雄主义

morbidness /'mɔːbidnis/ *n.* （精神的）病态，不健全

conduct /'kɔndʌkt/ *n.* 行为，品行，操行，举止（特指道德观点上的行动）

hasty /'heisti/ *adj.* 匆忙的，仓促的，草率的

undertaking /ˌʌndə'teikiŋ/ *n.* 任务，事业，企业；接受任务，承担责任

faculty /'fækəlti/ *n.* ＜旧＞能力，才能，本领

参考译文【Suggested Translation】

自　制

自制是幸福快乐与有所作为所不可或缺的。它主宰着一切美德，并根植于自尊之中。假若一个人屈服于其冲动突兀和感情用事，则从那一刻起他便放弃了他的道德自由。

正是自律使人能够更加勤奋和冷静地去追求成功。历史上的许多伟人都例证了这种特质。在日常生活之中，自律的运用也同样如此。想要领导他人的人必须先要掌控自我。每个人激动或是生气的时候，考验的时刻便到了，这时心平气和的心态便应冲锋陷阵了。

目前是特别需要培养这种特质的时候。没有受过良好教育或训练的年轻人匆匆进入商界，做起事情来一定既差劲又毛躁。忍耐要比逞英雄更能考验人的品格。

适度的自我检讨是可取的。若有自知之明方可自我制约。过度的自我检讨会导致病态；检讨不足则会使得行事粗心草率。不过，有两样东西肯定会增强我们的自制力。其一是注重良知，其二是心怀善意。不管一个人从事多么伟大的事业，要想成功就必须妥善掌控自己的才能；这些才能必须要先加以约束和磨炼，而后它们才会迅速而又令人愉快地服从人的意愿。◆

The Four Freedoms *

In the future days, which we seek to make secure, we look forward to a world founded upon four essential human freedoms.

The first is freedom of speech and expression — everywhere in the world.

---

* 作者富兰克林·德拉诺·罗斯福(Franklin Delano Roosevelt, 1882—1945),美国第 32 任总统,他一直被视为美国历史上最伟大的总统之一,是 20 世纪美国最不负众望和最受爱戴的总统,也是美国历史上惟一连任 3 届总统的人。执政后,他以"新政"对付经济危机,颇有成效。第二次世界大战初,美国采取不介入政策,但对希特勒采取强硬手段,以"租借法"支持同盟国。1941 年底,美国参战后,罗斯福代表美国两次参加同盟国"三巨头"会议,后来罗斯福政府提出了轴心国必须无条件投降的原则并得到了实施。罗斯福提出了建立联合国的构想,也得到了实施。63 岁时由于突发脑溢血而与世长辞。美国一位记者曾这样评价罗斯福:"他推翻的先例比任何人都多,他砸烂的古老结构比任何人都多,他对美国整个面貌的改变比任何人都要迅猛而激烈。"本文为 1941 年 1 月 6 日罗斯福致美国国会的国情咨文中最为精彩的一部分。

The second is freedom of every person to worship God in his own way — everywhere in the world.

The third is freedom from want — which, translated into world terms, means economic understandings which will secure to every nation a healthy peace time life for its inhabitants — everywhere in the world.

The fourth is freedom from fear — which, translated into world terms, means a world-wide reduction of armaments to such a point and in such a thorough fashion that no nation will be in a position to commit an act of physical aggression against any neighbor — anywhere in the world.

That is no vision of a distant millennium. It is a definite basis for a kind of world attainable in our own time and generation. That kind of world is the very antithesis of the so-called new order of tyranny which the dictators seek to create with the crash of a bomb.

To that new order we oppose the greater conception — the moral order. A good society is able to face schemes of world domination and foreign revolutions alike without fear.

Since the beginning of our American history we have been engaged in danger — in a perpetual peaceful revolution — a revolution which goes on steadily, quietly adjusting itself to changing conditions — without the concentration camp or the quicklime in the ditch. The world order which we seek is the cooperation of free countries, working together in a friendly civilized society.

This nation has placed its destiny in the hands and heads and hearts of its millions of free men and women; and its faith in freedom under the guidance of God. Freedom means the supremacy of human rights everywhere. Our support goes to those who struggle to gain those rights or keep them. Our strength is in our unity of purpose.

　　To that high concept there can be no end save victory. ✳

Vocabulary List 【词汇清单】

secure /si'kjuə/ *adj.* 安全的,安心的,安定的

inhabitant /in'hæbitənt/ *n.* 常住(或永久)居民,居住者

reduction /ri'dʌkʃən/ *n.* 减少,缩减

armament /'ɑːməmənt/ *n.* ＜常用复数＞(一国的)武装力量,军备

aggression /ə'greʃən/ *n.* 侵略,侵犯,侵袭

attainable /ə'teinəbl/ *adj.* (通过努力)可达到的,可获得的

antithesis /æn'tiθisis/ *n.* 对比,对照,对立(面)

tyranny /'tirəni/ *n.* 专制统治,集权政治;暴政,专制

dictator /dik'teitə/ *n.* 独裁者,专制君主,暴君

perpetual /pə'petʃuəl/ *adj.* 永远的,永久的,持续不停的

quicklime /'kwik‚laim/ *n.* 生石灰

ditch /ditʃ/ *n.* 沟,沟渠,壕沟

supremacy /sju'preməsi/ *n.* 至高无上(的性质或地位)

参考译文【Suggested Translation】

论 四 大 自 由

在未来的日子里,我们将试图寻求安宁稳定,我们将期待在人类四项必不可少的自由的基础之上建立一个新世界。

　　第一项自由,是在世界上的每一个地方,人人都享有言论自由。

　　第二项自由,是在世界上的每一个地方,每个人都有以自己的方式信奉上帝的自由。

　　第三项自由,是在世界上的任何地方脱离贫困的自由。从全球意义上说,就是达成经济上的相互理解,以确保任何一个国家的居民都可以过上健康与祥和的生活。

第四项自由,是在世界上的任何地方远离恐惧的自由。从全球意义上说,就是进行世界范围内的彻底裁军,从而使得任何一个国家都不会向其邻国采取武力侵略行动。

这并非对于遥远的太平盛世的幻想。在我们这个时代,我们这一代人有能力在这个确定的基础之上建立一个新世界。这样的世界,与那些独裁者企图用炸弹创造所谓的"新秩序"暴政截然对立。

我们用一种更加伟大的观念来对抗那种"新秩序"——这就是道德观念。一个良好的社会,能够毫不畏惧地面对主宰世界和在别国发动叛乱的种种阴谋企图。

自从美国有史以来,我们就一直致力于变革——致力于长期不断的和平革命,这场革命持续稳定地进行着,并沉静地调整其自身以适应不断变化的形势。我们的革命没有集中营,也没有万人坑。我们所寻求的世界秩序,是自由国家彼此合作,是在友好文明的社会中携手工作。

我们这个国家已经将其命运放在千百万自由的男男女女手中、头脑中和心中,并将其自由的信念置于上帝的指引之下。自由意味着无论在何处,人权都是至高无上的。我们坚决支持那些为争取或者捍卫人权而奋斗的人们。共同的目标使我们坚强有力。

为了实现这一崇高的设想,我们必定以胜利而告终。◆

第　篇

A Psalm of Life*

——What the Heart of the Young Man Said to the Psalmist

Tell me not, in mournful numbers,
Life is but an empty dream!
For the soul is dead that slumbers

---

　　* 作者亨利·沃兹沃思·朗费罗（Henry Wadsworth Longfellow，1807—1882），美国著名诗人，其抒情诗受德国浪漫主义诗人的影响，深受 19 世纪欧美读者的欢迎。1839 年他出版了第一部诗集《夜吟》（Hymn to the Night），包括著名的《人生礼赞》（A Psalm of Life）、《夜的赞歌》（Voices of the Night）等音韵优美的抒情诗，其最有名的其他作品还有《奴役篇》（Poems on Slavery）以及叙事诗《伊凡吉林》（Evangeline）等，并且翻译了但丁（Dante）的《神曲》（Devine Comedy）。朗费罗晚年创作依然不减，并且备受尊崇，牛律大学和剑桥大学曾分别授予他荣誉博士学位，其逝世后，伦敦威斯敏斯特教堂诗人之角安放了他的胸像，他是获得这种尊荣的第一位美国诗人。《人生礼赞》是传诵一时、极富教育意义的名篇，着重指出一个人要充分利用短暂的一生，自强不息，而不要沉溺于无谓的悔恨与沮丧。

And things are not what they seem.

Life is real! Life is earnest!
And the grave is not its goal;
Dust thou art, to dust returnest,
Was not spoken of the soul.

Not enjoyment, and not sorrow,
Is our destined end or way;
But to act, that each to-morrow
Find us farther than to-day.

Art is long, and Time is fleeting,
And our hearts, though stout and brave,
Still, like muffled drums, are beating
Funeral marches to the grave.

In the world's broad field of battle,
In the bivouac of Life,
Be not like dumb, driven cattle!
Be a hero in the strife!

Trust no Future, howe'er pleasant!
Let the dead Past bury its dead!
Act, act in the living Present!
Heart within, and God o'erhead!

Lives of great men all remind us
We can make our lives sublime,
And, departing, leave behind us
Footprints on the sands of time;

Foot prints, that perhaps another,
Sailing o'er life' solemn main,
A forlorn and shipwrecked brother,
Seeing, shall take heart again.

Let us, then, be up and doing,
With a heart for any fate;
Still achieving, still pursuing,
Learn to labour and to wait. ✽

 **Vocabulary List【词汇清单】**

psalm /saːm/ *n.* 赞美诗,圣诗,圣歌

psalmist /'saːmist/ *n.* 赞美诗作者,诗篇作者

mournful /'mɔːnful/ *adj.* 悲哀的,哀伤的,沮丧的

number /'nʌmbə/ *n.* <复数>韵律,诗;<古>拍子,调子,节奏

slumber /'slʌmbə/ *v.* 睡眠,以睡眠度过

earnest /'əːnist/ *adj.* 认真的,不开玩笑的;热心的,诚挚的;重大的,重要的

grave /greiv/ *adj.* 墓穴,坟墓

Dust thou art, to dust returnest: 相当于 You are dust, you return to dust. 本句源于《旧约·创世纪》,意思是人的肉体是尘土做的,人死后仍旧要回到尘土之中去。

destined /'destind/ *adj.* 命运注定的,天定的

fleet /fliːt/ *v.* 疾驰,飞逝,掠过

stout /staut/ *adj.* 勇敢的,无畏的,刚毅的

muffle /'mʌfl/ *v.* 包住,裹住;蒙住(铃、鼓等)使其减音

bivouac /'bivuæk/ *n.* <原义>夜晚警戒以防突然袭击;<军事>(战士)露营,宿营,露营地

dumb /dʌm/ *adj.* 哑的,无说话能力的;缄默的,沉默寡言的

strife /straif/ *n.* 斗争，冲突，竞争

howe'er = however

o'erhead = overhead

sublime /sə'blaim/ *adj.* 高贵的，崇高的；（伟大、美丽得）令人
　　崇敬的

o'er = over

forlorn /fə'lɔːn/ *adj.* 可怜的，悲惨的，不幸的；（几乎）无望的，
　　绝望的

shipwreck /'ʃiprek/ *v.* 船只失事，遇难

参考译文【Suggested Translation】

人 生 礼 赞

——年轻人对歌者的心语

事物的外表并不等同于真相，
灵魂麻木却是与死去没有什么两样，
因此请别用绝望的诗句哀叹：
"人生只不过是梦一场！"

人生真切而实在，
坟地荒山并非它真正的归宿；
灵魂无时不在，躯壳的写照才是：
"质本尘土，回归尘土。"

耽于享受，溺于忧愁，
并非命中注定如此，
行动起来，每一个明天，
都会有超越今天的进步。

智艺虽然无穷无尽，

但光阴一去不等人，
我们的心再充满刚勇坚毅，
也无从阻止丧钟那鼓点般的声音。

要在斗争中做一名无畏的闯将，
别学哑口无言、任人驱使的牛羊，
整个世界都是我们的战场，
到处都是人生扎寨的营帐。

过去的让它过去，把握今天，
可爱的未来坐等不来，
行动起来，从现在开始，
趁着赤心在胸、苍天在上！

伟人们的一生告诉我们，
人活着就应该活得崇高纯洁，
即便离开了人间，
也可流芳百世。

在人生大海航行中受挫的后来者，
仰视我们积极的行为，
或许会沿着我们的足迹，
重新站起，重新振奋精神。

让我们行动起来吧，
不计得失成败；
不断追求进取，
在劳动中迎接胜利的到来。◆

第 076 篇

Conservatism of the English People[*]

Conservatism refers to the acceptance of anything familiar and refusal of anything strange or foreign. There are numerous facts that tell the conservatism of the Englishmen.

The monarchy as nominal head of the state still exists in the highly developed capitalist country.

The national anthem was, is and will be in the near 1000 years the old "God Save the King (or Queen)".

English judges as usual wear long wigs in law courts, as shown in many films shot in Hong Kong. (As a colony of the

---

　　* 作者佚名。英国人不就是整天一套深色西服、腋下夹着雨伞、头顶圆顶小礼帽,在暗灰色的天空下不苟言笑的"绅士"吗？生长在和谐宁静的文化氛围里的英国人一向以保守著称。他们性格孤僻,生活刻板,办事认真,对外界事情不感兴趣,往往寡言少语,对新鲜事物持谨慎态度,具有独特的冷静的幽默。他们保守、冷漠,感情轻易不外露,即便有很伤心的事,也常常不表现出来……

British Empire, Hong Kong was once forced to adopt the British legal system.)

Despite the fact that the feudal class is a term of only history significance, noble titles are conferred on distinguished persons, who would accept the titles as something of the greatest honor.

Many Englishmen still spend lots of money keeping dummy fireplaces that are of no value at all, although their rooms are heated by gas or electric fire. They find it difficult to say goodbye to the past.

As the first country to complete the industrial revolution, Britain refused to introduce decimal system until 1971. Pence, shilling, pound and inch, foot, yard... all these are hard to be forgotten.

English people are always suspicious of any new plans of the government. Today they are still doubtful of the Europe integration plan, thus they are reluctant to allow pound to be integrated into Euro Dollars.

Never talk about any kind of reform to an Englishman, he would surely be silent and keep away from you! ✳

Vocabulary List 【词汇清单】

conservatism /kən'səːvətizəm/ *n.* 保守主义,守旧性

numerous /'njuːmərəs/ *adj.* 数目众多的,许多的

monarchy /'mɔnəki/ *n.* 君主政体,君主制;君主国,君主政府

nominal /'nɔminl/ *adj.* 名义上的,有名无实的

capitalist /'kæpitəlist/ *n.* 资本家,资本主义者 *adj.* 资本主义（者）的,资本家的

anthem /'ænθəm/ *n.* （旧指宗教应答轮唱的）赞美诗或（通常摘自《圣经》的）圣歌,现多指国歌（亦即 national anthem）

wig /wig/ *n.* 假发（通常指覆盖整个头发之物,如为部分假发则称为 hairpiece. 假发是 17、18 世纪盛行于欧洲的男人发饰。至今,英国法官和律师在法庭上都须戴此物）

adopt /əˈdɔpt/ *v.* 采用,采纳,采取（某种态度、习惯做法等）

feudal /ˈfjuːdl/ *adj.* 封建的,封建制度的,封建主义的

significance /sigˈnifikəns/ *n.* 意义,旨趣,重要性

confer /kənˈfəː/ *v.* 授予（称号、学位等）,赐与,把⋯赠与

distinguished /disˈtiŋgwiʃt/ *adj.* 卓越的,卓著的,杰出的,高贵的

dummy /ˈdʌmi/ *adj.* 虚设的,摆样子的（如空容器、假抽屉等）

decimal /ˈdesiməl/ *adj.* 十进位的,十进制的（decimal system/fraction：十进制）

pence /pens/ *n.* ＜英＞（penny 的复数形式）便士（英国及其他英镑国家的货币单位）

shilling /ˈʃiliŋ/ *n.* 先令（1971 年以前的英国货币单位,合二十分之一镑）

integration /ˌintiˈgreiʃən/ *n.* ＜美＞结合,尤指使不同的种族自由、平等交往;整合,综合

 参考译文【 Suggested Translation 】

英国人的保守

保守是指一种乐于接受熟悉的东西、而拒绝陌生或新奇事物的心态。有很多的事实可以证明英国人是多么的保守:

在这样一个高度发达的资本主义国家,君主作为国家名义上的统治者而仍然存在。

英国的国歌过去是、现在是、也许再过 1000 年还是那首古老的"上帝拯救国王（或女王）"。

正如在香港拍摄的许多电影里所看到的那样,英国的法官在法庭上依然戴着长长的假发。（香港曾经作为英国的殖民地而被迫采用英国的法律制度。）

虽然在事实上，封建阶级早已成为历史意义上的专用名词，但是英国仍给声名显赫的人授予贵族封号，而他们也把这种封号视作莫大的荣誉。

虽然许多英国人的房子早就用暖气或者电暖器取暖了，但是他们还在大把大把地花费金钱去保养毫无价值的仿制壁炉。对他们而言，和过去告别难上加难。

作为世界上第一个完成工业革命的国家，英国直到 1971 年还拒绝采用十进制。便士、先令、英镑，英寸、英尺、码……这些实在让他们难以忘怀。

英国人对政府制定的任何新政策总是持怀疑态度。直到今天，他们对欧洲的统一计划仍然心存疑虑。因而，他们不愿意把英镑纳入欧元计划之中。

千万别跟英国人谈论任何种类的改革——对此他们必定会沉默不语，并对你避而远之！ ◆

● Offense is the best defense.（进攻是最好的防御。）

● A light heart lives long.（静以修身。）

● Reading enriches the mind.（开卷有益。）

● What we do willingly is easy.（愿者不难。）

You Are What You Do *

If the past has taught us anything, it is that every cause brings effect — every action has a consequence. This thought, in my opinion, is the moral foundation of the universe; it applies equally in this world and the next.

We Chinese have a saying: "If a man plants melons, he will reap melons; if he sows beans, he will reap beans." And this is true of every man's life: good begets good, and evil

---

＊ 作者宋美龄（Mayling Soong，1897—2003），生于上海，幼年赴美留学，就读于波士顿的威斯理女子学院（Wellsely College），1917 年回国，从事教会工作。1927 年 12 月与蒋介石结婚，任蒋的秘书和英文翻译。在国民党政权于 1949 年被推翻后，她随蒋介石逃往台湾。蒋介石去世后，她长期居住在美国。她曾致力于中国人民抗日战争，反对国家分裂，期盼海峡两岸和平统一和中华民族的兴盛。宋美龄兼具中国古典气质和西方优雅风度，而又带有犀利、精明的作风。宋美龄有与生俱来的聪明、美丽与手腕，加上孔宋家族的强力支援与美国背景，使她在权力、财力与魅力的交织中，成为中国近代百年史上最有影响与争议的女人。

leads to evil.

True enough, the sun shines on the saint and sinner alike, and too often it seems that the wicked wax and prosper. But we can say with certitude that, with the individual as with the nation, the flourishing of the wicked is an illusion, for, unceasingly, life keeps books on us all.

In the end, we are all the sum total of our actions. Character cannot be counterfeited, nor can it be put on and cast off as if it were a garment to meet the whim of the moment. Like the markings on wood which are ingrained in the very heart of the tree, character requires time and nurture for growth and development.

Thus also, day by day, we write our own destiny, for inexorably we become what we do. This, I believe, is the supreme logic and the law of life. ✳

Vocabulary List 【词汇清单】

melon /ˈmelən/ *n.* ＜植物＞瓜（如西瓜、甜瓜等）

beget /biˈget/ *v.* ＜书面语＞ 招致，产生，引起

saint /seint/ *adj.* 神圣的，圣洁的

sinner /ˈsinə/ *n.* 罪人，恶人，做坏事者

wicked /ˈwikid/ *adj.* 邪恶的，恶劣的，有恶意的

wax /wæks/ *v.* （在大小、数量、力量或密集度上）变大，增加

certitude /ˈsəːtitjuːd/ *n.* 深信，确信，满有把握的感觉

flourish /ˈflʌriʃ/ *v.* 繁荣，茂盛；活跃，手舞足蹈；兴旺，处于旺盛时期

unceasingly /ʌnˈsiːsiŋli/ *adv.* 从不停止地，继续不断地

counterfeit /ˈkauntəfit/ *v.* 伪造，假冒；假装，装作

garment /ˈgɑːmənt/ *n.* 衣服（一般指长袍、外套等）

whim /wim/ *n.* 一时的兴致，心血来潮

ingrained /in'greind/ *v.* 根深蒂固的,固有的,天生的
nurture /'nə:tʃə/ *n.* 养育,培养,滋养
inexorably /in'eksərəbli/ *adv.* 无动于衷地,无情地,冷酷地

 参考译文【Suggested Translation】

你是你的所为

假如说过去的日子曾经教给我们一些什么的话,那就是有因必有果——每一个行为都有一种结果。在我看来,这种想法是全宇宙的道德基础;它不仅适用于今生,也适用于来世。

我们中国人有一句俗语说:"种瓜得瓜,种豆得豆。"而这就是每个人生活的真实写照:善有善报,恶有恶报。

说实在话,圣人与罪人皆会受到阳光的披泽,而且常常似乎是恶者大行其道。但是我们可以确信地说,不管是对个人或是对国家而言,恶人猖獗只是一种幻象,因为生活无时无刻不在将我们的所作所为像账本一样一笔一笔记录下来。

最终,我们就是我们行为的总和。品性是无法伪装的,也无法像衣服一样随兴地穿上或脱下来丢在一旁。就像木头的纹路发端于树木深邃的中心,品性的生长与发育也需要时间和滋养。

也因此,我们日复一日地写下我们自身的命运,因为我们的所作所为毫不留情地决定着我们的命运。我坚信,这就是人生的最高逻辑和法则。◆

April Fool's Day[*]

While popular in the U. S. , the April Fool's Day tradition is even more prevalent in European countries, such as France and Great Britain. Although the roots of the traditional trickings are unclear, the French and the British both have claims on the origin of the celebration.

One theory holds that the first April Fool's Day was on A-

---

　　* 作者佚名。每年的 4 月 1 日，是许多国家人民最开心的日子。在这一天，人们可以充分发挥自己的想像力，尽可能编造出一些耸人听闻的谎言，玩弄一些小把戏，去调侃、哄骗、取笑和愚弄别人，以得到一点看西洋镜的乐趣，例如新婚的妻子可能会收到告发丈夫不忠的信件，碌碌无为的公务员会接到提升的调令，儿子会接到某亿万富翁竟是自己失散多年的舅舅的电报……只要在午夜 12 点以前，无论你做得多么过分，多么肆无忌惮，也不负法律和道义上的任何责任。而且，如果你能制造出荒诞至极的"新闻"，又能让人信以为真，还能荣获骗术"桂冠"呢！这一天，就是举世闻名的愚人节。

pril 1 of the year when King of France instituted the new calendar. This new system placed the day that had formerly been the first day of a new year on April 1. Many people were reluctant to adjust to the new calandar and continued to celebrate New Year's Day on what had become the first day of April. Thus, they become the first April fools. Others began to give gag gifts on the day to mock the foolishness of those who continued to celebrate the new year on April 1.

An English story about the day, however, holds that it began sometime during the 1200s. At the time, King John of England was in the habit of making a road out of nearly every path he walked regularly. The citizens of one particular farm village were aware of this. To avoid having their green village were aware of this. To avoid having their green meadows and pastures disturbed with one of the king's roads, they built a fence that prevented the king from walking through their countryside. The king sent a group of messengers to inform the villagers that they must remove the barrier. Upon hearing that the king was planning to do this, however, the villagers developed a plan of their own. When the messengers arrived, they found what appeared to be a community of lunatics, with people behaving in a bizarre manner, throwing things and running around wildly. The messengers, alarmed at what they had found, reported to king John that these people were so mad as to be beyond punishment. So, the villagers saved their farmland by tricking the King. In Great Britain, tradition only allows April Fool's tricks from midnight to noon on April 1. Those who try to play tricks in the afternoon become the fools themselves. ✳

 Vocabulary List【词汇清单】

prevalent /'prevələnt/ *adj.* 普遍的,流行的,盛行的

tricking /'trikiŋ/ *n.* 诡计,骗局,恶作剧

celebration /ˌseli'breiʃən/ *n.* 庆祝,庆典,纪念

institute /'institjuːt/ *n.* 创立,制定,(开始)实行

calendar /'kælində/ *n.* 日历,历法

formerly /'fɔːməli/ *adv.* 从前,以前,原来

gag /gæg/ *n.* 恶作剧,戏弄,哄骗

mock /mɔk/ *v.* 嘲笑,奚落,愚弄

meadow /'medəu/ *n.* 草地,草旬;(河边或湖边的)低草地

pasture /'paːstʃə/ *n.* 牧地,草原,牧场

lunatic /'luːnətik/ *n.* 疯子,狂人,大傻瓜(现仅用于夸张说法)

bizarre /bi'zaː/ *adj.* (举止、外表等)怪异的,稀奇古怪的

trick /trik/ *v.* 欺骗,诈骗,哄骗

 参考译文【Suggested Translation】

愚 人 节

愚人节的习俗在美国是很流行的,在欧洲国家如法国和英国就更是如此了。虽然这种愚弄人习俗的起源不甚清楚,但是法国人和英国人却都宣称这种庆祝活动是由他们开始的。

有一种说法认为,第一个愚人节始于法国国王设立新历法那一年的 4 月 1 日。这种新历法将以前新的一年的第一天定在 4 月 1 日。很多人都不愿意按照新的历法行事,还继续在根据新的历法已经是 4 月的第一天庆祝新年,于是他们就成了第一批愚人。另有一些人开始在这一天送戏弄人的礼物来取笑那些继续在 4 月 1 日庆祝新年的人。

然而关于愚人节这一天,英国的一则故事却认为它始于 13 世纪的某一天。那时,英格兰的约翰国王习惯于将他经常走的几乎每条小道都修成一条路。有一个乡村的居民觉察到了这一点。为了保护他们绿油油的草地和牧场免受国王修路所造成的破坏，他们筑了一道篱笆来阻挡国王在他们的乡间穿行。国王派遣了一队使者去通报村民们必须撤掉障碍。在听到国王正要打算这么做时，村民们也想出了自己的办法。当使者到达的时候，他们看到这里的人像一群疯子似的，举止古怪，乱扔东西，并且四下疯跑。此情此景令使者们惊恐万分，后来赶紧向约翰国王报告说，这些人疯疯癫癫的，根本没办法处置。村民们就这样骗过了国王，保护了自己的农田。在英国，按习俗在 4 月 1 日这一天只允许从子夜到中午的这段时间搞恶作剧，到下午还这么做的人自己就成了愚人了。◆

（《英语沙龙》康坚 译）

- He who risks nothing gains nothing.（收获与风险并存。）
- Actions speak louder than words.（事实胜于雄辩；行胜于言。）
- Time past cannot be called back again.（时间不能倒流。）
- No cross, no crown.（不经历风雨，怎么见彩虹。）

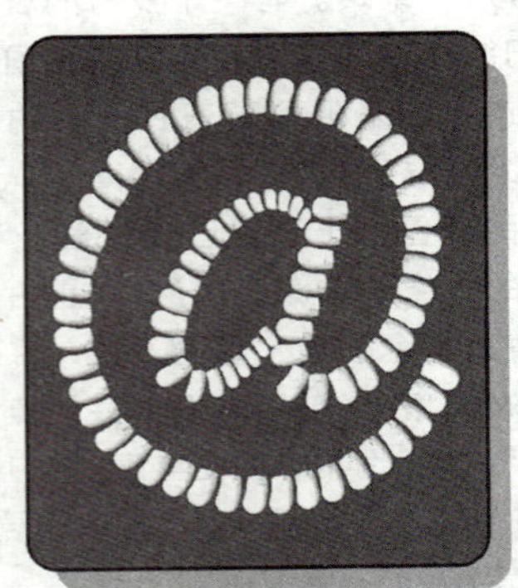

第 **079** 篇

Bill Gates' Speech to Qinghua University(Ⅰ)*

It's great to be here and have a chance to share some of my excitement with you.

I got involved with computers at 18. And the computer

---

* 作者威廉·亨利·盖茨三世（William Henry Gates Ⅲ,1955— ），昵称比尔·盖茨(Bill Gates),肄业于哈佛大学,被誉为电脑奇才、20 世纪最伟大的计算机软件行业巨人,一手创办了世界上最成功的企业之———微软公司,现任微软公司董事长兼首席软件架构师。盖茨曾是一名非常出色的学生,而且以极端个人主义闻名。根据他的一名高中同学的回忆,盖茨曾断言自己会在 25 岁时成为亿万富翁。现今,他已经连续十年位居《福布斯》杂志全球富豪排行榜首位,其一个人的财富要比全世界最贫穷的 50% 人口的财富总额还要多。1999 年 10 月 18 日出版的《时代》周刊将他评为在数字技术领域影响重大的 50 人之一,1998 年和 1999 年连续两年被英国《金融时报》评为全球最受尊重的企业家,2004 年被英国女王册封为爵士。其主要著作有《未来之路》、《未来时速》等。

was a very limited teletype that had to be connected through a phone line up to a mainframe-like computer, but my friends and I became fascinated with understanding what the computer can do, what was the future, and how would it be used. When we found out about chip technology, and the miracle of being able to improve the power of the chip exponentially, we realized that computers had a very bright future. We spent a lot of our time writing software because we loved writing software, because we thought that the software being written by a lot of big hardware companies wasn't as good as what we could do.

I was 19 when I realized that if I wanted to be the first to do a software company for these new cheap computers, I needed to get my friends together and start right away, so Microsoft became the first company doing software for these new machines. Our vision was a computer on every desk and in every home. In the last 20 years, that vision is certainly becoming a reality. If we had to change it today, we would simply add that now we also want to have a computer in every pocket, every car — many other places that we had not thought about when we first started doing development. I believe software is the key element that really unlocks the power of all this technology, and the idea of making it easy to find information, easy to create information, easy to communicate with other people. Software is at the center of that, and so software will be the fastest growing industry in the world and one that will create lots and lots of great jobs. Certainly here in China the opportunity for hundreds of thousands of great jobs should be very exciting because there is a global shortage in terms of computer skills.

The personal computer revolution got started in 1975,

that's when I left college and started Microsoft. These last 22 years have really been amazing, every prediction we've made about improvements have all come true. As we look ahead, that pace of innovation is not slowing down, in fact if anything it's speeding up. Very high speed processors like 300MHz Pentiums, or new 64-bit processors that we're already developing Windows NT for; incredible storage capacity, which will let us store, not just data, but also digital video as well; great screen technology to create a tablet-like device that would be good enough for reading and writing; advanced graphics and now the ability to connect computers together at very high speed.

The Internet is the way that all these machines can be connected together. And those standards, and the improvement of those standards, is very very important. Some people like to think about how the computer industry compares to other industries. I've shown before what the cost of the typical car was in 1980 in US, and that rose up to be about from 8,000 to 19,000 today, and likewise cereal has increased in price. How does that compare to PCs? If the same model was followed for PCs, you can buy a car for 27 cents and cereal for less than one cent, so there's no other area of the economy that has this rapid improvement, and people just aren't used to it. You almost have to tell people, "What would you do if Internet computing power was free." Because that's what we'll be able to deliver with all these improvements.

Microsoft's vision of computing is global computing. We see PCs connected to the Internet making the world a smaller place, and that's positive in so many ways: to bulid understanding between people, to share research in key science areas, including medicine, to allow world commerce to work very well. And the Internet is driving this already. Microsoft has set up cooperations around the world, and we are very pleased with the success we're having here in China. We are doing significant software development on products here, and that will continue to increase, and key for us is having very very high quality software people, and we've been lucky to hire a great number of people from this university. Really I'd say that the core of the teams we've put together have come from here, and I've listed some of those employees here, and we certainly hope that in the future this list will increase dramatically, and the quality of our work continues to rise. (To be continued) ✲

Vocabulary List 【词汇清单】

teletype /ˈtelitaip/ *n.*　<通讯>电传打字机,电报交换机

exponentially /ˌekspəuˈnenʃəli/ *adv.*　<数学>指数级地,几何级地

shortage /ˈʃɔːtidʒ/ *n.*　<美>不足,缺乏(额)

innovation /ˌinəuˈveiʃən/ *n.*　改革,革新,创新,变革

processor /ˈprəusesə/ *n.*　(电脑中的)处理机,处理器

Pentium /ˈpentəm/ *n.*　<计>Intel 公司生产的电脑 CPU 芯片,中文称为"奔腾"

graphic /ˈgræfik/ *n.*　<自动数据处理>图形,图像

cereal /ˈsiəriəl/ *n.* 谷类,谷类植物;<美>由谷类制成的食物

PC：(= personal computer)个人电脑

commerce /ˈkɔmə(ː)s/ *n.*　商业,商务,买卖,生意,贸易;交际,交往,(思想、意见、感情等的)交流

core /kɔː/ *n.*　中心,核心,(事物)最重要的部分

dramatically /drəˈmætikəli/ *adv.* 戏剧性地,引人注目地,显著地

参考译文【Suggested Translation】

比尔·盖茨在清华大学的演讲（一）

十分高兴来到这里并有机会与诸位分享我的兴奋之情。

我是在 18 岁的时候开始接触电脑的。当时的电脑只是一台功能很有限的电传打字机，并需要通过电话线连接在一台类似于大型机（主机）的计算机上。但是，我的朋友们和我都被电脑深深地吸引住了。我们急于想知道，电脑能够做些什么，它的前景怎样，并且人们将如何使用电脑。当我们发现了芯片技术，以及人们可以奇迹般地以几何级的速度增强芯片的功能时，我们认识到电脑的前景无限广阔。我们花了很多时间编写软件，因为我们喜欢编写软件，并且因为我们觉得许多大的硬件公司编写的软件不如我们编写得好。

在我 19 岁的时候，我认识到如果我想要创办第一家专为新型的便宜的电脑开发软件的公司，就必须召集我的朋友，然后马上开始行动，于是微软作为第一家软件公司就此诞生了。我们当时的设想是让每一张办公桌上、每一个家庭里都拥有一台电脑。在过去的 20 年当中，这个设想无疑变成了现实。假如我们今天要修改一下这个设想的话，我们只是想补充一点，那就是现在我们还想让每个人的口袋里，每辆车中，以及在我们起初开始发展时没想到的许多其他地方都摆放一台电脑。我相信，软件是能够真正开发电脑技术潜力的关键因素，并是使电脑帮助人们更简便地查询信息、创造信息、与他人交流信息的好方法。软件处于其核心地位，因此，软件将成为世界上发展最快的产业，并且它将创造许许多多巨大的就业机会。在中国，当然也不例外，数以十万计的绝佳的就业机会将是十分激动人心的，因为全球都急需计算机领域的人才。

个人电脑的革命起步于 1975 年，那时候我刚刚离开大学并开始创办微软。过去的这 22 年实在令人惊讶，我们关于电脑发展的一切预言都变成了现实。放眼未来，我们发现，革新的步伐非但没有减慢，而且事实上还在加快。超高速处理器，如 300 兆赫的奔腾处理器或新的 64 位（比特）处理器，我们已经在为它们开发 Windows NT 操作系统；令人难以置信的存储容量，不但可以存储数据，还可以存储数字视频；妙不可言的屏幕技术能创造出一种适于读和写的刻录装置；此外还有先进的图像技术以及现有的电脑非常快速的联网能力。

　　因特网是能够使所有电脑联接起来的方法。至于这些标准及其完善，是非常非常重要的。有些人想知道计算机产业较之其他产业是怎样的一种状况。以前我曾经指出一辆典型的汽车 1980 年在美国的价格，如今这个价格已经涨到大概 8000 至 19000 美元；同样，谷物也在涨价。与它们相比，个人电脑的价格如何呢？如果按照个人电脑价格的下跌方式计算，你只要花 27 美分就可以买到一辆汽车了，而谷物则还不到 1 美分，所以没有什么经济领域有电脑业这样快的发展速度，只是人们还不太习惯而已。你差点儿就得告诉人们："如果因特网免费，你打算怎么办呢？"因为随着电脑业的发展，我们将能够做到这一点。

　　微软公司在计算机业发展的前景是全球计算机化。我们看到，联上因特网的个人电脑正在使世界变小，而这在许多方面会起到积极作用：架起人与人之间理解的桥梁，分享包括医学在内的重点科学领域的研究成果，保证世界贸易的顺利进行。而因特网正在朝着这个方向努力。微软公司也和世界各地的人们建立了合作关系，并且我们对于和中国的合作成功感到十分高兴。我们在中国的软件发展非常迅速，而且速度还将继续提升。对我们来讲，其关键是要拥有高素质的软件工程师，而我们很幸运地从贵校聘请到了很多人才。的确，我想说，我们这个团队的核心成员都毕业于贵校。我在此列出了其中一些雇员的名单，当然我们希望将来这个名单上的名字会大大增加，而我们的工作质量也会进一步提高。（未完待续）◆

Bill Gates' Speech to Qinghua University (Ⅱ)

Microsoft believes in doing a lot of research because the software of today is not adequate for tomorrow. It's come a long way, such as the graphics interface, the application, and the way we deal with linguistics; it's much better than it was a year ago. Building the Internet into the software has come a long way. Some of the more ambitious things, like teaching the computer to speak or listen or see, still require a lot of software work that's not yet done, and so we've been investing in research, and building the number of research locations which will be increasing in the years ahead. One advance is teaching the computer to pick up sentences and understand them, and not just think of them as a series of characters.

Here we have an example where the word processor is looking at an English sentence, and suggesting that the grammar is not correct, and showing exactly how the grammer might be fixes. That kind of thing has proven to be extremely popular, and (it's just a step on the road to getting computers to actually understand what's going on) in the same way that humans do. That pursuit of artificial intelligence is the most exciting thing in computer science. Although the progress in that has been fairly slow, I'm confident that that will be accelerating quite a bit.

Another interesting area that I think people aren't expecting is computer vision. The actual digital cameras that allow you to have an image and scan that image are going down in cost; and software to recognize users, see what they're looking at, what kind of gestures they're making, that kind of software is coming along quite well. In fact I brought a short little film of a demonstration that someone from our vision group did, so let's take a quick look at some of the progress that's been made.

〔Demo video〕

That just gives you a glimpse of one area that is expected to make the personal computer really disappear into the environment and connect up in a rich way. Tomorrow's PC will be quite different from what we have today, tomorrow's Internet will be much better than what we have today, but it will all evolve out of this technology that we have right now.

It's clear that the reason we refer to this as the information age is that the capabilities available in the information age will let people reach out and get what they need, whether it's business, learning, or for entertainment. Microsoft feels in a very lucky position to be helping to drive these things, and key for us is working with other software companies so that they can build other applications on top of the system. Every industry needs a lot of software work there, and so I talk about the software industry creating so many great jobs in the years ahead. I think you picked a great field to be in, and we look forward to working with you.

Thank you. ✳

# Vocabulary List【词汇清单】

adequate /'ædikwit/ *adj.* 足够的,充分的

interface /'intəfeis/ *n.* ＜计＞界面(在相关区域、实体、物质或阶段之间所形成共同界限的面)

linguistics /liŋ'gwistiks/ *n.* 语言学(研究人类语言的性质和结构的学科)

ambitious /æm'biʃəs/ *adj.* 有极大进取心的,抱负不凡的,有雄心壮志的,

artificial /ˌaːti'fiʃəl/ *adj.* 人工的,人造的,人为的(artificial intelligence:人工智能,智能模拟,是指机器用以执行通常认为要具备智力才能完成那些活动的能力)

accelerate /ək'seləreit/ *v.* (使运动物体)加速,加快

gesture /'dʒɛstʃə/ *n.* 手势,姿势,动作

demonstration /ˌdeməns'treiʃən/ *n.* 示范(表演),展示(下文的 demo /'deməu/与之同义)

glimpse /glimps/ *n.* (粗略的)一瞥,一看,扫视

evolve /i'vɔlv/ *v.* ＜美＞进展,发展,演进

# 参考译文【Suggested Translation】

比尔·盖茨在清华大学的演讲(二)

软坚信还有大量的研究工作要做,因为今天的软件到明天就不够用了。我们在这方面的工作由来已久,例如图形界

面、应用程序以及我们处理语言学的方式。与一年之前相比，我们已经取得了很大进步。我们在把因特网编制成软件方面也取得了长足进步。一些更加宏伟的计划，如教电脑说、听、看，仍然需要做很多现在还没有做的软件工作。因此，我们一直在研究开发软件、增加研究网点，在今后几年里，研究网点的数量还会继续增加。我们已经取得的一个进展是教电脑识别和理解句子，而不仅仅是把它们看成一串串字符。

这里有一个例子，说的是文字处理程序看到一个英语句子，可以指出其语法错误，并准确地提出应该如何予以改正。像这类东西已经被证明极受人们欢迎，但是这仅仅是我们在使电脑像人那样真正知道发生了什么新的情况方面向前迈出了一小步。人工智能的探究是计算机科学中最为激动人心的部分。尽管这方面的进展还相当缓慢，但是我深信它会有很大进步的。

我猜想，另一个人们没料到的有趣领域是计算机视觉。能够用来照相和扫描的数码相机的价格正在下跌；而能够识别用户、注意用户正在看什么以及用户手势的这些软件的开发进展很快。事实上，我带来了一小段演示影片，它是我们视觉小组的人员制作的，那么，让我们快速看一下我们研究的进展情况吧。

〔一段录像演示〕

诸位看到的只是未来个人电脑发展的一个方面。未来的个人电脑将完全融入环境之中，并以各种方式互相联接起来。明天的个人电脑将和我们今天的大不相同，明天的因特网要比我们今天的好得多，但是它们都将由我们现有的技术发展而来。

显然，我们之所以称今天的时代为信息时代，是因为在信息时代里，人们可以获取所需要的一切信息，无论是商业、学习还是娱乐信息。微软很幸运地处在这样的一个位置，它将有助于促进这些事物的发展。对我们来讲，关键在于和其他软件公司进行合作，使其能够在这个系统之上组建其他应用程序。每种产业都需要许多软件工作，所以我说，未来的软件产业将创造很多巨大的就业机会。我认为你们选择了一个伟大的发展领域，而我们期待着与诸位的合作。

谢谢大家。◆

第 081 篇

Love Your Life*

However mean your life is, meet it and live it; do not shun it and call it hard names. It is not as bad as you are. It looks poorest when you are richest. The faultfinder will find faults even in paradise. Love your life, poor as it is. You may perhaps have some pleasant, thrilling, glorious hours, even in a poor-house. The setting sun is reflected from the windows of the almshouse as brightly as from the rich man's abode; the snow melts before its door as early in the spring. I do not see but a quiet mind may live as contentedly there,

---

* 作者亨利·大卫·梭罗（Henry David Thoreau, 1817—1862），美国著名博物学家、散文家和思想家，19 世纪超验主义运动的重要代表人物，其代表作《瓦尔登湖》（Walden）出版于 1854 年，是一本寂寞、恬静、智慧的书，以"深沉而敏感的抒情"和"超凡入圣"而著称，是 19 世纪美国文学非小说著作中最受读者欢迎的书籍，此书业已成为美国文学中的一本独特的、卓越的名著。同时，梭罗的许多散文语语惊人，字字闪光，沁人心肺，动人衷肠，极富思想内容，在美国 19 世纪散文中独树一帜。

and have as cheering thoughts, as in a palace. The town's poor seem to me often to live the most independent lives of any. Maybe they are simply great enough to receive without misgiving. Most think that they are above being supported by the town; but it often happens that they are not above supporting themselves by dishonest means, which should be more disreputable. Cultivate poverty like a garden herb, like sage. Do not trouble yourself much to get new things, whether clothes or friends. Turn the old, return to them. Things do not change; we change. Sell your clothes and keep your thoughts. ✳

 **Vocabulary List【词汇清单】**

mean /miːn/ *adj.* （社会地位）低贱的,出身寒微的

shun /ʃʌn/ *v.* 回避,躲开,避免

faultfinder /ˈfɔːltˌfaində/ *n.* 喜欢挑剔者,吹毛求疵的人,揭人短处者

paradise /ˈpærədais/ *n.* 伊甸园,天堂,乐园

glorious /ˈglɔːriəs/ *adj.* 光荣的,荣耀的,可称颂的

almshouse /ˈaːmzhaus/ *n.* ＜美＞（用公费设立的）贫民院,救济院,贫民所;＜英＞（私人资助的）贫民院,救济院

abode /əˈbəud/ *n.* 住所,寓所

contentedly /kənˈtentidli/ *adv.* 满足地,满意地,心满意足地

misgive /misˈgiv/ *v.* 疑虑,担忧,害怕

disreputable /disˈrepjutəbl/ *adj.* 名誉（或声誉）不好的,声名狼藉的,不体面的

herb /həːb/ *n.* 药草,香草（尤指薄荷、麝香草）;在本文中泛指花草。

sage /seidʒ/ *n.* 贤人,圣人,年高望重的人

参考译文【Suggested Translation】

热 爱 生 活

不论你的生活如何卑微，你都得面对与度过；不要逃避，也莫以恶言相加。生活不像你认为的那般坏。当你富甲天下之时，生活却显得贫瘠乏味。即使在天堂，吹毛求疵之人也能挑出缺点。即使生活贫穷，你也该热爱生活，因为就是在贫济院，你也有自己快乐、激动与光荣的岁月。夕阳照在贫济院窗上的反光与富人宅第上的一样夺目；其门前的积雪同样是在早春融化。我只是看到，一个心绪宁静的人就算居住在贫济院，生活起来也会心满意足，思想愉悦，如同生活在皇宫中一样。在我看来，城镇中的贫民大凡过着最为无拘无束的生活。或许他们只是超乎寻常，不然岂会毫无疑惧地接受这一切。大多数人认为自己超凡脱俗而无须依赖城镇的资助，然而情况往往是，他们谋生靠的是不正当的手段，这更会让他们声名扫地。如圣人一般，视贫穷如园中的花草去慢慢地耕耘吧。不要自找麻烦地去追求新花样——衣服也好，朋友也好。翻开故往，回归故往。万物未变，我们在变。你的衣装可以卖掉，但要保留你的思想。◆

Privacy as Border*

There are quite a few questions that are supposed never to be asked about. It is impolite or rude even to mention them in a conversation. These topics include one's age, income, marriage, religious belief and political position as well as any other fields of privacy. In order to understand the American or western idea of a personal concept of privacy, one may think of the concept of "territory". As well known, a nation has borders or boundaries with other countries and everything within

---

* 作者佚名。隐私权(The Right to Privacy)的理论产生于美国。一般认为,构成隐私权有两个要件:一是"私",二是"隐"。前者指纯粹是个人的,与公共利益、群体利益无关的事情,这是隐私权的本质所在;后者则是指某个事物、某个信息不为人知的事实状态。因此,隐私权是自然人享有的对其个人的,与公共利益无关的个人信息、私人生活和私有领域进行支配的权利。作为一项人身权,只要权利人没有言明放弃自己的禁止权,任何人均无权泄露和公开与此相关的信息和内容。那么,从社会这个更广泛的意义上讲,隐私又包括哪些内容呢?

the border belongs to the nation alone and no one else.

One's home — one's castle

Is one able to enter another country without a passport — a permit from another? Absolutely not. It is the same for one's home.

If one enters someone else's home without asking for permission, he is likely to be charged with trespassing or even burglary. Inside the house everything is within the territory of the owner, no one else. A bedroom is his or her castle. No one may visit it without permission.

Inside the room — confidential

No one has the right to open a closet, desk or drawer in the room — these are something secret in the host or hostess' castle. On top of the desk there may be letters, business papers or exercise books, these too are within the owner's territory. Never touch them or read them! Similarly never read over one's shoulder when he or she is reading something! You don't want to behave like a spy, do you? Anything one is reading is his or her private property. Don't invade it!

Income — a top secret

In the United States, one's income is the top secret. Never even try to ask any questions about it! Avoid asking for dishonor. In the same way, it is impolite to inquire about one's property or the cost of some articles. You may say how cool something is, but never ask about the price.

Age — taboo for everyone

Age is considered a taboo, especially for the ladies. They hate any topics about age, simply because they hate to get old, because they want to stay young forever! They are very sensitive to questions like: "When were you born?" or "Do you have artificial teeth?" Never make any comment like

"You have grey hair", otherwise the males and females alike will beat you black and blue.

Religion — sensitive

Religion is what one believes in personally. It is totally a personal matter. Never ask, "Why do you worship as a Christian", it is none of your business. Everyone has the freedom to believe as they choose in belief.

Politics — big men's affairs

Politics is a sensitive topic too. It's completely of personal opinion. There is no argument about taste, anyway. Besides, such questions as "Do you believe Israel will accept the conditions for peace talks?" should be on the agenda of those "big men", not for a "nobody" like you and me. ✳

Vocabulary List 【词汇清单】

territory /'teritəri/ *n.* 领土,领地;＜美＞(按某种目的划定的)区域

boundary /'baundəri/ *n.* 边界,分界线

trespass /'trespəs/ *v.* 非法侵入,未经许可进入私人土地;＜法律＞(非法)侵害,侵入私宅

burglary /'bə:gləri/ *n.* 入室行窃,夜盗行为

confidential /ˌkɔnfi'denʃəl/ *adj.* 机密的,秘密的

invade /in'veid/ *v.* 侵略,侵入,侵犯

dishonor /dis'ɔnə/ *n.* 不名誉,不光彩;羞耻,丢脸(的事、行为)

taboo /tə'bu:/ *n.* ＜宗教＞(社会习俗或传统方面的)禁忌,禁讳

Israel /'izreiəl/ *n.* 以色列(西南亚的一个国家,位于地中海东岸,1948 年 5 月 14 日在联合国推荐下建国,耶路撒冷是其首都。此后,以色列与其阿拉伯邻国的不和睦导致了许多战争。在国际社会的斡旋下,巴以双方开始寻找政治解决的途径。国际社会先后提出了一系列和平方案,但均遭沙龙政府

拒绝。2003 年,联合国、美国、欧盟和俄罗斯中东问题四方正式公布并启动了实现巴以和平的中东"路线图"计划。但因以色列坚持其强硬政策,巴以冲突再起,"路线图"计划被搁浅至今。)

 参考译文【Suggested Translation】

隐私如国境

有一些话题在谈话中永远不要涉及,提一提都是无礼、甚或粗鲁的行为。这些话题包括一个人的年龄、收入、婚姻状况、宗教信仰、政治立场以及其他个人领域的事物。为了理解美国以及其他西方国家有关个人隐私的观念,我们不妨从"领土"这个概念说起。众所周知,一国总以边境或边界与他国为界,而之内的一切事物仅属于该国所有,别国不得侵犯。

住宅——个人城堡

假如没有护照(进入一国的许可证),任何人能够进入他国吗?绝不可能。同理,进入他人住宅也必须得到许可。

如果未经允许就闯进别人家里,轻则告你"擅闯民宅",重则告你"入室行窃"。同样,家里的一切都是主人领土上的财产,他人不得擅动。而卧室简直就是他或她的"城堡"——未经允许不得参观。

室内——保密

任何人都无权乱翻他人室内的衣柜、书桌或者抽屉——这些是主人城堡里的秘密!书桌上也许有信件、商务文函或练习本——这些也是他人境内的财产。千万别碰它们,也别拿来读。同样,当别人在阅读什么的时候,千万不要站在别人后面"偷"看!你不想成为一个间谍,是吧?别人正在阅读的一切都是他的私人财产,千万不要侵犯!

收入——最高机密

在美国,个人收入是最高机密。你甚至不要试图去打听有关的问题,不要自讨没趣!同样,询问他人的财产或某件物品的价格也是不礼貌的。你可以说某样东西多么多么酷，但就是别问价格！

年龄——个人禁忌

年龄是一个非常忌讳的问题，对于女士尤其如此。她们讨厌任何与年龄有关的话题，只因为她们害怕衰老，总想永葆青春！她们对和年龄有关的问题十分敏感，诸如"您什么时候出生的？"或者"您戴假牙吗？"。千万不要说"您的头发都白了"一类的话，否则人家会把你揍得鼻青脸肿！

宗教——敏感的话题

宗教纯粹属于个人信仰，其完全是个人的事情。千万别问"您为什么信仰基督教"之类的话，这不关你的事。再者说，人人都有信仰自由。

政治——大人物的事

政治也是一个敏感的话题。它完全属于个人看法，无论如何也没什么好争论的。更何况，诸如"您认为以色列会接受和谈条件吗？"之类的问题是"大人物"们关心的事，不是你我这样的"无名小卒"该管的。◆

- It never rains but it pours. （不鸣则已，一鸣惊人。）
- All work and no play makes Jack a dull boy. （只会用功不玩耍，聪明孩子也变傻。）
- The early bird catches the worm. （捷足先登。）
- Do as you would be done by. （己所不欲，勿施于人。）

Of Studies *

Studies serve for delight, for ornament, and for ability. Their chief use for delight, is in privateness and retiring; for ornament, is in discourse; and for ability, is in the judgment and disposition of business. For expert men can execute, and perhaps judge of particulars, one by one; but the general counsels, and the plots and marshalling of affairs, come best from those that are learned. To spend too much time in studies is sloth; to use them too much for ornament, is

---

　　* 作者弗兰西斯·培根（Francis Bacon，1561—1626），英国著名的唯物主义哲学家和科学家，第一个提出"知识就是力量"，在文艺复兴时期的巨人中被尊称为哲学史和科学史上划时代的人物。马克思称培根是"英国唯物主义和整个现代实验科学的真正始祖"，罗素则尊称他为"给科学研究程序进行逻辑组织化的先驱"。培根的处女作《论说随笔文集》表现了自己对于人生、对于社会的种种现象、种种问题的独到的见解与鞭辟入里的议论，其中名言警句俯仰皆是，深受广大读者的欢迎。本文是该文集最著名的篇章之一。

affectation; to make jugment wholly by their rules, is the humour of a scholar. They perfect nature, and are perfected by experience: for natural abilities are like natural plants, that need pruning by study; and studies themselves do give forth directions too much at large, except they be bounded in by experience. Crafty men contemn studies, simple men admire them, and wise men use them; for they teach not their own use; but that is a wisdom without them, and above them, won by observation. Read not to contradict and confute; nor to believe and take for granted; nor to find talk and discourse; but to weigh and consider. Some books are to be tasted, others to be swallowed, and some few to be chewed and digested; that is, some books are to be read only in parts; others to be read, but not curiously; and some few to be read wholly, and with diligence and attention. Some books also may be read by deputy, and extracts made of them by others; but that would be only in the less important arguments, and the meaner sort of books, else distilled books are, like common distilled waters, flashy things.

Reading maketh a full man; conference a ready man; and writing an exact man. And therefore, if a man write little, he had need have a great memory; if he confer little, he had need have a present wit; and if he read little, he had need have much cunning, to seem to know that he doth not. Histories make men wise; poets witty; the mathematics subtitle; natural philosophy deep; moral grave; logic and rhetoric able to contend. Abeunt studia in mores. Nay there is no stand or impediment in the wit, but may be wrought out by fit studies: like as diseases of the body may have appropriate exercises. Bowling is good for the stone and reins: shooting for the lungs and breast; gentle walking for the stomach; riding for the head; and the like. So if a man's wit be wandering, let him study the mathematics; for in demonstrations, if his wit be called away never so little, he must begin again. If his wit be not apt to distinguish or find differences, let him study the Schoolmen; for they are cymini sectores. If he be not apt to beat over matters, and to call up one thing to prove and illustrate another, let him study the lawyers' cases. So every defect of the mind may have a special receipt. ✳

Vocabulary List【词汇清单】

ornament /'ɔːnəmənt/ *n.* 装饰,修饰

discourse /'diskɔːs/ *n.* 交谈,谈话;演讲,演说

disposition /ˌdispə'ziʃən/ *n.* 部署,安排;(事务的)处理,处置

marshal /'maːʃəl/ *v.* 排列,安排,整理

sloth /sləuθ/ *n.* 怠惰,懒散

prune /pruːn/ *v.* 修剪(树枝等),删节

crafty /'kraːfti/ *adj.* 狡猾的,狡诈的,诡计多端的

contemn /kən'tem/ *v.* 轻视,轻蔑,藐视,蔑视

confute /kən'fjuːt/ *v.* 驳斥,驳倒(某人、论据等),辩驳

swallow /'swɔləu/ *v.* 吞下,咽下

distilled /dis'tild/ *adj.* 蒸馏;<引申>(精华)被提取出来

confer /kən'fəː/ *v.* 讨论,磋商,商讨,交换意见

doth /dʌθ/ (= does) <古> do 的第三人称单数现在时的陈述语气(主要用于助动词用法)

subtle /'sʌtl/ *adj.* 敏锐的,明察的,精细的

rhetoric /'retərik/ *n.* 修辞学,修辞技巧

Abeunt studia in mores: <拉丁文>凡有所学,皆成性格。

nay /nei/ *adv.* <书>不仅如此,而且,甚至

impediment /im'pedimənt/ *n.* <罕用>妨碍,阻碍,障碍

wrought /rɔːt/ *v.* <古> work 的一种过去式和过去分词

reins /reinz/ *n.* <古>肾脏;腰部

be apt to: 易于…,倾向于…

cymini sectores: <拉丁文>过分讲究细节的人

receipt /riˈsiːt/ *n.*（recipe 的旧体）处方，药方

参考译文【Suggested Translation】

谈 读 书

读书足以怡情，足以博彩，足以长才。其怡情也，最见于独处幽居之时；其博彩也，最见于高谈阔论之中；其长才也，最见于处世判事之际。练达之士虽能分别处理细事或一一判别枝节，然纵观统筹、全局策划，则舍好学深思者莫属。读书费时过多易惰，文采藻饰太盛则矫，全凭条文断事乃学究故态。读书补天然之不足，经验又补读书之不足，盖天生才干犹如自然花草，读书然后知如何修剪移接；而书中所示，如不以经验范之，则又大而无当。有一技之长者鄙读书，无知者羡读书，唯明智之士用读书，然书并不以用处告人，用书之智不在书中，而在书外，全凭观察得之。读书时不可存心诘难作者，不可尽信书上所言，亦不可只为寻章摘句，而应推敲细思。书有可浅尝者，有可吞食者，少数则须咀嚼消化。换言之，有只须读其部分者，有只须大体涉猎者，少数则须全读，读时须全神贯注，孜孜不倦。书亦可请人代读，取其所作摘要，但只限题材较次或价值不高者，否则书经提炼犹如水经蒸馏、淡而无味矣。

读书使人充实，讨论使人机智，笔记使人准确。因此不常作笔记者须记忆特强，不常讨论者须天生聪颖，不常读书者须欺世有术，始能无知而显有知。读史使人明智，读诗使人灵秀，数学使人周密，科学使人深刻，伦理学使人庄重，逻辑修辞之学使人善辩：凡有所学，皆成性格。人之才智但有滞碍，无不可读适当之书使之顺畅，一如身体百病，皆可借相宜之运动除之。滚球利睾肾，射箭利胸肺，慢步利肠胃，骑术利头脑，诸如此类。如智力不集中，可令读数学，盖演题须全神贯注，稍有分散即须重演；如不能辨异，可令读经院哲学，盖是辈皆吹毛求疵之人；如不善求同，不善以一物阐证另一物，可令读律师之案卷。如此头脑中凡有缺陷，皆有特药可医。◆

（王佐良　译）

The Urgency*

June 24

If a man is ever going to abmit that he belongs to the earth, not the other way round, it probably will be in late June. Then it is that life surpasses man's affairs with incredible urgency and outreaches him in every direction. Even the farmer, on whom we all depend for the substance of existence, knows then that the best he can do is cooperate with wind and weather, soil and seed. The incalculable energy of chlorophyll, the green leaf itself, dominates the earth, and the root in the soil is the inescapable fact. Even the roadside weed ignores man's legislation.

---

* 作者赫尔·波兰德（Hal Borland，1900—1978），美国著名作家和诗人。本文体裁属于日记体散文，描绘的是初夏时节自然界的动植物繁衍生息之时一片欣欣向荣的景象。"本文尤其着重写只有短暂生命的小生物抓紧时机完成其生命历程的紧迫性，使人不禁对生命珍惜、时光宝贵产生震撼感。"（陈文伯语）

The urgency is everywhere. Grass blankets the earth, reaching for the sun, spreads its roots, flowers and comes to seed. The forest widens its canopy, strengthens its boles, nurtures its seedlings, ripens its perpetuating nuts. The birds nest and hatch their fledglings. The beetle and the bee are busy at the grassroot and the blossom, and the butterfly lays eggs that will hatch and crawl and eat and pupate and take to the air once more. Fish spawn and meadow voles harvest the wild meadows, and owls and foxes feed their young. Dragonflies and swallows and nighthawks seine the air where the minute winged creatures flit out their minute life spans.

And man, who glibly calls the earth his own, neither powers the leaf nor energizes the fragile wing. Man participates, but his dominance is limited. It is the urgency of life, or growth, that rules. Late June and early Summer are the ultimate, unarguable proof. ✳

Vocabulary List 【词汇清单】

surpass /səːˈpaːs/ *v.* （数量、程度等）超越,超过,胜过

outreach /autˈriːtʃ/ *v.* 超出…范围,胜过,占…上风

incalculable /inˈkælkjuləbl/ *adj.* 数不清的,数不胜数的,无数的,极大的

chlorophyll /ˈklɔrəfil/ *n.* ＜生化＞叶绿素（在植物体内能够吸收太阳光以促进其生长的一种绿色物质）

dominate /ˈdɔmineit/ *v.* 统治,支配,主宰

inescapable /ˌiniˈeskeipəbl/ *adj.* 不可避免的,无法规避的,逃避不了的,必然（发生）的

canopy /ˈkænəpi/ *n.* （床或宝座上的）顶盖,天篷,华盖

bole /bəul/ *n.* 树干,主干

nurture /ˈnəːtʃə/ *v.* 养育,给与营养物,滋养

perpetuate /pəˈpetʃueit/ *v.* 使永久存在,使不朽

fledgling /ˈfledʒliŋ/ *n.* 刚生羽毛（或刚会飞）的小鸟，雏鸟，幼鸟

crawl /krɔːl/ *n.* （虫、蚁等）爬行，蠕动，缓慢的行进

pupate /ˈpjuːpeit/ *v.* ＜昆＞化蛹，变成蛹

spawn /spɔːn/ *v.* （鱼等）产卵

vole /vəul/ *n.* ＜动物＞田鼠，仓鼠

owl /aul/ *n.* ＜动物＞猫头鹰，枭

nighthawk /ˈnaithɔːk/ *n.* ＜动物＞夜鹰

seine /sein/ *v.* 用围网（拉网）捕鱼或打捞

flit /flit/ *v.* （鸟、蝙蝠等）轻快地飞过，掠过

life span：某种生物可预期的最长寿命；平均生命期

glibly /ˈglibli/ *adv.* 圆滑地，随便地；油嘴滑舌地，油腔滑调地

 参考译文【Suggested Translation】

紧 迫 性

6 月 24 日

如果一个人愿意承认他是属于地球的而不是地球属于他，那很可能就是在 6 月份的晚些时候。这个时候，自然生机那种只争朝夕的精神比起人类事务来真是紧迫得令人难人置信，在各方面都胜人类一筹。就连农民（我们依靠他们生产的东西维持生存）也知道这时候最好是能顺应风雨天候，照料土壤种子。主宰着大地的是叶绿素无法估算的能源以及绿叶本身，土壤中有根的存在，这是自不待言的。即使是路边的野草也都冲破人为的制约蔓生开来。

那种只争朝夕的紧迫感无处不在。草如绿毯，铺满大地，一直伸向太阳；它四处伸延根须，开花结籽。森林拓展其华盖，强固其主干，给其秧苗输送养分，并使长了许久的坚果渐趋成熟。鸟雀筑巢并孵化雏鸟。甲虫在草根旁奔忙，蜜蜂在花丛中飞逐。蝴蝶则在产卵，将来孵出的小虫从爬行、吃食、化蛹到振翅飞舞再经历一次循环。鱼儿也在产卵，田鼠则在野生的牧场上采获食物。猫头鹰和狐狸给它们的幼仔喂食。蜻蜓、燕子和夜鹰在天空中像围网似地捕食，而极小的有翼动物在空中轻快地飞来

飞去,顷刻间其短暂的生命便结束了。

　　然而,人类扬言地球属于他们,可是既不能给叶片以能量又不能给脆弱的翅膀以力量。人类只是参与其中,而其主导地位是有限的。驾御一切的是生命或生长只争朝夕的紧迫性。6 月份晚些时候的初夏时节从根本上无可争辩地证明了这一点。◆

● All that ends well is well. (结果好则一切皆好。)

● Every advantage has its disadvantage. (凡事有利必有弊。)

● We shall never have friends if we expect to find them without fault. (欲求完美无缺的朋友必然成为孤家寡人。)

● Life is not all roses. (人生并不是康庄大道。)

The Happy Door *

Happiness is like a pebble dropped into a pool to set in motion an ever-widening circle of ripples. As Stevenson has said, being happy is a duty.

There is no exact definition of the word happiness. Happy people are happy for all sorts of reasons. The key is not wealth or physical well-being, since we find beggars, invalids and so-called failures who are extremely happy.

Being happy is a sort of unexpected dividend. But sta-

---

　　* 作者米尔德里德·克拉姆(Mildred Cram)，生平不详。快乐，是人真实的、相对的感觉。它反映人在物质上或精神上的一种满足，一种愉悦的心情。它既有人的本性一面，也有人的情操成分。现实生活中，快乐的确是很难有统一标准的。有的人认为很平常的事，对于其他人来说则是快乐的；有的人认为很快乐的事，对于另一些人来说则是痛苦的；有的人其实已经很快乐，可他还认为不快乐而四处寻求快乐；有的人非常痛苦没有快乐但他却从痛苦中去感悟快乐。"宠辱莫惊，闲看庭前花开花落；去留无意，漫随天外云卷云舒。"笑对生活，知足常乐；享受快乐，顺其自然。你打开你的快乐之门了么？

ying happy is an accomplishment, a triumph of soul and character. It is not selfish to strive for it. It is, indeed, a duty to ourselves and others.

Being unhappy is like an infectious disease; it causes people to shrink away from the sufferer. He soon finds himself alone, miserable and embittered. There is, however, a cure so simple as to seem, at first glance, ridiculous：If you don't feel happy, pretend to be!

It works. Before long you will find that instead of repelling people, you attract them. You discover how deeply rewarding it is to be the center of wider and wider circles of good will.

Then the make-believe becomes a reality. You possess the secret of peace of mind, and can forget yourself in being of service to others.

Being happy, once it is realized as a duty and established as a habit, opens doors into unimaginable gardens thronged with grateful friends. ✽

Vocabulary List【词汇清单】

pebble /ˈpebl/ *n.* 小圆石,小鹅卵石

ripple /ˈripl/ *n.* （水、草等）呈波状起伏,波纹

Stevenson /ˈstiːvnsn/ （全名 Robert Louis Balfour Stevenson）罗伯特·路易斯·鲍尔福·斯蒂文生（1850—1894,苏格兰小说家、诗人和随笔作家）

well-being /ˈwelˈbiːiŋ/ *n.* 幸福,福利,健康欢乐

invalid /inˈvælid/ *n.* 病弱者,久病衰弱者

strive /straiv/ *v.* 努力,奋斗,力争（for）

embitter /imˈbitə/ *v.* （使）难受,（使）怨恨,（使）愁眉不展

ridiculous /riˈdikjuləs/ *adj.* 可笑的,荒谬的

repel /riˈpel/ *v.* 使厌恶,使反感,使不愉快

unimaginable /ˌʌniˈmædʒinəbl/ *adj.* 无法想像的,想像不到

的,不可思议的
throng /θrɔŋ/ *v.* 拥挤,挤满,群集(with)
grateful /'greitful/ *adj.* 感谢的,感激的,致谢意的

 参考译文【Suggested Translation】

快 乐 之 门

快乐好似掷入池塘里的一枚鹅卵石,会激起不断扩散的一圈圈涟漪。正如斯蒂文生所说:"快乐是一种责任。"

快乐这个字眼并没有确切的定义。快乐的人可以因种种理由而快乐。其关键并非在于财富或健康,因为我们可以发现有些乞丐、病弱的人和所谓的失败者却极其快乐。

快乐是一种意料不到的收益。而能保持快乐则是一项成就,也是灵魂与品性的胜利。努力追求快乐算不上是自私。事实上,追求快乐不仅是对我们自己,也是对别人的一种责任。

闷闷不乐就像是一种传染病;染上这种疾病的人大家都避之如蛇蝎。这种人很快就会发现自己感到孤单、痛苦和难过。然而,有一种很简单的治疗方法,乍看起来似乎荒谬可笑,那就是:如果你觉得不快乐,就假装快乐吧!

这个方法很有效的。不久你就会发现自己非但不会使人反感,反而还能吸引别人。你会发现,能够成为广结善缘的中心人物是多么值得的事。

于是,原本装扮的快乐就变成了真正的快乐。你会拥有心境平和的秘诀而又能忘情于服务他人。

一旦快乐被认作一种责任履行并成为一种习惯的时候,它就会开启大门,引领我们进入无法想像的花园中,里边云集着满怀感激的朋友。◆

Success Is a Choice *

All of us ought to be able to brace ourselves for the predictable challenges and setbacks that crop up everyday. If we expect that life won't be perfect, we'll be able to avoid that impulse to quit. But even if you are strong enough to persist the obstacle course of life and work, sometimes you will encounter an adverse event that will completely knock you on your back.

Whether it's a financial loss, the loss of respect of your peers or loved ones, or some other traumatic event in your

---

* 作者佚名。成功者宣言:我不会选择做一个普通人,我要成为一个不寻常的人,我寻找机会,但不是寻找安稳,我要做有意义的冒险,我要梦想,我要创造,我要失败,但我也要成功! 我决不用刺激来换取施舍,宁愿向生活挑战,而不要过安定的生活;宁要达到目的时的激动,不要"桃花源"式毫无活力的平静。我决不会在任何一位大师面前发抖,也决不会被任何恐吓所屈服。我要勇敢地面对这个世界,我要选择我想过的生活,我要选择我认为的成功!

life these major setbacks leave you doubting yourself and wondering if things can over change for the better again.

Adversity happens to all of us, and it happens all the time. Some form of major adversity is either going to be there or it's lying in wait just around the corner. To ignore adversity is to succumb to the ultimate self-delusion.

But you must recognize that history is full of examples of men and women who achieved greatness despite facing hurdles so steep that easily could have crashed their spirit and left them lying in the dust. Moses was a stutterer, yet he was called on to be the voice of God. Abraham Lincoln overcomes a difficult childhood, depression, the death of two sons, and constant ridicule during the Civil War to become arguably our greatest president ever. Helen Keller made an impact on the world despite being deaf, dumb, and blind from an early age. Franklin Roosevelt had polio.

There are endless examples. These were people who not only looked adversity in the face but learned valuable lessons about overcoming difficult circumstances and were able to move ahead. ✻

Vocabulary List 【词汇清单】

brace /breis/ *v.* 准备经受冲击（或压力）（常与反身代词连用）

predictable /pri'diktəbl/ *adj.* 可推断的,可预见的,可预想的

setback /'setbæk/ *n.* 挫折,阻碍

peer /piə/ *n.* 同辈,同等的人（尤指同等地位的公民）

traumatic /trɔː'mætik/ *adj.* ＜医学＞损伤的,外伤的;＜精神病学＞（精神）心灵创伤的

adversity /əd'vəːsiti/ *n.* 悲惨的境遇,不幸,逆境

succumb /sə'kʌm/ *v.* 屈服,屈从（to）

self-delusion /'selfdi'luːʒən/ *n.* （ = self-deception）自欺欺人

（行为），自欺

hurdle /ˈhəːdl/ *n.*　＜英＞篱笆，围栏；＜引申＞（有待克服的）困难，障碍

steep /stiːp/ *adj.*　陡峭的，险峻的；＜旧＞（极）高的

Moses /ˈməuziz/ *n.*　＜圣经＞摩西（古代犹太人的首领、先知和立法者，率领以色列人逃出埃及）

stutterer /ˈstʌtərə/ *n.*　口吃者，（说话）结结巴巴的人

ridicule /ˈridikjuːl/ *n.*　嘲笑，奚落，嘲弄（的话或举动）

Helen Keller /ˈhelən ˈkelə/　海伦·凯勒（1880—1968，美国传记作家、演说家。从小盲聋，后跟随其老师安妮·莎丽文学会读书、写字和讲话。她毕业于赖德克利芙学院，曾代表盲人在各处演讲，并著有《走出黑暗》一书）

polio /ˈpəuliəu/ *n.*　＜医＞（poliomyelitis 的缩略形式）脊髓灰质炎，小儿麻痹症

参考译文【Suggested Translation】

成功是一种选择

我们每个人都应该让自己做好准备，迎接每天可以预见的挑战和突如其来的挫折。假如我们相信生活并非十全十美，我们就能够避免因一时冲动而放弃追求。但是即使你足够坚强并能够在生活和工作的障碍重重的道路上挺进，有时候你也会遭遇逆境，它将会在背后给你狠狠一击。

不管是出现经济损失，或是失去同辈及亲人的尊敬，或是遭受其他的生活重创，这些巨大的挫折都会使你对自己产生怀疑，并且想知道情况是否能够好转。

我们每个人都可能遭遇困境，而且它时常发生，有些灾祸不是即刻发生就是藏于角落以待时机。而忽视逆境则无异于彻头彻尾的自我欺骗。

但是你必须认识到历史上有许许多多的事例都讲述了克服重重困难之后才成为卓越不凡之人。而他们曾面对的困难如此之大，以至于足以轻易粉碎他们的意志，并让他们流落于尘俗之

中。摩西曾有口吃，但他后来却成为传播上帝福音的使者。亚伯拉罕·林肯战胜了童年的艰难困苦、绝望沮丧、丧失两子之痛以及内战中纷至沓来的嘲弄，最终成为美国历史上无可争辩的最伟大的总统。海伦·凯勒从小就双目失明，双耳失聪，又是个哑巴，但她还是对世界产生了深刻影响。而富兰克林·罗斯福则患有小儿麻痹症。

　　类似的例子不胜枚举。这些人不仅大胆地直面逆境，而且从中学到了征服困境的宝贵经验，然后能够勇往直前。◆

●History repeats itself.（历史会重演。）

●Every little helps a mickle.（聚沙成塔，集腋成裘。）

●Send a wise man on an errand, and say nothing to him.（智者当差，不用交代。）

●A man can do no more than he can.（凡事都应量力而行。）

Living in Big Cities[*]

Why are so many people so anxious to get away from the small town or village where they were brought up, and to make for the big cities? They usually describe their home-town as "boring" or "dead," or — the harshest criticism of all — as "provincial."

If we examine the question from a distance, as if we were viewing the whole country from a long way off, we start to get a clue about what it is that lures us into the big cities. The main point to notice about big cities is that they are big: there are a lot of people, and there are a lot of things going on. If you look down on a city, literally from a great distance,

---

* 作者佚名。啊,大都市！高楼林立,车水马龙,环境优雅,生活便利……然而,这些可以给人们带来精神上的愉悦么？繁华确实是繁华,可是繁华却掩盖不了人们的内心的压力和落寞。交通、环境、住房、犯罪等等问题的解决又岂是轻易之举？我们在追求繁荣的同时,不要忘了还有许多值得去关注的问题。

from an airplane at night, you will be struck by the incredible brightness of a city: there are so many lights that you cannot help feeling that all the bright things of life are down there waiting for you. But a feeling of disappointment will set in shortly after you land, because you will discover as you drive into the city center from the airport that the lights are just that: lights, miles and miles of street lights and neon signs. They are not in themselves sources of joy and happiness: city lights are not friendly, they are merely lights. In fact, the effect will probably be to make you feel lonely and isolated.

And yet the city lures us, because it is not provincial like the dead little town we have left behind us. "Provincial" is in fact our way of describing not the town but the attitude of the people. In our little town, we know (or think we know) everybody. And what we know about them is that they do not want to go anywhere, or to do anything outside to normal routine of their everyday lives. Unlike us, they have no sense of adventure, no longing for new experiences or new horizons.

So we look down on them, pity or despise them, pack our bags, and make for the big world which we know is out there, where the bright lights are. Then a curious thing happens. We find a job, make a small circle of friends and acquaintances, and move into some cramped accommodation. Gradually we get to know our section of the city, its shops and its people, and for a while, we begin to feel at home. It is small enough, our part of the city, for us not to feel lost or anonymous. We, in effect, create another little village for ourselves within the big city. The ultimate irony comes when we rent a television set so that we can stay in at night and watch exactly the same programs that our despised country cousins watch. Soon we too become "provincial", and others who live round us will be glad to get up and leave us behind. ✳

Vocabulary List【词汇清单】

harsh /haːʃ/ *adj.* 苛刻的,极严厉的,严格的

provincial /prəˈvinʃəl/ *adj.* 狭窄的,偏狭的,狭隘的

lure /ljuə/ *v.* 吸引,诱惑,不断引诱

literally /ˈlitərəli/ *adj.* 事实上,实际上

neon /ˈniːən/ *n.* ＜化＞氖,氖气(neon signs:霓虹灯广告)

horizon /həˈraizn/ *n.* 地平线;(常用复数)(视野、经验、兴趣、知识等的)限度,范围,眼界

despise /disˈpaiz/ *v.* 轻视,蔑视,鄙视

acquaintance /əˈkweintəns/ *n.* 相识的人(或人们),熟人

cramped /kræmpt/ *adj.* 狭窄的,(范围等)受限制的

accommodation /əˌkɔməˈdeiʃən/ *n.* (通常用复数形式)住宿设备,(租住的一间或几间)房间

anonymous /əˈnɔniməs/ *adj.* 匿名的,不知名的,无名的

参考译文【Suggested Translation】

住 在 大 都 市

为什么那么多人那么急切地想离开自己从小长大的小城镇或村庄,而奔向大都市呢?他们常称自己的家乡"枯燥乏味",或者"死气沉沉",甚或最为刺耳地评判为"偏狭"。

假如我们从更高的层面来审视这个问题,就像我们远距离地一览整个国家一样,我们就会对到底是什么诱使我们到大城市来这个问题有一点线索了。大城市值得注意的主要一点就是"大":人口众多,发生的事情也多。假如你确实从一个很远的距离——如夜晚航行的飞机上——俯视一座城市,你会被一座城市难以置信的明亮所打动:那么多的灯光,以至于你会情不自禁地感觉五彩缤纷的生活正在那里等着你。然而,一旦你乘坐的飞机着陆,一股失望之情便会油然而生,因为当你驱车从机场驶向市中心的时候，你会发现那种光亮不过是绵延几英里的路灯和霓虹灯招牌。它们本身并非快乐与幸福的源泉：城市之光并不友善，它们仅仅是灯光而已。事实上，其灯光效果很可能还会让你感觉到孤独与落寞。

然而，大城市依旧诱惑着我们，因为它们不像我们背弃的那个死气沉沉的小城镇那样偏狭。实际上，"偏狭"一词是我们用来描述人们态度的方式而非城镇本身。在我们的小城镇，我们认识（或者我们以为认识）那里的每一个人。我们对他们的了解就是：他们不想到任何地方去，或者不想做任何与他们的日常生活相距甚远的事情。不像我们，他们没有冒险意识，没有寻求新体验或者新视野的渴望。

所以我们瞧不起他们，可怜或者鄙视他们。于是我们自己打点好行囊，来到这个我们知道确确实实存在着的、灯火通明的大千世界。随后却发生了令人感到不解的事情。我们找到了工作，结识了一小群朋友与熟人，又搬进了拥挤的住房。渐渐地，我们了解了城市的这一区域，它的商店和它的居民。有一段时间，我们开始有了一种家的感觉。这块地方很小，我们并不感到失落或被人遗忘。实际上，我们正是在一座大都市中营造了一个小村庄。当我们租来一台电视机，我们就能够在晚上待在家里，与曾被我们藐视的乡下亲戚收看同一套节目，而这真是一个绝大的讽刺。不久，我们也变得"偏狭"了，居住在我们周围的人也会兴冲冲地准备行装而远走他乡。◆

Speech Given by Colin Lucas at Bejing University*

Ladies and Gentlemen, Dear Colleagues：

Because I am the Vice-Chancellor of the oldest of the foreign universities represented here today, I have been chosen to speak on their behalf. I am pleased to be their voice in presenting our heartfelt congratulations to the professors, teachers, researchers and students of Peking University on

---

　　* 作者科林·卢卡斯（Colin Lucas,1940—　　），毕业于英国牛津大学林肯学院，现为牛津大学常务副校长，是研究 18 世纪法国革命史的著名专家，也是法国革命史学新潮的著名代表人物之一，北京大学、法国里昂大学、谢菲尔德大学、格拉斯哥大学、西澳大利亚大学荣誉博士以及牛津大学林肯学院和 Balliol 学院荣誉研究员，同时兼任梅隆基金会和罗德基金会理事，其主要学术著作有《超越恐怖》（Beyond the Terror）、《重写法国革命》（Rewriting the French Revolution）、《法国革命的政治文化》（The Political Culture of the French Revolution）等。本文是科林·卢卡斯在北京大学 100 周年校庆之时对北京大学的致辞。

the 100th anniversary of its foundation.

Our universities form a great intellectual community round the world. Science has no nationality; knowledge belongs to everyone.

Our universities create new knowledge. They teach this knowledge, together with that of other universities and also the best of the great storehouse of knowledge, which those who came before us have uncovered, tested and accumulated.

All universities contribute to the prosperity and success of their country. They also conserve the culture and inheritance specific to their country's civilization. But, they do more. Knowledge is secure only when it is hard won by the independent tests of accuracy, rational explanation and truth. So, when we teach our students skills, we also give them values. On the one side, these are values for personal and civic conduct. On the other side, these values underwrite the personal need for independent understanding which is the source of human creativity.

These duties give universities a high responsibility. They are rooted in a great and fine tradition of honesty, free fearless enquiry and independence. Each university is a beacon of light in its own society and, by its association with its sisters, its knowledge and its values are spread wide.

A tradition is not built easily or quickly. During one hundred years, Peking University has been fashioning its tradition. Present and future members of the University! We hope to see you elaborate and consolidate your tradition. We hope to see you become a keystone of the intellectual community. In your next century, we hope to see you contribute to the international academic movment as a whole, as more and more of your numbers come to participate in the activities of your sister universities.

　　Congratulations, Peking University on your first century of achievement! ✳

Vocabulary List【词汇清单】

vice-chancellor /ˈvaisˈtʃɑːnsələ/ *n.* （英国的）大学副校长
（chancellor 仅是名誉职务, vice-chancellor 才是实际上的最高负责人）

accumulate /əˈkjuːmjuleit/ *v.* 积聚, 积累, 堆积

conserve /kənˈsəːv/ *v.* 贮存, 保存, 保藏

inheritance /inˈheritəns/ *n.* 继承（物）, 遗产, 遗物

civic /ˈsivik/ *adj.* 城市的, 市民的, 公民的

enquiry /inˈkwaiəri/ *n.* （＝inquiry）询问, 探问; 调查, 查究, 探究

elaborate /iˈlæbəreit/ *v.* 尽心竭力地做, 精心制作, 苦心经营

consolidate /kənˈsɔlideit/ *v.* 巩固, 加强, 强化

参考译文【Suggested Translation】

牛津大学副校长科林·卢卡斯

在北京大学的演说

女士们, 先生们, 亲爱的同道们:

　　由于我是今天在此派有代表的各外国大学中最古老的大学的副校长, 我就被推选来代表他们讲话。我很高兴作为大学的代言人, 在北京大学成立 100 周年之际, 向北京大学的教授们、教师们、研究员们和学生们表示我们衷心的祝贺。

　　我们这些大学在全世界形成一个很大的知识型社区。科学没有国籍; 知识属于每一个人。

　　我们这些大学创造新的知识。我们讲授这种知识, 也讲授其他大学所创造的新知识，还讲授我们的前辈们所发现、试验和积累的伟大知识宝库中的最佳的知识。

所有的大学都对它们本国的繁荣和成功作出贡献。它们也保存它们国家的文明所特有的文化和遗产。但是，它们所做的比这还要多。只有经过准确、合理解释和真理的独立试验而辛苦获得的知识，才是牢靠的知识。因此，当我们教给学生技能的时候，我们也是在教给他们价值观。一方面，这些是对于个人行为和社会行为的价值观；另一方面，这些价值观强调个人需要有独立的理解力，其是人类创造力的源泉。

这些职责赋予了大学一种高度的责任。这些职责植根于诚实、自由无畏的探究和独立性这三者构成的伟大的优良传统。每一所大学是其本国社会里的一座灯塔；通过与其兄弟院校的联系交流，它的知识和价值观得以广泛传播。

传统的树立并非易事，也并非一日之功。一百年以来，北京大学已形成了自己的传统。北大在今天和将来的成员们，我们希望看到你们精心发展和巩固你们的传统。我们希望看到你们成为这知识型社区的一块拱顶石。在你们的第二个百年中，我们希望看到，随着你们越来越多的成员参与兄弟院校的活动，你们会为整个国际学术运动作出贡献。

为了北京大学第一个百年的成就，向北大表示祝贺！　◆

O Captain! My Captain!*

O CAPTAIN! my Captain! our fearful trip is done,
The ship has weather'd every rack, the prize we sought is won,

The port is near, the bells I hear, the people all exulting,

While follow eyes the steady keel, the vessel grim and daring;

＊ 作者瓦尔特・惠特曼（Walt Whitman, 1819—1892）,19 世纪美国著名浪漫主义诗人、《草叶集》是惠特曼一生创作的总汇,也是美国诗歌史上一座灿烂的里程碑,其中的作品包含了丰富而深刻的思想内容,充分反映了19 世纪中期美国的时代精神。它是世界闻名的佳作,开创了美国民族诗歌的新时代。作者在诗歌形式上有大胆的创新,创造了"自由体"的诗歌形式,打破了传统的诗歌格律,以断句作为韵律的基础,节奏自由奔放,汪洋恣肆,舒卷自如,具有一泻千里的气势和无所不包的容量。本诗写于林肯被刺后不久,是惠特曼为了纪念这位伟大的总统而做的,也是其广为人知的一首诗。林肯是伟大的,他将熊熊的自由之火在美国点燃。但不幸的是,林肯自己却看不到自由之火的燃烧。然而,人民永远不会忘记他! 惠特曼在诗中就表达了这种深切挚烈的感情,这是一种巨大的承认和承诺。

But O heart! heart! heart!
　O the bleeding drops of red!
　　Where on the deck my Captain lies,
　　Fallen cold and dead.

O Captain my Captain! rise up and hear the bells;
Rise up — for you the flag is flung — for you the bugle trills,
For you the bouquets and ribbon'd wreaths — for you the shores crowding,
For you they call, the swaying mass, their eager faces turning;
　Here, Captain! dear father!
　This arm beneath your head!
　　It is some dream that on the deck
　　You've fallen cold and dead.

My Captain does not answer, his lips are pale and still,
My father does not feel my arm, he has no pulse nor will;
The ship is anchor'd safe and sound, its voyage closed and done,
From fearful trip the victor ship comes in with object won;
　Exult, O shores! and ring, O bells!
　But I, with mournful tread,
　　Walk the deck my Captain lies.
　　Fallen cold and dead. ✳

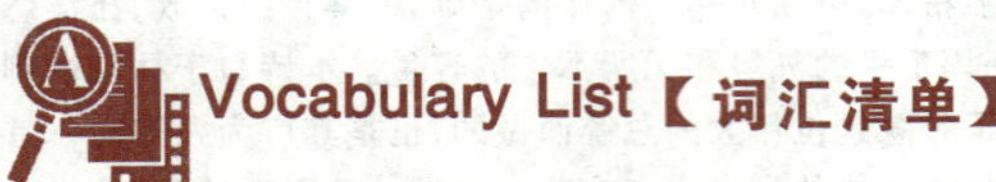

Vocabulary List 【词汇清单】

weather /'weðə/ *v.* 渡过（暴风雨、困难等），经受住（风雨），对风雨等能耐久

rack /ræk/ *n.* （身体或精神上的）巨大痛苦；激变，动乱；＜书面语＞行云，流云

exult /ig'zʌlt/ *v.* 狂喜，狂欢；＜旧＞欢跃，雀跃

vessel /'vesl/ *n.* 船，（尤指）大船

grim /grim/ *adj.* 坚强的，坚定的，不屈不挠的

bugle /'bju:gl/ *n.* 军号，喇叭（一种铜制的风动乐器，比小号要短，没有键或阀）

trill /tril/ *v.* 发出颤音，发出抖动的声音

bouquet /bu:'kei/ *n.* 一束花，花束

wreath /ri:θ/ *n.* 花环，（象征荣誉和胜利的）花冠

sway /swei/ *v.* 摇摆，摇动；＜引申＞人潮涌动

anchor /'æŋkə/ *n.* 锚，锚状物（用缆绳或粗绳系在船只上的重物，将其抛出后船只可因其重量或锚钩紧水底而固定住）

voyage /'vɔidʒ/ *n.* 航程，航海，航行

mournful /'mɔ:nful/ *adj.* 悲哀的，哀伤的；令人悲伤的，令人沮丧的

tread /tred/ *n.* 步态，踩（的动作、方式或声音）；足印

 ## 参考译文【Suggested Translation】

哦，船长！我的船长！

哦，船长！我的船长！我们险恶的航程已经告终，我们的船安然渡过惊涛骇浪，我们所寻求的奖赏已赢得手中。

港口已经不远，钟声我已听见，万千人众都在欢呼呐喊，
无数目光迎着我们的船从容返航，我们的船威严而又勇敢。
　　可是，心啊！心啊！心啊！
　　哦，殷红的血滴正流泻，
　　　在甲板上，那里躺着我的船长，
　　　　他已倒下，已死去，已冷却。

哦，船长！我的船长！起来听听这钟声，

起来吧，——旌旗在为你招展——号角在为你长鸣。

为你，岸上挤满了人群——为你，人们准备了无数的花束、彩带和花环。

为你，熙攘的群众在呼唤，转动着多少殷切的脸。

这里，船长！亲爱的父亲！

让你的头颅枕着我的手臂！

真像是梦，在甲板上

你已倒下，已死去，已冷却。

我们的船长不作回应，他的双唇惨白、寂静，

我的父亲感觉不到我的手臂，他已没有脉搏、没有生命，

我们的船已安全抛锚碇泊，航行已完成，已告终，

胜利的船从险恶的旅途归来，我们寻求的已赢得手中。

欢呼，哦，海岸！轰鸣，哦，钟声！

可是，我却轻移悲伤的步履，

在甲板上，那里躺着我的船长，

他已倒下，已死去，已冷却。◆

◉ Courtesy on one side only lasts not long.（来而不往非礼也。）

◉ Keep good men company and you shall be of the number.（近朱者赤，近墨者黑。）

◉ It is easy to open a shop but hard to keep it always open.（创业容易守业难。）

◉ Misfortune tests the sincerity of friends.（患难见真情。）

The Strenuous Life[*]

A life of slothful ease, a life of that peace which springs merely from lack either of desire or of power to strive after great things, is as little worthy of a nation as an individual.

We do not admire the man of timid peace. We admire the man who embodies victorious efforts, the man who never wrongs his neighbor, who is prompt to help a friend, but who has those virile qualities necessary to win in the stern strife of actual life. It is hard to fail, but it is worse never to have tried

---

　　* 作者西奥多·罗斯福(Theodore Roosevelt, 1858—1919)，美国第 26 任总统，其继任总统时，不到 43 岁，所以成为美国历史上最年轻的总统。同时，他博览群书，是博物学家、历史学家、演说家，被认为是美国最多才多艺的总统之一。他曾经发表了演说《勤奋地生活》，旨在遏制 19 世纪末美国社会盛行的骄奢淫逸、贪图享乐之风，而本文则与之类似，反映了他反对怠惰安逸、崇尚倾力奋斗的人生思想。

to succeed. In this life we get nothing save by effort. Freedom from effort in the present merely means that there has been effort stored up in the past. A man can be freed from the necessity of work only by the fact that he or his fathers before him have worked to good purpose. If the freedom thus purchased is used aright, and the man still does actual work, though of a different kind, whether as a writer or a general, whether in the field of politics or in the field of exploration and adventure, he shows he deserves his good fortune.

But if he treats this period of freedom from the need of actual labor as a period, not of preparation, but of mere enjoyment, even though perhaps not of vicious enjoyment, he shows that he is simply a cumberer on the earth's surface; and he surely unfits himself to hold his own place with his fellows, if the need to do so should again arise. A mere life of ease is not in the end a very satisfactory life, and, above all, it is a life which ultimately unfits those who follow it for serious work in the world.

As it is with the individual, so it is with the nation. It is a base untruth to say that happy is the nation that has no history. Thrice happy is the nation that has a glorious history. Far better it is to dare mighty things, to win glorious triumphs, even though checkered by failure, than to take rank with those poor spirits who neither enjoy much nor suffer much, because they live in the gray twillight that knows neither victory nor defeat. ✳

Vocabulary List 【词汇清单】

strenuous /ˈstrenjuəs/ *adj.* 奋发的,使劲的,艰辛的
slothful /ˈsləuθful/ *adj.* 怠惰的,懒散的,行动迟缓的

timid /'timid/ *adj.* 胆小的,畏怯的,怯懦的

victorious /vik'tɔːriəs/ *adj.* 胜利的,凯旋的,表示胜利的

virile /'virail/ *adj.* 有男子气概的,精力充沛的,强壮的

stern /'stəːn/ *adj.* 严峻的,严肃的,严酷的

store up：把…贮存(或积蓄)起来,贮藏,储备

adventure /əd'ventʃə/ *n.* 冒险(活动),冒险的经历

deserve /di'səːv/ *v.* 值得,应得,应受(赏罚等)

vicious /'viʃəs/ *adj.* 邪恶的,堕落的,恶意的,有害身心的

cumberer /'kʌmbərə/ *n.* 拖累,累赘,赘疣

thrice /θrais/ *adv.* 三次地,三倍地;很,非常,十分

triumph /'traiəmf/ *n.* (古罗马庆祝获胜将军极其军队归来的)凯旋式;胜利,成功,成就

checker /'tʃekə/ *v.* 使多变(指生活上的坎坷或命运的多变等),人生沉浮

twilight /'twailait/ *n.* 薄暮,暮色,晨昏蒙影;<引申>(充分发展、兴盛、荣耀等之后随之而来的)衰落状态,没落时代

 参考译文【Suggested Translation】

艰辛的人生

一种怠惰安逸的生活,一种仅仅是由于缺少追寻伟大事物的渴望或能力而导致的悠闲生活,这对国家与个人都是毫无价值的。

我们不欣赏那种怯懦安逸的人。我们钦佩那种表现出奋力向上的人,那种永不屈待邻人,能随时帮助朋友,但是也具有那些刚健的品质,足以在现实生活的严酷斗争中获取胜利的人。失败是难以忍受的,但更为糟糕的是从来不去努力争取成功。在人的这一生中,任何的收获都要通过努力去得到。目前不作任何的努力,只不过意味着在过去有过努力的积储。一个人不必工作,除非他或其先辈们曾经努力工作过,并取得了丰厚的收获。假如他能够把获得的这种自由加以正确地运用,仍然做些实际的工作,尽管那些工作是属于另一类的,不论是做一名作家

还是将军,不论是在政界还是在探险和冒险方面做些事情,都表明了他没有辜负自己的好运。

但是,假如他未将这段需要从事实际工作的自由时期用于准备,而仅仅是用于享乐(即使他所从事的或许并非不良的享乐),那也就表明了他只是地球表面上的一个赘疣;而且如果那种需要再度出现的话,他肯定无法在同僚之中维持自己的地位。一种纯粹安逸的生活终究并不是一种令人很满意的生活,而且,最主要的是,过那种生活的人最终肯定没有能力担当起世上之重任。

对于个人是如此,对于国家也是这样。有人说一个没有历史的国家是得天独厚的,这是根本错误的。一种得天独厚的优越感来源于一个国家所具有的光荣历史。敢于挑战非比寻常的事物,去赢得光辉的胜利,即使其中掺杂着失败,那也远胜于与那些既没有享受多大快乐也没有遭受多大痛苦的平庸之辈为伍,因为他们生活在一个既享受不到胜利也不会遭遇挫败的灰暗的境界中。◆

On the Fear of Death[*]

Perhaps the best cure for the fear of death is to reflect that life has a beginning as well as an end. There was a time when we were not: this gives me no concern — why then should it trouble us that a time will come when we shall cease to be? I have no wish to have been alive a hundred years ago, or in the reign of Queen Anne. Why should I regret and lay it so much to heart that I shall not be alive a hundred years hence, in the reign of I cannot tell whom?

To die is only to be as we were born; yet no one feels any remorse, or regret, or repugnance, in contemplating this last idea. It is rather a relief and disburdening of the mind; it seems to have been a holiday time with us then; we were not

---

* 作者威廉·赫兹里特（William Hazlitt, 1778—1830），英国浪漫主义散文家、文学评论家和画家，主要作品有《莎士比亚剧作中的人物》、《英国诗歌演讲集》、《关于作家的谈话》和《谈读旧书》等。他的文笔生动流畅、清新明朗，其文体对后世影响极大。

called to appear upon the stage of life, to wear robes or tatters, to laugh or cry, be hooted or applauded; we had lain perdu all this while, snug out of harm's way; and had slept out our thousands of centuries without wanting to be waked up; at peace and free from care, in a long nonage, in a sleep deeper and calmer than that of infancy, wrapped in the softest and finest dust. And the worst that we dread is, after a short fretful, feverish being, after vain hopes, and idle fears, to sink to final repose again, and forget the troubled dream of life! ✽

Vocabulary List【词汇清单】

cure /kjuə/ *n.* （疾病的）治疗法（药）；对策，克服的方法

Queen Anne /kwiːn æn/ 安妮女王（1665—1714，大不列颠及爱尔兰的女王（1702—1714），斯图亚特王朝的末代君主）

remorse /riˈmɔːs/ *n.* 懊悔，悔恨，自责

repugnance /riˈpʌgnəns/ *n.* 深恶痛绝，极为反感

contemplate /ˈkɔntempleit/ *v.* 考虑，深想，沉思，细究

disburden /disˈbəːdn/ *v.* 解除…的负担（或累赘之物），卸下…的重负（或精神负担）

robe /rəub/ *n.* < 古 >（复数）衣服，制服

tatter /ˈtætə/ *n.* （撕下的或悬挂着的）破布条，碎布；< 复数 > 破衣服

hoot /huːt/ *v.* 用呵责声表示（轻蔑、不满等）；（以叫喊声）轰赶（或驱逐）

applaud /əˈplɔːd/ *v.* 鼓掌欢迎，拍手喝彩；称赞，赞扬

perdu /pəːˈdjuː/ *n.* 隐藏的，潜伏的，看不见的

snug /snʌg/ *adv.* 舒适地，整洁地

nonage /ˈnəunidʒ/ *n.* 早期，未成熟（期）

fretful /ˈfretʃul/ *adj.* 烦燥的，焦躁的；易怒的，不安的

repose /riˈpəuz/ *n* 休息，睡眠，长眠

参考译文【Suggested Translation】

谈 怕 死

也许克服对死亡恐惧的最好方法是想一想，人生有始也就必有终。在过去一段时期我们并不存在：这一事实并未让我们担心过——那为什么我们还要为了有一天将不存在而感到困扰呢？我既然不期望活在一百年之前，或是生活在安妮女王统治的时代，我何以要因为不能活在一百年以后说不出谁统治的时代，深感遗憾而耿耿于怀呢？

死亡只不过是恢复到生前状况而已。当我们在思忖这个新观念时，没有人会感到一丝丝的懊悔、遗憾或是厌烦，反而感到心灵的舒缓慰藉和如释重负。我们在生前仿佛在度假一般：我们没有被召唤而出现在人生舞台上，穿着华贵的礼袍或褴褛的衣衫、大笑或是哭嚎、被人呵斥或是接受喝彩；相反地，我们埋伏了很久很久，安详自在而且远离伤害，熟睡千百个世纪也不愿意被唤醒，平和惬意而无忧无虑，长期处于胚胎阶段，远比婴儿时期睡得更为深沉和静谧，并被最轻柔和最细致的尘埃所包裹着。而最糟糕的是，我们担心在短暂的烦躁和狂热的生存之后，在空虚的期盼以及无谓的恐惧之后，再度沉入最终的长眠，而忘却了人生烦恼痛苦的梦境！◆

On the Instability of Human Glory[*]

What then is the work of life? What the business of great men, that pass the stage of the world in seeming triumph as these men we call heroes have done? Is it to grow great in the mouth of fame and take up so many pages in history? Alas! That is no more than making a tale for the reading of posterity till it turns into fable and romance. Is it to furnish subjects to the poets, and live in their immortal rhymes as they call them? That is, in short, no more than to be hereafter turned into ballad and song and be sung by old women to quiet children, or at the corner of the street to gather crowds in aid of the pickpocket and the poor. Or is their busi-

---

　　* 作者丹尼尔·笛福（Daniel Defoe, 约 1659—1731）,18 世纪英国极具影响力的小说家和散文家,开创了英国现实主义小说之先河,其代表作《鲁滨逊漂流记》是一部描述人类返朴归真情结的童话,它的发行量超过了欧洲其他所有读物,此外,他还著有《辛格尔顿船长》、《彼得大帝记》、《不列颠岛周游记》等。

ness rather to add virtue and piety to their glory, which alone will pass them into eternity and make them truly immortal? What is glory without virture? A great man without religion is no more than a great beast without a soul. What is honour without merit? And what can be called true merit but that which makes a person be a good man as well as a great man? ✳

 ## Vocabulary List 【词汇清单】

instability /ˌinstəˈbiliti/ *n.* 不稳定（性），不稳固，摇摆不定

posterity /pɔsˈteriti/ *n.* 子孙，后裔；后代，后世

fable /ˈfeibl/ *n.* 寓言，神话，传说

furnish /ˈfəːniʃ/ *v.* 供给，供应，提供

rhyme /raim/ *n.* 韵（脚），押韵；＜复数＞韵文，诗篇

hereafter /hiərˈaːftə/ *adv.* 此后，今后，从此以后

ballad /ˈbæləd/ *n.* 民谣，民歌，歌谣

pickpocket /ˈpikˌpɔkit/ *n.* 扒手（从口袋里偷东西的人）

piety /ˈpaiəti/ *n.* 虔诚，虔敬（行为）

religion /riˈlidʒən/ *n.* 宗教，信仰

merit /ˈmerit/ *n.* 优点，价值，长处

 ## 参考译文【Suggested Translation】

论人类荣誉之虚渺

那么，人生的工作是什么？那些伟大的人物们，还有那些被我们称为英雄的人们，他们春风得意地走过世界的舞台时又做了些什么呢？难道就是要在众口喧称中变得伟大，并且还要在历史上占据许多篇章吗？唉！那只不过是编了一个故事供后人阅读，直到它变成了神话或是传奇罢了。难道就是要供给诗人们以吟咏的题材，并生活在他们那些所谓不朽的诗篇之中

吗？简而言之，那只不过是在将来变成歌谣，由老奶奶唱给静心聆听的孩子，或由卖唱的在街角唱出，以吸引大批的听众，使扒手和穷人多了一个谋生机会而已。他们所应做的事情，是不是要为自己的荣耀添加上美德和虔诚呢？只有这两样东西才可以使他们进入永生，让他们真正不朽！如果没有美德，荣耀又算得了什么呢？一个没有宗教信仰的伟人只不过是一只没有灵魂的巨兽。如果没有价值存在，荣誉又算得了什么呢？而被称作真正有价值的东西，除了那种不仅把一个人造就成伟人，并且使他具有好人的品质之外，还能有什么呢？◆

⦿ Do nothing by halves.（凡事不可半途而废。）

⦿ The darkest hour is nearest the dawn.（黎明前是最黑暗的时刻。）

⦿ A miss is as good as a mile.（失之毫厘，差之千里。）

⦿ Confidence in yourself is the first step on the road to success.（自信是走向成功的第一步。）

A Message to Garcia *

In all this Cuban business there is one man stands out on the horizon of my memory like Mars at perihelion.

When war broke out between Spain and the United States, it was very necessary to communicate quickly with

---

　　* 作者阿尔伯特·哈伯德（Elbert Hubbard，1856—1915），美国著名出版家，伟大的职业成功学家、作家。百余年以来，他所著的《致加西亚的信》（1899 年）一书仍然在全世界广为流传，2000 年被美国《哈奇森年鉴》和《出版商周刊》评选为有史以来世界最畅销图书第六名。哈伯德的《致加西亚的信》及姊妹篇《怎样把信送给加西亚》、《自动自发》、《鼓舞人心的剪贴本》、《一生的智慧》等书中推崇的敬业、忠诚、勤奋、自信、主动性等思想观念影响了一代又一代人，一个国家又一个国家。这些作品除了深入地阐释哈伯德的职业思想外，还用诗一样的语言，阐发了众多足以激励人类灵魂和精神的人生智慧、生命真谛。这些作品随着时间的推移、社会的变迁而越发显得光芒四射、撼人心魄。只要有人类社会及各种组织存在，这些作品中所弘扬的勤奋、敬业、忠诚、自信等职业精神和闪光的人生哲理就具有普遍永久的价值和魅力。哈伯德的职业思想上承美国开国元勋富兰克林在其自传和《穷理查年鉴》中阐释的勤俭、忠诚等商业精神，下启当代伟大社会学家马克斯·韦伯在《新教伦理与资本主义精神》中总结的美国人勤奋、视获取财富为上帝使命的新教精神。哈伯德的职业思想是美国精神的基石之一，是美国商业之所以繁荣强大的精神资源之一。

the leader of the Insurgents. Garcia was somewhere in the mountain fastnesses of Cuba — no one knew where. No mail or telegraph message could reach him. The President must secure his cooperation, and quickly. What to do?

Some said to the President, "There's a fellow by the name of Rowan who will find Garcia for you, if anybody can."

Rowan was sent for and given a letter to be delivered to Garcia. How the "fellow by the name of Rowan" took the letter, sealed it up in an oilskin pouch, strapped it over his heart, in four days landed by night off the coast of Cuba from an open boat, disappeared into the jungle, and in three weeks came out on the other side of the Island, having traversed a hostile country on foot and delivered his letter to Garcia — are things I have no special desire now to tell in detail. The point that I wish to make is this: McKinley gave Rowan a letter to be delivered to Garcia; Rowan took the letter and did not ask, "Where is he at?"

By the Eternal! There is a man whose form should be cast in deathless bronze and the statue placed in every college of the land. It is not book-learning young men need, nor instruction about this and that, but a stiffening of the vertebrae which will cause them to be loyal to a trust, to act promptly, concentrate their energies: do the thing — "Carry a message to Garcia."

General Garcia is dead now, but there are other Garcias. No man who has endeavored to carry out an enterprise where many hands were needed, but has been well-nigh appalled at times by the imbecility of the average man — the inability or unwillingness to concentrate on a thing and do it.

Slipshod assistance, foolish inattention, dowdy indifference, and half-hearted work seem the rule; and no man succeeds, unless by hook or crook or threat he forces or bribes other men to assist him; or mayhap, God in His goodness performs a miracle, and sends him an Angel of Light for an assistant. ✳

 ## Vocabulary List 【词汇清单】

Cuban /'kju:bən/ *n.* 古巴人　*adj.* 古巴（人）的

perihelion /ˌperi'hi:liən/ *n.* ＜天文＞近日点（绕太阳运行的行星或其他天体的椭圆轨道上离太阳最近的一点）

Spain /spein/ *n.* 西班牙（欧洲西南部国家）

insurgent /in'sə:dʒənt/ *n.* （起来反抗现政权的）起义者，反叛者，造反者

Cuba /'kju:bə/ *n.* 古巴（由古巴岛及其临近诸小岛组成的国家，首都为哈瓦那）

oilskin /'ɔilskin/ *n.* 油布，防水布

pouch /pautʃ/ *n.* （随身携带的）小袋，烟草袋；＜美＞邮袋

traverse /'trævə(:)s/ *v.* 横过，穿过，经过，横越

Mckinley /mə'kinli/ （全名 William Mckinley）威廉·麦金莱（1843—1901，美国第 25 任总统，其在职期间发动西班牙—美国战争（美西战争），后被无政府主义者刺杀）

stiffening /'stifniŋ/ *n.* （使）变强劲（或有力），（使）变坚挺

vertebra /'və:tibrə/ *n.* （复数形式 vertebrae）＜解剖＞椎骨，脊椎骨

endeavor /in'devə/ *v.* 尽力，努力，力图（做某事）（to）

well-nigh /'welnai/ *adv.* 几乎，差不多

appall /ə'pɔ:l/ *v.* 使惊愕，使惊骇，使震惊

imbecility /ˌimbi'siliti/ *n.* 低能，痴愚，愚钝

slipshod /'slipʃɔd/ *adj.* 马虎的，漫不经心的

dowdy /'daudi/ *adj.* （衣服或外观）不整洁的，衣衫褴褛的，邋遢的

by hook or by crook：不择手段，用种种方法，无论如何

mayhap /'meihæp/ *adv.* ＜古＞可能，或许；希望，但愿（亦作 mayhappen）

 参考译文【Suggested Translation】

致加西亚的信

在所有与古巴有关的事情中，有一个人常常令我无法忘怀。美西战争爆发以后，美国必须马上与反抗军首领加西亚将军取得联系。加西亚将军隐藏在古巴辽阔的崇山峻岭中——没有人知道确切的地点，因而无法送信或电报给他。但是，美国总统必须要尽快与他建立合作关系。怎么办呢？

有人对总统推荐说："有一个名字叫罗文的人，假如有人能找到加西亚将军，那个人一定就是他。"

于是，他们将罗文找来，交给他一封信——写给加西亚的信。关于那个"名字叫罗文的人"如何拿了信，将它装进一个油纸袋里并打封，吊在胸口藏好，如何用 4 天的时间乘坐一条敞口船连夜抵达古巴海岸，而后消失在丛林之中，如何在 3 个星期之后出现在古巴岛的另一端，其间徒步穿越一个危机四伏的国家，将信交到加西亚手上——这些都不是我现在想要详细讲述的。我希望强调的重点是：美国总统麦金莱将一封写给加西亚的信交给了罗文，而罗文接过信后，并没有问"他在哪里？"

像罗文这样的人，我们应该为他塑造不朽的青铜雕像，将其放在美国每一所大学里。年轻人所需要的不仅仅是学习书本上的知识，也不仅仅是聆听他人的种种教诲，更需要的是对于一种责任的忠诚，能够立即采取行动，全心全意去完成任务——"把信送给加西亚"。

加西亚将军已不在人世，但是现在还有其他的"加西亚"。没有人能经营好这样的一家企业——虽然需要众多人手，但时常几乎让人惊骇的是，其中大部分人庸庸碌碌——他们要么能力不足，要么根本不愿意全心全意去工作。

懒懒散散、漠不关心、马马虎虎和心不在焉的工作态度，对于许多人来说似乎已成常态。除非苦口婆心、威逼利诱地强迫他们做事，或者，请善意的上帝创造奇迹，并派一名光芒天使相助，否则，这些人将一事无成。◆

Autumn*

There is no month in the whole year, in which nature wears a more beautiful appearance than in the month of August! Spring has many beauties, and May is a fresh and blooming month, but the charms of this time of year are enhanced by their contrast with the winter season. August has no such advantage. It comes when we remember nothing but clear skies, green fields and sweet-smelling flowers when the

---

* 作者查尔斯·狄更斯(Charles Dickens, 1812—1870),英国小说家,19 世纪英国批判现实主义文学的杰出代表,其一生共创作了 14 部长篇小说,许多中、短篇小说和杂文、游记、戏剧、小品,其中最著名的作品是描写劳资矛盾的长篇代表作《艰难时世》(1854)和描写 1789 年法国革命的另一部代表作《双城记》(1859),其他作品有《奥列佛·特维斯特》(即《雾都孤儿》)、《老古玩店》(1841),《董贝父子》(1848),《大卫·科波菲尔》(1850)和《远大前程》(1861)等。狄更斯在艺术上以妙趣横生的幽默、细致入微的心理分析以及现实主义描写与浪漫主义气氛的有机结合而著称。马克思将他和萨克雷等称誉为英国的"一批杰出的小说家"。

recollection of snow, and ice, and bleak winds, has faded from our minds as completely as they have disappeared from the earth and yet what a pleasant time it is! Orchards and corn-fields ring with the hum of labour; trees bend beneath the thick clusters of ripe fruit, which bows their branches to the ground; and the corn, piled in graceful sheaves, or waving in every light breath that sweeps above it, as if it wooed the sickle, tinges the landscape with a golden hue. A mellow softness appears to hang over the whole earth; the influence of the season seems to extend itself to the every wagon, whose slow motion across the well-reaped field, is perceptible only to the eye, but strikes with no harsh sound upon the ear. ✳

Vocabulary List【词汇清单】

blooming /ˈbluːmiŋ/ *adj.* 兴旺,茂盛,繁盛;鲜艳,发亮,艳丽

recollection /ˌrekəˈlekʃən/ *n.* 回忆,记忆,回忆起的事

orchard /ˈɔːtʃəd/ *n.* 果园,果园里的全部果树

cluster /ˈklʌstə/ *n.* (同类事物的)一束,一串,一簇,一团,一丛

sheaf /ʃiːf/ *n.* (sheave 是其复数形式)束;(稻草、书、纸等)捆

woo /wuː/ *v.* 向(女子)求爱(求婚),追求,想得到

sickle /ˈsikl/ *n.* 镰刀(用来切割谷物或高杆草的一种工具,有一连接在一短柄上的半圆形刀刃)

tinge /tindʒ/ *v.* 着淡色于…,微染

hue /hjuː/ *n.* 色调,颜色,色彩(的浓淡)

wagon /ˈwægən/ *n.* 四轮马车;<美>(19 世纪美国西部拓荒者用的)有帆布篷顶的大马车

perceptible /pəˈseptəbl/ *adj.* 感觉得到的,可察觉的,可感知的

harsh /haːʃ/ *adj.* (声音)尖得(或粗得)令人不快的,刺耳的,不和谐的

参考译文【Suggested Translation】

秋

一年四季之中，大自然的外貌最美不过的一个月就是八月。春天有许多美的地方，五月是新鲜和娇艳的月份，但是这种时节的媚人之处是由于和冬季的对照而加强起来的。八月没有这种有利的条件。它来的时候，我们所记得的只有晴朗的天、绿色的田野和芬芳的花——雪、冰和凛冽的寒风已经完全被我们的脑子遗忘了，正如它们已经完全从地面消失了一样，——然而这八月是何等可爱的时节啊！果园里和谷田里震荡着嘈杂的劳作的声音；结了一丛丛丰硕果实的枝条垂到地面，连树干都坠得发弯了；谷物呢，整整齐齐地束束堆着，或者被不时掠过的一阵阵的微风吹得摇摇摆摆，像是在向镰刀求爱，它们给这片风景染上一片金色。似乎有一种丰美的柔和气氛笼罩着整个地面；时节的影响像是连大车也受了感染，它在收割过的田野里缓慢地移动，唯有眼睛可以看得出来，而耳朵却听不到粗浊的声音。◆

Tribute to Diana, Princess of Wales*

Today is our chance to say thank you for the way you brightened our lives, even though God granted you but half a life. We will all feel cheated always that you were taken from us so young, and yet we must learn to be grateful that you came along at all. Only now you are gone do we truly appreciate what we are now without and we want you to know that life without you is very, very difficult. We have all despaired at our loss over the past week and only the strength of the message you gave us through your years of giving has afforded us the strength to move forward.

There is a temptation to rush to canonize your memory, there is no need to do so. You stand tall enough as a human being of unique qualities not to need to be seen as a saint.

---

* 作者查尔斯·斯宾塞(Charles Spenser)，生平不详。本篇演讲辞节选自斯宾塞伯爵于 1997 年 9 月 6 日在伦敦威斯敏斯特大教堂为英国威尔士王妃戴安娜举行追悼会时的献词。本文情感深挚，文笔优美，极富感染力。

Indeed, to sanctify your memory would be to miss out on the very core of your being, your wonderfully mischievous sense of humour with a laugh that bent you double. Your joy for life, transmitted wherever you took your smile, and the sparkle in those unforgettable eyes. Your boundless energy, which you could barely contain. But your greatest gift was your intuition and it was a gift you used wisely. This is what underpinned all your other wonderful attributes and if we look to analyse what is was about you that had such a wide appeal we find it in your instinctive feel for what was really important in all our lives... ✳

 ## Vocabulary List 【词汇清单】

tribute /ˈtribjuːt/ *n.* 献词,颂词(表示感激、尊重或仰慕等情感的声明或其他形式的表示)

Wales /weilz/ *n.* 威尔士(英国大不列颠岛西部半岛的一个地区,自联盟令(the Act of Union)(1536 年)后与英格兰合并,它同时保持了自己的独特文化风格和强烈的民族主义情感,加的夫(Cardiff)为其首府)

temptation /tempˈteiʃən/ *n.* 引诱,诱惑

canonize /ˈkænənaiz/ *v.* 封(死者)为圣徒,使加入圣徒之列;褒扬,推崇

sanctify /ˈsæŋktifai/ *v.* 使神圣化,使圣洁,把…奉若神明

mischievous /ˈmistʃivəs/ *adj.* 淘气的,顽皮的

transmit /trænzˈmit/ *v.* 传送,传达,传导,传播

sparkle /ˈspaːkl/ *n.* 火花,火星;闪耀,闪光;光彩,生气,活力

boundless /ˈbaundlis/ *adj.* 无边无际的,无限的,广阔的

intuition /ˌintju(ː)ˈiʃən/ *n.* 直觉,直觉力(未经过理性的论证过程便能知道或感觉的行为或能力)

underpin /ˌʌndəˈpin/ *v.* 加强…的基础,巩固,强化

instinctive /inˈstiŋktiv/ *adj.* 本能的,天生的,天性的

致威尔士王妃戴安娜的献词

即使上帝只赐予了你一半的生命，我们今天还是趁此机会来感谢你以自己的那种方式使我们的生命熠熠生辉。我们大家永远都会有一种上当受骗的感觉，因为你过早地香销玉殒，但是我们仍然必须学会感恩，因为你毕竟曾与我们同在。唯在此刻，当你已离我们远去，我们才真正意识到我们现在损失了什么。我们想让你知道，没有你，我们的生活会是十分、十分困难的。我们大家都在过去的一周内因为失去了你而感到绝望。在过去的岁月里，你不断给别人以奉献的启示，唯有这种启示的威力才为我们提供了朝前迈进的力量。

人们情不自禁急于想要尊你为圣徒，其实，并没有必要这么做。因为作为一个具有无与伦比特质的凡人，你足够超凡，无须被视做圣徒。确实，把你尊为圣徒来纪念，或许将会遗漏你性格的核心，那就是你用开怀大笑所表达的绝妙的童心未泯的幽默感。你对生活的欣喜，通过你的微笑和你令人难忘的双眸中的闪光，传遍了你的所到之处。还有你那几乎无法抑制的无穷的活力。但你最杰出的天赋是你的直觉，而你又把它加以睿智地使用。这种能力加强了你其他一切出类拔萃的特质。假如我们特意要分析你身上的什么东西会有这么普遍的吸引力，我们就会发现你对所有我们大家生活中真正重要的东西都有一种本能的同情……◈

Tips for Getting Promoted[*]

A Chief Executive officer is not necessarily someone who has had a lot of formal training. So, I doubt more schooling would help you climb up that ladder of success.

Maybe you should try and change your work habits or character. You cannot just sit around in an organization waiting for people to promote you. You have to let people know you are ambitious and waiting for bigger and more rewarding challenges. You should tell your supervisor or boss that you want to be promoted and rise up that management ladder. A good manager will accept, even respect the fact that you wish for career development. If this is not the case, you should find a new job or new company that will allow you to

---

* 作者雷曼（Lehman），生平不详。对于步入职场的人们来讲，谁不想平步青云？谁不想飞黄腾达？谁不想一路高歌，迈向自己事业的珠穆朗玛峰之巅？世界如梯——The world is a ladder for some to go up and for others to go down. 而站在职场阶梯上的你又该如何去登攀呢？

grow.

You must start out small. Hoping that one day you will suddenly become director of a company is doubtful. Getting ready for a slow ascent is more likely. Accept it, and commit yourself, realizing that it may be a long climb.

You will need some skills to propel you up that ladder of success. You must be competent, that is you need to develop skills in many areas, such as marketing, human resources, public relations and finances.

You must also be a good people person, always cultivating relationships with the people around you. Having "guanxi" is a necessary characteristic of any successful CEO. ✱

Vocabulary List【词汇清单】

executive /ig'zekjutiv/ *adj.* 实行的,执行的,经理主管的
ambitious /æm'biʃəs/ *adj.* 有雄心的,有抱负的,胸怀大志的
supervisor /'sju:pəvaizə/ *n.* 监督者,管理人,主管
ascent /ə'sent/ *n.* （职位、社会地位、声望等）上升,提高,擢升
propel /prə'pel/ *v.* 推动,推进,鼓励
competent /'kɔmpitənt/ *adj.* 有（充分）能力的,能胜任的
characteristic /ˌkæriktə'ristik/ *n.* 特性,特征,特质

参考译文【Suggested Translation】

晋升的诀窍

公司的首席执行官未必都是经过许多正规培训的人。所以,我认为接受更多的学校教育未必就能促使你在成功的阶梯上步步高升。

也许，你应该试着改变工作习惯或性格。不能仅仅在一个单位里坐等别人来提升你。必须让人们知道你胸怀大志，正在等待更大的、回报更多的挑战。应该告诉你的上司或老板：你想得到提拔，登上管理者的阶层。一位好经理将会理解，甚至尊重你发展事业的愿望。假如情况不是这样的话，你就应该另谋高就，以使自己得到发展。

必须从小处开始做起。幻想着有一天突然当上某公司的领导是不太现实的。作好准备慢慢地升迁，可能性更大。接受现实，全力以赴，要意识到这可能是一种漫长的攀登。

你需要掌握一些促使自己往上爬升的技能。你必须具备胜任工作的各种能力。换句话说，你必须具备诸如市场营销、人力资源、公关和财务等方面的技能。

你也必须要有良好的人缘，营造与周围的人融洽的关系，好的"关系"是任何一位成功的首席执行官必备的要素。◆

◉A man is known by his friends.（从其交友知其为人。）

◉Don't trouble trouble until trouble troubles you.（不要自找麻烦。）

◉Every man has his faults.（金无足赤，人无完人。）

◉The fire is the test of gold, adversity of strong man.（烈火试真金，逆境磨意志。）

The Other Side of the Olympics[*]

The Olympics represents the noble ideal of sports overcoming the barriers of politics with champion athletes of all nations gathering in the spirit of sportsmanship. However, the stakes go beyond who wins the gold medal. Shortly after each competition, nations begin to vie afresh for the bid to host the next game. Winning the vote to host is not merely an honor, it is a political conquest in global recogni-

---

[*] 作者佚名。奥运会是奥林匹克运动会的简称,起源于古希腊的奥林匹亚竞技。第一次全希腊性的运动竞赛会是在公元前 77 年(希腊纪年之始)在希腊南部伊利斯境内的奥林匹亚举行的,故名奥林匹亚竞技会。1896 年 4 月 6 日至 15 日,第一届现代奥运会终于在雅典隆重举行。奥林匹克运动从此开始了一个崭新的纪元。现代奥林匹克运动的口号是:"更快、更高、更强!"这句格言从奥运会复兴到现在,已成为体育运动爱好者的座右铭,是奥林匹克标志的一部分。它希望运动员有高度的思想境界,有勇往直前、不断进击的精神。本文视角独特,文笔深婉,向我们展示了现代奥运会不为人注意的另一面……

tion. It also spins revenue from the influx of tourists, participants and Olympic related paraphernalia.

However, all that glitters is not gold. For some residents of Beijing, the site of Olympic 2008, the impact of winning the bid cuts deep and far into their personal lives. The capital is expecting to pour billions of dollars into sports facilities and related upgrades such as roads, public transport, landscaping and sanitation. For the bustling city of bicycles and traffic jams tucked among imperial relics, the Olympics is an opportunity for urban renewal. Yet for those within the areas, something must give way to make room for the model Olympic Village.

Decades of family homes will be uprooted and dispersed among apartments on the outskirts of the city. Although modern plumbing and sanitation will replace chamber pots, the move is an upheaval of a community and its way of life and social dynamics. It will be interesting to follow up on these and study the effects of the transplant.

The Olympics upgrades are not disposable stage props that can be easily discarded after the show. Experts are afraid that without the heartbeat of ordinary people dwelling in the ancient city, the high tech Olympic City would become culturally dry. Careful urban planning and stringent regulations such as building restrictions can preserve the impression of an intact neighborhood. Nevertheless, without the residents, aesthetic is lost and only the facade remains, waiting to be filled by tourists and businesses.

Nonetheless who can begrudge anyone a more comfortable living environment? Even without the Olympics, can the drumbeat of modernization be stopped? And whether the changes are for better or worse, who should presume to judge such things other than those whose lives bear the brunt of the impact? ✳

Vocabulary List 【词汇清单】

stake /steik/ *n.* ＜复数＞奖品,奖金,悬赏

vie /vai/ *v.* ＜古＞竞争,较量(for)

influx /'inflʌks/ *n.* (人或物的)涌进,接踵而来,汇集

paraphernalia /ˌpærəfə'neiliə/ *n.* 设备,装置,工具;随身用具

glitter /'glitə/ *v.* 闪闪发光,闪烁,闪耀

sanitation /ˌsæni'teiʃən/ *n.* (环境)卫生;(尤指下水道等)卫生设施

bustle /'bʌsl/ *v.* (使)忙乱,(使)奔忙,(使)喧闹

imperial /im'piəriəl/ *adj.* 皇帝的,皇家的,帝国的

relic /'relik/ *n.* 遗物,遗俗;＜复数＞遗迹,遗址

renewal /ri'njuːəl/ *n.* 更新,复兴,翻新

uproot /ʌp'ruːt/ *v.* 连根拔起,根除

disperse /dis'pəːs/ *v.* (使)分散,(使)散开,疏散

outskirt /'autskəːts/ *n.* ＜复数＞(城镇等的)郊区,市郊,郊外

plumbing /'plʌmiŋ/ *n.* (煤气管、水管等的)管道工程;(建筑物内部的)管道(系统)

chamber pot：(寝室用)便壶,夜壶

upheaval /ʌp'hiːvəl/ *n.* (社会等的)剧变,激变,大变动

dynamics /dai'næmiks/ *n.* 动力学;动力,原动力

disposable /dis'pəuzəbl/ *adj.* 用完便扔的,可(任意)处置(或处理)的

discard /dis'kaːd/ *v.* 丢弃,抛弃,扔掉(废物、习惯等)

stringent /'strindʒənt/ *adj.* (规则等)严格的,严厉的

restriction /ris'trikʃən/ *n.* 限制,限定,约束

intact /in'tækt/ *adj.* 未动(没碰)过的,原封不动的,完整无缺的

aesthetic /iːs'θetik/ *adj.* 美学(的原则),审美,美感

facade /fə'saːd/ *n.* ＜法语＞(虚有其表的)外观,外表,表面

nonetheless /ˌnʌnðə'les/ *adv.* 虽然如此,但是;然而;不过

begrudge /bi'grʌdʒ/ *v.* 妒忌、嫉妒(别人);对…抱怨(发牢骚)

drumbeat /'drʌmˌbiːt/ *n.* 击鼓声,鼓音

presume /pri'zjuːm/ *v.* ＜书面语＞胆敢做…,冒昧地做…

bear the brunt of：（在…面前）首当其冲

参考译文【Suggested Translation】

奥运会的另一面 （林为慧 译）

奥运会所代表的崇高理想，就是各国的运动选手用运动员精神超越政治障碍聚集在一起。可是，其利害关系不仅在于谁获得金牌。每一届奥运会后不久，各国又重新开始争夺下一届奥运会的主办权。获得主办权不仅仅是一种荣誉，也代表着在政治上被全球认同的胜利。此外，还可以通过接踵而来的游客、参赛者和和奥运会有关的设备迅速增加税收。

然而，我们不能只看其表面（该句亦可直译为"闪闪发光的未必都是金子"）。对于北京2008年奥运会场地的那些居民来说，获得主办权对他们生活的影响是深远的。首都预计要在运动设施及其相关的改进，如道路、公共交通、环境景观和公共卫生等方面投入数十亿美元。对于其皇家遗址中到处存放自行车、交通拥堵的繁忙城市，奥运会是一次都市翻新的机会。可是对于那些住在规划用地的人而言，他们必须放弃一些东西来为一个现代化的奥运村腾地儿。

几十年的家园被连根拔起，而被分散到城市郊区的公寓。虽然现代化的管道和卫生设备将取代便盆，但是迁移对一个社区及其生活方式和社会变迁过程仍然是一个大变动。追踪这些人并研究迁移给他们带来的影响将是很有意义的。

为奥运会所做的改进工程，并非是戏剧演出结束后轻易就可以丢弃的舞台小道具。专家们担心在这座古城中缺乏了普通居民的声迹，高科技的奥运城会在文化上几近枯竭。即使细心的城市规划和严厉的法规，例如建筑管制可以保留原封不动的社区外观，然而没有了居民，美感仍会失落，而只留下空壳，等待游客和商业的填充。

不过，谁能妒忌一些人有较舒适的居住环境呢？即使没有奥运会，现代化的鼓点声是否能被阻挡？而且社会变迁的好与坏，除了那些深受其影响的人以外，还有谁能擅自判断呢？◆

Liberty Is Order*

Liberty is order. Liberty is strength. Look round the world, and admire, as you must, the instructive spectacle. You will see that liberty not only is power and order, but that it is power and order predominant and invincible — that it derides all other sources of strength. And shall the preposterous imagination be fostered, that men bred in liberty — the first of humankind who asserted the glorious distinction of forming for themselves their social compact — can be condemned to silence upon their rights? Is it to be conceived that

---

＊ 作者查尔斯·詹姆斯·福克斯（Charles James Fox，1749—1806），英国政治家，辉格党领袖。本篇演说词发表于 1794 年，意在反对托利党政府废除《人身保护法》，其主旨在于：自由前进的趋势不可更改！人类社会的历史，是一部不断追求自由和进步的历史。从人治走向法治，是这种追求的必然结果。人类理想的法治社会的形态是：人权受到广泛尊重，自由得到充分保障，执法公正如山，社会秩序井然。而法律的各种价值大小并不相同，自由居首，公正次之，秩序再次之。在某种意义上，自由就是秩序！同时，自由也意味着力量！

men who have enjoyed, for such a length of days, the light and happiness of freedom, can be restrained, and shut up again in the gloom of ignorance and degradation? As well, sir, might you try, by a miserable dam, to shut up the flowing of a rapid river! The rolling and impetuous tide would burst through every impediment that man might throw in its way; and the only consequence of the impotent attempt would be, that, having collected new force by its temporary suspension, enforcing itself through new channels, it would spread devastation and ruin on every side. The progress of liberty is like the progress of the stream. Kept within its bounds, it is sure to fertilize the country through which it runs; but no power can arrest it in its passage; and short-sighted, as well as wicked, must be the heart of the projector that would strive to divert its course. ✻

Vocabulary List【词汇清单】

spectacle /ˈspektəkl/ *n.* （印象深刻的）景象,光景,壮观（场面）

predominant /ˌpriˈdɔminənt/ *adj.* 占优势的,支配其他的,优越的

invincible /inˈvinsəbl/ *adj.* 不可征服的,不可战胜的,无敌的

deride /diˈraid/ *v.* 嘲弄,嘲笑,取笑,揶揄

preposterous /priˈpɔstərəs/ *adj.* 荒谬的,乖戾的,愚蠢的

foster /ˈfɔstə/ *v.* 助长,促进;抱有（希望等）,心怀

assert /əˈsəːt/ *v.* 坚持、维护（权利、要求等）,坚决要求自己的权利（被承认）

condemn /kənˈdem/ *v.* 把（某人）逼入某种状态,使（某人）注定（to）

degradation /ˌdegrəˈdeiʃən/ *n.* （地位的）降低,降级;堕落,败坏

dam /dæm/ *n.* 堤坝,水坝,水闸

impetuous /im'petjuəs/ *adj.* 猛烈的，狂暴的，奔腾的，迅疾的

impediment /im'pedimənt/ *n.* 妨碍，阻碍，障碍物

impotent /'impətənt/ *adj.* 软弱无力的，虚弱的，衰弱的

temporary /'temprəri/ *adj.* 暂时的，临时的，一时的

suspension /səs'penʃən/ *n.* 暂停，中止；悬而未决

devastation /ˌdevəs'teiʃən/ *n.* 毁坏，破坏，损毁

projector /prə'dʒektə/ *n.* 计划者，规划者

divert /dai'vəːt/ *v.* 转移，使（人或物）转向

参考译文【Suggested Translation】

自由就是秩序

自由就是秩序，自由就是力量。放眼寰球，你定然会对那些具有启发性的景象钦佩不已。你会看到，自由不仅仅是力量和秩序，而且是占据统治地位的不可征服的力量和秩序——它使其他一切力量的源泉都相形见绌。那些在自由中被养育的人们，是人类当中第一批主张拥有订立自己的社会契约的殊荣的人，难道应该促进他们对其权利选择缄默不语的荒谬幻觉吗？试想，那些长期沐浴在自由的幸福光辉下的人们可能被压制、被重新禁锢在无知和堕落的黑暗之中吗？是的，先生，你完全可以尝试用一道可怜的堤坝去围堵奔腾湍急的河流！翻腾的急流会冲垮人们设置在河道上的任何障碍物；这种于事无补的尝试只会产生一个后果，那就是：河水经过暂时的停留而聚集了新的力量，强行冲破新的河道，会导致两岸四处受到损毁，并损毁一切。自由的前进如同河流的前进。假如它保持在自己活动的弹性范围之内，它必然会肥沃它所流经的土地；但是，任何势力都无法阻碍它按照自己的路径前进；那些力图改变其路径的谋划者必定是目光短浅而且令人憎恶之人。 ◆

We Were Dear to Each Other*

Stray birds of summer come to my window to sing and fly away.

And yellow leaves of autumn, which have no songs, flutter and fall there with a sign.

O Troupe of little vagrants of the world, leave your footprints in my words.

The world puts off its make of vastness to its lover.

---

* 作者罗宾德拉纳特·泰戈尔（Rabindranath Tagore, 1861—1941），印度著名诗人、作家、艺术家和社会活动家，1913 年荣获诺贝尔文学奖。泰戈尔是一位具有世界影响力的作家，其大量的文学艺术作品可以构成印度文艺复兴运动和民族独立运动的一个重要历史侧面；内容几乎无所不包，无所不精，主要反映了印度人民在帝国主义和封建种族制度压迫下要求改变自己命运的强烈愿望，描写了他们不屈不挠的反抗斗争，充满了鲜明的爱国主义和民主主义精神，同时又富有民族风格和民族特色，具有很高的艺术价值，深受人民群众喜爱。他一生共创作 50 多部诗集，被称为"诗圣"，几乎影响了一代诗风。其主要诗作有诗集《吉檀迦利》（Jitanjali）、《新月集》（Crescent Moon）、《飞鸟集》（Stray Bird）等。

It becomes small as one song, as one kiss of the eternal.

It is the tears of the earth that keep her smiles in bloom.

The mighty desert is burning for the love of a blade of grass who shakes her head and laughs and flies away.

If you shed tears when you miss the sun, you also miss the stars.

The sands in your way beg for your song and your movement, dancing water. Will you carry the burden of their lameness?

Her wishful face haunts my dreams like the rain at night.

Once we dreamt that we were strangers.

We wake up to find that we were dear to each other. ✽

# Vocabulary List 【词汇清单】

stray /strei/ *adj.* 漂泊的,迷路的,离群的

flutter /ˈflʌtə/ *v.* （鸟）鼓翼,振翅,拍翅

troupe /truːp/ *n.* ＜美＞群,队;剧团,文艺团体

vagrant /ˈveigrənt/ *n.* 流浪者,漂泊者,游民

vastness /ˈvaːstnis/ *n.* 浩瀚,广阔,无边无际

blade /bleid/ *n.* ＜植物＞（尤指草的）叶,叶片

lameness /ˈleimnis/ *n.* 跛足,瘸足

haunt /hɔːnt/ *v.* （思想、回忆等）萦绕;（气氛）充满,弥漫

 参考译文【Suggested Translation】

我们相亲相爱

天的飞鸟,飞到我的窗前唱歌,又飞去了。

秋天的黄叶,它们没有什么可唱,只叹息一声,飞落在那

里。

　　世界上的一队小小的漂泊者呀，请留下你们的足印在我的文字里。

　　世界对着它的爱人，把它浩翰的面具揭下了。

　　它变小了，小如一首歌，小如一回永恒的接吻。

　　是大地的泪点，使她的微笑保持着青春不谢。

　　无垠的沙漠热烈追求一叶绿草的爱，她摇摇头笑着飞开了。

　　如果你因失去了太阳而流泪，那么你也将失去群星了。

　　跳舞着的流水呀，在你途中的泥沙，要求你的歌声，你的流动呢。你肯挟瘸足的泥沙而俱下么？

　　她的热切的脸，如夜雨似的，搅扰着我的梦魂。

　　有一次，我们梦见大家都是不相识的。

　　我们醒了，却知道我们原是相亲相爱的。◆

（郑振铎 译）

●All that glitters is not gold.（发光的未必都是金子。）

●There are two sides to every question.（问题皆有两面。）

●All roads lead to Rome.（条条大路通罗马。）

●The water that bears the boat is the same that swallows it up.
（水能载舟，亦能覆舟。）

Born to Win [*]

Each human being is born as something new, something that never existed before. Each is born with the capacity to win at life. Each person has a unique way of seeing, hearing, touching, tasting and thinking. Each has his or her own unique potentials — capabilities and limitations. Each can be a significant, thinking, aware, and creative being — a productive person, a winner.

The word "winner" and "loser" have many meanings. When we refer to a person as a winner, we do not mean one who makes someone else lose. To us, a winner is one who

---

　　[*] 本文选自美国心理学畅销书《天生赢家》(Born to Win)，该书是两位心理学女博士穆里尔·詹姆斯(Muriel James)和多萝西·琼基瓦德(Dorothy Jongeward)合作的结晶。在我们的日常生活、工作、恋爱婚姻等方面，赢家之所以成为赢家、输家之所以成为输家的真正原因，其实在很多时候并不在于个人能力和素质，而在于日常习惯与生活态度……

responds authentically by being credible, trustworthy, responsive, and genuine, both as an individual and as a member of a society.

Winners do not dedicate their lives to a concept of what they imagine they should be; rather, they are themselves and as such do not use their energy putting on a performance, maintaining pretence, and manipulating others. They are aware that there is a difference between being loving and acting loving, between being stupid and acting stupid, between being knowledgeable and acting knowledgeable. Winners do not need to hide behind a mask.

Winners are not afraid to do their own thinking and to use their own knowledge. They can separate facts from opinion and don't pretend to have all the answers. They listen to others, evaluate what they say, but come to their own conclusions. Although winners can admire and respect other people, they are not totally defined, demolished, bound, or awed by them.

Winners do not play "helpless", nor do they play the blaming game. Instead, they assume responsibility for their own lives. They do not give others a false authority over them. Winners are their own bosses and know it.

A winner's timing is right. Winners respond appropriately to the situation. Their responses are related to the message sent and preserve the significance, worth, well-being, and dignity of the people involved. Winners know that for everything there is a season and for every activity a time.

Although winners can freely enjoy themselves, they can also postpone enjoyment, can discipline themselves in the present to enhance their enjoyment in the future. Winners are not afraid to go after what they want, but they do so in appropriate ways. Winners do not get their security by controlling others. They do not set themselves up to lose.

A winner cares about the world and its peoples. A winner is not isolated from the general problems of society, but is concerned, compassionate, and committed to improving the quality of life. Even in the face of national and international adversity, a winner's self-image is not one of a powerless individual. A winner works to make the world a better place. ✳

Vocabulary List 【词汇清单】

capacity /kə'pæsiti/ *n.* （做某事的）能力，才能，才智（to）

capabilitiy /ˌkeipə'biliti/ *n.* （实际）才能，能力，本领

authentically /ɔː'θentikəli/ *adv.* 真实地，真正地

trustworthy /'trʌstˌwəːði/ *adv.* 值得信任的，可靠的，可信赖的

genuine /'dʒenjuin/ *adj.* 真诚的，诚实的，诚恳的，坦率的

pretence /pri'tens/ *n.* （= pretense）虚饰，矫饰；伪装，假装

knowledgeable /'nɔlidʒəbl/ *adj.* 有知识的，有见识的，学识渊博的

demolish /di'mɔliʃ/ *v.* 推翻，驳倒；轻易而彻底地打败

appropriately /ə'prəupriitli/ *adv.* 适宜地，合适地，恰当地

dignity /'digniti/ *n.* 尊严，自尊

enhance /in'haːns/ *v.* 增加，提高，增强

compassionate /kəm'pæʃənit/ *adj.* 慈悲的，怜悯的，富于同情心的

commit to：承诺…，许诺…，答应负责…

参考译文【Suggested Translation】

天 生 赢 家

个人生来就是新的事物，是前所未有的事物。每个人天生就具有在生活中获取成功的能力。每个人都有自己观察、

聆听、触摸、品尝和思考的独特方式。每个人也各有其独特潜能——各有所长也各有局限。每个人都有可能成为一个重要、好思考、头脑清醒而富于想像的人———个创造性的人，一个赢家。

"赢家"一词和"输家"一词都有多种不同的含义。当我们认为某人为赢家，并不意味着他会让别人输掉什么。在我们看来，一个赢家不管是作为个体还是社会的一分子，他都会以可靠、诚信、感怀、坦率的态度真切地对一切作出反应。

赢家不会置身于想像他们应当成为何种人的观念之中；相反，他们就是本真的自我。因此，他们不会费神费力地装模作样，故作姿态，以及玩弄他人。他们很清楚爱与装爱、傻与装傻、真才实学与故作高深之间的区别。赢家们不需要用面具掩饰自己。

赢家们不惧怕进行独立思考和运用自身的知识。他们既能够区分事实与想法，又不会装作通晓一切。他们倾听他人意见，评估他人的言论，从而得出自己的结论。虽然赢家们能够敬佩和尊重他人，但是却不会完全被他人所限制、伤害、束缚或吓倒。

赢家们不会装作"无助"，也不会玩弄怨天尤人的把戏。相反，他们承担生活中自己应尽的责任。他们不会给别人名不符实的权威，让别人凌驾于他们之上。赢家们主宰着自己的命运，对此他们一清二楚。

赢家们擅于掌握时机，会对形势作出适当的应对。他们能根据得到的信息做出反应，维护有关人员的地位、价值、利益和尊严。赢家们知道，每件事情都有其适宜的时机，每个行动都有其恰当的时刻。

虽然赢家们能自由自在地享受生活，但是他们也能推迟享乐的时间。他们能够在目前约束自己，以便在将来享受更大的快乐。赢家们不惧怕追求心中想要的东西，但是行为方式恰如其分。赢家们不会通过控制他人来获取自身的安全感。他们不会把自己推向失败。

赢家关注世界和世间民众。赢家不会置身世外，不理睬普遍存在的社会问题，他对此充满关心和热情，并致力于改善生活的质量。即使面对全国性甚至全球性的灾难，赢家也不会显得无能为力。赢家致力于让世界变得更加美好。◆

第 **101** 篇

Leaning into the Afternoons[*]

Leaning into the afternoons I cast my sad nets
towards your oceanic eyes.

There in the highest blaze my solitude lengthens and flames,
  its arms turning like a drowning man's.

---

[*] 作者巴勃罗·聂鲁达(Pablo Neruda, 1904—1973),20 世纪最伟大的拉丁美洲诗人,智利外交官。在其近半个世纪的情歌创作中,情诗一直是他最脍炙人口的主题,也使得聂鲁达的名字几乎成为情诗的代名词。他的诗歌既继承西班牙民族诗歌的传统,又接受了波德莱尔等法国现代派诗歌的影响;既吸收了智利民族诗歌特点,又从惠特曼的创作中找到了自己最倾心的形式。由于"他的诗具有自然力般的作用,复苏了一个大陆的命运和梦想",1971 年荣获诺贝尔文学奖。聂鲁达的代表作包括《二十首情诗与绝望的歌》、《船长之歌》和《一百首爱的十四行诗》等,其中《二十首情诗与绝望的歌》一书是聂鲁达最受欢迎并且在拉丁美洲畅销达数百万册,被誉为 20 世纪"情诗圣经"。本诗即选自该诗集。

I send out red signals across your absent eyes
that move like the sea near a lighthouse.

You keep only darkness, my distant female,
from your regard sometimes the coast of dread emerges.

Leaning into the afternoons I fling my sad nets
to that sea that beats on your marine eyes.

The birds of night peck at the first stars
that flash like my soul when I love you.

The night gallops on its shadowy mare
shedding blue tassels over the land. ✳

 # Vocabulary List【词汇清单】

oceanic /ˌəuʃiˈænik/ *adj.* 海洋的,海洋般的,无边无际的

blaze /bleiz/ *n.* （燃烧得通红的）火焰,火苗;强光,亮光

solitude /ˈsɔlitjuːd/ *n.* 孤独,独居,寂寞

drown /draun/ *v.* 淹没,浸水,溺水

lighthouse /ˈlaithaus/ *n.* 灯塔（上面装有大功率照明灯的一种高建筑,用作指示海上航行的信标或标志）

dread /dred/ *n.* 恐惧,恐怖,可怕,畏惧

fling /fliŋ/ *v.* （猛）投,抛,掷,扔

marine /məˈriːn/ *adj.* 海洋的,海洋一般的

peck /pek/ *n.* 啄,啄食

gallop /ˈgæləp/ *n.* （马等）飞跑,疾驰,骑马奔驰飞跑

shadowy /ˈʃædəui/ *adj.* 有阴影的,虚幻的,朦胧的

shed /ʃed/ *v.* 散发,放（出）;放射（光、热等）,散布

tassel /ˈtæsl/ *n.* （玉蜀黍的）穗,缨,流苏

参考译文【Suggested Translation】

倚身于暮色中

倚身于暮色中，我向你海洋般的双眼
投掷我忧愁的网。

我的孤独，在那极度的光亮中不断延长并燃起火焰，
它的双臂扭转翻动，仿佛一个溺水之人在求救。

穿过你茫然的双眼，我送出红色的讯号，
你的双眼涌动着涟漪，如靠近灯塔的海洋。

你保有惟一的黑暗，我远方的女子，
有时惊怖的海岸从你的凝视之中浮现。

倚身于暮色中，在拍打你海洋般双眼的海上
我抛掷出我忧愁的网。

夜晚的鸟群啄食第一阵闪烁的群星，
如同爱上你时我的灵魂。

夜在它阴郁的梦魇上疾驰，
在大地上撒下湛蓝的穗须。◆

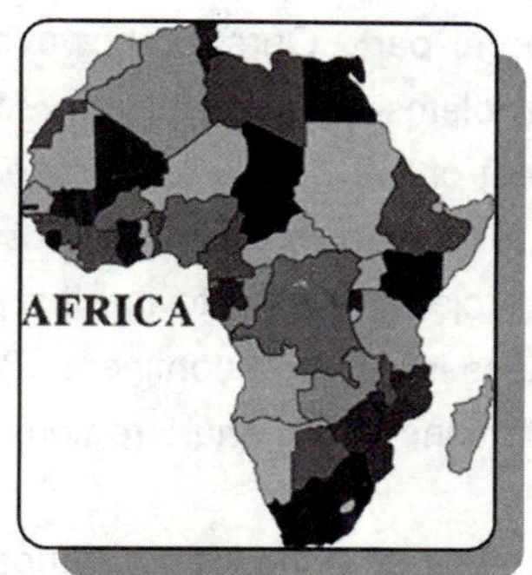

On the Future of Africa*

We are in a period of decisive historical significance for Africa and its place in the world. We are determined that this 21st century shall be the African century.

The idea of an African renaissance has taken hold in our continent with all the resonance of an idea whose time has come. The rebirth we are engaged in is not one that will culminate, as European renaissance did, in colonization and

---

　＊ 作者纳尔逊·曼德拉（Nelson Mandela, 1918—　），不结盟运动主席、南非前总统、非洲人国民大会前主席，1993 年荣获诺贝尔和平奖。他曾在 1964 年 6 月被控"企图以暴力推翻政府"，被判终身监禁，1990 年 2 月 11 日获释出狱。曼德拉本人曾经这样说道："他们关了我 27 年，夺走我的一切，我的黄金岁月；害得我婚姻破裂，无法亲见孩子成长，让我身心饱受摧残。但是别人夺不走的是我的思想和心灵，只要自己不放弃，别人就夺不走，你也不能放弃……。"本文为 2000 年 4 月 6 日曼德拉在伦敦经济学院发表的演说摘录，语调平缓，感情肃穆，通过将非洲和其他地区进行纵向和横向对比，自信地预言了非洲的复兴。

dominance of a world economic system, of which the slave trade was an integral part. Ours is, however, a rebirth that must deal with problems that derive from Africa's historical relation with the rest of the world, established in that period. And this must be achieved in a rapidly globalizing world. A second historical project, related to the first, is that of building strong institutions in a united continent. Political, economic and social institutions at national, regional and continental level ...

The vision expressed in the idea of African renaissance is that of the reconstruction and development of an Africa in which people's lives are constantly and rapidly improving towards standards broadly in line with the best in the world.

It is also a vision of an Africa that is integrated in the world on an equal basis. Africa collectively stands at the bottom of the world stage of development. This means for millions, the ills brought by poverty and under-development, the scourges of disease such as malaria, tuberculosis and HIV/AIDS, and educational programmes that are far from what is needed for Africa's full participation in the modern economy and society. As the world is seeing now in what the floods are doing to the people of Mozambique and part of South Africa, it means a vulnerability to environmental disaster.

If, despite all this, we talk with conviction of realizing our long-cherished dream of rebirth and reconstruction... ❋

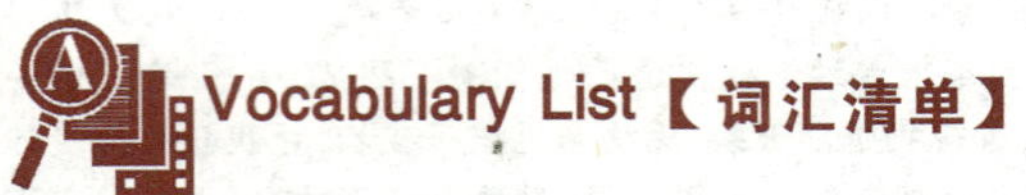

Vocabulary List 【词汇清单】

renaissance /rəˈneisəns/ *n.* 新生,复兴
resonance /ˈreznəns/ *n.* 反响,共鸣
culminate /ˈkʌlmineit/ *v.* 达到其最高点(顶点),结果是,告

终（in）

colonization /ˌkɔlənaiˈzeiʃən/ *n.* 殖民，殖民地化（建立殖民地的行为或过程）

derive /diˈraiv/ *v.* 引出，起源（于），出自（from）

globalize /ˈgləubəlaiz/ *v.* （在范围或应用上）使全球化（性）

scourge /skə:dʒ/ *n.* 灾害，苦难，灾祸

malaria /məˈlɛəriə/ *n.* ＜医＞疟疾（一种传染性疾病，症状为周期性地感到冷、热和发汗）

tuberculosis /tju(:)ˌbəkjuˈləusis/ *n.* ＜医＞结核（病）（由结合菌引起的人类和动物感染性疾病）；肺结核，肺痨（肺部的结核病，特征是咳出粘液或痰，发烧，体重减轻和胸口疼痛）

HIV：（＝Human Immunodeficiency Virus）人体免疫缺损病毒，艾滋病病毒

AIDS：（＝Acquired Immune Deficiency Syndrome）艾滋病，获得性免疫缺损综合症

Mozambique /ˌməuzəmˈbi:k/ 莫桑比克（非洲东南部国家）

vulnerability /ˌvʌlnərəˈbiliti/ *n.* 弱点，攻击

reconstruction /ˌri:kənˈstrʌkʃən/ *n.* 重建，再建（的行为或结果）

 ## 参考译文【Suggested Translation】

非 洲 的 未 来

我们非洲及其在世界上的地位正处于具有决定性历史意义的时期。我们决心要使21世纪成为非洲的世纪。

非洲复兴的理想引起大家的共鸣，并已深深扎根于我们这片大陆，这一理想实现的时刻已经到来。我们所从事的复兴，其结果将不同于欧洲复兴那样所导致的殖民主义——以贩卖奴隶为其必然组成部分的经济制度主宰世界。然而，我们的复兴必须处理解决一系列的问题，这些问题源自于在那个时期产生的非洲和其外部世界的历史性关系。而这在一个迅速全球化的世

界里必须着手进行。上述是第一个历史工程，而与此相关的第二个历史性工程就是在统一的非洲大陆上建立坚强的制度体系，包括在国家、区域以及整个大陆层面的政治、经济和社会体制……

非洲复兴的理想，就是重建和发展一个人民的生活持续而迅速改善的非洲，使其生活水平达到与世界最高水平大体相当。

这一理想也是对于非洲在平等的基础上融入世界的展望。就整体而言，非洲现在正处于世界发展的最低阶段。这意味着贫穷和发展不足给千百万人带来了弊病，如疟疾、肺结核和艾滋病等灾难性疾病，以及远未达到使非洲能充分参与现代经济和社会所需要的教育系统。全世界现在正看到水灾怎样祸害着莫桑比克以及南部非洲的部分地区，这意味着我们容易受到环境灾祸的损害。

尽管这样，我们还是能够自信地谈论实现我们长期怀有的重生和重建的梦想……◢

- Nothing is too difficult if you put your heart into it. （世上无难事，只怕有心人。）
- Grasp all, lose all. （样样都要，全都失掉。）
- Better master one than engage with ten. （会十事不如精一事。）
- Don't put off till tomorrow what should be done today. （今日事，今日毕。）

Man Is Here for the Sake of Other Men*

Strange is our situation here upon earth. Each of us comes for a short visit, not knowing why, yet sometimes seeming to divine a purpose.

From the standpoint of daily life, however, there is one thing we do know that man is here for the sake of other men

---

* 作者阿尔伯特·爱因斯坦（Albert Einstein, 1879—1955），20 世纪最伟大的自然科学家、物理学革命的旗手。爱因斯坦生于德国，后入瑞士籍，终入籍美国，曾任柏林大学、普林斯顿大学等校教授。1921 年获诺贝尔物理学奖。对于这一享誉全球的人物，巴内什·霍夫曼在《爱因斯坦》一书中曾这样说道："爱因斯坦的深刻本质藏在他的质朴个性之中；而他科学的本质藏在他的艺术性之中——他对美的非凡感觉。""他最出名的当然是他的相对论，那给他带来了世界性的声誉。但伴随名声而来的是一种爱因斯坦感到难以理解的盲目崇拜。令他惊讶的是，他成为一种活生生的神话，一个真实的民族英雄。他被人看作一个奇迹，并得到皇室人员、政治家和其他名人的招待，公众和新闻界把他当作一个电影明星而不是科学家。"

— above all for those upon whose smile and well-being our own happiness depends, and also for the countless unknown souls with whose fate we are connected by a bond of sympathy. Many times a day I realize how much my own outer and inner life is built upon the labors of my fellow men, both living and dead, and how earnestly I must exert myself in order to give in return as much as I have received. My peace of mind is often troubled by the depressing sense that I have borrowed too heavily from the work of other men.

To ponder interminably over the reason for one's own existence or the meaning of life in general seems to me, from an objective point of view, to be sheer folly. And yet everyone holds certain ideals by which he guides his aspiration and his judgment. The ideals which have always shone before me and filled me with the joy of living are goodness, beauty, and truth. To make a goal of comfort and happiness has never appealed to me; a system of ethics built on this basis would be sufficient only for a herd of cattle. ✱

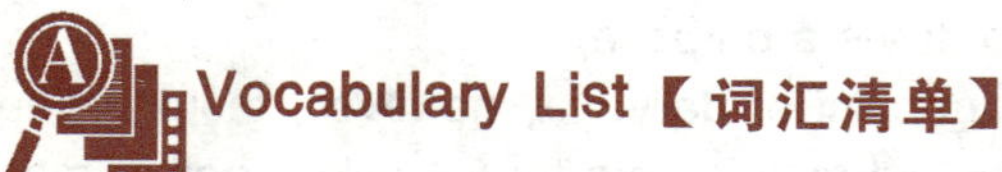

Vocabulary List 【词汇清单】

divine /di'vain/ *v.* 猜测,猜想,推测

sympathy /'simpəθi/ *n.* 同情,同情心,怜悯

exert /ig'zəːt/ *v.* 努力,尽力,竭尽全力（oneself）

ponder /'pɔndə/ *v.* 默想,沉思,考虑

interminably /in'təːminəbli/ *adv.* 没完没了地,无止境地,冗长地

sheer /ʃiə/ *adj.* 绝对的,全然的,彻底的

aspiration /ˌæspə'reiʃən/ *n.* 热望,渴望;志气,抱负

ethics /'eθiks/ *n.* （人、宗教、团体、职业的）伦理观,道德观,道德标准（或规矩）

sufficient /sə'fiʃənt/ *adj.* 充分的,足够的（for）

a herd of：　一群，一队，一伙

 参考译文【Suggested Translation】

人是为了别人而活着

人类在这个世界上的处境真是奇怪。我们每个人来到这个世界上，都是进行一次短暂的访问，不知道原因何在，然而有时候却似乎卜算出一种目的。

　　然而，从日常生活的观点来看，有一件事情我们是肯定知道的，那就是人在这个世界上是为了别人而活着——尤其是为了那些我们自身的幸福寄托在他们的微笑和福祉之上的人们，以及那些我们由于同情之感而同他们的命运联系在一起的无数的不知名的人们。每天，我几次三番地觉察到自己的物质生活和精神生活是如何建立在别人——包括活着的人和死去的人——的劳动之上，以及自己必须如何认真地奋发努力，从而使我对我所获得的予以同等的回报。我平和的心情时常被沮丧之感困扰，因为我觉得自己从别人的工作中承袭得太多太多了。

　　从一种客观的观点来看，我想没完没了地沉思着自己生存的理由或人生的意义是近似愚蠢的行为。可是，每个人都有一些特定的理想作为他的抱负和判断的指南针。经常在我的眼前闪闪发光，并使我充满了生活的快乐的理想，就是真、善、美。我从未以追求舒适和安逸作为生活的目标；建立在其基础上的一套伦理观念，只能满足一群牲畜的需要。◆

Game Playing[*]

In a game the moves are set up beforehand. In a non-game situation the moves are supposed to arise out of events as these develop. A girl wants to encourage her boyfriend so she pretends to be busy when he phones her or she pretends that someone else is courting her. A young child who is reluctant to go to bed deliberately spills milk from a cup on to the carpet so that in the ensuing fuss and scolding the immediacy of his bedtime will be forgotten. Diplomats at a

---

＊ 作者爱德华·德·波诺（Edward De Bono），英国人，牛津大学心理学、医学博士学位、剑桥大学医学博士，曾任职于牛津大学、伦敦大学、哈佛大学和剑桥大学。他在历史上第一次把创造性思维的研究建立在科学的基础上，是思维训练领域的国际权威。他是横向思维理论的创立者，有"横向思维之父"的美誉。如今，"横向思维"一词作为语言的一部分，已经被收入《牛津英语大词典》、《朗文词典》。爱德华·德·波诺这个名字已经成为创造力和新思维的象征。1994 年，国际思维大会因其对人类思维的杰出贡献，授予他"先驱者"称号。本文选自其名作《语言力》（Wordpower）一书。

conference make a great fuss over the shape of the table as they play the procedural game. An agent selling the film rights in a first novel casually mentions other parties who have shown an interest in buying the rights. A hostess deliberately places a seductive lady next to a husband with a jealous wife. Union negotiators go through a ritual of complaints before settling down to discuss the current issue.

The characteristic of a game is that a sequence of moves are recognisable as part of the game. The game may be played very seriously; it may also be played for a purpose rather than as an end in itself. Nevertheless each move in the sequence is determined by the requirements of the game rather than the realities of the situation itself. Someone who is aware that a game is being played sits back and waits for the game to be played out. Someone who is not aware that it is a game gets involved and manipulated by the games player who knows the moves of the game better. It is this expertise in the moves of the game which makes it worth playing. If the player knows, from long experience, the moves, reactions and counter-moves then he only has to entice the other person to play the game to achieve success. If the situation works itself out naturally neither side has an advantage. But if one side sets up a game with which only he is familiar then that side immediately acquires the advantage of skill and foreknowledge.

A good games player not only knows how to make the next move, he can think one, two or three moves ahead. This is extremely diffcult for an inexperienced player. Thus the player who sets up a familiar game can lay traps several moves ahead with very little chance of the opponent noticing what is being done.

Just as a philosopher will always try to run an argument

according to his own definitions so a games player will always try to make an opponent play his special game. ✳

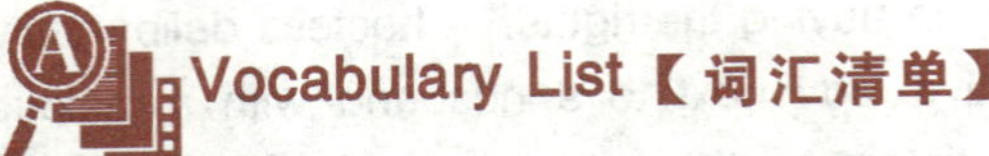

Vocabulary List【词汇清单】

beforehand /biˈfɔːhænd/ *adv.* 预先，事先；提前，提早

court /kɔːt/ *v.* 向…献殷勤，追求，求爱

deliberately /diˈlibəritli/ *adv.* 故意地，蓄意地，有意地

fuss /fʌs/ *n.* 忙乱，大惊小怪，小题大作

scold /ˈskəuld/ *v.* 责骂，叱责

diplomat /ˈdipləmæt/ *n.* 外交家，外交官，有外交手腕的人

procedural /prəˈsiːdʒərəl/ *adj.* 程序上的，程序性的，有关程序的

seductive /siˈdʌktiv/ *adj.* 诱人（堕落）的，有诱惑力的

ritual /ˈritjuəl/ *n.* （日常的）仪式般的行为，应遵循的惯例

recognisable /ˈrekəgnaizəbl/ *adj.* (= recognizable) 可认知的，可认识的，可辨认的

manipulate /məˈnipjuleit/ *v.* （熟练地）操作，巧妙地处理；（用权势或不正当手段）操纵（人或市价、市场等），摆布

expertise /ˌekspəˈtiːz/ *n.* ＜法语＞专门技能（或知识），专门技术

entice /inˈtais/ *v.* 引诱，诱惑，诱使

foreknowledge /ˈfɔːˈnɔlidʒ/ *n.* 预知，先知，先见之明

参考译文【Suggested Translation】

玩 游 戏

在一场游戏里，步骤是事先设计好的。如果不是在游戏的情况下，采取什么步骤则要看事态的发展。一位姑娘想激励她的男友，就会在其男友打电话来时故意说自己很忙，或者说另外有人对她献殷勤。一个小孩儿不愿意上床睡觉，会故意把杯

子中的牛奶泼到地毯上，造成忙乱并引起责备，于是家人就会立刻忘记让他上床睡觉的时间。谈判中的外交官在程序问题上玩游戏时，会对谈判桌的形状小题大作。一位经纪人就新出版的小说推销电影改编权时，会向对方间或提及另有买家对于购买该改编权表现出兴趣。一位女主人会故意将一个风骚女郎安排在一位男士身旁就座，该男士的妻子正好嫉妒心很重。某机构的谈判人员会在切入正题之前照老规矩先发一通牢骚，如此等等。

游戏的特点是其中的一系列步骤都可以看清楚，这也是游戏的内容。游戏可以玩得很认真，也可以只为达到某一意图，而不把游戏本身作为目的。无论如何，步骤序列中的每一步都是按照游戏本身的要求而决定的，而不是按照形势的实际情况而定。明白这是在玩某一游戏的人会泰然处之，坐等游戏玩完。而不明白这是在玩游戏的人则会卷入其中，被比他更清楚游戏步骤的玩游戏者所操控。正是懂得游戏步骤这种专门知识才使游戏值得一玩。假如玩游戏者从长期经验知晓该采取什么步骤，对方会做何反应，以及应如何对付，那么他只需要诱导对方一步步玩下去就能够取胜。假如让形势自然发展自行了结，则双方均无优势。但是如果游戏是由一方设局，只有他熟悉局势，那么他便立刻拥有技术优势和先见之明。

一个出色的玩游戏者不但懂得下一步该怎么走，而且能够提前设想两步或是三步之后改如何去走。而没有经验的玩游戏者就很难做到。因此，玩游戏者设定其熟悉的游戏格局，就能够提前好几步布下陷阱，而对手则几乎不会觉察正要发生的事情。

正如哲学家总是试图按照他自己的定义来展开论辩一样，玩游戏者也总是试图让对方跟他玩他自己特设的游戏。◆

Paradox of Our Times *

Today we have bigger houses and smaller families; more conveniences, but less time; we have more degrees, but less common sense; more knowledge, but less judgment; We have more experts, but more problems; more medicine, but less wellness.

We spend too recklessly, laugh too little, drive too fast, get to angry too quickly, stay up too late, get up too tired, read too little, watch TV too often, and pray too seldom.

We have multiplied our possessions, but reduced our

＊作者奥尔加·希尔（Olga Scheel），生平不详。这是一个伟大的时代么？当权威已经消失，统计社会和个人独创精神有机地结合在一起，这个时代已经属于我们每一个人。诚然，我们无法选择时代——生在何时，是男是女，父母是谁，属何民族，这些你我说了都不算，只有认命。然而，这并不能抑止我们对这个光怪陆离时代信笔涂鸦。本文笔触颇深，将我们这个时代引发的种种悖论娓娓道来，令人读罢不禁掩卷深思：我们到底生活在一个什么样的时代？我们生存的这个时代究竟将何去何从？

values. We talk too much, love too little and lie too often. We've learned how to make a living, but not a life; we've added years to life, not life to years.

We have taller buildings, but shorter tempers; wider freeways, but narrower viewpoints. We spend more, but have less; we buy more, but enjoy it less.

We've been all the way to the moon and back, but have trouble crossing the street to meet the new neighbor. We've conquered outer space, but not inner space. We've split the atom, but not our prejudice; we write more, but learn less; plan more, but accomplish less.

We've learned to rush, but not to wait; we have higher incomes, but lower morals. We build more computers to hold more information, to produce more copies, but have less communication. We are long on quantity, but short on quality.

These are the times of fast foods and slow digestion; tall men and short character; steep profits and shallow relationships. More leisure and less fun; more kinds of food, but less nutrition; two incomes, but more divorce; fancier houses, but broken homes.

That's why I propose, that as of today, you do not keep anything for a special occasion, because every day that you live is a special occasion. Search for knowledge, read more, sit on your front porch and admire the view without paying attention to your needs. Spend more time with your family and friends, eat your favorite foods, and visit the places you love. Life is a chain of moment of enjoyment, not only about survival.

Use your crystal goblets. Do not save your best perfume, and use it every time you feel you want it. Remove from your vocabulary phrases like "one of these days" and "someday". Let's write that letter we thought of writing "one of these days". Let's tell our families and friends how much we love them. Do not delay anything that adds laughter and joy to your life. ✲

 **Vocabulary List【词汇清单】**

paradox /'pærədɔks/ *n.* 似是而非的评论，自相矛盾的事，逆说，悖论

convenience /kən'viːnjəns/ *n.* 便利，方便，舒适，适宜

degree /di'griː/ *n.* 学位，学衔（由大学或学院授予完成学业学生的学术称号）

common sence：常识

judgment /'dʒʌdʒmənt/ *n.* 判断，鉴定

wellness /'welnis/ *n.* 良好状态

recklessly /'reklisli/ *adv.* 不在乎地，粗心大意地

stay up：熬夜

multiply /'mʌltiplai/ *v.* 使成倍增加，增多

possession /pə'zeʃən/ *n.* ＜复数＞财产，财富

make a living：谋生，营生

freeway /'friːwei/ *n.* 高速公路

split /split/ *v.* ＜化学＞使（分子等）分裂，使产生裂变

prejudice /'predʒudis/ *n.* 偏见，成见，损害，侵害

digestion /dai'dʒestʃən/ *n.* 消化，领悟

steep /stiːp/ *adj.* 陡峭的，险峻的，急剧升降的，不合理的

shallow /'ʃæləu/ *adj.* 浅的，浅薄的

nutrition /njuː'triʃən/ *n.* 营养，营养学

divorce /di'vɔːs/ *n.* 离婚；脱离

porch /pɔːtʃ/ *n.* 门廊，走廊

crystal /'kristl/ *adj.* 水晶的，晶体的

goblet /'gɔblit/ *n.* 高脚玻璃杯，酒杯

perfume /'pəːfjuːm/ *n.* 香味，芳香，香水

delay /di'lei/ *v.* 使延迟，使耽搁，使耽误

参考译文【Suggested Translation】

我们这个时代的尴尬

今天，我们居住的房屋越来越宽敞，家庭却越来越小型化；可以享受的生活便利日益增多，属于自己的时间却日趋减少；我们获得了一张又一张学位证书，却愈加频繁地陷入对常识的茫然之中；我们广泛地涉猎各类知识，却越来越缺乏对于外界事物的准确把握和判断；我们的专家越来越多，问题却也日渐增加；药物越吃越多，健康却每况愈下。

我们花钱太疯，笑容太少，开车太快，怒气太盛，熬夜太晚，起身太累，文章读得太少，电视看得太勤，祷告做得太少。

我们不断聚敛物质财富，却逐渐失去了自我价值。我们的话语太多，真爱太少，谎言泛滥。我们掌握了谋生手段，却不懂得生活真谛；我们让年华付诸流水，却不曾将生命倾注其中。

我们的住房越来越好，脾气越来越糟；我们行驶的道路越来越宽阔，眼光却越来越狭隘。我们付出很多，可获得的很少；我们购买了很多，可从中得到的乐趣却很少。

我们能够往返于地球与月球之间，却不乐于穿过马路向新邻居问好。我们可以征服外部空间，却懦于走进内心世界。我们可以击碎原子，却不能突破思想偏见；我们写得很多，可学到的很少；计划很多，可完成的很少。

我们学会了追赶时间，却没有学会耐心等待；我们拥有的财富越来越多，道德品质却日益沦丧。我们生产更多的电脑用于存储更多的信息和制造更多的拷贝，而相互间的交流与沟通却越来越少。我们拥有的是数量，缺乏的却是质量。

这是一个快餐食品和消化迟缓相伴的时代；一个体格高大和性格病态并存的时代；一个追名逐利和人情冷漠相生的时代。我们的闲暇多了，乐趣却少了；食品种类多了，营养却少了；双薪家庭增加了，离婚率也激升了；居室的装修华丽了，家庭却残缺破碎了。

因此我奉劝大家，在当今这个时代，不必为某个特别时刻保留什么，因为我们生活的每一天都是特别的。探索知识，遨游书海，坐在门廊前欣赏眼前的景色，把所有烦恼抛在脑后。留出更多的时间与家人和朋友一起分享，吃遍天下美食，游遍你心中向往的名山大川。生命是由快乐时光组成的一个链条，而绝不仅仅是一种生命的存在。

举起你那水晶酒杯开怀畅饮吧，不要吝惜你最好的香水，只要想用就尽情地用吧。将"今后某一天"这类的话从你的词汇中删除，现在就把你想在"今后某一天"写的信件写了寄走。不要把对家人和朋友的爱深藏心中，大胆地告诉他们。对于能给你的生命增添快乐的事情，不要押后拖延。◆

● A man cannot spin and reel at the same time. （一心不能二用。）

● Take things as they come. （既来之，则安之。）

● Respect yourself, or no one else will respect you. （要人尊敬，必先自重。）

● Everybody's business is nobody's business. （众人之事是无人之事。）

Fleeting Time（Ⅰ）*

Can it really be sixty-two years ago that I first saw you? It is truly a lifetime, I know. But as I gaze into your eyes now, it seems like only yesterday that I first saw you, in that small café in Hanover Square.

From the moment I saw you smile, as you opened the door for that young mother and her newborn baby. I knew, I knew that I wanted to share the rest of my life with you.

I still think of how foolish I must have looked, as I gazed at you, that first time. I remember watching you intently, as you took off your hat and loosely shook your short dark hair with your fingers. I felt myself becoming immersed in your every detail, as you placed your hat on the table and cupped

---

* 作者佚名。本文是一位深情款款的老人在自己的爱妻离开人世之后回忆他们当年相遇相识相知相爱直到步入婚姻殿堂的诸多生活片断，浓情厚意，沁人肺腑，将似水年华演绎得淋漓尽致，是一部浓缩的情感世界的编年史。其情切切，其意脉脉，读之犹可感觉到一种真情所以。

your hands around the hot cup of tea, gently blowing the steam away with your pouted lips.

From that moment, everything seemed to make perfect sense to me. The people in the café and the busy street outside all disappeared into a hazy blur. All I could see was you.

All through my life I have relived that very first day. Many, many times I have sat and thought about the first day, and how for a few fleeting moments I am there, feeling again what is like to know ture love for the very first time. It pleases me that I can still have those feelings now after all those years, and I know I will always have them to comfort me.

Not even as I shook and trembled uncontrollably in the trenches, did I forget your face. I would sit huddled into the wet mud, terrified, as the hails of bullets and mortars crashed down around me. I would clutch my rifle tightly to my heart, and think again of that very first day we met. I would cry out in fear, as the noise of war beat down around me. But, as I thought of you and saw you smiling back at me, everything around me would be become silent, and I would be with you again for a few precious moments, far from the death and destruction. It would not be until I opened my eyes once again, that I would see and hear the carnage of the war around me.

I cannot tell you how strong my love for you was back then, when I returned to you on leave in the September, feeling battered, bruised and fragile. We held each other so tight I thought we would burst. I asked you to marry me the very same day and I whooped with joy when you looked deep into my eyes and said "yes" to being my bride.

I'm looking at our wedding photo now, the one on our dressing table, next to your jewellery box. I think of how young and innocent we were back then. I remember being on the church steps grinning like a Cheshire cat, when you said how dashing and handsome I looked in my uniform. The photo is old and faded now, but when I look at it, I only see the bright vibrant colors of our youth. I can still remember every detail of the pretty wedding dress your mother made for you, with its fine delicate lace and pretty pearls. If I concentrate hard enough, I can smell the sweetness of your wedding bouquet as you held it so proudly for everyone to see. (To be continued) ✳

Vocabulary List【词汇清单】

Hanover /ˈhænəuvə/ 汉诺威（德国西北部、不莱梅东南部的一个城市）

intently /inˈtentli/ *adv.* 目不转睛地，专心致志地，全神贯注地

immersed /iˈməːst/ *adj.* 浸入的，沉浸的；专心的，全神贯注的（in）

pout /paut/ *v.* 撅嘴，绷脸，板脸

hazy /ˈheizi/ *n.* 有雾的，雾蒙蒙的；模糊的，朦胧的

blur /bləː/ *n.* （轮廓或形状）模糊不清；黯淡，阴暗

uncontrollably /ˈʌnkənˈtrəuləbəli/ *adv.* 无法控制地，无法掌控地

trench /trentʃ/ *n.* 沟渠，堑壕，战壕

huddle /ˈhʌdl/ *v.* 蜷缩，缩成一团

mortar /ˈmɔːtə/ *n.* 迫击炮（一种可移动的、前装式的大炮，用来发射较低速度、近程和高弧形行程的炮弹）

clutch /klʌtʃ/ *v.* 抓住，抓牢，握紧

rifle /ˈraifl/ *n.* 步枪，来复枪（为使子弹回旋，在枪膛内加螺旋状沟纹的步枪）

destruction /disˈtrʌkʃən/ *n.* 灭绝，毁灭（的事实或情况）

carnage /ˈkaːnidʒ/ *n.* （尤指在战场上的）残杀，大屠杀

batter /ˈbætə/ *v.* 捣碎，打烂，敲碎；磨损，磨破（本文中的 battered 是形容人精疲力竭的样子）

bruised /bruːzd/ *adj.* 使（精神、感情等）受创伤；青肿的，有伤

痕的

whoop /huːp/ *v.* 高声叫喊,大声吼叫

jewellery /ˈdruːəlri/ *n.* <总称>珠宝,珠宝饰物

grin /grin/ *v.* 露齿而笑,(表示高兴、愉快、满足或窘迫时的)咧开嘴笑

Cheshire /ˈtʃeʃə/ 柴郡(英国英格兰西部的郡)

vibrant /ˈvaibrənt/ *adj.* 有活力的,活跃的;精力充沛的,充满生命力的

bouquet /bəuˈkei/ *n.* <法语>一束花,花束

 ## 参考译文【Suggested Translation】

似 水 流 年(一)

我们初次相遇,难道真的是六十二年之前吗?

年华似水,倏忽间我们已相携一世。可是当我望着你的双眼,当年的邂逅历历如在昨昔,也就是在汉诺威广场的那间小咖啡馆里。

那一刻,你正在为一位年轻的母亲和他的小宝宝开门,而从见到你当时的盈盈笑靥之刻起,我就明白我只愿与你执手携老,共度此生。

我仍然不时想起,那天自己第一次那样地盯着你,一定很傻;我的目光就那样情不自禁怔怔地投向你,追随你摘下帽子,用手指松了松短短的黑发,追随你把帽子放在桌前,双手捧起那杯热茶,追随你微微撅起的樱唇,轻轻吹走飘腾的热气。我的目光始终追随着你,感觉自己在你温柔的举止间慢慢融化。

从那一刻起,一切对于我似乎都有了完美的意义。咖啡馆里的来来往往和外面闹市的熙熙攘攘都变得模糊不清了。我的眼睛所能看到的,只有你。

光阴似箭,那一天却不断在我的记忆里重演,鲜活如初。数不清多少回了,我再次坐下,不断追忆那天的点点滴滴,不断回味那些飞纵的瞬间,重新体会一见钟情的美丽。让我欣喜的是,岁月的流逝却并没有带走那些爱恋的感觉,这些体验会永远伴

随着我，安抚我的寥寥余生。

即使当我在战壕中控制不住地颤抖和战栗，我也不曾忘记你的容颜。飞蹿的子弹和迫击炮弹如雨点般在我身边开了花，我蹲坐着蜷缩在稀泥里，惊恐万分。我把步枪紧紧地握在胸前，还是想起了我们初遇的那一天。萧萧的战火在我的周身呼啸着，我恐惧得几乎要大声呼叫。但是，当我想起你，仿佛看见你在我身后盈盈浅笑，我周围的一切忽然沉寂下来，并且在这珍贵的瞬间，我觉得自己暂时远离了死亡和毁灭，又和你待在了一起。我沉浸在这种美好之中，直到我忽然再次睁开双眼，看到的却是依然围困着我的血与火的生死战场。

九月我休假回到你身边，深感疲惫和脆弱，而那时我重又燃起对你的爱火却无法用语言来形容。我们紧紧拥抱在一起，仿佛将要把对方挤碎。也正是在那一天，我请求你嫁给我，而当你深深地凝望我的眼睛并答应做我的新娘时，我早已欢喜地大喊大叫。

我现在正注视着我们的结婚照，就是放在我们梳妆台上你首饰盒旁边的那一张。那时候，我们多么年轻，多么纯真。我记得当站在教堂的台阶上，你说我穿着制服是多么英武俊朗的时候，你咧嘴一笑的样子俨然如一只英国柴郡的小花猫。现在照片已经旧得泛黄了，但是我所看到的，却只有我们年轻时的明媚姿彩。我仍然能够记得你母亲为你做的那件漂亮的结婚礼服，上面镶嵌着精致的花边和美丽的珍珠。让我再仔细体会一下，我还能闻到我们婚礼上花束的甜香，你那么骄傲地捧着花，让每个人都分享你的幸福时光。（未完待续）◆

第 107 篇

Fleeting Time (Ⅱ)

I remember being so over-enjoyed, when a year later, you gently held my hand to your waist and whispered in my ear that we were going to be a family.

I know both our children love you dearly; they are outside the door now, waiting.

Do you remember how I panicked like a mad man when Jonathon was born? I can still picture you laughing and smiling at me now, as I clumsily held him for the very first time in my arms. I watched as your laughter faded into tears, as I stared at him and cried my own tears of joy.

Sarah and Tom arrived this morning with little Tessie. Can you remember how we both hugged each other tightly when we saw our tiny granddaughter for the first time? I can't believe she will be eight next month. I am trying not to cry, my love, as I tell you how beautiful she looks today in her pretty dress and red shiny shoes, she reminds me so much of you that first day we met. She has her hair cut short now, just like yours was all those years ago. When I met her at the door her smile wrapped around me like a warm glove, just like yours used to do, my darling.

I know you are tired, my dear, and I must let you go. But I love you so much it hurts to do so.

As we grew old together, I would tease you that you had not changed since we first met, But it is true, my darling. I do not see the wrinkles and grey hair that other people see. When I look at you now, I only see your sweet tender lips and youthful sparkling eyes as we sat and had out first picnic next to that small stream, and chased each other around that big old oak tree. I remember wishing those first few days together would last forever. Do you remember how exciting and wonderful those days were?

I must go now, my darling. Our children are waiting outside. They want to say goodbye to you.

I wipe the tears away from my eyes and bend my frail old legs down to the floor, so that I can kneel beside you. I lean close to you and take hold of your hand and kiss your tender lips for the very last time.

Sleep peacefully my dear.

I am sad that you had to leave me, but please don't worry. I am content, knowing I will be with you soon. I am too old and too empty now to live much longer without you.

I know it won't be long before we meet again in that small café in Hanover Square.

Goodbye, my darling wife. ✳

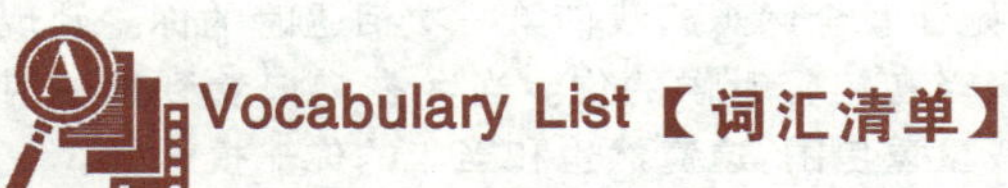

Vocabulary List 【词汇清单】

whisper /'wispə/ *v.* 低声地说, 耳语, 窃窃私语

panick /'pænik/ *v.* 恐慌,惊慌失措

clumsily /'klʌmzili/ *adv.* 笨手笨脚地,(手脚)笨拙地

hug /hʌg/ *v.* 拥抱,紧紧拥抱

tiny /'taini/ *adj.* 极小的,微小的

remind /ri'maind/ *v.* 提醒,使想起(某事)(of)

tease /ti:z/ *v.* 逗弄,戏弄

sparkle /'spa:kl/ *v.* (宝石、目光等)闪闪发光,闪耀,闪光

oak /əuk/ *n.* <植物>栎数,橡树

frail /freil/ *adj.* 虚弱的,脆弱的,体弱的

kneel /ni:l/ *v.* 跪下,跪着

peacefully /'pi:sufuli/ *adv.* 平静地,安宁地,太平地

 ## 参考译文【Suggested Translation】

似 水 流 年 (二)

一年之后,你轻轻地把我的手放在你的腹前,对着我的耳朵悄悄透露那个让我欣喜若狂的好消息:我们就快有宝宝啦。

我知道我们的两个孩子都深深地爱你,他们现在就在门外等候着。

你还记得乔纳森出生的时候我像疯子一样惊慌失措的样子吗?我现在还能描绘出当我笨拙地把他抱在怀里时你笑话我的样子。我看着你的笑意渐渐混合着泪水;我又看着他,也情不自禁地涌出了开心的泪花。

今天早晨,撒拉和汤姆带着小缇西也赶到了。你还记得吗?第一次看到这个可爱的小孙女,我们俩紧紧地拥抱在一起。真让人难以置信,她下个月就八岁了。亲爱的,我不得不强忍着眼泪告诉你,小家伙今天穿着美丽的裙子和闪亮的红色小鞋,看上去多么漂亮啊!她让我全然想起我们第一次相遇时的你。她现在留着短发,正像当初年轻时候的你。当我在门口看到她的时候,她的笑容将我重重包围,这竟然也和当年的你一模一样。

亲爱的,我知道你累了,而我应该让你离开。可是爱人即

逝，孤侣何伤！

这些年我们相濡以沫，白首到老，我总是逗你说你的容颜依然如昔。可亲爱的，这是千真万确的。我的确看不到在他人眼中你的皱纹和白发。现在我望着你，却只能看到你娇嫩温柔的红唇和秋水流盼的双眸，这情景仿佛我们第一次在那条小溪边野餐，在那棵巨大的老橡树周围追逐嬉戏。我记得那时候我们刚刚在一起，总是盼望那样的日子生生世世。你还记得吗？那些日子是多么激情荡漾，让人不忍回首……

亲爱的，我应该走了。我们的孩子都等在外面。他们要和你道别了。

我擦去了眼角的泪水，将虚弱的两条老腿跪在地板上，这样就能凑在你的身边。让我轻轻靠近你并握住你的手，最后一次吻你柔软的嘴唇。

亲爱的，安心地睡吧。

这种分离扯碎了我的心。可是请别担心，我知道我很快就会去陪伴你，对此我已心满意足。现在我已衰老不堪，内心空乏，以至于没有你我将无以度日。

我想不会很久，我们就能在汉诺威广场的那间小咖啡馆里再次相逢。

再会了，我的爱妻。◆

I Have a Dream（Ⅰ）*

I am happy to join with you today in what will go down in history as the greatest demonstration for freedom in the history of our nation.

---

　　* 作者马丁·路德·金（Martin Luther King, Jr., 1929—1968），美国著名黑人民权运动领袖，基督教牧师和律师，1964 年荣获诺贝尔和平奖。他一生曾三次被捕，三次被行刺，1968 年 4 月 4 日被种族主义分子枪杀。马丁·路德·金被誉为近百年来八位最具有说服力的演说家之一。1983 年，美国政府规定，从 1986 年起，每年 1 月的第三个星期一为小马丁·路德·金全国纪念日。本文背景：1963 年，马丁·路德·金组织的伯明翰黑人争取自由平等权利的大规模游行示威，把黑人运动从南方推向北方。8 月 28 日，斗争达到高潮。25 万人聚集首都华盛顿，以和平集会方式举行"自由进军"的示威，就在林肯纪念堂前，他向示威群众发表了这篇激动人心的经典演说——《我有一个梦想》，表达了他的非暴力主义思想以及他对自由平等公正的追求与憧憬。这次讲演义正并且辞严，愤懑而有节制，被赞誉为"充满林肯和甘地精神的象征和圣经的韵律"。

Five score years ago, a great American, in whose symbolic shadow we stand today, signed the Emancipation Proclamation. This momentous decree came as a great beacon light of hope to millions of Negro slaves who had been seared in the flames of withering injustice. It came as a joyous daybreak to end the long night of their captivity.

But one hundred years later, the Negro still is not free. One hundred years later, the life of the Negro is still sadly crippled by the manacles of segregation and the chains of discrimination. One hundred years later, the Negro lives on a lonely island of poverty in the midst of a vast ocean of material prosperity. One hundred years later, the Negro is still languishing in the corners of American society and finds himself an exile in his own land. So we have come here today to dramatize a shameful condition.

In a sense, we have come to our nation's Capital to cash a check. When the architects of our republic wrote the magnificent words of the Constitution and the Declaration of Independence, they were signing a promissory note to which every American was to fall heir. This note was a promise that all men, yes, black men as well as white men, would be guaranteed the unalienable rights of life, liberty, and the pursuit of happiness.

It is obvious today that America has defaulted on this promissory note insofar as her citizens of color are concerned. Instead of honoring this sacred obligation, America has given the Negro people a bad check; a check which has come back marked "insuffcient funds". But we refuse to believe that the bank of justice is bankrupt. We refuse to believe that there are "insufficient funds" in the great vaults of opportunity of this nation. So we have come to cash this check — a check that will give us upon demand the riches of freedom and the security of justice.

We have also come to this hallowed spot to remind America of the fierce urgency of "now" . This is no time to engage in the luxury of cooling off or to take the tranquilizing drug of gradualism. "Now" is the time to make real the promises of Democracy. "Now" is the time to rise from the dark and desolate valley of segregation to the sunlit path of racial justice. "Now" is the time to lift our nation from the quicksands of racial injustice to the solid rock of brotherhood. "Now" is the time to make justice a reality fo all of God's children.

It would be fatal for the nation to overlook the urgency of the moment. This sweltering summer of the Negro's legitimate discontent will not pass until there is an invigorating autumn of freedom and equality. Nineteen sixty-three is not an end, but a beginning. Those who hope that the Negro needed to blow off steam and will now be content will have a rude awakening if the nation returns to business as usual. There will be neither rest nor tranquility in America until the Negro is granted his citizenship rights. The whirlwinds of revolt will continue to shake the foundations of our nation until the bright day of justice emerges.

But there is something that I must say to my people who stand on the warm threshold which leads into the palace of justice. In the process of gaining our rightful place we must not be guilty of wrongful deeds. Let us not seek to satisfy our thirst for freedom by drinking from the cup of bitterness and hatred. We must forever conduct our struggle on the high plane of dignity and discipline. We must not allow our creative protests to degenerate into physical violence. Again and again we must rise to the majestic heights of meeting physical force with soul force.

The marvelous new militancy which has engulfed the Negro community must not lead us to a distrust of all white people, for many of our white brothers, as evidenced by their presence here today, have come to realize that their destiny is tied up with our destiny and their freedom is inextricably bound to our freedom. We cannot walk alone.

As we walk, we must make the pledge that we shall always march ahead. We cannot turn back. There are those who are asking the devotees of civil rights, "When will you be satisfied?"

We can never be satisfied as long as the Negro is the victim of the unspeakable horrors of police brutality.

We can never be satisfied as long as our bodies, heavy with the fatigue of traveling, cannot gain lodging in the motels of the highways and the hotels of the cities.

We cannot be satisfied as long as the Negro's basic mobility is from a smaller ghetto to a larger one.

We can never be satisfied as long as our children are stripped of their selfhood and robbed of their dignity by signs stating "For Whites Only."

We can never be satisfied as long as a Negro in Mississippi cannot vote and a Negro in New York believes he has nothing for which to vote.

No, no, we are not satisfied, and we will not be satisfied until justice rolls down like waters and righteousness like a mighty stream. (To be continued) ❋

Vocabulary List 【词汇清单】

demonstration /ˌdemənsˈtreiʃən/ *n.* 示威,示威游行
emancipation /iˌmænsiˈpeiʃən/ *n.* （从支配、束缚等的）解放

proclamation /ˌprɔkləˈmeiʃən/ *n.* 声明（书），宣言（书）（注：the Emancipation Proclamation：<美>《黑奴解放宣言》（美国总统林肯于 1862 年 9 月颁布，1863 年 1 月 1 日生效））

momentous /məuˈmentəs/ *adj.* 重大的，重要的

decree /diˈkriː/ *n.* 法令，政令，教令

beacon /ˈbiːkən/ *n.* （山上、杆上用作信号的）烟火，烽火；（用作警告或导航的）信号灯；灯塔

sear /siə/ *v.* 使干枯，使凋谢；烧灼，烧焦

withering /ˈwiðəriŋ/ *adj.* 摧毁性的，极有毁灭性的

injustice /inˈdʒʌstis/ *n.* 不公平，不公正，非正义（的行为）

captivity /kæpˈtiviti/ *n.* 关押，囚禁，束缚，奴役

cripple /ˈkripl/ *v.* 使损伤，使丧失活动能力，使失去战斗力

manacle /ˈmænəkl/ *n.* 手铐，脚镣，镣铐

segregation /ˌsegriˈgeiʃən/ *n.* 种族隔离

discrimination /disˌkrimiˈneiʃən/ *n.* （对少数集团的）歧视，种族歧视

languish /ˈlæŋgwiʃ/ *v.* 受折磨，憔悴，潦倒

exile /ˈeksail/ *n.* 流亡者，被流放（放逐、充军）者

architect /ˈaːkitekt/ *n.* 建筑师；设计师；缔造者

magnificent /mægˈnifisnt/ *adj.* 高尚的，崇高的，宏伟的

the Declaration of Independence：<美>《独立宣言》（于 1776 年 7 月 4 日第二次大陆会议发表并获得通过，并分送十三州的议会签署及批准。独立宣言包括三个部分：第一部分阐明政治哲学——民主与自由的哲学；第二部分列举若干具体的不平事例，以证明乔治三世破坏了美国的自由；第三部分郑重宣布独立，并宣誓支持该项宣言。）

promissory /ˈprɔmisəri/ *adj.* 允诺的，约定的，有约束力的（注：promissory note：<商业>本票，期票）

heir /ɛə/ *n.* 后嗣，（根据遗嘱或法定的）继承人

inalienable /inˈeiljənəbl/ *adj.* （权利等）不能让与（或转让）的，不能剥夺的

default /diˈfɔːlt/ *v.* 不履行职责，食言；拖欠，不支付

insofar /ˌinsəuˈfaː/ *adv.* 在…的范围（或限度）内（通常与 as 连用）

vault /vɔːlt/ *n.* 地下拱顶室，地下储藏室，地窖

hallowed /ˈhæləud/ *adj.* 神圣的，受崇敬的

fierce /fiəs/ *adj.* 凶猛的,凶暴的;猛烈的, 强烈的

tranquilize /ˈtræŋkwilaiz/ *v.* （使）安定,（使）镇静

gradualism /ˈgrædjuəlizəm/ *n.* <美>渐进主义,按步就班主义

desolate /ˈdesəlit/ *adj.* 荒凉的,孤寂的,荒无人烟的

quicksand /ˈkwiksænd/ *n.* 流沙;危险而捉摸不定的事物

fatal /feitl/ *adj.* 致命的,重大的,生死攸关的,决定命运的

sweltering /ˈsweltəriŋ/ *adj.* 热得发昏的,酷热的,中暑的

legitimate /liˈdʒitimit/ *adj.* 合法的,合理的,合乎逻辑的

invigorating /inˈvigəreitiŋ/ *adj.* 爽快的,令人精神充沛的

tranquillity /trænˈkwiliti/ *n.* （亦即 tranquillity）安定,镇静,平
　　静,宁静

whirlwind /ˈwəːlwind/ *n.* 旋风;旋风般急剧的势力

revolt /riˈvəult/ *n.* 反抗,起义,反叛,造反

threshold /ˈθreʃhəuld/ *n.* (= doorsill)门槛,门口

degenerate /diˈdʒenəreit/ *v.* 堕落,退化,变质

majestic /məˈdʒestik/ *adj.* 宏伟的,庄严的,崇高的

marvelous /ˈmaːviləs/ *adj.* 不可思议的,令人难以置信的;
　　<口语> 非凡的,极好的

militancy /ˈmilitənsi/ *n.* 战斗精神,尚武精神

engulf /inˈgʌlf/ *v.* 卷入,吞没,淹没,席卷

inextricably /inˈekstrikəbli/ *adv.* 无法摆脱（或解脱）地,息息
　　相关地

pledge /pledʒ/ *n.* 誓言,誓约,保证

devotee /ˌdevəuˈtiː/ *n.* 皈依者,信徒,热心之士

brutality /bru(ː)ˈtæliti/ *n.* 残忍,残酷,兽性;<复数> 兽行,
　　暴行,野蛮行为

fatigue /fəˈtiːg/ *n.* （身体或精神上的）疲劳,疲倦,疲乏

motel /məuˈtel/ *n.* <美>汽车旅馆（一种为乘汽车旅行的人提
　　供屋内住宿设施,房间通常有直接通往室外停车场的通道）

mobility /məuˈbiliti/ *n.* 流动性,移动性,迁移

ghetto /ˈgetəu/ *n.* （城市中）少数民族的集中居住区;贫民区

Mississippi /ˌmisiˈsipi/ 密西西比州（美国南部州名）

righteousness /ˈraitʃəsnis/ *n.* 严格,严厉;公正,正义

 参考译文【Suggested Translation】

我有一个梦想（一）

我很高兴今天和你一起参加这次集会，其将作为我们国家历史上为争取自由而举行的最伟大的示威集会而永垂史册。

一百年前，一位伟大的美国人正式签署了黑奴解放宣言，今天我们就是站在他的雕像前集会。这项重要法令的颁布犹如一座伟大的灯塔，照亮了当时在不义之火中备受煎熬的数百万黑奴的希望；它像欢快的黎明曙光，结束了束缚黑人的漫漫长夜。

然而，一百年后的今天，我们必须面对这个悲惨的现实：黑人仍然没有得到自由。一百年后的今天，黑人仍然被种族隔离的镣铐和种族歧视的锁链羁绊着，举步维艰。一百年后的今天，在物质充裕的汪洋大海之中，黑人却仍然独自生存于贫穷的孤岛之上。一百年后的今天，黑人仍然瑟缩在美国社会的阴暗角落里向隅而泣，在自己的土地上却仍然感到流离失所。因此，我们今天来到这里，把这种骇人听闻的情况公之于众。

就某种意义而言，我们今天来到国家的首都是为了兑现一张支票。当我们共和国的缔造者在撰写美国宪法以及独立宣言的壮丽篇章时，就签署了一张本票，并规定每个美国人都有权继承。这张本票承诺，所有的人，是的，——不论白人还是黑人——都拥有不可剥夺的生存、自由和追求幸福的权利。

就有色公民而言，今天美国显然没有承兑这张本票。美国拒不履行这项神圣的义务，只是退给黑人同胞一张空头支票，上面盖着"现金不足"的印戳。但是，我们绝不相信正义的银行已经破产。我们绝不相信，这个国家装满机遇的巨大宝库居然会出现现金不足的窘况。因此，我们要求兑现这张支票——这张支票一经兑现将给予我们宝贵的自由和正义的保障。

此外，我们来到这个神圣之地，也是为了提醒美国，事情的解决已经迫在眉睫，再没时间让我们奢谈冷静，或拿渐进主义当镇静剂了。现在是实现民主诺言的时候了；现在是走出种族隔离的荒芜阴暗的深谷，踏上种族平等的光明大道的时候了；现在是向上帝所有的儿女打开机会之门的时候了；现在是把我们的国家从种族不平等的流沙中拯救出来，安放在手足之情铸就的磐石之上的时候了。

忽视时间的紧迫性和低估黑人的决心，这对美国来讲，后果不堪设想的。自由平等的爽朗秋天不到来，黑人义愤填膺的酷暑就不会过去。1963 年并不意味着斗争的结束，而仅仅是一个开始。如果这个国家依然无动于衷，我行我素，那么，那些曾希望黑人只要发泄一下怒火就会心平气和的人就会猛醒。黑人一天得不到他的公民权利，美国就不可能安宁和平静。抗争的飓风将继续动摇这个国家的基石，直至光明璀璨的正义之日浮现眼前。

但是，对于站在通向正义殿堂温暖的门槛上的同胞们，有些话我是必须要说的。在争取合法地位的过程中，我们切不可因错误之举而犯罪；我们切不要为了满足对自由的渴望而而捧着敌对和仇恨之杯痛饮。我们在斗争中必须要自尊自重，纪律严明。我们不能容忍我们富于创造的抗争沦为粗野的暴动。我们应该一次次地将自己升华到用灵魂的力量对抗对手的有形暴力的崇高境界。

席卷整个黑人社会的了不起的新战斗精神，不应该把我们引入不信任所有白人的歧途——因为许多白人兄弟已经认识到：我们彼此的命运紧紧相连，我们彼此的自由密不可分——今天，他们来参加我们这个集会就是对此最好的证明。我们不能独自前行。

而当我们行动时，我们就必须确保勇往直前，我们无路可退。有人问热衷于民权运动的人："你们什么时候才能满足？"

我们绝不会满足，只要黑人仍然是警察不堪形容的野蛮暴行的牺牲品。

我们绝不会满足，只要我们在外奔波而自己疲倦的身躯仍然不能栖身于公路旁的汽车旅馆和城市里的旅馆。

我们绝不会满足，只要黑人的基本活动范围只能从小的贫民区转移到稍大的贫民区。

我们绝不会满足，只要我们诵孩子仍然会看到"白人专用"的告示——那些剥夺了他们的人格，践踏了他们自尊的告示。

我们绝不会满足，只要密西西比州的黑人依然不能参加选举投票，而纽约的黑人依然认为自己的投票毫无意义。

不，不，我们并不满足，也将不会满足，除非正义和公正犹如江河之波涛，汹涌澎湃，滚滚而来。（未完待续）◆

I Have a Dream (Ⅱ)

I am not unmindful that some of you have come here out of great trials and tribulations. Some of you have come fresh from narrow jail cells. Some of you have come from areas where your quest for freedom left you battered by the storms of persecution and staggered by the winds of police brutality. You have been the veterans of creative suffering. Contiue to work with the faith that unearned suffering is redemptive.

Go back to Mississippi, go back to Alabama, go back to South Carolina, go back to Georgia, go back to Louisiana, go back to the slums and ghettos of our Northern cities, knowing that somehow this situation can and will be changed. Let us not wallow in the valley of despair.

I say to you today, my friends, and so even though we face the difficulties of today and tomorrow, I still have a dream. It is a dream deeply rooted in the American dream.

I have a dream that one day this nation will rise up and live out the true meaning of its creed: "We hold these truths to be self-evident: that all men are created equal."

I have a dream that one day on the red hills of Georgia the sons of former slaves and the sons of former slave-owners will be able to sit down together at the table of brotherhood.

I have a dream that one day even the state of Mississippi, a state sweltering with the heat of injustice, sweltering with the heat of oppression, will be transformed into an oasis of freedom and justice.

I have a dream that my four little children will one day live in a nation where they will not be judged by the color of their skin but by the content of their character.

I have a dream today.

I have a dream that one day, down in Alabama, with its vicious racists, with its governor having his lips dripping with the words of interposition and nullification; one day right down in Alabama little black boys and black girls will be able to join hands with little white boys and white girls as sisters and brothers.

I have a dream today.

I have a dream that one day every valley shall be exalted, every hill and mountain shall be made low, the rough places would be made plain, and the crooked places would be made straight, and the glory of the Lord shall be revealed, and all flesh shall see it together.

This is our hope. This is the faith that I will go back to the South with. With this faith we will be able to hew out of the mountain of despair a stone of hope. With this faith we will be able to transform the jangling discords of our nation into a beautiful symphony of brotherhood. With this faith we will be able to work together, to pray together, to struggle together, to go to jail together, to stand up for freedom together, knowing that we will be free one day.

This will be the day , this will be the day when all of God's children will be able to sing with a new meaning.

My country, 'tis of thee,

Sweet land of liberty,

Of thee I sing.

Land where my fathers died,

Land of the pilgrims' pride,

From every mountainside,

Let freedom ring.

And if America is to be a great nation, this must become true. So let freedom ring from the prodigious hilltops of New Hampshire.

Let freedom ring from the mighty mountains of New York.

Let freedom ring from the heightening Alleghenies of Pennsylvania!

Let freedom ring from the snowcapped Rockies of Colorado!

Let freedom ring from the curvaceous slopes of California!

But not only that; let freedom ring from Stone Mountain of Georgia!

Let freedom ring from Lookout Mountain of Tennessee!

Let freedom ring from every hill and molehill of Mississippi.

From every mountainside, let freedom ring.

And when this happens, When we allow freedom ring, when we let it ring from every village and every hamlet, from every state and every city, we will be able to speed up that day when all of God's children, black men and white men, Jews and Gentiles, Protestants and Catholics, will be able to join hands and sing in the words of the old Negro spiritual, "Free at last! free at last! Thank God almighty, we are free at last!" ✹

 # Vocabulary List 【词汇清单】

unmindful /ʌnˈmaindful/ adj. 不留心的,不注意的;漫不经心的,疏忽的

tribulation /ˌtribjuˈleiʃən/ n. 苦难,困苦,磨难

persecution /ˌpəːsiˈkjuːʃən/ n. 迫害,残害,困扰

stagger /ˈstægə/ v. (使)摇晃,(使)蹒跚,(使)摇摇摆摆

veteran /ˈvetərən/ n. n. (尤指参加过战争的)退伍军人,老兵;老手,富有经验的人

unearned /ˈʌnˈəːnd/ adj. 不相称的,不应得的

redemptive /riˈdemptiv/ adj. 用以赎回(或买回)的,用以赎救的,用于补偿的

Alabama /ˌæləˈbæmə/ 阿拉巴马州(美国州名)

Carolina /ˌkærəˈlainə/ 卡罗莱纳州(美国州名)

Georgia /ˈdʒɔːdʒə/ 乔治亚州(美国州名)

Louisiana /lu(ː)ˌiːziˈænə/ 路易斯安那州(美国州名)

slum /slʌm/ n. (城市中的)贫民区,贫民窟

wallow /ˈwɔləu/ v. (猪等在泥、脏水中)打滚;<喻>溺于,沉迷(in)

oasis /əuˈeisis/ n. 绿洲(沙漠或不毛之地中因为有水而产生的肥沃土地或绿地)

interposition /inˌtə(ː)pəˈziʃən/ n. 干涉,干预,提出异议;<美>一种有争论主张:州政府可抵制侵犯其主权的联邦法令

nullification /ˌnʌlifiˈkeiʃən/ n. 无效,废弃,取消;<美>州对联邦法令的拒绝执行

transform /trænsˈfɔːm/ v. 使改变,改造,变换(性质、机能等)

exalted /egˈzɔːltid/ adj. 举起,升起,使提高

hew /hjuː/ v. (用斧、刀等)砍,劈,伐

discord /ˈdiskɔːd/ n. 不一致,不和谐;喧闹声,嘈杂声

stand up for：争取，坚决要求；维护，捍卫

thee /ði:/ *pron.* ＜古＞（thou 的宾格）汝，你，你自己

pilgrim /'pilgrim/ *n.* 圣地朝拜者，朝圣者，香客；＜美＞1620
年移居美洲的英国清教徒

prodigious /prə'didʒəs/ *adj.* 巨大的，庞大的

Hampshire /'hæmpʃiə/ 新罕布什尔州（美国州名）

Alleghenies /ˌæli'geiniz/（即 Allegheny Mountains）阿勒格尼山
脉（北美阿巴拉契亚山系西部的分支）

Pennsylvania /ˌpensil'veinjə/ 宾夕法尼亚州（美国州名）

Colorado /ˌkɔlə'ra:dəu/ 科罗拉多州（美国州名）

curvaceous /kə:'veiʃəs/ *adj.* ＜口语＞（女人）曲线美的，婀
娜多姿的

California /ˌkæli'fɔ:njə/ 加利福尼亚，加州（美国州名）

Tennessee /ˌtenə'si:/ 田纳西州（美国州名）

molehill /'məulhil/ *n.*（由鼹鼠打洞扒出的泥土堆成的）鼹鼠
丘（窝）

hamlet /'hæmlit/ *n.* 村子，小村庄

Gentile /'dʒentail/ *n.* 非犹太人，不信犹太教的人

Protestant /'prɔtistənt/ *n.*（除罗马天主教及东正教以外的）
基督教徒，新教徒

Catholic /'kæθəlik/ *n.*（罗马）天主教徒

spiritual /'spiritjuəl/ *n.* ＜美＞黑人的圣歌，灵歌

参考译文【Suggested Translation】

我有一个梦想（二）

我并非没有注意到，你们当中有些人是经过重重磨难才能来
到这里，有的人刚刚走出狭小的牢房，有的人来自那些地
方——你们追求自由，但却惨遭迫害暴雨捶打和警察暴力飓风
肆虐。你们是久经人为磨难的老兵。那么，继续奋斗下去吧，要
坚信：总有一天，无辜受难的人们终会得到拯救。

　　让我们回到密西西比去吧，回到阿拉巴马去吧，回到南卡罗

来纳去吧,回到佐治亚去吧,回到路易斯安那去吧,回到我们北方城市中的贫民区和黑人居住区去吧。要知道,这种处境是可以而且必将会改变的。我们切莫再陷入绝望而不能自拔的深谷之中。

朋友们,今天我要告诉你们,尽管此时此刻我们面临种种困难和挫折,但是我仍然有一个梦想。这个梦想深深扎根于伟大的美国之梦。

我梦想有一天,这个国家奋然而起,实现其信条的真谛:"我们认为这些真理是不言自明的:人人生而平等。"

我梦想有一天,在佐治亚州的红土山坡上,昔日奴隶的儿子与昔日主人的儿子能够如兄弟手足一般同榻而坐。

我梦想有一天,就算是密西西比州这片蒸腾着不公与压迫热浪的沙漠也将会变为一块流淌着自由与公正清泉的绿洲。

我梦想有一天,我的四个孩子将生活在一个不是以他们的肤色,而是以他们内在品质来评价他们的国度中。

今天,我有一个梦想。

我梦想有一天,阿拉巴马州能够有所不同,尽管该州州长今天仍然满口异议,不执行联邦法令,但是有朝一日,那里的黑人男孩和女孩能够与白人的男孩和女孩情同骨肉,携手同行。

今天,我有一个梦想。

我梦想有一天,我们会填平所有的峡谷,夷平所有的山丘,崎岖之地将变为坦荡的平原,曲折之路将变为笔直的大道;主的荣光将会显现,满照天地人间。

这就是我们的希望,也是我返回南方时怀有的信念。有了这个信念,我们就能从绝望之峰劈出一块希望之石。有了这个信念,我们就能把我们国家里种族争斗的不和谐之音,转化为一支洋溢手足之情的动人交响曲。有了这个信念,我们就能共同工作,共同祈愿,共同战斗,共同昂首入狱,共同维护自由。因为我们知道,总有一天,我们会获得自由。

当这一天到来之时,上帝所有的子民都能以全新的涵义高唱:

我亲爱的祖国,

美丽的自由之邦,

我为您歌唱。

您是先辈们安息的故园,

您是朝圣者为之自豪的地方，
让自由之声响彻每个山岗！

如果美国要成为一个真正伟大的国家，这一切必将实现。
因此，让自由之声从新罕布尔州的巍峨高峰响起来！
让自由之声从纽约州的崇山峻岭响起来！
让自由之声从宾夕法尼亚州高耸的阿勒格尼山顶峰响起来！
让自由之声从科罗拉多州白雪皑皑的落基山响起来！
让自由之声从加利福尼亚州的逶迤的群峰响起来！
不仅如此，还要让自由之声从佐治亚州的石岭响起来！
让自由之声从田纳西州的了望山响起来！
让自由之声从密西西比州的每一座山岗，每一座丘陵响起来！
让自由之声从每一片山坡响起来！
当我们让自由之声响起来时，当我们让自由之声从每一个大小村庄，每一个州和每一座城市响起来时，我们就能让这一天早日来临。到那时，上帝所有的儿女——白人与黑人，犹太教徒与非犹太教徒，基督教徒与天主教徒——携手同唱那首古老的黑人灵歌："终于自由啦！终于自由啦！感谢全能的上帝，我们终于自由啦！"◣

I Remember, I Remember*

I remember, I remember
The house where I was born,
The little window where the sun
Came peeping in at morn;
He never came a wink too soon,
Nor brought too long a day,
But now I often wish the night
Had borne my breath away!

I remember, I remember
The roses red and white,

　　＊ 作者托马斯·胡德(Thomas Hood,1799—1845),英国著名诗人,其诗作多为抗议不合理的社会现象。同时,其写实主义的诗歌和幽默诗亦颇负盛名,主要作品有诗集《衬衣之歌》(Song of the Shirt)和《伤心桥》(The Bridge of Sighs)以及幽默喜剧《约克和兰开斯特》(York and Lancaster)。本诗是胡德颇具灵性的一首诗,借此我们足以管窥作者的诗才何其厚重。

The violets, and the lily-cups,
Those flowers made of light!
The lilacs where the robin built,
And where my brother set
The laburnum of his birth-day, —
The tree is living yet!

I remember, I remember
Where I was used to swing,
And thought the air must rush as fresh
To swallows on the wing；
My spirit flew in feathers then,
That is so heavy now,
And summer pools could hardly cool
The fever on my brow!

I remember, I remember
The fir-trees dark and high；
I used to think their slender tops
Were close against the sky：
It was a childish ignorance,
But now it is little joy
To know I'm further off from heaven
Than when I was a boy. ✽

 ## Vocabulary List 【词汇清单】

morn /mɔːn/ *n.* ＜诗歌＞早晨（ ＝ morning）

wink /wiŋk/ *n.* 瞬息，一瞬间，霎时

violet /ˈvaiəlit/ *n.* ＜植物＞紫罗兰（花）

cup /kʌp/ *n.* ＜生物＞杯状器官或结构；（花的）花萼

lilac /ˈlailək/ *n.* ＜植物＞丁香（尤指西洋丁花），丁香花，紫丁香

robin /ˈrɔbin/ n.　<鸟>知更鸟
laburnum /ləˈbəːnəm/ n.　<植物>金链花
swallow /ˈswɔləu/ n.　<鸟>燕子,雨燕及类似禽鸟
fir-tree /fəːtriː/ n.　<植物>枞树,冷杉,白冷杉
slender /ˈslendə/ adj.　细长的,纤细的,苗条的
ignorance /ˈignərəns/ n.　无知,不知,无学

 ## 参考译文【Suggested Translation】

我记得,我记得

我记得,我记得
我出生的那所房屋,
还有那扇小窗,
清晨太阳向里面窥探。
它从不提前一瞬来临,
也不使人感到白天太长。
可现在我却常常希望,
黑夜能使我安息长眠!

我记得,我记得
那红色的和白色的玫瑰,
还有紫罗兰和百合花瓣,
那些光彩斑斓的花朵!
那知更鸟筑巢的紫丁香,
我弟弟在他生日那天
将金链花种在它旁边——
这棵树至今生机勃勃!

我记得,我记得
我常去荡秋千的地方,
心想那扑向飞翔着的燕子的清风,
必定是同样地令人心旷神怡;

我的心啊，那时犹如插翅飞翔，
现在却沉重无比，
即使夏日的水潭也难以
消退我额头上的高热！

我记得，我记得
那些枞树苍郁而高耸；
我常思量它们纤细的树梢
几乎紧贴着天空；
那是孩子的天真无知，
但现在我却很少欢乐，
由于知道自己离开天国
比儿时更加遥远。◆

（唐力行 译）

特别鸣谢

　　《英文诵典》是专门为英语文学爱好者编写的经典英语小品文合集。在编写过程中,我们查阅了国内外大量的资料和文献,搜集了一大批被广为传诵的英语文章精品。由于受到客观原因的限制,我们无法与部分资料的原作者及时取得联系,在此特别向这些作者表示衷心感谢。同时也请这些作者在读到本书后,尽快与我编辑部取得联系,领取稿酬。

　　编辑部电话:010 – 8274 – 2036

　　邮箱:t82742036@ sina. com

世界知识出版社笃志英语图书编辑部